1:00 - 2nd
2:45 - 3rd

THE SCEPTICAL VISION OF MOLIÈRE

THE SCEPTICAL VISION OF MOLIÈRE

A Study in Paradox

Robert McBride, B.A., Ph.D.

Senior Lecturer in French
The Queen's University of Belfast

BOOKS
10 East 53d St., New York 10022
(a division of Harper & Row Publishers, Inc.)

© Robert McBride 1977

First published 1977 by
THE MACMILLAN PRESS LTD
London and Basingstoke

Published in the U.S.A. 1977 by
HARPER & ROW PUBLISHERS, INC.
BARNES & NOBLE IMPORT DIVISION

Printed in Great Britain

Library of Congress Cataloging in Publication Data

McBride, Robert.
The sceptical vision of Molière.

Bibliography: p.
Includes index.
1. Molière, Jean Baptiste Poquelin, 1622-1673 —
Criticism and interpretation. I. Title.
PQ1860.M24 1977 842'.4 76-7847
ISBN 0-06-494676-2

To the memory of my mother, and to my father

Contents

Acknowledgements

I would like to express my thanks to Professor H. T. Barnwell for his constructive criticism and constant encouragement; to Emeritus Professor H. J. G. Godin for the many things I have learnt from him as teacher, colleague and friend; to Dr H. Gaston Hall for his helpful comments on my typescript; to Mrs M. Hatch, Mrs G. Carse and Miss G. Greig for typing the manuscript so efficiently and so cheerfully; and lastly, but by no means least, to my wife.

Introduction

To the student of Molière, attempting not only to grapple with the voluminous amount of critical judgements which three centuries have produced on his author, but also to formulate his own, the wry observation of D. Mornet might not seem inappropriate: 'Que de Molières en effet dont chacun est la négation d'un autre Molière.'[1] Molière the impious author of *Tartuffe,* Molière the precursor of the French Revolution, Molière the sombre Romantic of the early nineteenth century, Molière the unfortunate husband of the latter half of that century, Molière the apostle of the golden mean in the early twentieth century, and Molière of the more recent new criticism - all differing Molières, who evince a seemingly unending variety of interpretation to which the work of Jean-Baptiste Poquelin has been subjected.[2]

It is therefore with no little apprehension that one approaches the almost legendary problem of his thought, which has obsessed generations of *Moliéristes* and which could aptly be termed the philosopher's stone of Molière studies. When one investigates past attitudes to this question, however, one is surprised to discover that there is not only a general agreement about the existence of a *morale de Molière* (generally taken to mean the moral thought and opinions which he wished to express in his plays), but also about the fact that this *morale* is at once obvious and demonstrable. The adverse judgement originating from prejudice of the moment might be later replaced by more rational discussion, and the excessive harshness of the opponents of *Tartuffe* give way to more equitable opinion: the fact remains, however, that like his contemporary critics, the majority of their successors have, with certain notable exceptions, tended to view his *morale* unfavourably.

The stern denunciation of the 'morale du théâtre' by Bossuet overshadows the diffident defence of his comedy by a Père Caffaro, and is contradicted only by the more nuanced and elegant expression of a Bourdaloue or a Fénelon, but not by their thought on the subject.[3] The Jansenist Baillet, judging Molière to be a dangerous enemy to morality, is supported from a secular standpoint by Rousseau's rigorous diatribe against the author of *Le Misanthrope*.[4] On the other hand, the more balanced attitudes of Fontenelle and of Bayle in the early part of the century, and of the *Encyclopédie* and especially Voltaire in the latter, provide ample evidence of a more unbiased approach to the subject in the *siècle des lumières* - for the latter, Molière was not only a *philosophe,* but also the founder of 'l'école de la vie civile', 'ce législateur dans la morale et dans les bienséances du monde.'[5] The view that Molière's *morale* exemplified reason and virtue subsisted in the early nineteenth century in the criticism of Marmontel and La Harpe.[6] If the later critics of the century displayed the more moderate attitude of the Enlightenment to a study of his philosophy, they nevertheless tended to view him once more within the context of Christian tradition and orthodoxy. Thus Molière became the free-thinker, the disciple of Gassendi, the follower of a natural religion, yet not so much the hostile opponent of Christianity as one who, by nature and instinct, was alien to its spirit.[7] The thesis of Molière the militant *libertin* and implacable enemy of the Church was revived and stated in a particularly trenchant way by L. Veuillot and F. Brunetière.[8]

Moliéristes at the beginning of the present century tended to restate this view of Molière the exponent of a philosophy of nature. The range of opinions extended from that of a Molière overtly and aggressively tendentious in his *morale* to that of a Molière representing a somewhat mediocre and unedifying philosophy — at its highest level, a tranquil form of paganism, disregarding the more noble and challenging virtues, at its lowest a corroding and insidious form of *libertinage érudit*.[9]

These assumptions about his philosophy rested largely upon a paragraph in the first biography of Molière, which stated that the playwright had followed a course in philosophy given by the foremost interpreter of the ideas of Epicurus in the seventeenth century, Pierre Gassendi.[10] One of several factors which have contributed profoundly to a complete reorientation of Molière studies was the extremely cogent argument expounded by G. Michaut against this tradition. He stressed in particular that there was no single period of any duration during which Molière could have followed a systematic course of instruction from Gassendi.[11] The immediate result of Michaut's research was that it opened the door to an interpretation of Molière as a sincere Christian, though not perhaps of the most fervent kind.[12] A second and more far-reaching consequence has been the subsequent tendency on the part of scholars to minimize the importance of external factors such as the possible influence of Gassendi in an appreciation of his plays, and the application to them of an internal criterion of interpretation.[13] This has more recently culminated in the 'new criticism' which emphasizes that an expression of opinion may have been far from Molière's mind, and that the plays should consequently be studied primarily as drama, and not as literature or philosophy.[14]

One other important factor in the evolution of Molière studies in the twentieth century was the publication in 1900 of Bergson's celebrated essay on the meaning of the comic. His formula underlying the comic — 'raideur' contrasting with the 'élasticité' of life — has led critics to concentrate their attention on the importance of comic form rather than on moral content. As such, it has provided powerful reinforcement for the central idea of the 'new criticism.'[15] The older view of Molière the free-thinker intent on expressing a personal view of life still survives, although in a much less systematic form than previously.[16]

Molière studies would thus appear to have reached an extremely interesting stage in their development. Without exaggeration, it seems true to say that the wheel has indeed come full circle — for whereas critics of preceding generations were categorical about the nature as well as the existence of *la morale de Molière,* the trend of contemporary studies is towards an acceptance of the view that his thought is at best obscure, at worst unknowable.[17] This shift of attitude is amply reflected in the increasing attention which *Moliéristes* now seem to be giving to consideration of the style and the poetic nature of Molière's plays, rather than to the opinions expressed by his characters.[18]

The purpose of this study is to attempt to look afresh at the whole question of thought in Molière's theatre, to ask in what way it seems meaningful to speak of its existence within a comic framework, and to consider how thought in comedy may change as the nature of the comedy which underlies it evolves. Part I discusses the apparently conflicting views of Molière the *moraliste* and Molière the creator of comic forms, and seeks to define the characteristic mode of Molière's comic conception at its most elementary level (that of verbal comedy) and at the level of comic structure (with particular reference to *Sganarelle ou Le Cocu Imaginaire* and *Dom Garcie*). I have selected these plays not only because they seem to me to illustrate clearly and systematically the basic structure common to most, if not all, of Molière's plays, but also because they represent important stages in the evolution of his comic technique from farce to comedy of character. Analysis of the structure of other plays would therefore have been pedantic as well as superfluous.

Part II is concerned with the progression of the comic idea to the idea set in the dramatic structures of *Tartuffe, Dom Juan, Le Misanthrope, Amphitryon* and *Les Femmes Savantes.* The choice of these plays is by no means arbitrary, as they appear to me to illustrate, within very different thematic and comic frameworks, the vision of comedy and the comic vision of things. In particular, they seem to me to allow a comparison with the sceptical view of life, as set forth notably by La Mothe Le Vayer, the Sceptic philosopher and friend of Molière. I have not viewed the analogy between the sceptical thought of Le Vayer and the comedy of Molière from the point of view of sources and borrowings (although it is possible to see certain resemblances of expression). I have tried rather to view them in the wider perspective of the visions of life and man which they present in their own individual forms, and to consider the principal ideas or *leitmotifs* of those visions.

(Élsewhere, some of the themes which recur regularly in Molière's comedies, such as marriage and fashion, are discussed and viewed in relation to their sceptical treatment at the hands of Le Vayer.)[19]

I have adopted a two-part approach in order to reduce the subject to manageable proportions, but I am only too aware that it may run the risk of being considered as a schematic reconstruction of an evolving conception of comedy, a conception which almost certainly did not take place on a conscious level. Molière is the most *unschematic* of authors, and this is scarcely surprising since he was not at all a *littérateur* as such. But some schema is nevertheless necessary if the common pattern underlying the comic idea and the philosophy of comedy is to be illustrated at all. I hope that the conclusions of this study will in some way embody this dual feature of his comic creation.

Part One

The Idea of Paradox

1 The Double Vision of Comedy

(1)

The return to Molière the comic dramatist and technician of comedy must be welcomed as a salutary corrective to the point of view illustrated by those critics who have considered him as a moralist and philosopher rather than as a comic playwright. As W. G. Moore has rightly stated, such an approach has often assumed what has still to be proved — that Molière did in fact wish to express his precise personal opinion upon specific topics;[1] in addition, it has been seen to owe too much to uncontrolled subjective opinion, in the ascription to Molière of ideas which his presumed circle of friends shared, or which squared with preconceived notions of what those ideas were meant to be. Recourse to external criteria, such as autobiographical and philosophical data, falsified the perspective of Molière studies, and contributed much to the tendency to overlook the fundamental fact that the plays themselves constitute the only basis for the discussion of what Molière may or may not have believed.[2]

The value of the 'new criticism' lies then in the necessary shift of emphasis which it marks to Molière as the creator of comedy. The plays are seen as having been written primarily to entertain an audience, and not to fulfil a didactic purpose on the part of the author.[3] Molière himself provides unambiguous confirmatory evidence for this view in *la Critique de l'Ecole des Femmes,* where his *porte-parole* Dorante (one of the rare characters whom we may accept as Molière's representative) enunciates the principle which underlies his dramatic art, and directs it specifically against the pedantic 'spéculatifs' to whom Corneille also makes slighting reference in his *Discours:* 'Je voudrois bien savoir si la grande règle de toutes les règles n'est pas de plaire, et si une pièce de théâtre qui a attrapé son but n'a pas suivi un bon chemin' (Sc.6).[4] Several years later, Molière was to take a somewhat more moralistic view of the goal of comedy: and the German critic C.S. Gutkind has commented in this connexion on the discrepancy between his view in the *Critique* and the view expressed in the *Tartuffe* polemics: in fact it was not until the moral worth of that play was impugned that its author invoked the Horatian concept of comedy: 'castigat ridendo mores.'[5]

The question then arises: if the plays are to be considered as plays, does this mean that there is no *morale* and no thought which they can be said to express? Of the 'new critics', R. Bray in particular has argued strenuously in favour of an affirmative answer to the question, and in so doing, illustrates the ambiguity latent in it which has bedevilled Molière studies for generations. There can be no moral thought or philosophy in

3

the plays, he claims, since they were intended only to be performed in the theatre, and thus represent a world of unreason, 'folie', imagination, and poetic exaggeration. One may quote two central points from his argument which he stresses at considerable length: 'Son dessein est celui d'un technicien, nullement d'un psychologue ou d'un moraliste' and '. . . le comique ne peut comporter ni moralité ni immoralité.'[6] If by the first of these two quotations it is meant that a consciously didactic purpose was extraneous to Molière's concern in writing his plays, then the second sentence would be accurate within that restricted sense of moral. Yet the question is evidently much more complex than that, as Bray illustrates when he admits (paradoxically?) that 'le comique réside dans une certaine vue du monde' and when he accepts 'le comique satirique' as an intrinsic part of Molière's comedy.[7] The particular way in which Molière saw life took shape in an imaginative recreation of reality, or, to use the same critic's description, 'un royaume enchanté';[8] but 'un royaume enchanté' which can and does possess its own internal moral structure and coherence. (If we think that the hypocrisy of a Tartuffe is morally bad, it is so only because the family have judged him before we do, since he threatens to disrupt the moral order of their world and not of ours; such judgement on our part is therefore not an external and unnatural criterion which we clumsily insist on applying in a world different to that of the real world which we have just left for the theatre, but rather a principle implanted by the poet in the minds of those characters who oppose Tartuffe's design.)

The implicit contradiction between Bray's world of the imagination and his admission of a certain view of life which shapes the comedy, stems from the unnecessarily exclusive way in which the question of the thought of Molière has been posed. The choice offered between Molière the writer concerned above all with the expression of a moral viewpoint on the one hand, and Molière the man of the theatre and inventor of comic forms and situations on the other, is a deeply false as well as a deeply irrational one: it amounts to saying solemnly that Molière is either a propagandist of gnomic platitudes, or quite simply a mindless creator. In his excellent book *The Life of the Drama,* Eric Bentley warns us opportunely against the error of conceiving of thought and imagination as two separate elements in a work of art which must be mutually exclusive. Molière can indeed depict the full range of human absurdity and folly in a world of poetic imagination, yet it will remain true, as Bentley says, that '. . . the created work not merely is written from the viewpoint of reason but is itself a rational structure.'[9] It was not Molière, after all, who was an *imaginaire,* but rather the author who creates him and who places him in situations where his folly can be comically and rationally exploited. Reason and thought are therefore not only at the origin of his drama, but also ever present in its structure and content. But whilst affirming the presence of the judgement of the author at each stage of his work, one must beware of concentrating one's attention solely on ideas to the exclusion of form and structure (and at this point one can understand why Bray felt it necessary to stress that Molière was nothing more than a man of the theatre), or of expecting and attempting to discover what Bentley has termed '. . . the elaborations which would be required either in the novel or in a historical or philosophic treatise.'[10]

One must not expect a coherent, well-organised philosophy free from contradictions in Molière's plays; had he striven for coherence and completeness in the domain of thought he would certainly have taken care to compose a moral treatise. Yet it does seem not only justifiable but also necessary to look for a view of life couched in comic and dramatic form, since at each moment of the play the thought is inseparable from the form which it underlies. It is here that W.G. Moore is likely to prove a more perspicacious guide than Bray, when he writes sensitively that '. . . the view of life . . . is not where scholars have been too ready to find it, lying scattered on the surface, in the speeches of the most "reasonable" and often least dramatic character in any given play, but is hidden deep in the philosophical conception of the whole dramatic situation.'[11]

Starting from this point, I should like to explore the possibility of finding a general objective principle situated in the dramatic as well as in the comic structure of the plays, which may be indicative of the way in which that view of life is transmitted as well as of the dominant elements which go to form it.

(2)

One might well begin this inquiry by suggesting the possible bearing which dramatic structure in general might have upon the expression of ideas. Here I am not at all concerned with the discussion of specific ideas in Molière (that will be a matter for later chapters), but solely with a consideration of the way in which the *expression of ideas* in drama is liable to be affected and moulded by the structure of the *genre* in which they are cast. But Molière's plays belong not only to drama, but to comic drama as well; at a later stage of this chapter the structure of the comic is also investigated, with the same question in mind. In short, what follows represents an attempt to erect, from dramatic and comic first principles, a theoretical framework in which to study the views expressed in the comedies.

The most common way in which ideas have been attributed to Molière consists in equating them with the *raisonneur,* the most reasonable character in any given play, as W.G. Moore has said. Michaut in particular has been the best known and the most consistent advocate of this method of interpreting the plays.[12] According to this critic, the lines which Philinte speaks in *Le Misanthrope* epitomized the philosophy of *juste-milieu* and moderation which Molière wished to express:

> La parfaite raison fuit toute extrémité,
> Et veut que l'on soit sage avec sobriété (Act I, Sc. 1, ll. 151-2)

His method for penetrating to Molière's opinion was based upon the following procedure; ask who the ridiculous character is in the play, discover what he says, and then take precisely the opposite view (i.e. that of the *raisonneur*) as being necessarily that of the author.[13] It must be acknowledged that such a view is, in theory at any rate, reasonable. It is as natural for us to assume that the playwright is in disagreement with the views which he appears to ridicule (the *dénouement,* after all, it is argued, shows the invariable triumph of the *raisonneur's* ideas) as it is to feel gratified that we have more in common with the slightly more lucid characters. But on reflection, there would seem to me to be at least two fundamental disadvantages in the application of such a rigorous method to Molière's plays. Considering the character in a purely literary way by categorising neatly his ideas, one overlooks his presence in the play, and, more importantly, the role he plays, which varies as the play's circumstances demand; and by its very nature such a viewpoint as that of Michaut takes an extremely restricted view of the creator's attitude to his play (we are dealing here with mysterious processes which require that we should approach the question in the widest and least rigid manner possible). Nevertheless, we are fully entitled to base our approach to the plays on the affirmation that Molière is the creator both of the so-called *ridicule* and of his apparently more reasonable counterpart, the *raisonneur,* and that consequently his experience of his play is neither one-sided nor fragmentary but total and absolute. It is no coincidence that the dramatist George Meredith was one of the first students of Molière to express this emphatically when he wrote that his thought did not '. . . hang like a tail, or preach from one character incessantly cocking an eye at the audience . . . but is in the heart of his work, throbbing with every pulsation of an organic structure.'[14]

What does it mean dramatically to say that his is the total experience of the creator, enabling him to be 'in the heart of his work'? It means above all that he is prescient, that is, able to shape what the characters say and do in the light of what he wishes them to say and do, and of the way in which he wishes an audience to react to them; he is also omnipresent, that is, able to be in each character as he pleases in the sense of supplying them with mutually incompatible opinions most conducive to dramatic contrast. If one looks at the lines quoted from Philinte's role for example, one will see that his apparent moderation may well appear to be *excessive* moderation, which Molière calculatingly opposes to the full-blooded fixation of his other character.[15] From a purely dramatic point of view then, it seems very tenable to argue that characters such as Sganarelle, Arnolphe, Orgon, Alceste, Chrysale, etc. would all be but pale imitations of themselves if they did not gain in comic relief from the character most calculated to exacerbate them beyond all measure.

When Molière is thus viewed as a comic dramatist, necessarily involved with the basic mechanics of his art, it seems very difficult to speak meaningfully of him having a single view in and of any particular play (even if the *dénouement* could invariably be regarded as expressing his own view on the subject in question — an assumption which is extremely hazardous to make — the significant point to note would be that it is reached in each play only *after* the dramatic conflict of opposing opinions has taken place). But on the other hand it does seem possible to speak of a double view of the author and creator which enables him to be in both his contrasting pairs of characters whilst placing them in a certain comic and dramatic perspective, shaping it as he pleases. (It is remarkable that even in the only play in which Molière avowedly articulates his own opinion, through Cléante in *Tartuffe,* this is still true to a large extent.) Michaut saw a unity in the ways in which Molière expressed his opinion through successive *raisonneurs*[16] — but if there is any unity in the way the thought is expressed it may be said to lie in the mode of presentation of the various subjects, whether they be marriage, education of women, religion, or one's attitude to the human condition; and this is achieved in and by the systematic presentation of opposites, the pattern which underlies not only the structure of his plays but of all drama as well: 'To see drama in something is both to perceive elements of conflict and to respond emotionally to these elements of conflict.'[17]

If this is at all correct, one can speak with more certainty of the thought behind the 'elements of conflict' which Molière dramatizes than of the thought of Molière the man. The only sense in which it would seem possible to subscribe to the view represented by Michaut of Molière the exponent of avoidance of all excess would be in a very general and therefore limited one, from which we could conclude that, to the extent that they are written about unreasonable characters, the comedies are written from the standpoint of reason. But to say that is to view him implicitly as a creative artist, for the same could be said of the creator of Phèdre and of Horace, both of whom lose their reason, whilst their authors view them from the standpoint of reason. What this does not and cannot tell us is what constitutes the tragic vision of Racine or of Corneille, or, in this case, the comic vision of Molière.

The dramatist perceives opposing elements in a situation, and drama mediates the conflict to the spectator in the theatre. If the dramatist has

been successful in his play, the spectator responds emotionally to the
dramatic conflict: like the author, he is not committed to the single view
of a character in a given situation. He too can lead a double life scarcely
conceivable in reality: indeed, his acceptance of this double life is the
sine qua non of all theatre: as Henri Gouhier expresses it, 'Par l'acte de
bonne volonté que le théâtre me demande, un jugement d'existence
pose comme réel un monde créé par le poète et recréé par les
interprètes.'[18] In a world maintained by his 'bonne volonté', the
spectator can do what he cannot do in reality: that is, identify himself
with one or more characters on stage, simultaneously or alternately. He
too can re-create, in an imperfect way of course, the original double
vision of the author which conceives and sustains the situation. Like
Molière, he can be Alceste or Philinte, Tartuffe or Cléante, or both
together; unlike Molière, he cannot create Alceste or Philinte. But
comedy disposes of a process peculiarly its own whereby the spectator
re-creates the double vision of the creator more concretely and directly
than is afforded in drama in general — namely, the comic. It achieves
this by detaching the spectator from the dramatic illusion by means of
what Bergson called picturesquely 'une anesthésie momentanée du
coeur' on his part.[19]

The comic process *par excellence,* the double vision, is analysed by
the *Lettre sur la Comédie de l'Imposteur,* which was certainly written in
close collaboration with Molière, if not, as is my view, by the playwright
himself.[20] Commenting upon the comic aspects of Panulphe, the *Lettre*
says that the general principle behind the comic (or *ridicule* as it is
qualified) is to be found in any *disconvenance,* that is, in any element
which offends our reason. The *Lettre* then goes on to give as an example
of such irrational *disconvenance* the behaviour of Panulphe during his
interview with Elmire. When we perceive the saintly Panulphe in the
guise of a seducer we judge him to be comic 'à cause que les actions
secrètes des bigots ne conviennent pas à l'idée que leur dévote grimace
et leur austérité de discours a fait former d'eux au public.' The comic in
Panulphe derives, as the *Lettre* makes explicit, not merely from the
contradiction between his actions and his devout appearances (such a
contradiction could arguably appear as tragic) but rather from our
perception of him as both *dévot* and seducer *simultaneously.* We have
momentarily two irreconcilable images of the same person at the same
moment: our reason cannot reconcile the apparent double truth
(Panulphe speaking precisely the language of a *dévot* whilst going
through the motions of a seducer) or, as the *Lettre* terms it, 'une
contrariété qui procède d'un même principe', because of its manifestly
irrational nature. Yet the irrational proposition can be entertained by
our imagination 'qui est le réceptacle naturel du ridicule', which can
accept appearances diametrically opposed to reason. Whilst reason
marks its refusal of such an absurdity by laughter at Panulphe, our

imagination is still capable of creating and maintaining the same double vision after his exit, if the slightest pretext is offered to it.[21]

The simultaneous perception of 'elements of conflict' which goes to form the conception of the dramatic situation as well as our imaginative participation in it, is also the first principle behind the conception of the comic and our reaction to it. With its function in drama as well as in comedy, is not the concept of the double vision therefore a useful instrument with which to explore Molière's comedy, from its most elementary and uncomplicated level to its most complex dramatic manifestations? D. Romano has reminded us that '. . . la fonction première du comique n'est pas de faire rire de ceci plutôt que de cela, mais de faire rire tout court.'[22] Molière did not begin to write comedies because he wished to express a personal philosophy of life: if, as R. Fernandez remarks, one can write *Sganarelle* or *Scapin* without changing the intellectual order of the world, this is, however, no longer possible when one writes *Tartuffe* or *Le Misanthrope*[23]. A study of the conception of the double vision in comedy may well tell us much, not only about the meaning of comedy, but eventually about the mind of the author of *Le Misanthrope* and *Tartuffe*.

(3)

Arthur Koestler has elaborated the theory of the comic adumbrated in the *Lettre sur la Comédie* in a way which is particularly illuminating for an understanding of the idea behind the double vision of comedy.[24] The interest in Koestler's treatment of the subject lies in the fact that he neither considers it as a purely mechanistic phenomenon like Bergson (whose famous formula 'du mécanique plaqué sur du vivant' summed up the essence of the comic) nor as a purely affective phenomenon like Freud (for whom the comic was the result of the mind moving suddenly from a state of tension into one of deception),[25] but from an intellectual viewpoint, which is precisely the approach adopted by the slightly pedantic analysis of the *Lettre*.

According to Koestler, all coherent thinking and behaviour are subject to some specifiable code of rules to which they owe their character of coherence - even though these codes may function partly or entirely on unconscious levels of the mind. In conversation, for example, grammar and syntax may be said to be the codes which function unconsciously and which are 'condensations of learning into habit'.[26] We can escape from these more or less automatized routines of thought and action in two ways, both closely related: either we can plunge into a dream-like state where the codes of rational thinking are suspended, or we can move in the opposite direction by seeing a familiar situation or idea in a new way by connecting it with some idea which we had not previously related to it. This Koestler calls the state of the creative act, which differs from the routine skills of thinking on a single plane, in that it invariably operates as a double-minded state making us 'understand what it is to be awake, to be living on several planes at once.'[27]

The comic is seen as one of the branches of what he calls the creative state of mind, and the formula which characterizes (but obviously does not and cannot explain) its basic idea is '. . . the perceiving of a situation or idea . . . in two self-consistent but habitually incompatible frames of reference.'[28] The collision of two ideas which have their own inner and coherent logics, but which are rationally incompatible, formed the paradox underlying the comedy of Panulphe. But it also is seen both at the simplest and most subtle levels of Molière's comic dialogue. It can appear as a simple *jeu de mots*: at the end of *Amphitryon* Sosie says to Mercure

> Et je ne vis de ma vie
> Un Dieu plus diable que toi (Act III, Sc. 9, ll. 1888-9)

The idea of Mercure the divine messenger of Jupiter is neatly connected with the more ribald Mercure, who has played a leading role in the very human act of cuckolding Amphitryon. The two codes which collide and co-exist in incompatibility may be more subtle than this simple play with words. In *Les Précieuses Ridicules* Magdelon tells her father, who is anxious that she and Cathos should marry La Grange and Du Croisy: 'Quoi? débuter d'abord par le mariage?' To which he replies brusquely 'Et par où veux - tu donc qu'ils débutent? par le concubinage?' (Sc. 4). The logic with which Magdelon interprets the meaning of marriage is that of the *Carte de Tendre,* in which a girl only yields to the claims of a suitor when she has ascended the hierarchical steps of *précieux* courtship. Her reaction to her father is fully consistent and logical within the understood code which she follows. But Gorgibus too follows a logic which is equally consistent and which is also the only one he knows — the literal one, in which marriage is devoid of sophisticated connotation and means precisely what it says. In the creation of such verbal comedy, however, nothing can ever mean what it literally means; deeper levels of meaning are unexpectedly discovered with such effect that it is the common or garden logic of the literalist code which is invariably defeated by appearances. In the first scene of *Le Médecin Malgré Lui,* Sganarelle's wife Martine reproaches him for his inactivity: 'J'ai quatre petits enfants sur les bras.' He escapes from the pressing logic of the literalist code by a riposte which, paradoxically, makes a shift of emphasis from the figurative to the literal level: 'Mets-les à terre.' When his wife complains of his extravagance, calling him '. . . un débauché, un traître, qui me mange tout ce que j'ai', he escapes in more subtle fashion from her meaning: 'Tu as menti; j'en bois une partie.'She has used *manger* in the figurative sense of 'to consume'; he chooses to answer her according to the logic of a different code, involving the displacement of emphasis from whole to part, to a previously neglected level of meaning.[29] This is not the logic by which we expected him to answer, and our intellect is forced to concede his clever invention.

A similar pattern underlies the famous *ruban* scene in *L'Ecole des Femmes* (Act II, Sc. 5), although it involves a clash of different codes. Arnolphe asks Agnès if Horace has taken anything from her at their meeting: her reiteration of the equivocal 'le' is calculated to evoke all sorts of expectations in our mind. With the transparently innocent answer ('il m'a pris le ruban que vous m'aviez donné' l. 578), the logic of our emotions, which led us to expect a more *piquant* conclusion, collides with the logic of reason, which tells us that, in spite of appearances, nothing at all has happened. Our laughter at such a situation is, in Koestler's terms, 'the puffing away of emotion discarded by thought.'[30]

The double vision of the comic is also to be found in the gestures of Molière's characters. Sganarelle is seen examining Célie who has just fainted. We see him make an ambiguous gesture — 'lui passant la main sur le sein' — and then hear him say solemnly

Elle est froide partout et je ne sais qu'en dire,
Approchons - nous pour voir si sa bouche respire.
Ma foi, je ne sais pas, mais j'y trouve encor, moi,
Quelque signe de vie *(Sganarelle ou Le Cocu Imaginaire,* Sc. 4, ll. 113-
16)

Visually, the logic behind his gesture is that of the lecherous *bourgeois;* aurally, it is that of the passer-by who has to assume hastily the role of doctor. In *Le Médecin Malgré Lui,* there is a similar case of visual and aural ambiguity — while examining Jacqueline, the would-be doctor Sganarelle assures her gravely that his procedure is, despite strong appearances to the contrary, strictly medical (Act II, Sc. 3).

The double vision of comedy often forms the basis of a scene or a situation in Molière — indeed, the crossing of two independent causal chains through coincidence, mistaken identity or misunderstanding forms one of the most common formulae for comedy.[31] There are three examples of this *quiproquo* in Molière which may be quoted as examples of the thought implicit in the situation. In *L'Ecole des Femmes* (Act IV, Sc. 2). Arnolphe talks in imagination to himself. The notary answers him, and a dream-like conversation ensues in which Arnolphe meditates on his plan for preventing Horace cuckolding him, while the notary gives his professional advice in answer to Arnolphe's anguished queries. A *dialogue de sourds* ensues, in which each pursues his own logic: both blend in a sequence of questions and answers which in themselves form a coherent conversation. In fact, it is nothing less than a *reductio ad absurdum* of conversation and language, in which words can simultaneously be seen to form sense and nonsense:

Le Notaire	Ah! le voilà! Bonjour. Me voici tout à point Pour dresser le contrat que vous souhaitez faire.
Arnolphe, sans le voir	Comment faire?
Le Notaire	Il le faut dans la forme ordinaire.
Arnolphe, sans le voir	A mes précautions je veux songer de près.
Le Notaire	Je ne passerai rien contre vos intérêts.
Arnolphe, sans le voir	Il se faut garantir de toutes les surprises.
Le Notaire	Suffit qu'entre mes mains vos affaires soient mises. Il ne vous faudra point, de peur d'être déçu, Quittancer le contrat que vous n'ayez reçu.
Arnolphe, sans le voir	J'ai peur, si je vais faire éclater quelque chose, Que de cet incident par la ville on ne cause.
Le Notaire	Hé bien! il est aisé d'empêcher cet éclat, Et l'on peut en secret faire votre contrat.
Arnolphe, sans le voir	Mais comment faudra-t-il qu'avec elle j'en sorte?
Le Notaire	Le douaire se règle au bien qu'on vous apporte.
Arnolphe, sans le voir	Je l'aime, et cet amour est mon grand embarras.
Le Notaire	On peut avantager une femme en ce cas. (ll. 1039-55).

In *Le Malade Imaginaire* there is a similar conversation between two supposedly conscious characters, Monsieur Diafoirus and Argan (Act II, Sc. 5), as the former begins to greet the hypochondriac:

Monsieur Diafoirus	Nous venons ici, Monsieur. . .
Argan	Avec beaucoup de joie. . .
Monsieur Diafoirus	Mon fils Thomas, et moi. . .
Argan	L'honneur que vous me faites. . .
Monsieur Diafoirus	Vous témoigner, Monsieur. . .
Argan	Et j'aurais souhaité. . .
Monsieur Diafoirus	Le ravissement où nous sommes. . .
Argan	De pouvoir aller chez vous. . .
Monsieur Diafoirus	De la grâce que vous nous faites. . .
Argan	Pour vous en assurer. . .
Monsieur Diafoirus	De vouloir bien nous recevoir. . .

Argan	Mais vous savez, Monsieur. . .
Monsieur Diafoirus	Dans l'honneur, Monsieur. . .
Argan	Ce que c'est qu'un pauvre malade . . . (etc.)

The compliments of Diafoirus are 'completed' by Argan with the appearances of verbal coherence — yet we see words being stretched out to form a seemingly unending spiral of linguistic absurdity and empty sounds.

In *L'Avare* (Act V, Sc.3), Harpagon and Valère are also at linguistic loggerheads — thinking that the miser's accusation of theft refers to his love for Elise, Valère answers each successive question consistently in the light of Harpagon's obsession with his stolen 'cassette'. But it is much more than a mere sustained *malentendu*. Beginning from the simple misinterpretation of a single word, Molière exploits language so cleverly that the same words (*honneur, amour, foi, flamme*, etc.) are gradually made to carry the most divergent meanings that it is possible to incorporate in them — that of an inanimate object, and that of a person. The double interpretation of a single line of thought surely goes much further than Bergson's explanation of this type of comic as the 'boule de neige' which from small beginnings gathers ever-increasing momentum as it rolls on.[32] What the comic points to here is the different but self-consistent value of judgements which may shape the individual's use and interpretation of language.

The clash of logics is nowhere better exemplified than in the language of Molière's doctors. Tomès inquires about a certain patient: Lisette answers that he is 'Fort bien; il est mort', and he can deny it on the most impressive medical authority: 'Cela est impossible. Hippocrate dit que ces sortes de maladies ne se terminent qu'au quatorze, ou au vingt-un; et il n'y a que six jours qu'il est tombé malade.' (*L'Amour Médecin*, Act II, Sc. 2). It is not merely the discrepancy between subjective notion and fact that is comic, but that according to the medical code of rules he *cannot* be dead. Tomès is right, and can invoke irrefutable theory to prove his point and Lisette cannot. When Angélique pleads with Diafoirus not to force her to marry him, he can *prove* that she is wrong — 'Nego consequentiam . . .' (*Le Malade Imaginaire*, Act II, Sc. 6). A wrong diagnosis on his part can be corrected by judicious use of medical jargon (Act II, Sc. 6). Sganarelle can use burlesque reasoning with impeccable form to reassure Géronte that medicine has changed the respective positions of heart and liver (*Le Médecin Malgré Lui*, Act II, Sc. 4). The burlesque reasoner, whether medical or lay, cannot be proved formally wrong however absurd he appears, whilst the characters who are in possession of indubitable fact cannot prove formally that they are right. Our double attitude to what he says is best epitomized by Sganarelle's bewildered observation to Dom Juan: 'Ma foi! j'ai à dire . . . je ne sais; car vous tournez les choses d'une manière, qu'il semble que vous avez raison; et cependant il est vrai que vous ne l'avez pas' (Act I, Sc. 2).

It is this double-minded state that we enjoy as spectators which is both effect and cause of Molière's comedy, as we enter into the collision of appearances and reality provoked by it on every level — whether it be of character-comedy, of comedy of situation, of the simple verbal joke, of dialogue, of gesture. It is in perceiving the mode of thought behind this state that we are brought not only to suspend our code of disciplined thinking on the single level of reason (on entering the 'royaume enchanté' of the theatre we have already done that), but also to participate in the comedy implicit in that thinking, hidden in reality but brought to the surface and exploited by comedy in its manifold forms.[33] By living momentarily on two planes of thought at once we re-enact the idea behind that comedy. That idea, consisting of the simultaneous perception of two self-consistent but rationally incompatible ideas, characterizes through and through the purely intellectual form of Molière's comedy. Does it also characterize the view of life transmitted by the plays? Speaking of the meaning of plot for the dramatist, Bentley writes that 'to imitate an Action is to find objective equivalents of a subjective experience.'[34] The basic contention of this study will be that it is not in terms of moral teaching or of reason that Molière objectifies his thought, but rather in terms of paradox, which — as I hope to show in the following chapter — underlies intellectual comedies such as *Sganarelle* and *Dom Garcie* as well as the moral outlook of comic dramas such as *Tartuffe* and *Le Misanthrope*.

2   Les Apparences trompeuses

(1)

If we are to believe Grimarest's *Vie de Monsieur de Molière* (1705), one of the objections formulated by contemporaries against *Sganarelle ou le Cocu Imaginaire* was that 'le titre de cet ouvrage . . . n'est pas noble.'[1] The title certainly does suggest that the play's subject will be rather banal and farcical; it is true that it has little or none of the satirical interest of the successful *Les Précieuses Ridicules* which preceded it, and its relative neglect at the hands of critics is probably due to the controversy aroused by that *petit divertissement* as well as to the banality of its own subject-matter. Its general theme, which is the confusion of reality with appearances, was in addition a fairly conventional one at the time; *La Fausse Apparence* by Scarron, for example, had been performed several years earlier. Dom Carlos finds Dom Sanche hidden in the room of his *amante* Léonor, and concludes, not unnaturally, that she has deceived his trust. Appearances however are deceptive, and in the end the innocence of Léonor is duly vindicated. It is she who utters the moral of the play, to the effect that 'Une fausse apparence est un dangereux mal' (Act V, Sc. 7). Boisrobert's *Apparences trompeuses* also offers multiple examples of jealousy confusing appearances with reality. Fleride is glimpsed by her *amant* in her room with his rival, disguised as the *amant*. Dom Alonce, father of the virtuous Ismène, finds her alone with the reprobate Dom César who summarizes the play's theme when he says:

> . . . un soupçon conçu sans apparence,
> Porta ma jalousie à quelque extravagance.

J. Rousset has demonstrated that other *genres* such as the *ballet de cour,* the pastoral and tragi-comedy made extensive use of related themes such as illusion, disguise, deception, both conscious or unconscious on the part of the characters.[2] Yet if the general nature of the theme could be said to be conventional, the manner in which it was treated by Molière was so strikingly original that it evoked admiration from his friends as well as from the enemies he had made during the first years in Paris after his stay in the provinces. A zealous but importunate admirer, La Neufvillaine, averred that he had learnt the entire play by heart, and published, without Molière's knowledge, *La comédie Sganarelle avec des arguments sur chaque scène,* in which he repeatedly extols the incomparable comic genius of the author.[3] On the other hand Donneau de Visé who was at the time ill-disposed towards

15

Molière, wrote that 'Le Cocu imaginaire . . . est, à mon sentiment et à celui de beaucoup d'autres, la meilleure de toutes ses pièces et la mieux écrite.'⁴ Although his praise may well have contained some trace of irony (he was writing during '*la querelle de l'Ecole des Femmes*'), a contemporary critic as ardently devoted as he was to discovering the 'plagiarisms' of which Molière was supposedly guilty would not have failed to draw attention to borrowings, real or imaginary, in *Sganarelle*.⁵

The paradox of appearances and reality underlies every aspect of this play — its structure and theme, as well as the motivation of the characters. Its originality resides in the highly intellectual and rigorous manner in which the paradox is developed on all these levels: appearances and reality provide the two mutually incompatible but self-consistent interpretations of the same event, which clash, not arbitrarily (or with an illusion of arbitrariness) but with extreme precision and impeccable regularity. Each interpretation is governed by its own exact logic, and the logic followed by each character is no less rational and exact than that of the spectator who enjoys the double vision of comedy. All the characters are forerunners of the more famous *imaginaires* who people Molière's theatre, as they systematically interpret successive events in the light of their own preconceptions of reality. Each character has therefore his own subjective vision of things, fully coherent and rational, but at variance not only with that of his neighbour, but also with the true situation of the play.

As an epigraph to his play, Molière might well have chosen a quotation from Montaigne which expresses exactly the use which he makes of, and the idea behind, the paradox of appearances and reality in the play: 'Il est bien aisé, sur des fondemens avouez, de bastir ce qu'on veut; car, selon la loy et ordonnance de ce commencement, le reste des pièces du bastiment se conduit aysément, sans se démentir. Par cette voye nous trouvons notre raison bien fondée, et discourons à boule veue...'⁶

The basic 'loy et ordonnance' which govern the erection of a rational construction on subjective premises are to be found in Scenes 4 and 5. Célie, having been informed by her father Gorgibus that she must marry a person of his choice, and not Lélie, to whom she has been promised, falls in a faint and drops the portrait of him which she is carrying. The *bourgeois* Sganarelle rushes to her aid; as he tries to revive her, his wife glimpses him in what she imagines to be a compromising situation. She suspects his fidelity at the precise moment when he is thinking of running off with Célie in his arms to seek help. What he undertakes in a spirit of helpfulness is promptly interpreted by his pursuing wife as evidence of her worst fears. This is the first of a series of mistakes which the characters make about events external to themselves; but *Sganarelle* is not merely a play turning on the simple confusion of appearances and reality, for each confusion merely serves as a pretext for the characters to consolidate the erroneous impression with closely reasoned argument. The event is subordinate to the propensity which the characters have for deduction and induction which makes up their very elementary psychology. It does not therefore seem completely accurate to say, like J. D. Hubert, that '. . . the initial blunders remain mostly external to the characters who have committed them and can therefore have very little to do with their psychology.'[7]

Thus the psychological trait which dominates all the characters enables Sganarelle's wife to substantiate immediately the somewhat tentative evidence of her senses both by deduction and induction: she remembers the apparent coldness of his recent behaviour towards her, connecting logically what appears to be his present action with his past tendencies, and interprets each attitude in the light of the other. And from this particular argument, she even derives a proverb-like truth which she applies to husbands in general:

Je ne m'étonne plus de l'étrange froideur
Dont je le vois répondre à ma pudique ardeur;
Il réserve, l'ingrat, ses caresses à d'autres,
Et nourrit leurs plaisirs par le jeûne des nôtres.
Voilà de nos maris le procédé commun:
Ce qui leur est permis leur devient importun. (Sc. 5, ll. 127-32)

The second stage of the confusion is both an extremely skilful repetition and a reversal of the first error. Sganarelle sees his wife looking at Lélie's portrait, which Célie had just dropped. Just as Sganarelle is moved by a 'fort vilain soupçon' (Sc. 6, l. 149), his wife is doing nothing more harmful than admire the craftsmanship with which it has been made (ll. 150-3). His initial suspicions, therefore, are not even probable, but his wife gives him apparently adequate grounds for disquiet by admiring Lélie. On the strength of seeing the portrait in his wife's possession as well as hearing her praise him, he accuses her of infidelity. The proof of her duplicity is to him as concrete in its nature as that which Alceste will presume to have in the form of the *billet* supposedly written by Célimène to Oronte.[8] Sganarelle tells his wife euphemistically:

La chose est avérée, et je tiens dans mes mains
Un bon certificat du mal dont je me plains. (Sc. 6, ll. 175-6)

The extremely delicate irony in the situation lies precisely in the fact that he sees in the portrait tangible proof for what he is saying, whereas a portrait is, by its very nature, only a symbol of verisimilitude, a mere substitute for reality. The words he uses to express what he feels are also figurative symbols: he cannot utter the thought which presents itself forcefully to his mind, because his vanity and phobia of cuckoldry prevent him from crystallizing his cuckoldry:

> Sganarelle est un nom qu'on ne me dira plus,
> Et l'on va m'appeler seigneur Corneillius, (ll. 191-2)
> D'un panache de cerf sur le front me pourvoir,
> Hélas! voilà vraiment un beau venez-y-voir! (ll. 199-200)

His ambiguous and oblique references to horns are not only the effect of his elementary psychology, but are also the reason for the complication of the comic confusion. They have the immediate effect of making his wife unable to accept them literally:

> Parle donc sans rien feindre . . .
> Tu prends d'un feint courroux le vain amusement (ll. 197, 203)

she tells him. The motive which she can with all logic suspect behind his 'feint courroux' is that of wishing to distract her attention from his own guilt. It is a stratagem to forestall the force of her legitimate grievances: injured innocence is therefore the attitude imposed on her by reason.[9] Sganarelle can do no more than admire the impertinence which calmly assumes the mask of a prude (ll. 203-8). With each applying his or her own logic to the appearances offered by the other, no explanation is possible. We are forced to concede that both are correct in protesting their innocence, and both wrong in supposing that the other is trying to outwit them. And both are simultaneously deceiving themselves, rather than deceiving, or being deceived by, the other.

The basic situation is repeated and intensified when Lélie finds Sganarelle in possession of his *portrait* in Scene 9. He informs Lélie that he found it in the hands of someone whom he, Lélie, ought to know, proceeds to tell him how distasteful a husband finds such attention given to his wife, and further complicates the issue for the distraught suitor of Célie when he hints that his wife has cuckolded him. It is now Lélie's turn to make what he thinks he has heard fit his previous knowledge of the situation, as he now remembers (Sc. 10) that Célie had been promised to a decrepit and wealthy husband. The appearance of the *bourgeois* fits this description, and any existing ambiguity in what he has told Lélie is immediately clarified by a true fact, which Gorgibus indeed mentioned earlier (Sc. 1, ll. 49 ff.).

A pause is introduced into the furious sequence of erroneous perceptions with the first and only appearance of Le Parent in the play (Sc. 12). Le Parent comes in at the precise centre of the action, when all the characters, with the exception of Célie, have been drawn into the mounting confusion. His central position in the structure of the play serves as a temporary balance between the two halves, and what he says emphasizes this. It is true, he tells Sganarelle, that one ought to approve the most rigorous conduct on the part of husbands whenever their marital honour is threatened, but he points out that the would-be cuckold has insufficient evidence before him to prove his suspicions. In his advice, Le Parent therefore embodies a dual attitude of approval and caution. Sganarelle is right to show concern, but wrong to reach precipitate conclusions. Confronted with the problem of discriminating between appearances and truth, the only course one can follow is to investigate patiently what *appears* to be the case. The appearance of Le Parent has the effect of slowing up the tempo of the play, as his ponderous wisdom appears to prevail on Sganarelle. It also fulfils a function similar to that of Eliante and Philinte in *Le Misanthrope*, who give substantially the same advice to the jealous Alceste: 'Une lettre peut bien tromper par l'apparence' (Act IV, Sc. 2, l. 1241), Philinte tells him. Both the *raisonneurs* of that play and Le Parent give objective appraisals of a situation which is being exclusively interpreted according to a subjectively coherent view of things. Without enjoying as much knowledge as the spectators, for whom the paradox of true and false appearances can only be of an artificial nature, Le Parent is both in the play as well as standing on its periphery, both within and without at the same time. His answer to the confusion of appearances and reality (or rather to a possible confusion, for he does not conclude that Sganarelle is either right or wrong) is itself a paradox in its dual nature, fully consistent with his position of actor-spectator in the play. The first in the long line of the *raisonneurs* gives a sketchy but basic *résumé* of what his more famous successors will develop in more elaborate form.

The judicious counsel of Le Parent has an importance in the subsequent action out of all proportion to the eleven lines which contain it. It has the apparent effect of retarding Sganarelle's rashness, but in actual fact intensifies the comedy of errors by inducing a more rational frame of mind in him, for which future perceptions will have but additional urgency. It is reason, after all, which has been responsible for all the doubtful deductions which he has hitherto made. Just when he is giving an impression of lucidity, thereby contradicting all his previous actions which he dismisses as 'ces visions cornues' (Sc. 13, l. 325), he receives fresh visual evidence of the strongest possible nature, overthrowing all his resolutions. He sees his wife not with the portrait of Lélie, but with Lélie himself. Le Parent had successfully suggested to him that Lélie might well know his wife, and that this would provide an innocuous explanation of how she came to be in possession of the portrait, and Sganarelle himself had recognised this. Having vowed to suspend his judgement of appearances in future, he cannot extend the same principle to meet each contingency. The pause provided by his new-found lucidity is merely a case of 'reculer pour mieux sauter', and his subsequent actions illustrate the comedy of rationalization at a correspondingly higher level.

The comedy restarts with renewed vigour as Sganarelle sums up what Lélie has said to his wife in their formal conversation by saying 'Ce n'est

point s'expliquer en termes ambigus' (Sc. 16, 1. 343). He now explains
his present situation to Célie in more direct terms than before:

> Ce damoiseau, parlant par révérence,
> Me fait cocu, Madame, avec toute licence; (ll. 373-4)

Célie follows the course which each character has taken in turn, and
uses an external event to corroborate her own presentiment. Her
suspicion about Lélie's secret return is now amply confirmed.

With the confusion now embracing all four parties, there is a second
pause in the action as Sganarelle resolves on a more pragmatic course of
conduct (Sc. 17). The paradox of appearances and reality is now given a
new development in his character: his reasoning from his perceptions
leaves him in no doubt about the truth, but this creates additional
problems for his honour. How can he square his desire for revenge with
his pusillanimous nature? His answer is a subtle variation on the theme
which all the characters have illustrated so well, that of rationalization:

> Je hais de tout mon coeur les esprits colériques,
> Et porte grand amour aux hommes pacifiques;
> Je ne suis point battant, de peur d'être battu,
> Et l'humeur débonnaire est ma plus grande vertu. (ll. 421-4)

Yet he reverts to his preoccupation — 'Il faut absolument que je prenne
vengeance' (1. 426) — only to reverse immediately this absolute resolve,
as he begins to analyse the concept of honour. What will he achieve if he
maintains his honour and is killed? 'Il vaut mieux être encor cocu que
trépassé' (1. 436), he reasons. The next stage of his rationalization of
his position involves a consideration of the actual state of *cocuage* as
opposed to its traditional image. It does not affect in the slightest degree
our personal appearance, and since it is not our fault, we cannot be
blamed. Besides, there are plenty of real problems in everyday life

> Sans s'aller, de surcroît, aviser sottement
> De se faire un chagrin qui n'a nul fondement (ll. 455-6)

All the effort of his reason has been devoted to proving without doubt
his betrayal to himself: when successful in this, however, it is then
devoted to making that 'reality' evaporate.

The logic of reason is convincing, but the logic of instinct he finds
even more convincing, and arrives armed to challenge Lélie to a duel
(Sc. 21). He now rationalizes once more his position, but in the inverse
direction, as he attempts to work himself up to the required pitch of
courage by his heroi-comic language:

> Ma colère à présent est en état d'agir;
> Dessus ses grands chevaux est monté mon courage;
> Et si je le rencontre, on verra du carnage.
> Oui, j'ai juré sa mort; rien ne peut l'empêcher.
> Où je le trouverai, je le veux dépêcher. (ll. 512-16)

When Lélie asks what is wrong, he can save face by yet another rationalization of his warlike attitude in banal and inoffensive terms: his armour is 'un habillement' put on for the rain (ll. 519-20); he can also rationalise his inaction to himself: 'si je n'étois sage, on verroit arriver un étrange carnage' (ll. 541-2).[10]

The following scene marks the climax of all the misunderstandings: all the characters are now on stage together, whereas previously the one character who could have explained the *malentendu* was generally absent from the scene. All the characters can explain the true nature of their actions in the light of the subjective interpretations of them. In spite of this, La Suivante is the only character free from preconception, and consequently the one who unravels all the complications; she tells them with a high degree of justification:

Vous voyez que sans moi vous y seriez encore,
Et vous aviez besoin de mon peu d'ellébore. (ll. 601-2)

Reason and logic, she implies, are not necessarily to be equated with common sense. More often than not 'le bon sens' must rescue them from the folly into which they lead those who practise their use too systematically.

Sganarelle and his wife illustrate the point which she has just made, by the dubious manner in which they accept each other's explanations (ll. 603-6). He is, however, quite happy with his apparent escape from cuckoldry and offers a formula for a solution:

...mutuellement croyons-nous gens de bien:
Je risque plus du mien que tu ne fais du tien;
Accepte sans façon le marché qu'on propose. (ll. 607-9)

The final paradox in this play of paradoxes is, therefore, one which Sganarelle willingly imposes on himself, for he accepts the apparent solution engineered by La Suivante and does not try to substantiate it by reason. His acceptance of it enables him to formulate the witty concluding line: 'Et, quand vous verriez tout, ne croyez jamais rien' (l. 657). In advising us not to trust appearances, he himself is the first to contradict his own maxim, by his all too ready acceptance of his wife's apparent fidelity. Sganarelle here amplifies burlesquely the advice formerly given by Le Parent, as he advises a suspension of reason as the best method of avoiding the confusion of true and false appearances. Better instead to be satisfied, or appear to be satisfied, with things as they appear to be, than to continue to afflict oneself needlessly by attempting to plumb the unfathomable depths of appearances. But what happens if one cannot bring oneself to limit judgement to the surface of appearances? That is the problem which confronts the hero of Molière's next play, *Dom Garcie de Navarre*.

(2)

Dom Garcie de Navarre ou Le Prince Jaloux has traditionally been regarded as a 'tragédie manquée', and its failure ascribed to the fact that the public at the Palais-Royal were not accustomed to see Molière in a serious role.[11] Only one critic, W.D. Howarth, has attempted to show that it does not differ radically from plays generally held to be comic in Molière's theatre: Molière did, after all, entitle it 'comédie', and it was only in the 1734 edition of his plays that it was called 'comédie héroïque'.[12]

Although the play does appear at first sight to be closer to the *genre* of tragi-comedy than of comedy, it has the same recurrent comic pattern as that of *Sganarelle,* namely a character making systematic and logical deductions from reality which are seen to be erroneous. However, in spite of having the same general pattern, there are very important differences in *Dom Garcie,* as Molière moves away from farce to comedy of character. In *Sganarelle,* the confusion of appearances and reality arose initially from external reality, and was then confirmed by the characters' own individual logic. In *Dom Garcie,* the source of this confusion is situated primarily in the mind of the character, and this confusion is subsequently confirmed by reality. Sganarelle's 'visions cornues' are merely of a temporary nature: but Dom Garcie's doubt is a permanent feature of his character, deriving from and sustained by his jealous temperament, which provides the initial premise on which his imagination works. There is also an additional element in his confusion which is present from the beginning, rendering it all the more natural and inevitable — the deliberately ambiguous attitude adopted by the *précieuse* Elvire towards her suitor. In the first scene, she illustrates the posture which she will maintain until the end of the play. Faced with the choice of Dom Garcie or Dom Sylve as her suitor she confesses that objectively and rationally there is no ground why the former should merit her love. He has no qualities or merits which his rival does not possess in at least equal measure. Inexplicably, she feels drawn towards Dom Garcie. Elise underlines this ambiguous attitude when she tells her mistress that

Cet amour que pour lui votre astre vous inspire,
N'a sur vos actions pris que bien peu d'empire (ll. 15-16)

Elvire admits that she has even tried to balance any preference that may have been shown towards Dom Garcie by a display of friendship for Dom Sylve (ll. 33-6). Her intellectualized approach towards love demands adherence to a *précieux* code of courtship which deems that the most discreet 'avowals' of love must suffice for any suitor: she will not declare her affection verbally, but in 'un soupir', 'un regard', 'une simple rougeur', 'un silence' (ll. 69-70). Since her rigorous code of *précieux* honour has no place for unequivocal statement of feeling, jealousy is considered to be both irrational and offensive (ll. 100 ff).[13]

The comedy is constructed around the conflict between Dom Garcie, who perpetually doubts appearances, and Elvire, who, by her belief that an *amant* ought to accept appearances unquestioningly, provides the liveliest encouragement for those doubts. The conflict is focused most sharply in four 'tests' which confront the hero: on each occasion he promises not to fall victim to his jealous temperament, and each time he is in fact mastered by his pathological suspicions about Elvire's fidelity to him. For these episodes, as well as for the theme and principal characters of his play, Molière drew on an Italian source, *Le Gelosie fortunate del Principe Rodrigo* by Cicognini, published in 1654. But there are fundamental features in the French play which mark it off definitively from the Italian one. In *Dom Garcie,* the extreme subtlety of Elvire gives some initial credibility to the hero's suspicions, whereas in the Italian play, the corresponding character, Delmire, is not at all reticent or ambiguous in her avowals of love to Dom Rodrigue; in spite of his jealousy, she admits to her *confidente* that if she does not marry him, she will not marry at all (Act I, Sc.1), and she assures him many times of her love for him (e.g. Act II, Sc.2, Act II, Sc.7, Act III, Sc.4, etc.).[14] In the French version, it is Dom Lope, a scheming courtier, who contrives to implant the seeds of suspicion in Dom Garcie's jealous mind; the naïve *bouffon* Arlequin is unwittingly responsible for the confusion in the Italian play. Molière changes the order of the successive 'tests' which confront Dom Garcie, making them proceed from the stage of purely imaginary ambiguity to highly probable ambiguity; in Cicognini's play, on the other hand, these episodes are extremely arbitrary, and the possibility of comic progression is entirely overlooked. The most important consequence of these changes is to be found in the hero of the French play; if Despois and Mesnard are accurate in describing Dom Rodrigue as being 'jaloux sans motif suffisant', the opposite description of 'jaloux avec motif suffisant' would be nearer to the truth of Molière's character.[15]

The first of the 'tests' which his jealousy undergoes is to be found in Act I, Sc.3. Elvire has asked her suitor

...désirez-vous savoir
Quand vous pourrez me plaire, et prendre quelque espoir? (ll. 245-6)

She elaborates in three different forms the indispensable condition for his courtship, before announcing that he will find favour in her eyes

...quand d'un injuste ombrage
Votre raison saura me réparer l'outrage (ll. 255-6)

He has no sooner forsworn his jealousy when Dom Pèdre brings in a letter for Elvire. Instinctively, his suspicions betray themselves so much that she can only exclaim: 'Prodigieux effet de son tempérament!' (1. 329). It is perfectly obvious that Dom Garcie's jealousy originates here primarily from his temperament, and is thus of an imaginary character. On this occasion at least, Elvire is correct in her assessment of his behaviour, as she adjures him: 'Guérissez-le, ce mal: il n'est que dans l'esprit' (1. 342). By allowing him to see that the letter is addressed by Done Ignès to herself, she merely confirms something which is self-evident to all with the exception of Dom Garcie. It is significant that this, the weakest of all the Dom's deductions from appearances, forms the initial 'test' in the play, whereas in Cicognini it constitutes the second episode, in which Dom Rodrigue sees Delmire in the act of writing a letter (Act III, Sc.4).

It is the arch-schemer Dom Lope who engineers the subsequent 'test'. He leaves half of a letter, written by Elvire and tantalizingly incomplete, in view of Dom Garcie (Act II, Sc. 4). Before he comes to read it, Dom Garcie follows the same course as Sganarelle after his encounter with Le Parent, and lucidly reminds himself that he must at all costs avoid precipitate conclusions. Like Sganarelle, however, his apparent lucidity only gives a presentiment of the logical cecity of the true *imaginaire:*

> Consulte ta raison, prends sa clarté pour guide;
> Vois si de tes soupçons l'apparence est solide;
> Ne démens pas leur voix; mais aussi garde bien
> Que pour les croire trop, ils ne t'imposent rien (ll. 484-7)

To appeal to appearances is, for Dom Garcie, to be convinced by appearances, not only because he is an *imaginaire,* but also because the part of the letter which he reads *appears* as a betrayal of his passion. It makes mention of a 'rival' (l. 494), an 'obstacle' (l. 497), and of a desire on the part of Elvire to free herself from someone (ll. 499-501). According to appearances, therefore, his premonition is more sure and more probable than that in the first 'test'. This episode makes up the first 'test' in Cicognini. Arlequin has snatched part of a letter written by Delmire, to Florante, the *amant* of her *confidente* Delia, who was unable to write it herself on account of an injured hand. The fragment shown by the valet to Dom Rodrigue is signed 'Del'. . . (Act II, Sc. 3). Delmire, however, still declares her love for her suitor after his outburst of jealousy (Act II, Sc. 7), whereas Elvire merely lends probability to the Dom's assumption. When the latter conjectures that the *billet* has probably been written to a woman friend or a relative, she replies enigmatically

> Non, c'est pour un amant que ma main l'a formé,
> Et j'ajoute de plus, pour un amant aimé (Act II, Sc. 5, ll. 574-5)

It is paradoxical but fully consistent with the character of the *précieuse* that this, the most direct declaration of love for Dom Garcie (for the letter is written to him) is made with the intention of intensifying his doubts beyond endurance. For he is only too aware that she has not discouraged the attentions paid to her by his rival, Dom Sylve. Even when the completed letter is read to him, he has at least a point when he counters Elvire's anger by saying to her

Vous-même, dites-moi si cet événement
N'eût pas dans mon erreur jeté tout autre amant
(Act II, Sc. 6, ll. 646-7)

The essence of her long reply, to the effect that a true *amant* would not
let his faith be shaken by appearances, however compromising they
seemed to be, rests on the somewhat casuistical assertion that she would
be incapable of deceiving him (ll. 649-53, ll. 663 ff). Even in what
purports to be a *billet doux*, she praises Dom Garcie's past deeds whilst
criticizing bitterly his present humour!

Dom Garcie's third 'test' comes in Act III, Sc. 3, and has been
engineered by Dom Lope, as Dom Alvar will presently tell Elvire (Act
IV, Sc. 1, ll. 1104-5). Dom Garcie finds her alone with his presumed
rival, Dom Sylve. In the previous scene, Elvire has told the latter of her
preference for Dom Garcie, but the Dom himself can be excused if he is
still in some doubt about her intentions. When he confronts his 'rival',
he is merely curious about this unexpected visit (ll. 972 ff). But it is
Elvire once more who gives his uncertainty and curiosity a firm
foundation, as she chooses to remain obstinately enigmatic. Eventually
she does speak in an apparently definite way, but her unambiguous
words can only serve to heighten and prolong the ambiguous situation
as she tells him '...on ne me verra point le butin de vos feux' (l. 1035).
She deliberately intensifies this paradox to its highest pitch by stressing
that she speaks nothing but the truth:

Voilà mon coeur ouvert, puisque vous le voulez,
Et mes vrais sentiments à vos yeux étalés (ll. 1038-9)

It is scarcely surprising that the combination of Elvire's ambiguity and
his own jealous temperament should render him more certain than
hitherto in the play about his fate. He is confirmed in his logic by the
studied pose struck by Dom Sylve in the following scene and by the
latter's hasty withdrawal from his presence.

The fact that appearances have now assumed a more cogent form is
borne out by the two characters best placed to give an objective
appraisal of the action, namely the *raisonneurs* Dom Alvar and Elise.
Both perceive clearly how appearances contrive against Dom Garcie:
the former attenuates the Prince's error by emphasizing the role played
by external events (Act IV, Sc. 1, ll. 1104 ff). Elvire rejects this
reasoning scornfully, but Elise, the principal *raisonneur* of the play,
makes allowances for Dom Garcie's jealousy. She does this in an
interesting way, placing the Dom's jealous humour and Elvire's attitude
towards it in the same natural perspective, as she tells him that

. . . nous avons du Ciel ou du tempérament
Que nous jugeons de tout chacun diversement.
Et puisqu'elle vous blâme, et que sa fantaisie
Lui fait un monstre affreux de votre jalousie,
Je serois complaisante . . . (Act IV, Sc. 6, ll. 1182-6)[16]

In her view, Dom Garcie is as justified in following his subjective vision of reality as Elvire is in adhering to 'sa fantaisie', which envisages jealousy as a monstrous offence. The inference to be drawn from this and other speeches by the *raisonneur,* whose role is completely original to Molière's play and has no equivalent in Cicognini, is important — namely that Elvire, by her refusal to recognize the equally valid but necessarily diverse interpretations of the same situation, is partially responsible for Dom Garcie's misconstruction of it. When it is recalled that in Cicognini the corresponding episode simply consists of Dom Rodrigue seeing Delmire's brother Dom Pèdre, disguised, in her room, (Act III, Sc. 5 and 6), it is clear how much Molière elaborated it in order to make it fit into his own comic schema.

It is the fourth and last 'test' which presents Dom Garcie with the greatest of all difficulties, as he sees Elvire embrace a man. With unconscious irony he says that he just witnessed 'le renversement de toute la nature' (Act IV, Sc. 7, 1. 1232), for the 'man' whom he has seen will prove to be none other than Done Ignès, disguised as a man. His language at this point takes on a new certainty:

Faut-il que je m'assure au rapport de mes yeux?
Ah! sans doute ils me sont des témoins trop fidèles (ll. 1223-4)

In all his previous 'tests', what he saw had in fact no unambiguous visual relation to his own interpretation of it. The letter handed to Elvire, the fragment of the *billet* in her writing, the presence of Dom Sylve in Elvire's room, all had to be seen in the distorting perspective of his jealous humour before they could become totally unambiguous. But what he sees now is, for the first time in the play, totally at one with his interpretation of it. The advice of Dom Alvar, which is basically the same as that given by Le Parent to Sganarelle, is however much less objectively valid at this stage of the play:

Seigneur, nos passions nous font prendre souvent
Pour chose véritable un objet décevant.
Et de croire qu'une âme à la vertu nourrie
Se puisse...(ll. 1246-9)

Le Parent was well-founded in advising Sganarelle to be cautious, since the latter is forced to admit that appearances have never actually coincided with his interpretation of them (Sc. 12). It seems to me that the interpretations given of the Dom's actions in this scene by G. Michaut and J. D. Hubert do not take fully into account the complex nature of this comic climax, towards which Molière has progressively and skilfully orientated his play. For the first critic 'Convaincu de son erreur, il n'y devrait pas retomber aussitôt ...' and for the second 'He rejects, by such irrational means, all previous assurances of Done Elvire's innocence, and considers his ill-founded and frequently refuted suspicions as premonitions of the absolute, the eternal, the awful truth.'[17]

But Elvire's sincerity if not her fidelity is highly debatable, and there has been an undeniable progression from the realm of 'the purely imaginary to the apparently certain'.[18] Michaut attributes the failure of Dom Garcie's character, and therefore of the comedy, to his inability to correct his faulty apprehension of each occurrence.[19] But this is surely beside the point, since it is the prerogative of the *imaginaires* in Molière never to see the incidents of the present in the light of their past experience. On the contrary, their nature inevitably inclines them to see each fresh event solely in terms of itself: the fact that Arnolphe has repeatedly failed to control the action in no way detracts from the overweening confidence with which he envisages each successive occurrence. We find that the opposite is true, for he is paradoxically more confident as his failures become more and more disastrous.

The comedy of Dom Garcie proceeds in an almost inverse direction to that of Arnolphe, as he appears increasingly more justified in his assessment of each fresh situation. The fact that he appears correct in his judgement does not take away from his comic side, but rather enhances it. He has hitherto been wrong in each case, appearances to the contrary, and although appearances are stronger than ever in the fourth episode, the spectators know and expect to see the familiar comic mechanism of logical but erroneous appearances come into play again. And what can be more comic than the man who has evident and logical justification for thinking that he is right, and who inevitably is proved to be wrong? The final 'test' of Dom Garcie illustrates the fact that what might seem superficially to be a straightforward comedy of errors involves in reality the ever-ascending comedy of rationality constantly thwarted by the intrusion of the irrational. That this is fundamental to Molière's comic design may be seen from the fact that the very perceptible progression from the third to the fourth 'test' is not present in Cicognini: he merely repeats the preceding one with no essential variation, as Rodrigue discovers the Duchesse Bélise disguised as a man in Delmire's room (Act V, Sc. 3).

The final 'test' represents not only the climax of Dom Garcie's comedy, but also of Elvire's *précieux* attitude towards him. Throughout the play, each fresh outburst on the part of her suitor has occasioned a firmer rebuke from her and a threat to discontinue her friendship with him. Now she couches both rebuke and threat in the most extreme form, as she demands no less than 'Un sacrifice entier de vos soupçons jaloux' (Act IV, Sc. 8, l. 1375). Dom Garcie must decide whether he is going to remain true to his suspicious nature, and thereby forfeit her love, or gain her love at the expense of his own need for certainty. Since he persists in demanding an explanation from her, she has an ideal opportunity for strengthening her resolve. She utters this resolve in terms which echo ironically those employed by Dom Garcie when vowing to resist his future doubts:

> Et si je puis jamais oublier mes serments
> Tombent sur moi du Ciel les plus grands châtiments!
>
> (Act IV, Sc. 9, ll. 1466-7)[20]

The last Act is thus predictably concerned with the gradual weakening of her decision, until she capitulates utterly by admitting that she will marry Dom Garcie without conditions: 'jaloux ou non jaloux' (Act V, Sc. 6, l. 1870).

In the actions of both principal characters, an exact comic parallel is cleverly worked out in inverse directions. Dom Garcie progresses with apparent logic towards certainty, and is finally most certainly and most comically wrong. Elvire obtains more and more evidence to support her initial premise that she ought logically to choose a different suitor. In both cases, the logics of appearances are swept aside, and a happy ending is assured in spite of and at the expense of reason. Elvire cannot explain rationally her choice of Dom Garcie as husband, and is finally forced to make room for the irrational as the prime motivating factor in one's actions in a much more real if no less puzzled manner than she did at the beginning of the play:

> . . . je vois qu'on doit quelque indulgence
> Aux défauts où du ciel fait pencher l'influence (ll. 1868-9)

Part Two

The Philosophy of Paradox

3 Tartuffe

The paradox of appearances and reality assumes a different and much more complex form in *Tartuffe* from that of the two plays discussed in the last chapter. In those and in previous plays, the basis of the comic situation, the *malentendu,* was soon resolved and the original order existing at the start of the play restored. Questions such as those of guilt and innocence, right and wrong, did not arise in any philosophical sense, because they belonged to the moral order of the play, which the *dénouement* left intact. The confusion of appearances and reality is more intellectual in its nature than moral. Neither Sganarelle's wife nor Elvire are guilty of moral duplicity in any real sense; they are both caught up in circumstances from which Sganarelle and Dom Garcie logically but erroneously infer that they were guilty. They are, it is true, guilty of using appearances to implant suspicion in the minds of Sganarelle and Dom Garcie as regards their fidelity; they are, however, never guilty of actual infidelity. In *L'Ecole des Maris* and *L'Ecole des Femmes* the paradox appears in a slightly modified form. Both Léonor and Agnès are admittedly guilty of deceiving their guardians, but their deception is necessary to re-establish the difference between the hypocritical and ascetic morality of Sganarelle and Arnolphe, and their own complete innocence. It is not the proof of moral ambiguity, but rather that of the permanent gulf which separates right from wrong in Molière's dramatic universe. It is a fact that at no time throughout these two plays does the spectator or reader experience the slightest feeling of doubt either about the inevitability or the desirability of the trick practised upon the *barbons.* It is they who place their wards in situations to which deception offers the only issue, and since they remain rigidly true to their obsessions, a *dénouement* requires that they be deceived.

Tartuffe is also a play centring around the confusion of appearances and reality which forms the basis of religious hypocrisy. To the extent that such hypocrisy is ultimately defeated in the play, one could perhaps think that the *dénouement* leaves the moral order intact just as it is left intact at the end of *Sganarelle ou Le Cocu Imaginaire* or *Dom Garcie.* In *Tartuffe,* however, circumstances do not merely contrive to lend an air of reality to appearances, as was the case in those plays; the moral order is here wilfully overturned by hypocrisy, and cannot be re-established from within the dramatic universe of the play. Recourse must therefore be made to a *deus ex machina* in the form of Louis XIV, who opportunely intervenes to reward good and to punish evil. The paradox of *Tartuffe* lies not only in the confusion of hypocrisy with true religion, but in the permanently precarious balance in which good and evil are seen to stand in relation to each other.

This paradox is obviously at the centre of the vision and thought behind the play. But the *Tartuffe* of 1669 stands at the end of five years of development and controversy, and it is not surprising that its vision and thought evolve accordingly, making it Molière's most ambiguous play. The history of the present play shows that it is a compromise between the original version of 1664 and an artificial *Tartuffe,* the product of an enforced afterthought, since the original conception had to be modified by considerations extraneous to the creation of a work of art, such as pressure from organized religion.[1] This is most clearly seen in the development of the roles of Tartuffe and Cléante. From 1664 to 1667 Tartuffe's role underwent considerable modifications, if we are to judge from Molière's second *Placet* (1667). There Panulphe, as the character was then named, is described as being a man of the world, fashionably dressed and thus less liable to offend the enemies of the first version in respect of his costume at least.[2] On the basis of the description of Panulphe in the second *Placet* and contemporary documents, G. Couton has argued cogently that the costume of the first Tartuffe was as follows: 'soutane, ou cette soutane courte qu'on appelait la soutanelle, petit collet; tout indique qu'il était autre chose qu'un laïc, même pieux, mais bien un homme d'Eglise, tonsuré sûrement, peut-être diacre, peut-être prêtre.'[3] In other words, that of at least a semi-ecclesiastic or spiritual director fulfilling definite clerical functions.[4] Of the Tartuffe of the final version the same scholar has also written: 'Mais l'adoucissement essentiel, par rapport au texte de 1664, est sans doute que Tartuffe n'apparaît plus comme d'Eglise. Il porte un costume sobre certes, comme un homme qui s'est 'mis dans la réforme', mais ce costume ne sent plus autant l'ecclésiastique.'[5] Similar attenuations are also discernible in the development of Cléante. We know from the detailed description of the 1667 play in the *Lettre sur la Comédie de l'Imposteur* that his role was much more dramatic and aggressive in attacking religious bigotry than in the final version, in which he appears as the epitome of the *honnête homme*.[6] If the role existed in 1664, it could scarcely have taken the present form of the *raisonneur*; in a comedy of three Acts there would have been little place for the lengthy arguments on true and false piety of 1669. The modifications in the conception of the role of Tartuffe (1664-9) and to a much lesser extent in that of Cléante (1667-9) serve then to illustrate the more unambiguous nature of the earlier versions for Molière and doubtless also for the audience. It seems to me that the most promising indication of the meaning of *Tartuffe* for his author lies in the changing expression of his subject, symbolized in the evolution of the role of Tartuffe.

According to the secretary of the troupe, La Grange, the first version of 1664 comprised '...trois actes de *Tartuffe,* qui estoient les trois premiers.'[7] The perennial question of whether or not they constituted a complete play need not be discussed here. La Grange obviously refers to the first three Acts of the 1669 play. This means that the 1664 performance ended with the events set in motion by the accusation of Damis that Tartuffe is attempting to seduce Orgon's wife. The hypocrite's unexpected avowal of his sins and Orgon's equally unexpected justification of his guest's behaviour would have followed. Far from advising Tartuffe to avoid Elmire in future, her husband encourages him to frequent her company, contributing richly to his own future *cocuage* and making for an hilarious ending in the nature of the *dénouement* in *George Dandin.*[8]

The content of these three Acts may well have differed from those of the final version, and may well have formed a complete play — that is a matter for speculation. What La Grange *is* at pains to underline in his *Registre* is that the 1664 performance certainly did not proceed beyond the ending to Act III of the present play, which represents one of the comic apexes of *Tartuffe.* The contemporary description of the 1664 performance in the *Relation des Plaisirs de l'Ile Enchantée* as 'fort divertissante' would thus square with the essential part of La Grange's statement.[9] Accordingly, the episode of Tartuffe ordering the family out of the house (Act IV, Sc. 7), and the consequent intervention of the King (Act V) were not part of the original version of the play. Even without the confirmation of La Grange's statement, it is patent that the *deus ex machina* is a later addition, which, whilst present in 1667, is meant to symbolize Molière's gratitude to Louis XIV for his support during the *Tartuffe* controversy. The political motivation for Tartuffe's threats to the family (involving a 'donation' and 'certaine cassette': see Act IV, Sc. 8) are also later additions, for they serve both as pretext and condition for the King's intervention. But more importantly, they constitute, with the final Act, a fresh and more sinister turn of events for the family, which were entirely absent from the 'comédie divertissante' of 1664.

In 1664 the Tartuffe of the three-Act performance at Versailles was therefore unequivocally comic, even farcical in his nature. By 1667-9 he had become a complex figure, no longer simply a figure of fun but one capable of threatening the existence of Orgon and his family. The judgement of E. Rigal on the 1669 character of Tartuffe has been re-echoed by critic and actor alike: '...Tartuffe reste dans son ensemble un personnage à la fois sinistre et comique.'[10] In the present version of the play, it is possible to see how the character of the hypocrite evolves from its original conception to that of the later versions. By following the dramatic development of Tartuffe in the 1669 play, it is also possible to trace the evolution of Molière's thought, of which *Tartuffe* is the changing aesthetic expression.

(2)

The first three Acts of the 1669 play are faithful in spirit, if not necessarily in content, to the 'comédie divertissante' of 1664. Indeed, there is little room for ambiguity in Molière's portrayal of the hypocrite. The first reference to him is made by Damis, who seems to provoke Mme Pernelle deliberately into mentioning his name: 'Votre Monsieur Tartuffe est bien heureux sans doute...' (l. 41). This slighting reference to Tartuffe allows Molière to give a description of him through the eyes of Mme Pernelle, that is, the character least liable to endear him to us. From the start of the play, she is presented as a grotesque caricature of religious austerity, so that we are, so to speak, conditioned to believe precisely the opposite of what she says.[11] Damis goes on to speak of Tartuffe contemptuously as 'un cagot de critique' (l. 45) and 'ce pied plat' (l. 59), and this initial impression of extreme mediocrity is reinforced by Dorine's reference to him as a 'gueux' (l. 63).[12] By insisting on the cecity of those who refuse to see the real contemptible Tartuffe, Molière ensures that our scorn for them reflects also onto the source of their cecity — namely Tartuffe. The absent Tartuffe and Orgon and Mme Pernelle — they are the comic heroes of the first Act.

This process of a double-edged satire is continued throughout the next Act. In the second scene, although Orgon is principally the comic subject, he is comic only because of his absurd obsession with Tartuffe, of whom Dorine gives a physically grotesque description (ll. 191-4). She repeats this description in Sc. 4 (ll. 233-40), and in the following scene Orgon attempts to convince Cléante of the worth of his guest. Once again Orgon and Tartuffe are comically discredited at one and the same time; all Orgon's grandiloquence only serves to convince us that Tartuffe is, in the words of the *Lettre sur la Comédie de l'Imposteur* '. . . un fourbe, un méchant, un traître et un animal très pervers dans le langage de l'ancienne comédie.'[13] The whole of the second Act is dominated by the impending threat of Orgon to marry Mariane to Tartuffe. This could of course seem to be the tragic sacrifice of innocence to his lust. But Tartuffe has not yet outgrown his comic stature of the previous Act; Dorine continues the process of creating a farcical Tartuffe by suggestion and depiction, drawing attention to the gross disparity between the youthful Mariane and the physically grotesque *faux dévot* (ll. 502-517). The serious import of Orgon's decision is further lessened by Dorine's verbal duel with him, and by her constant asides, in one of which she refers to Orgon's object of veneration as 'un beau museau' (l. 560). The retirement of Orgon, without having achieved his expected acquiescence from Mariane, is symbolic of the triumph of the comic spirit, incarnate here in Dorine, over potential disaster.

Scene 3 follows a similar pattern; Mariane realizes the serious consequences of Orgon's threats, and Dorine keeps the tone resolutely burlesque with her description of Tartuffe's appearance, and of their idyllic marriage and triumphant return to his provincial town (ll. 636 ff.). Her vision of Mariane's marriage to Tartuffe is in fact so inexpressibly comic that she has to invent a new word to describe the experience — that of being 'tartuffiée' (l. 674). Thus in spite of the fact that no stratagem has been adopted to prevent the marriage, the Tartuffe described in this scene is still too far removed from the *scélérat* of the later action to threaten the unreality of the comic spectacle.

Before Tartuffe's entrance in Act III Sc. 2, Dorine (and Molière) take care to suggest once again that the *faux dévot* is in love with Elmire:

Sur l'esprit de Tartuffe elle a quelque crédit;
Il se rend complaisant à tout ce qu'elle dit,
Et pourroit bien avoir douceur de coeur pour elle. (ll. 835-7)
(cf. also l. 84)

The suggested contradiction in Tartuffe's behaviour is comic within the terms of the *Lettre sur la Comédie*, that is '...toute apparence différente du fond ...toute contrariété entre actions qui procèdent d'un même principe'.[14] We are henceforth prepared to scrutinize the behaviour of the hypocrite to find the astonishing paradox suggested to us by Dorine — that of a saint who nourishes a romantic passion, an ascetic who happens also, according to Dorine, to be a glutton. In the presence of characteristics which seem to us so mutually exclusive, our astonishment gives way to that state of mind which Ramon Fernandez aptly termed 'la conscience critique', and which is the condition *par excellence* of the perception of the ridiculous.[15]

This preposterous paradox in theory, which we have so far refused to accept in any serious sense, assumes flesh and bones in the second scene, and the 'critical idea' receives instant confirmation of its suspicion, for before he speaks, his rubicund appearance has made an indelible impression upon us. He may well begin his famous speech 'Laurent, serrez ma haire avec ma discipline' — our imagination will continue to hold tenaciously these two contrary pictures of him, however convincing he may be verbally. The logic of our imagination is, we feel, preferable to the logic behind his words.[16]

G. Michaut did not find Tartuffe at all comic in this scene: 'Sa pudeur dans la scène du mouchoir est grotesque? Il l'a voulu; il joue son rôle.'[17] But this judgement does not take into account the important fact that Molière has carefully implanted the critical idea in our mind; Tartuffe is thus undeniably comic in this scene, because, although he is playing the verbal part of his role with consummate skill, he is still unaware of the contradiction implicit in the condemnation of Dorine's physical appearance by someone who, reason as he may, cannot camouflage his own ruddy exterior. How could one listen to him saying to the servant:

> Couvrez ce sein que je ne saurois voir;
> Par de pareils objets les âmes sont blessées,
> Et cela fait venir de coupables pensées. (ll. 860-2)

without becoming aware of the discrepancy between his spiritual sensitivity and his lecherous mien? Acting a part which is at variance with his physical appearance, he betrays his real thoughts more fully than he could know in the last of these lines. Here the guilty thoughts, Molière would have us believe, come more naturally to Tartuffe's mind than his lofty spiritual admonition. Dorine seizes immediately on such an interpretation of his lines, as truly revelatory of the man beneath the saint, and thus keeps him in comic perspective, suggesting:

> Vous êtes donc bien tendre à la tentation,
> Et la chair sur vos sens fait grande impression? (ll. 863-4)

Tartuffe may be rationally in control of his role in this scene, as Michaut suggested, but he is none the less comic because of the instinctive ascendancy of the logic of the imagination over reason, a logic which forces us to measure his solemn spiritual injunctions with Dorine's hypothetical picture of him:

> Et je vous verrois nu du haut jusques en bas,
> Que toute votre peau ne me tenteroit pas. (ll. 867-8)

The *Lettre sur la Comédie* draws attention to his more obvious comic side (or *disconvenance*) at the end of this scene, when Dorine gives him Elmire's message: '... il le reçoit avec une joie qui le décontenance et le jette un peu hors de son rôle: et c'est ici où l'on voit représentée mieux que nulle part ailleurs la force de l'amour, et les grands et les beaux jeux que cette passion peut faire par les effets involontaires...'[18]

But for us to see him as comic, it is not necessary that we should actually see the mask fall, but that Molière should subtly confront us with an interpenetration of contradictory images, which forces us to look for possible discrepancies in the character. This point seems to me to be worth stressing, because critics of Molière constantly speak of his comic as though it only occurred at a precise and given moment, that is, when the mask of the character is actually *seen* to fall. Naturally, the comic will be theatrically more obvious in such cases but only because the author has carefully orientated his play towards those central comic moments. It is, however, in the process of orientation that the psychological foundations of the comic are laid: in Tartuffe's case the spectator deduces his moral character from his physical appearance and his judgement is confirmed by the character's actions — without which the fall of the mask would greatly lose its impact.[19]

Michaut once again saw no comedy in the first of Tartuffe's *entretiens* with Elmire, in the following scene.[20] As I have tried to show, such a view does not take into account the fact that the dramatist has prepared us for this scene by his previous juxtaposition of extreme opposites, sexual lust and holiness, gluttony with asceticism. It has been left to the logic of the imagination to interpenetrate these opposites. Now, in the scene with Elmire, the comic is more direct because Tartuffe himself chooses to fuse these apparently incompatible elements, justifying his illicit passion in terms of high-flown devotion, immorality in the language of morality. It is important to note that he only makes use of the vocabulary of religion because he is speaking to the wife of his spiritual charge, just as 'apercevant Dorine' he had begun to speak of his spiritual obligations. His intellect is firmly in charge of the situation, at least at the outset of both scenes; the proof of this lies in the fact that he never ceases to couch his passion in religious terms. With line 930, 'Mon sein n'enferme pas un coeur qui soit de pierre', W.G. Moore sees Tartuffe beginning to leave his role of *dévot*.[21] I should prefer to say that rather than leaving his role, Tartuffe *extends* the scope of it to embrace even extramarital adventures. The crux of his speech illustrates this:

Mais les gens comme nous brûlent d'un feu discret,
Avec qui pour toujours on est sûr du secret;
Le soin que nous prenons de notre renommée
Répond de toute chose à la personne aimée,
Et c'est en nous qu'on trouve, acceptant notre coeur,
De l'amour sans scandale et du plaisir sans peur. (ll. 995-1000)

For the same critic 'This is the complete avowal, by the *masqué*, that his mask is a mask. It may not be funny; it is deeply comic.'[22] But nowhere throughout the play does Tartuffe choose to drop his mask of a *dévot*: even when he accuses himself (truthfully!) of heinous sins (ll. 1091-1106), he is not abandoning his mask. It is merely a case of 'reculer pour mieux sauter'. Even when he reveals his true nature to Orgon in Act IV Sc. 7, he will still cling to the fiction of his devotion, as he outlines his spiritual duty which compels him to evict the family (ll. 1563-4). The comic here derives not from the fact that he abandons his mask of *dévot,* but from his attempt to reconcile incompatibilities such as illicit passion and religious devotion, love of the creator with love of the creature, and from the dimension of irony which Molière inserts subtly into his lines 'Ah! pour être dévot, je n'en suis pas moins homme' (l. 966) and 'Mais Madame, après tout , je ne suis pas un ange' (l. 970), which produce a totally different impression on Elmire and the audience from that which he imagines he is giving. It is this dislocation of ends and means, the disharmony between effect and cause, that the writer of the *Lettre sur la Comédie* sees as one of the conditions of the comic of

Panulphe's actions in his scenes with Elmire: '...quand des moyens produisent une fin fort différente de celle pour quoi on les emploie, nous supposons, avec juste sujet, qu'on en a fait le choix avec peu de raison, parce que nous avons cette prévention générale qu'il y a des voies partout, et que quand on manque de réussir, c'est faute d'avoir choisi les bonnes.'[23]

Thinking that he is reconciling convincingly two irreconcilable modes of behaviour, he merely convinces us more firmly than ever of their irreconcilable nature. His expenditure on rational argument thus proves useless, for at each moment we are subtly assured by Molière that the hypocrite's 'thesis' cannot possibly be both rationally and emotionally acceptable to us at one and the same time. Whilst rationally we are obliged to accept his answer to Elmire's question as true ('Que fait là votre main?' to which he answers: 'Je tâte votre habit: l'étoffe en est moelleuse') (ll. 916-17), emotionally we refuse his explanation. In Pascalian terms 'La nature soutient la raison impuissante...'[24] If he is able to rationalize brilliantly his actions and desires, we know only too well that they are all too human in origin.

Nevertheless our attitude towards Tartuffe here is not merely one of detachment, as a reading of the play can too easily suggest. In the theatre we also identify ourselves with him, because we are aware that we are in the presence of a consummate actor who is able to rationalize sin by a brilliant *tour de force,* and to prove intellectually that he is not contradicting his profession of *dévot* in the slightest. As R. Bray points out, such identification belongs to the domain of the comedy of euphoria, as opposed to the comedy of satire which is founded upon detachment from the character:

> Non seulement le spectateur ne s'oppose pas au personnage dont il rit, mais il s'identifie à lui dans une sorte de communion. Le rire naît là dans une expansion de l'être, que facilite une disposition agréable du corps et de l'âme, le spectateur sentant qu'il est entré dans le royaume de la joie en même temps qu'il a quitté la rue pour passer les portes du théâtre, et qui s'appuie sur l'intuition de la fraternité qui lie les créatures.[25]

In this scene, we both laugh with Tartuffe and at him almost simultaneously; certainly no rigid line can be drawn here between the provinces of these two types of comedy.

When Damis has discovered Tartuffe's motives by overhearing his *entretien* with Elmire (Act III, Sc. 4 and 5), Orgon's expulsion and the disinheritance of his son in favour of the hypocrite ensue (Sc. 6 and 7). As in Act II, all the elements of a very poignant human tragedy are present, but this impression given by the text is quickly dispelled in the theatre. We admire once again the alacrity and ingenuity with which Tartuffe extricates himself from a seemingly irretrievable position, not by lying, as we unconsciously expect him to do, since dissimulation of the truth seems to be the only possible stratagem to employ, but by telling Orgon nothing less than the strict truth about himself. Of course Tartuffe is secure in the knowledge that Orgon will be deceived by his false parade of truthful humility, just as he was when he saw an impoverished penitent pray so fervently in Church.[26] In his discussion of this scene, W.G. Moore speaks of Tartuffe once again dropping the mask of a *dévot;* more exactly, Tartuffe is refining his role, giving his mask the maximum of flexibility as he deliberately pushes deception to its highest level — that of the supreme paradox in which truth is made to justify falsehood.[27] Verbally, his self-accusation (ll. 1074 ff) tells us the moral truth about his character, whilst intending to deceive Orgon into believing in his moral innocence. At the same time as apparently telling the objective truth about himself — as it appears to the rest of Orgon's family and the audience that is, — he adroitly evades Orgon's question about what has just happened, and takes refuge in generalities. His 'defence' of Damis in front of the enraged father sustains this masterly use of paradox:

> Ah! laissez-le parler: vous l'accusez à tort,
> Et vous ferez bien mieux de croire à son rapport.
> Pourquoi sur un tel fait m'être si favorable?
> Savez-vous, après tout, de quoi je suis capable?
> Vous fiez-vous, mon frère, à mon extérieur?
> Et, pour tout ce qu'on voit, me croyez-vous meilleur?
> Non, non: vous vous laissez tromper à l'apparence. (ll. 1091-7)

As he advises Orgon not to be deceived by appearances, he carefully calculates his future actions in the household upon the certainty that his host will do precisely that.

In this scene between Orgon, Damis and Tartuffe (Act III Sc. 6), which is probably one of the most comic scenes of the play when acted, it is nevertheless difficult to see Tartuffe himself as intrinsically comic. A situation in which Orgon wrongfully concludes in favour of the hypocrite's innocence when the hypocrite has just spoken the truth about his own baseness would admittedly exemplify the criterion of the comic elaborated in the *Lettre sur la Comédie*, namely the disharmony of ends and means. But from Tartuffe's *own* point of view, the result (the renewed favour with Orgon, the dismissal of the rightful heir) is *precisely* what he wished to achieve. Objectively, absolute truth is spoken concerning Tartuffe's character; spoken by Tartuffe it becomes falsehood masquerading as truth, whereas for Orgon it is complete and utter truth. Tartuffe is well aware of the paradox of the hypocrite telling the truth, because the ability to sustain this paradox in his actions grounds his very existence as a *faux dévot*. What *is* comic here is the hiatus which we and Tartuffe perceive between verbal truth on the one hand, and intention on the other, and Orgon's total blindness to it. Underlying the dramatic situation, however, is the idea of the extreme uncertainty of language and reason as means of revealing objective truth. They are unreliable because their correct interpretation may well depend, as it does here, on a hidden sense attached to them by the speaker; they may also be misinterpreted by the hearer, as they are in this scene; and the meaning which the hearer *thinks* he is giving to them may in fact be subtly predetermined by the form in which the speaker chooses to present his statement. An excellent example of such 'predetermined' judgement is to be found at the end of the following scene, where Tartuffe says to Orgon: 'Je fuirai votre épouse, et vous ne me verrez...' to which Orgon 'gives' the reply which Tartuffe has shaped discreetly for him: 'Non, en dépit de tous, vous la fréquenterez' (ll. 1171-2.)

In this scene Tartuffe refines the basic elements of hypocrisy (the confusion of truth and appearances) to the point where he compels us to be spectators, as he himself is one, of the comedy in which truth is continually mistaken for falsehood (Damis' statement disbelieved by Orgon, his self-description disregarded, Cléante's distinction between the true and false *dévot* dismissed as calumny of Tartuffe, etc.) and falsehood mistaken for truth (Tartuffe's intention to deceive Orgon taken as proof of his humility). A perspective is thus opened by this confusion of values, in which not only the normal assumptions of language are overturned (this is, after all, the basis for the most elementary type of comedy: see Part I), but in which those of language as a vehicle of truth, together with its dependent notions of right and wrong, are shown by systematic exploitation to be interchangeable and expendable at will. In short, Molière's conception of this scene has opened a sceptical perspective on language as the basis of human relationships.[28]

In Tartuffe's clever manipulation of language, we glimpse fleetingly something of the serious implications of his hypocrisy, which are developed in the following Act. But this does not mean that the end of this Act must be taken as serious or tragic. The expulsion of Damis by Orgon can no more be taken seriously in the theatre than the malediction which Harpagon pronounces on Cléante in *L'Avare,* for the spectator knows only too well the impotence concealed by this show of external violence on the part of the *barbon.* The comic of this scene is real and immediate; once again we admire Tartuffe's virtuosity in his use of language, but here he uses his skill not to make Orgon believe him, but rather to disbelieve him utterly; he gains a permanent foothold in the house and acquires a *carte blanche* as regards Elmire, by resolving to leave both immediately. Orgon is the puppet which Tartuffe can skilfully manipulate, because he has discovered the key in Orgon's pertinacious wish to 'faire enrager le monde'. But Tartuffe the hypocrite can also manipulate at will truth and falsehood, right and wrong. As he reveals their multiple contradictions, his successful manipulation of these values as well as of Orgon is certainly comic, but at the same time it shows up his limitations as a comic figure in himself, as he extends the domain of comedy to include the bases of society and its institutions.

The first scene of Act IV, between Cléante and Tartuffe, acts as an intermediate stage in the evolution of Tartuffe's hypocrisy; it is neither the hypocrisy of the end of Act III, where its serious implications were glimpsed but not emphasized, nor yet the sinister hypocrisy of the end of Act IV. In this scene we, and the most able representative of the family, Cléante, nevertheless realize for the first time the complex and alarming nature of Tartuffe's hypocrisy. Whilst there is once again admiration on our part for his verbal dexterity, as he answers objections to his acceptance of Orgon's estate and legacy by pretexting the will of heaven, the flexibility of his use of language and morality shades into elusiveness, which makes us realize how effortlessly superior he is to the arguments put forward by Cléante in the name of reason and justice. There is an important difference too in his attitude here which confirms this impression. In previous scenes, his existence in Orgon's household was grounded upon his ability to play his part as a true *dévot* convincingly (that is to say, as convincingly as possible in a play in which comic effect depends upon incompatibility in behaviour) in order to achieve his designs. When we see him in this scene, he has already achieved those designs and has displaced the rightful heir, Damis; he need not therefore be primarily concerned with the maintenance of his well-knitted pretence of devotion. He is here merely going through the motions of his role as a true *dévot* treating it as a perfunctory exercise, as does Dom Juan in the last Act of Molière's play. He knows that Cléante penetrates the hypocrisy of his performance, just as Dom Juan knows that Dom Carlos sees through his hypocritical gestures, but he keeps up the fiction of devotion (he invokes the authority of 'Le Ciel' no less than four times to cover his actions) in order to preserve his religious appearances — for appearances are not merely reality to Orgon, but eventually serve to render his position as heir virtually unassailable in law.

The analysis of Tartuffe as a comic figure solely on the basis of contradiction (*disconvenance, contrariété* according to the terms of the *Lettre sur la Comédie*) seems to me particularly vulnerable here, as he is far from blind to the contradiction of piety and unlawful dispossession. In fact he exploits this discrepancy between his profession and practice so subtly that he is able to practise his baseness to its maximum extent, whilst keeping up the mere appearance of a religious motivation for his actions. His instinct and nature, he tells Cléante, would like to restore Damis to his place as heir; yet heaven makes his harsh duty incumbent on him (cf. l. 1203; l. 1229; ll. 1237 ff). Indeed within the strict terms of *disconvenance* or lack of reason between ends and means, Cléante

would paradoxically be closer to a comic figure than Tartuffe, because
he vainly insists on reasoning with him on the inhumanity of his action
in dispossessing Damis, an argument which could only make an
impression on someone who recognized the moral premises of right and
wrong on which it is based. Tartuffe's aim, on the other hand, is to
achieve the permanent inversion of these values. The *fin de non-
recevoir* which Tartuffe opposes to Cléante's reasons is well
characterized by the commentary of the *Lettre sur la Comédie* on the
end of this scene:

> . . . la manière dont il met fin à la conversation est un bel exemple de
> l'irraisonnabilité . . . de ces bons Messieurs, de qui on ne tire jamais
> rien en raisonnant, qui n'expliquent point les motifs de leur conduite
> . . . et qui, par une exacte connoissance de la nature de leur intérêt, ne
> veulent jamais agir que par l'autorité seule que donne l'opinion qu'on
> a de leur vertu.[29]

In the light of Tartuffe's apparent invulnerability in this scene, his
second *entretien* with Elmire is potentially serious (Act IV, Sc.5). In his
first *entretien* with her he still needed Orgon, and success for him
depended upon his ability to escape compromise in his host's eyes; now
it does not matter if he is discovered in his attempt to seduce Elmire,
since he is independent of Orgon. But these implications are far from
the spectator's mind in the theatre. He sees the scene between Tartuffe
and Elmire set against the background of Orgon's obstinacy in clinging
to his belief in the hypocrite's saintliness. Orgon refuses to believe for
one moment that Tartuffe is capable of such deception: in Scene 3
Elmire asks him to consider the question even as a remote hypothesis:

> Mais supposons ici que, d'un lieu qu'on peut prendre,
> On vous fît clairement tout voir et tout entendre,
> Que diriez-vous alors de votre homme de bien?
> Orgon: En ce cas, je dirois que...Je ne dirois rien,
> Car cela ne se peut. (ll. 1345-9)

Like Elmire, we are further exasperated by his repeated and lofty
dismissals of the slightest possibility of such betrayal, and are therefore
disposed to welcome the scene between Tartuffe and Elmire with the
expectation that Orgon's arrogance will suffer public deflation.

Tartuffe himself once more reveals the comic side to his actions,
because, as in his first *entretien* with Orgon's wife, his intelligence,
which grounds his existence as a true *dévot,* is at variance with his
emotions. His initial wariness of Elmire's confidences — 'vous parliez
tantôt d'un autre style' he tells her (l. 1410) — is dispelled once he is
convinced that her fear of offending 'Le Ciel' is the only obstacle to his
passion, since he feels sure of his own ability to explain away her
scruples. He imagines that his rationalization of passion is successful in

convincing her of the moral rightness of his proposals; never in fact has he been so intellectually persuasive when he expounds his casuistry:

Selon divers besoins, il est une science
D'étendre les liens de notre conscience,
Et de rectifier le mal de l'action
Avec la pureté de notre intention. (ll. 1489-92)

But never has his intellect been at the mercy of such a violent passion as the one which, previously frustrated, is now promised satisfaction. Seeking to harmonize his casuistical arguments in order to reconcile passion and piety, he begins to lose control of the very instrument which he imagined was assuring his triumph, namely his reason. The *Lettre sur la Comédie* underlines the ascendancy of his passion over his intellect here: '... insensiblement ému par la présence d'une belle personne qu'il adore ...il commence à s'aveugler, à se rendre...'[30] Tartuffe also is the comic victim in a situation, the secrecy of which, he imagines, assures his triumph. 'Ce n'est pas pécher que pécher en silence' (l. 1506), he confides to Elmire, unaware that he is being overheard by the man against whom he is sinning. In addition, he betrays in confidence his opinion of Orgon:

C'est un homme, entre nous, à mener par le nez...
Et je l'ai mis au point de voir tout sans rien croire. (ll. 1524,26)

This is, of course, a perfectly apposite comment on Orgon's cecity, but it is wrong here, for Orgon *has* indeed seen everything. Perhaps Tartuffe's description of the husband would once again have been confirmed (as in Act III, Sc. 6), perhaps he would have been able to justify himself against all compromising appearances, had he not made this unfortunate remark about his host (for it was the husband who enjoined him earnestly to see Elmire as frequently as possible). It is not the truth about Tartuffe which makes the obtuse Orgon grasp finally the implications of the situation, for, as the *Lettre sur la Comédie* perceptively notes, he deems the personal insult to be more outrageous than the adulterous proposal of Panulphe to his wife.[31]

The hypocrite tries to repeat the tactic which worked so well in Act III, Sc. 6, but cannot develop his verbal ingenuity when faced with an Orgon enlightened by his hypersensitive *amour-propre*.[32] The tone changes drastically from pure farce (Tartuffe on re-entering the room finds Orgon instead of Elmire in his arms) to drama, as the hypocrite sees that the appearance of a *dévot* will no longer convince Orgon. According to W. G. Moore, who sees a comic contradiction in his reaction, his threat 'C'est à vous d'en sortir, vous qui parlez en maître' (ll. 1557 ff) contains 'a final glimpse of the real man'.[33] But once again the *Lettre sur la Comédie* provides us with an invaluable indication as to the way in which Molière wished his hypocrite to be played, since it emphasizes the basic *unity* of Panulphe's behaviour at this point:

Comme Panulphe voit que ces charmes ordinaires ont perdu leur
vertu, sachant bien que, quand une fois on est revenu de ces
entêtements extrêmes, on n'y retombe jamais, et pour cela même
voyant bien qu'il n'y a plus d'espérance pour lui, *il change de batterie;
et sans pourtant sortir de son personnage naturel de dévot* . . . il
répond à ces menaces par d'autres plus fortes . . .[34]

As in the scene with Cléante (Act IV, Sc.1), Tartuffe is fully aware
that he is now emphasizing a different aspect of the same role, namely
that of outraged innocence. His role here is compounded of the exact
amount of truth and falsehood which the circumstances demand from
him. His intellect, the foundation of his role as *faux dévot,* is once again
firmly in control of the situation: he still remembers to cover his action
in evicting the family with the sanction of heaven:

...j'ai de quoi confondre et punir l'imposture,
Venger le Ciel qu'on blesse, et faire repentir
Ceux qui parlent ici de me faire sortir. (ll. 1562-4)

The intimidating attitude of Tartuffe has, as its immediate
consequence, the introduction of the political elements (involving a
'certaine cassette' which Orgon has entrusted to Tartuffe and which, he
tells Cléante in Act V, Sc.1, compromises him legally) and the
intervention of the King. Tartuffe's menace of eviction is by no means
rhetorical — dull-witted though he is, Orgon shows the reality of it by
his frantic reaction (Act IV, Sc. 8, Act V, Sc. 1). For Tartuffe, the arch-
hypocrite, who has used dishonest means to dispossess the rightful heir
to Orgon's *bien* and *donation,* also has the secret papers which point to
Orgon's political guilt at the time of the Fronde. Now, he has not only
the appearances of justice and legal authority on his side, but their
tangible evidence also. Morally wrong, he is nevertheless judicially
correct within the framework of the play. It is, therefore, beside the
point to argue, as does A. Adam, for example, that the *donation* made
by Orgon to Tartuffe would have been illegal in reality under existing
practice of law.[35] This is to import a false standard of reference into the
play; on entering the theatre, we put aside reality, and consent to
inhabit, for the duration of the play, an imaginary world created by the
dramatist with its own coherent moral structure. The family, on the
other hand, though morally correct, is legally wrong within the context
of the play. Since we sympathize instinctively with the family, a tragic
outcome to the situation seems inevitable with the issue solely
dependent on the actual protagonists, that is.

This potentially tragic situation creates an unusual perspective on the
relationship between good and evil in a comedy, and makes us aware of
issues far transcending the purely localized incident of a clever rogue
insinuating himself into a Parisian *bourgeois* family. The

representatives of moral values within the play, namely the members of the family, are threatened seriously not only by the hypocrite Tartuffe, but also by the secret machinations of a *cabale* of *faux dévots,* the ramifications of which extend throughout each stratum of society, and of which the triumphant hypocrisy of a Tartuffe is not an isolated example. The arrival of Loyal (Act V, Sc. 4) to effect the eviction of the family, confirms the extent to which the leaven of hypocrisy has permeated the social orders outside the family. When commenting upon the appearance of Loyal the *Lettre sur la Comédie* draws attention to the concerted and insidious activity of people for whom hypocrisy has become a profitable way of life:

> Ce personnage est un supplément admirable du caractère bigot, et fait voir comme il en est de toutes professions, et qui sont liés ensemble bien plus étroitement que ne sont les gens de bien, parce qu'étant plus intéressés, ils considèrent davantage et connoissent mieux combien ils se peuvent être utiles les uns aux autres dans les occasions, ce qui est l'âme de la cabale.[36]

It is to this circle of hypocrites that Dom Juan has recourse, when he finds himself in an *impasse* at the end of the play:

> Le personnage de l'homme de bien est le meilleur de tous les personnages qu'on puisse jouer aujourd'hui, et la profession d'hypocrite a de merveilleux avantages . . . On lie, à force de grimaces, une société étroite avec tous les gens du parti. Qui en choque un, se les jette tous sur les bras . . . On a beau savoir leurs intrigues et les connoître pour ce qu'ils sont, ils ne laissent pas pour cela d'être en crédit parmi les gens . . . Que si je viens à être découvert, je verrai, sans me remuer, prendre mes intérêts à toute la cabale, et je serai défendu par elle envers et contre tous. Enfin c'est là le vrai moyen de faire impunément tout ce que je voudrai. (*Dom Juan*, Act V, Sc. 2)[37]

Molière's constant preoccupation from 1664 onwards with the reality of evil in the form of concerted hypocrisy is shown by the sinister development of this *vice* in the final two Acts of *Tartuffe,* which were added to the three Acts by the end of November of the same year, according to La Grange. The sinister aspects of Tartuffe's character foreshadow the preoccupations of *Dom Juan* (1665) and *Le Misanthrope* (1666). But unlike those plays, the heterogeneous nature of the principal character reflects with great force and clarity the changing dramatic vision of Molière after 1664, as it evolves from untroubled optimism to incorporate more sombre elements. As later additions to the earlier and more unambiguously comic conception of Tartuffe, these elements do not in any way contradict it, making the character a contradictory amalgam of the type described by J.

Lemaître. For this critic, Molière developed separately the 'pourceau béat' and the 'fourbe renommé', enlarging the first to include the second, but 'sans trop se soucier de le mettre d'accord avec le premier'.[38] Whilst it is true that chronologically there are two Tartuffes, one belonging to farce and the other to drama, dramatically they form a single coherent character. This unity derives from two sources: from the nature of hypocrisy, and from Molière's changing conception of it. However far the transparent hypocrisy of the Tartuffe who reprimands Dorine for her *décolleté* may appear to be from the cold inexorable hypocrisy of the Tartuffe who utters the dark warning to the family, the second is but a logical development of the first. The ruse of the first is based upon an inversion of appearances and reality which our laughter attacks because we do not imagine (nor are we given sufficient reason to imagine) that it can establish itself other than temporarily. The second is impervious to our laughter because it has merely succeeded in making the temporary into the permanent. Our attitude towards Tartuffe's evolution closely reflects Molière's own dramatic experience of the years 1664-69; having at first been inclined to treat the question of religious hypocrisy as merely a social phenomenon (compare, for example, his attitude to, the *précieuses*) capable of being dealt with by means of ridicule alone, he came to see it as constituting a more permanent moral problem as he met with determined opposition from 1664 onwards. A moral problem, not for himself alone, but for the whole of society, against which the weapon of ridicule blunts itself. It is from this discovery by Molière that comedy is powerless in the face of irreducible moral evil that the vision of life and man proceeds which I describe as 'philosophic'. What are the bases of that vision, and to what philosophy is it to be attributed?

(3)

The difference in tonality between the *Tartuffe* of 1664 (which did not proceed beyond the present Act III), and that of 1667-9 is that between farce and drama; the unifying factor is to be found in Molière's own changing experience of the nature of good and evil, as illustrated dramatically in the problem of religious hypocrisy. In the remarks on the role of Tartuffe, I tried to show that his limitations as a comic character (revealed in the extent to which he transcends any contradiction or *disconvenance* in the words of the *Lettre sur la Comédie*) are reached in the scenes in which he himself exploits systematically the *disconvenances* inherent in the common assumptions of speech and reason (Act III, Sc.6; III, Sc.7; IV, Sc.1; IV, Sc.7). He uses reason to exploit the lack of reason and the ambiguity of language: it is this ability which grounds his existence as a *faux dévot*.

Moral ambiguity, the wilful confusion of true and false devotion, is only possible in the play because language and reason are themselves exposed to ambiguity. Both kinds of ambiguity are interdependent and derive from the same philosophic vision, which is, as I hope to show, in complete opposition to that of the *Lettre sur la Comédie*, written to defend the moral value of the play.[39]

Tartuffe's success in manipulating language for his own ends is a measure of Molière's acute awareness of what has been called 'the philosophy of language'.[40] His understanding of the nature of language as illustrated in the role of his hypocrite is profoundly nominalist in inspiration; deeply embedded in the structure of the play is the notion that there is no objective or necessary correspondence between a word and the reality which it purports to represent; words are only subsequent approximations to reality, describing it but inevitably failing to coincide with its essence. They are, as Montaigne described them: 'une piece estrangere joincte à la chose, et hors d'elle.'[41] In addition, language is dependent upon subjective judgement, use and interpretation, hence the fact that ambiguity is one of its permanent concomitants. The dictum of Aulus Gellius and Chrysippus to the effect that 'omne verbum ambiguum esse' could stand as an epigraph to the philosophy of language in *Tartuffe*. By using Tartuffe to uncover the multiple contradictions and ambiguities to which even the simplest form of language is exposed, Molière shares this philosophy with Montaigne, when he illustrates the unreliability of language in his *Essais*:

. . . Prenons la clause que la logique mesmes nous presentera pour la plus claire. Si vous dictes: Il faict beau temps, et que vous dissiez verité, il fait donc beau temps. Voylà pas une forme de parler certaine? Encore nous trompera elle . . . Si vous dictes: Je mens, et que vous dissiez vray, vous mentez donc. L'art, la raison, la force de la conclusion de cette cy sont pareilles à l'autre; toutes fois nous voylà embourbez.[42]

As was seen in the preceding section, Tartuffe the dramatic creation is made to illustrate the same dichotomy of language and intention (speaking the verbal truth about himself to Orgon, whilst lying in that he intends to deceive his hearer, etc.). In such scenes as this he symbolizes dramatically the fallibility and malleableness of reason which may be employed to justify any course of action, provided that one possesses, as Tartuffe undoubtedly does, what Montaigne described as '...la suffisance de...sçavoir contourner' such a pliable instrument. [43]

Tartuffe then escapes regularly from the domain of the comic *disconvenance* because his sceptical awareness of the ambiguities obtaining in reason and language does not contradict but rather confirms a comic vision which is itself in the process of becoming a sceptical one. It is the central part of this vision, the moral ambiguity occasioned by Tartuffe's exploitation of the ambiguity inherent in reason and language which makes it totally incompatible with the arguments emphasized by the *Lettre sur la Comédie* and elsewhere by Molière to justify the moral innocence of his play.

The entire demonstration of the moral value of comedy contained in the *Lettre sur la Comédie* is based on a rational argument about the nature of the comic; according to this argument, there is no room for any ambiguity concerning either the comic of Tartuffe or the moral view of Molière: the *ridicule,* says the writer, is '...la forme extérieure et sensible que la providence de la nature a attachée à tout ce qui est déraisonnable, pour nous en faire apercevoir, et nous obliger à le fuir.' The *Lettre* goes on to equate *vice* (which is, according to Furetière, 'une habitude de l'âme qui porte au mal') with 'tout ce qui est déraisonnable', and therefore the object of comedy: '...*la providence de la nature a voulu que tout ce qui est méchant eût quelque degré de ridicule*...La raison de cela est que si le ridicule consiste dans quelque disconvenance, il s'ensuit que tout mensonge, déguisement . . . toute apparence différente du fond . . . est essentiellement ridicule.'[44]

Reason enables one to distinguish clearly between *vice* and *vertu*; and the comic or *ridicule* is but the sanction or sign of the fixed gulf between the two moral categories. Likewise Cléante, in his speeches on the differences between true and false religion (Act I, Sc. 5), claims to be able to discriminate with clarity between the type of religious impostor represented by Tartuffe and the true *dévot*. If there is always such a clear distinction to be drawn between them, it is because reason enables him to pierce through the disguise of the hypocrites and see them as they really are (cf. ll. 339-44). Both Cléante and the author of the *Lettre* use reason in the same neo-stoic sense, to mean the principle implanted by nature in man, which renders both the intellectual perception of the true and the false and the ethical choice between *vice* and *vertu* obvious. [45] Transgression against this principle is automatically to come under the judgement of the comic. It has already been seen how Tartuffe succeeds in obscuring the intellectual difference between the true and the false by his manipulation of language and reason, thus escaping the judgement of the comic. In so doing, he obscures the difference which the *Lettre* conveniently draws between 'vice déraisonnable' and 'vertu raisonnable'.

In fact the *méchanceté* of the hypocrite is not as uniformly comic as the author of the *Lettre* wishes us to believe, simply because his *vice* is not always irrational in the sense in which the *Lettre* understands the word. The only way in which Tartuffe at the end of Act IV could possibly be termed irrational within the definition of the *Lettre* would be by acting as he does without the awareness of the inevitable intervention of the King at the end to thwart his evil designs. And without this reference to a *deus ex machina*, which is by its very nature an intrusion into the dramatic universe of the play, Tartuffe's behaviour is strictly *rational* in this scene. There is an exact *convenance* between the means which he employs and his desired end. He can legally evict the family as he is the rightful proprietor of the house; both the family and he know that according to the logic of the situation Tartuffe cannot be defeated. Once this fact is realised, that *vicieux can* and indeed *do* act rationally, the whole argument of the *Lettre* and of Cléante about rational and moral distinctions crumbles. *Raison* and *vertu* on the one hand, and *ridicule* and *vice* on the other, are not so clearly demarcated within the play. Of course it could be argued (and the *Lettre* does suggest this) that Tartuffe's behaviour is irrational and therefore comic in the wider metaphysical sense of a wicked man thinking that he could escape the consequences of his own evil doing with impunity, unaware that a just providence (symbolized by the King) governs the world, ensuring the defeat of the wicked and the certain triumph of the weak and oppressed. But even the *Lettre* draws attention to the dramatically illogical aspect of such a *dénouement* when describing the situation of the family at the end of the fourth Act: '...il paroît que c'est une affaire sans ressource dans les formes, de sorte qu'à moins de quelque Dieu qui y mette la main, c'est-à-dire de la machine, comme parle Aristote, tout est déploré'.[46] The intervention *ex machina* of the Prince obviously represented in Molière's eyes an ideal poetic triumph over the enemies who opposed him tenaciously after the first performance of his play; perhaps it was also an expression of gratitude to the King for his support during the struggle over *Tartuffe*. In any case, it would appear to be a very flimsy basis for a theodicy in which truth and justice ultimately triumph over the forces of evil.

The contradiction between the ordered view of right and wrong as set forth by the *Lettre* and indicated by Cléante on the one hand, and the strong implication of the supremacy of evil in the dramatic situation on the other, bears witness to the uncertainty and necessary ambiguity which form the bases of the moral and dramatic structure of the play: both are also the cornerstones of the sceptical vision of life. I wish to illustrate *Tartuffe's* sceptical vision by reference to one of the central ideas which underlies the philosophy of La Mothe Le Vayer, the Sceptic philosopher and close friend of Molière.

In Le Vayer's philosophy, the argument of the *Lettre* and Cléante that *vice* can be easily discerned from *vertu*, and is ultimately defeated, is paralleled by a counter-argument which expresses the same sceptical implications of *Tartuffe*. Both arguments constitute equally an integral and permanent part of the Sceptic's thought, and indicate, as does the play, the unresolved tension which he and Molière see in the precarious balance of good and evil.[47] In a disquisition *De la Prudence*, he discusses the relationship of *vice* and *vertu*: here he speaks with the certainty of Cléante and the *Lettre*: 'En effet la méchanceté la plus fardée se remarque toujours, parce que Dieu permet qu'elle soit aussi toujours imprudente. Et que serait-ce de la vie humaine, si le Ciel n'en avait disposé de la sorte? Quelle Vertu pourrait se garantir de l'oppression des vicieux, s'ils avaient pu conjoindre la prudence avec leur malice?' Those who masquerade in the disguise of the virtuous, he goes on to say, have merely 'un masque trompeur de cette vertu', and their imposture is easily discerned and punished.[48] In *Des Habitudes Vertueuses*, however, he is less sanguine about this proposition as he reflects that life would be less problematic if '. . . le Ciel avait donné des marques certaines pour discerner un hypocrite d'un véritable vertueux, de même que nous en avons pour reconnaître une pièce de fausse monnaie, et pour la distinguer de la bonne . . .'[49]

He is more explicit in a treatise entitled *Du Mensonge,* where he expresses his sceptical misgivings about such an unambiguous view of life; he is not, he writes, of the opinion of Polybius, who stated categorically that virtue may be compared to a great goddess, who is always recognized immediately on account of truth, which she represents. He goes on to draw the same doubting inference as that in Molière's play, when he says that he is also led to doubt whether it is true to say that she triumphs naturally over deceit and untruth.[50] Elsewhere, in *De la Fortune,* he states his doubts concerning this view even more explicitly: from time immemorial it has been an observable fact that '... une infinité de gens Vertueux ont été de tout temps exposés aux injures de la mauvaise fortune...' Often it would appear that the inscrutable order of providence renders the most virtuous and innocent people incapable of avoiding disaster.[51] In *De la Vertu des Payens* the same basic doubt assumes a different form as he opposes the moral paradoxes and ambiguities of experience to the rational order which the dialecticians ascribe to it: '...le vice et la vertu se brouillent quelquefois de telle sorte, qu'on voit des hommes fort vicieux faire de très bonnes actions; et d'autres au contraire qui en commettent de très méchantes, bien qu'ils soient d'ailleurs dans l'exercice de beaucoup de vertus.'[52]

Vice and *vertu* are so inextricably entangled in *Tartuffe* that both aspects of this extreme sceptical paradox are clearly evident in the play. At the end of *Tartuffe,* the hypocrite is *objectively* performing an immensely valuable function for the state in denouncing Orgon to the Prince — Orgon is, after all, a traitor to the royal cause, having attempted to thwart the proper course of justice by his unlawful possession of the secret papers and 'cassette' entrusted to him by his accomplice Argas. Tartuffe the *vicieux* thus acts apparently as a responsible citizen, whose primary concern is the maintenance of truth and justice in society. Conversely, Elmire, acting in the name of the family, uses deceitful tactics in order to outwit Tartuffe.

If such moral ambiguity is a recurrent theme in the sceptic vision of *vice* and *vertu,* its attitude towards the hypocrisy of a Tartuffe who presents a danger to the social order is, paradoxically, unequivocal: Tartuffe must be unmasked at all costs because he threatens to disrupt the life of the family, which in the play is a microcosm of society, by a *vice* which is, as Molière wrote: '...dans l'État, d'une conséquence bien plus dangereuse que tous les autres.'[53] Some twenty years before *Tartuffe*, Le Vayer draws attention to the danger in the pernicious inversion of the normal meanings of language in terms similar to those of Molière:

> Si la parole de l'homme est l'unique lien de toutes les sociétés civiles, quand elle sert de fidèle interprète à l'esprit, on ne saurait nier qu'elle ne devienne l'instrument de leur destruction et la ruine certaine des Polices, lorsqu'elle s'acquitte mal de sa charge, et qu'elle substitue une chose fausse au lieu de la Vérité . . . entre tous les défauts de notre humanité, il n'y en a point qui soit d'une si grande conséquence que celui du Mensonge.[54]

Both Le Vayer and Molière share a similar notion of the uncertainty and relative nature of reason and moral values, but both unite in declaring that there are certain limits beyond which it is dangerous to exploit them in practice. But once hypocrisy is abroad in society, some compromise with its means, if not its ends, is necessary to defeat it: '...il y a des occasions où on doit mentir' says Le Vayer, and quotes as justification examples of deception undertaken to save the established order. His guiding principle in such cases is that lying should not be practised 'avec mauvaise intention'.[55] Faced with the reality of concerted hypocrisy, the virtuous may not be morally reprehensible for having recourse to the weapons of the *vicieux*.

The hypocrisy of Tartuffe obviously involves Elmire in such moral compromise, as she uses means no different from his in appearance to protect the order of family life. Just as hypocrisy masks itself with the appearance of truth, so its opposite must mask itself with the appearance of falsehood before being accepted as true by Tartuffe. For a moment virtue and deceit must appear to be thoroughly indistinguishable in the play, so much so that, although forewarned by Dorine of Elmire's stratagem, Damis is in doubt about her intentions after listening to the first *entretien* with Tartuffe. When his step-mother tells him that a woman ought to be able to laugh at such *galanteries* without troubling her husband, he replies that she has her own reasons for doing so (ll. 1034-5). In the following scene, he informs his father that she listened to Tartuffe's outburst of passion without objection, and insinuates that

> Elle est d'une humeur douce, et son coeur trop discret
> Vouloit à toute force en garder le secret. (ll. 1063-4)

But it seems gratuitous to suggest, as do several critics, that Molière might wish us to doubt her fidelity to her husband: the fact that the impetuous Damis rushes to this conclusion only confirms the central theme of the play — that appearances are an extremely uncertain indication of the moral quality of any action. Besides, Elmire, as a sophisticated *honnête femme*, is well used to worldly ways, and knows that she is dealing with a consummately skilful rogue. She must therefore convince Tartuffe in her *entretien* that she is not averse to his declaration of love, or else fail in her attempt to divert his attention from the projected marriage with Mariane. And if to convince him of this necessarily involves appearances casting doubt upon her fidelity to Orgon, the circumstances which make for such moral ambiguity must be blamed and not Elmire.[56]

At the end of the play, the Prince, 'ennemi de la fraude' (1. 1906), acts in a similar way to Elmire; he does not scruple to use slightly devious means to ensnare the hypocrite in order to protect society. His emissary, the Exempt, has orders to beguile Tartuffe into thinking that he has agreed to accompany him to Orgon's house in order to evict the family and arrest the owner. La Mothe Le Vayer is again in agreement with the principle behind such action when he states that '... le devoir des Rois les oblige souvent à mentir, pour le salut du peuple qui leur est soumis.'[57] In spite of this subterfuge, the Prince is still the representative of all truth and justice in society just as Elmire remains virtuous and exemplary in spite of her stratagem. In both cases, the end justifies the means, since hypocrisy renders an intentional and utilitarian criterion of actions necessary.

There is a particular aspect of Tartuffe's hypocrisy which brings into sharp relief the *leitmotif* of moral ambiguity so fundamental to the conception of the play — that is, Tartuffe's practice of casuistry. Critics have diligently underlined the satirical and contemporary import of his casuistry — for one of them it meant that Tartuffe was 'Escobar traduit sur le théâtre', and for others it provides proof of Molière's attack on some 'cabale des dévots' — but preoccupation with a particular aspect of the role is dangerous because it tends towards an interpretation of the whole in the light of the part, losing sight of the overall vision of the dramatist, to which any satirical element is necessarily subservient.[58] Allusions to what Molière himself recognized as common themes of contemporary satire leave unanswered the real question of why casuistry should become an integral part of the hypocrite's role.[59] If he did choose to incorporate important elements of casuistry, they presented a crucial point of analogy with the experience out of which the play developed — that of the realisation of the precarious proximity of *vice* and *vertu*, and the ease and apparent success with which the Tartuffes of the world could present deceit in the guise of truth. What could have been a mechanical addition, at one remove from the vision of the play, provides, with its rational reconciliation of apparently incompatible actions powerful confirmation of the ambiguity of language and ethical values which sustains it. As such, it merges easily into the sceptical outlook, and a quotation from Le Vayer's *Prose Chagrine* serves to illustrate this perfectly: 'Le vice et la vertu ne sont presque plus reconnaissables, et les cas de conscience ont quelquefois tellement sophistiqué le bien et le mal, qu'il est très difficile de les discerner.'[60]

There is one point in Tartuffe's development where his use of casuistry seems to me to make such implications very explicit — that is, as explicit as possible without making the play into a tragedy. It is not in his famous second *entretien* with Elmire, in which he explains to her the theory behind the *direction d'intention* (the fact that his passion is at variance with his professed purity of intention allows the spectator to dominate him), but in Act IV Sc.1. Here the hypocrite answers Cléante's charge that his devotion is not compatible with his acceptance of Orgon's *donation* in the following terms:

> Et si je me résous à recevoir du père
> Cette donation qu'il a voulu me faire,
> Ce n'est, à dire vrai, que parce que je crains
> Que tout ce bien ne tombe en de méchantes mains,
> Qu'il ne trouve des gens qui, l'ayant en partage,
> En fassent dans le monde un criminel usage,
> Et ne s'en servent pas, ainsi que j'ai dessein,
> Pour la gloire du Ciel et le bien du prochain. (ll. 1241-8)

The *direction d'intention* is here implicit in Tartuffe's reasoning, and assumes a less specialized and therefore more dangerous form: no casuistical theorizing need precede it (such as that employed with Elmire) because it constitutes, in itself, an argument which could and would be used naturally, with irreproachable propriety, by people completely opposed to Tartuffe. The reasons employed by 'l'âme de toutes la plus concertée' according to the description given of him by the *Lettre sur la Comédie*, could easily pass for virtue within the moral framework of the play — being those of an apparently public-spirited individual concerned with the protection of society from pernicious influences.[61]

For Molière, the practical consequences of casuistry seem to have been infinitely more dangerous than its theory, and he uses Orgon's less subtle usage of it to suggest this. 'Vous-voulez manquer à votre foi?' Cléante asks him with regard to his promise to marry his daughter to Valère: 'je ne dis pas cela' he temporizes, adopting Tartuffe's *direction d'intention* (Act I, Sc.5, ll. 415-16). As with hypocrisy, so with casuistry, which must be rejected not because it is tainted with untruth but because it is a particularly insidious form of hypocrisy which leads to dissolution both within family and state. Once more, Le Vayer's ironic comment on the use of mental reservations seems to sum up the view of the play: there are already too many people, he writes, prepared to break their word, who do not need the provision of additional pretexts and conditions such as those so neatly provided by casuistry: 'Dès l'heure que vous la [la Foi] voulez accommoder à toutes ces subtilités d'Ecole, il n'y a personne qui ne prétende avoir droit d'en penser à sa mode.'[62]

The analogies in idea and structure between scepticism and *Tartuffe* emphasize the predominant elements of the play's moral vision. The increasing awareness on Molière's part of the absence of a formal distinction between *vice* and *vertu*, resulting in the possible triumph of the Tartuffes of society with apparent impunity, is underlined by the similarity of the actions undertaken by the protagonists. Intention is obviously the principal moral factor to be considered in these actions, but even this criterion is subject to qualification, as Tartuffe can manipulate it to make seduction justifiable. The solvent of hypocrisy and casuistry can dissolve the apparently clear barriers which separate *vice* from *vertu* — the actions of the Prince and Elmire are not, after all, so apparently different from those of Tartuffe. The hypocrisy of Tartuffe must consequently be seen as both sign and cause of an all pervasive moral ambiguity which grounds the sceptical vision of *Tartuffe*, in which no one in society is or indeed can be exempt from some degree of moral corruption. For the sceptical mind, the most radical confirmation of this truth lies in the perception that not even religion escapes from the influence of such moral ambiguity. If Le Vayer writes that '...à peine pouvons-nous dire que nos Autels soient exempts de cette corruption', a similar vision animates *Tartuffe*: we find Molière writing in his *Préface* that 'Les choses mêmes les plus saintes ne sont point à couvert de la corruption des hommes.'[63] If in the sceptical vision not even religion can be exempted from the moral ambiguity which characterizes all actions, one may well ask what then are the implications of such a vision regarding the delicate subject of religious hypocrisy, in which the discrimination of true from false devotion is of such crucial importance?

The play's vision tends to embarrass the arguments which Molière and his friends used in all good faith to defend the play. For there is no evidence to suppose that he intended to attack religion under the guise of hypocrisy.[64] In *Préface* and *Placets* we have Molière's assurance that he took care to distinguish the hypocrite from the true *dévot*, and although these are polemical writings, it is unwise to assume that he must therefore be guilty of untruth.[65] The same conviction underlies the *Lettre sur la Comédie* and the speeches of Cléante. But this distinction is fundamentally at variance with the play's vision of ambiguity, and seems to be swept away by its momentum. Implication, as I hope to show, clearly outstrips the overt intention of the author. Reality within the play is rarely what appearances suggest it to be. Hypocrites pose as true *dévots,* and the latter survive only by employing the methods of the former. Molière makes sure that the spectator and reader are exempt, as he is, from any confusion about the character of Tartuffe — 'c'est un scélérat qui parle.'[66] But Act IV implies strongly that hypocrisy can and does pass for true religion. Like Cléante in Act I, Sc. 5, Molière sees through his hypocrite; but like Cléante in Act IV, Sc. 1, he is frustrated by elusive hypocrisy, which he cannot unmask as quickly as he would claim to see through it.

Molière goes a step further than Cléante, since he illustrates in his defence of his play the risk of confusing true and false religion, to which *Tartuffe* unconsciously exposes him. For there, the name Tartuffe is employed by him as a kind of generic title, synonymous with hypocrite or *faux dévot,* but designating in reality those people who opposed his play whether from hypocrisy, fanaticism, or sincere misgivings about the place of religion in comedy. Irrespective of the wide difference between such religious professions, they nevertheless find themselves readily assimilated into the category of hypocrites.[67] In the first *Placet,* for instance, he complains that the Tartuffes of society have insinuated themselves into favour with the King: and as an example of this, he makes unambiguous reference to the virulent pamphlet written by the imprudent Curé de St. Barthélemy, Roullé (*Le Roy Glorieux au Monde,* July-August 1664). His conclusion is significant: '...sans doute Elle [i.e. votre Majesté] juge bien Elle-même combien il m'est fâcheux de me voir exposé tous les jours aux insultes de ces Messieurs...' The term 'ces Messieurs' alludes to certain 'Tartuffes' previously mentioned, to whose number the intemperate *curé* now belongs.[68] The action of M. de Lamoignon, *Premier Président,* in imposing an interdiction on the second version of the play, fits him for a similar description. The principal reason for this ban was, as Molière himself heard Lamoignon say, that 'ce n'est pas au théâtre à se mêler de prêcher l'évangile.'[69] In his *Préface* of 1669, Molière spoke of *les hypocrites* who attempted to prevent the performance of his play. One of the reasons alleged by them against it was precisely that used by the *Premier Président:* '...pour répondre ces Messieurs tâchent d'insinuer que ce n'est point au théâtre à parler de ces matières' (i.e. of the difference between true and false religion).[70] It is true that in the same *Préface* Molière does appear to draw a theoretical distinction between hypocrites and the *zélés indiscrets* whom they provoke against him.[71] But in the hostile atmosphere of the polemics, such a fine distinction is quickly discarded. In reply to one of these *zélés indiscrets* which was certainly composed with Molière's active collaboration, we read of B. A. Sieur de Rochemont that 'son zèle est devenu indiscret.'[72] But if he has solicited support from the Queen Mother against Molière, her devotion is too solid to be deceived by his malicious rumours: 'qui ne sont de conséquence que pour des tartufles.'[73] Further on, the *Lettre* refers to this *zélé indiscret* as being 'le défenseur des tartufles', and eventually as a *faux dévot*. It is such *faux dévots* who calumniate Molière by insisting that he was attacking true *dévots*. How then are these *tartufles* to be recognized? The criterion of true and false devotion is, predictably, the same as that in Molière's *Placet* and *Préface:* 'Molière n'a fait que deux pièces que les tartufles reprennent...et le zélé réformateur des ouvrages du théâtre, le bras droit des tartufles...a écrit contre lui...'[74]

It is beyond doubt that terms which cover a wide range of true and false religion are used by Molière interchangeably — because all are opposed to *Tartuffe* and *Dom Juan,* all qualify as *tartufles.* The ambiguous use of terms such as *faux dévot, zélé indiscret, zélé réformateur, hypocrite,* etc. fully reflects Molière's confused attitude towards the essence of religious hypocrisy. *Dévots* vociferous in their objections to his play, such as Rochemont, Roullé, Lamoignon, Hardouin de Péréfixe, etc. were all characterized by a dogmatic piety — but they could not all conceivably be termed hypocrites, at least in the accepted traditional sense which Furetière in his *Dictionnaire Universel* gives to that word: 'déguisement en matière de dévotion, de probité, d'amitié, ou de vertu; feinte de ce qu'on n'est pas.' Intransigence or fanaticism is not quite the same religious phenomenon as hypocrisy. The point is of crucial importance for the thought of the play when one considers Molière's treatment of Orgon. He shares with those *dévots* mentioned the inflexible cast of mind of the rigorist *dévot.* Like a Roullé or a Rochemont he condemns unequivocally those who do not share his precise religious opinions (i.e. Cléante, Elmire, and the family). He is quite clearly neither a hypocrite nor a *vrai dévot;*[75] he is a religious fanatic, guilty, not of hypocrisy, but of what Fernandez has aptly termed 'une grave déformation du sentiment chrétien'.[76] The important point is not that he is a fanatic, but that Molière does not choose to present him simply as a fanatic, and his treatment of him bears out the ambiguity of the polemics. Instead, he draws attention to the multiple comic contradictions which underlie the religious fanatic. For instance, the perceptive Dorine referring to his excessive devotion exclaims: 'Ah! vous êtes dévot. et vous vous emportez?' (Act II, Sc. 2, l. 552). When Orgon tells Cléante that the religious fervour inspired in him by Tartuffe makes him wish to forget family and friends, the *raisonneur* deliberately draws attention to his misguided religious zeal with the ironic observation: 'Les sentiments humains, mon frère, que voilà!' (Act I, Sc. 5, l. 280).

Molière thus uses both the ready wit of Dorine and the sophisticated irony of Cléante to underline in the spectator's mind the comic contradictions between behaviour and profession of the choleric *imaginaire* — and the nature of the contradiction is such that it is tantamount to religious hypocrisy. Molière himself unwittingly confirms this interpretation of Orgon: in his *Préface*, he writes that his intention in writing his play was to correct hypocrisy. This must apply to Orgon first and foremost, for, as Michaut has pointed out, the real hypocrite Tartuffe is not corrected of his hypocrisy (all he learns is that he will have to be more cautious in future), but rather Orgon and his mother, Mme Pernelle. The exceptional violation of the normally immutable psychology of the comic hero at the end of the play (his conversion to a more humane outlook) emphasizes Molière's conscious attempt to illustrate the thesis of his *Préface*. Orgon is nevertheless corrected not of hypocrisy, as Molière imagined, but rather of fanatical religiosity.[77]

Orgon's hypocrisy is therefore closely bound up with his role as the principal comic character in the play. In fact, it is possible to see how his comic psychology contributes to the confusion of rigorist devotion and hypocrisy in Molière's eyes. He takes his place in Molière's theatre as one of the most famous of all his *imaginaires* — comic protagonists who fall prey to an obsessive fixation which so dominates them as to become the omnipresent motive behind thought and action. Hypnotized, so to speak, by their inner vision of reality, they attempt to remould it in conformity with that vision. So far, the psychological structure of Orgon may be said to differ in no essential way from that of Sganarelle, Arnolphe, etc. But his particular fixation assumes the form of religious fanaticism, and the combination of these elements makes of him a more complex and ambiguous character than any of his *confrères*. This may be seen in his dialogue with Cléante (Act I, Sc. 5), where he lauds Tartuffe's spirituality to his bemused interlocutor. The example of Tartuffe, he says, teaches him to divest himself of all affection for both family and kin and leaves him with no regard whatsoever for the world. On the level of comic psychology, his attitude reflects the usual state of mind induced in the *imaginaire* by his totalitarian vision of things — that is, complete imprisonment in his subjective universe and radical separation from the rest of the world. On another level, that of religion, he reflects, whether intended to or not by Molière, radical Christian separation from the temporal scene, and absolute commitment to higher spiritual reality. Fernandez has put this point pertinently when he writes: 'L'isolement chrétien devient le type de l'isolement comique.'[78] Perhaps it would be more equitable to Molière to reverse this order, and to say that comic technique, taking as its basis the typical *raideur* (to use Bergson's term) of the *imaginaire* detached from the world of empirical reality, fuses automatically with the *raideur* of the rigorist *dévot* attached to the supra-empirical order. As Bergson has so well demonstrated, the most elementary source of the comic lies in the tension between the *raideur* of the comic character and the *élasticité* of life to which he will not be reduced. In *Tartuffe,* this tension is translated in terms of the *raideur* of religious fanaticism, and *élasticité* of the true *dévot* (Cléante). Because the nature of *Tartuffe* is such that comic technique and religious attitude could not possibly be separated, opposition to Orgon, the 'fantoche ... lunaire et guignolesque', as Adam terms him, is, by the same token, unconscious opposition to the trans-empirical type of religion which he represents in distorted but essentially recognizable form.[79]

There is then implicit in Molière's comic technique, and without presupposing any irreligious intentions on his part, a natural scepticism with regard to the otherworldly dogmatism of Orgon. It is directly responsible for the character's ambiguity, making him both a comic hero as well as a hypocrite, or, to put it more precisely, a comic character who in this context automatically becomes a hypocrite. He becomes comic because he is prepared to dogmatize about something (his fixation) that is neither apparent nor evident to the representative of reality within the play, Cléante. Like the other *imaginaires,* he claims to see life through the eyes of reason. But unlike them, he claims to possess, in Tartuffe, heaven's supreme revelation, and proceeds to prove to his brother-in-law in Act I, Sc. 5 why he too ought to believe in Tartuffe. As this scene suggests, it is not Cléante but rather Orgon who is the real *raisonneur* of the play. The former limits himself to making one simple point to Orgon, concerning the difference between true and false religion, the substance and the shadow (ll. 318-45, ll. 351-407). Beyond this he does not and will not go. It is rather Orgon who claims the exclusive prerogative of reason for himself, here and elsewhere throughout the play. It is he who characteristically says to his daughter:

...comme sage
J'ai pesé mûrement toutes choses (Act II, Sc. 2, ll. 557-8)

He qualifies perfectly for the admirable description which Jouvet has given of the comic heroes in Molière who are 'des imaginaires ou des imaginatifs, des hommes en proie à eux-mêmes, des déraisonnables qui raisonnent dans la déraison.'[80] His interminable reasonings about heaven's will and Tartuffe bear this out: it is of his captious ratiocinations that Cléante says:

Avec de tels discours vous moquez-vous de moi?...
Voilà de vos pareils le discours ordinaire. (ll. 312, 318)

He is the supreme *sage* who possesses religious truth *in toto.* When Cléante ventures to contradict him, he replies in absolute terms which give the clearest insight into his own pretensions to wisdom:

Oui, vous êtes sans doute un docteur qu'on révère;
Tout le savoir du monde est chez vous retiré;
Vous êtes le seul sage et le seul éclairé,
Un oracle, un Caton dans le siècle où nous sommes;
Et près de vous ce sont des sots que tous les hommes. (ll. 346-50)

Cléante, on the other hand, distrusts such arrogant confidence in one's own reason. To Orgon's extravagant *discours*, he opposes his less pretentious idea of wisdom:

Les hommes la plupart sont étrangement faits!
Dans la juste nature on ne les voit jamais;
La raison a pour eux des bornes trop petites;
En chaque caractère ils passent ses limites. (ll. 339-42)

The deep paradox behind these simple words emphasizes the natural scepticism of Molière's comic technique. Taken in themselves, they are no more than platitudes about the golden mean and the *juste-milieu,* which have often been seen as Molière's philosophy. In their comic context, however, they express the fundamental thought implicit in the comedy, in the light of which Orgon is seen as a comic figure. Pleading that one should *control* one's speculations and reasonings, and not go beyond empirical reality to claim a supernatural basis for one's conduct, Cléante fulfils a similar function to Chrysalde, Ariste, Philinte and the other so-called *raisonneurs;* he provides the necessary perspective in which the comedy of Orgon may be viewed. And this comedy consists precisely in leaving reality behind for a subjectively fabricated world, from which Orgon claims to derive his vision of truth. That is to say that the comic perspective of Cléante here on Orgon is automatically a sceptical one. For the reason to which he alludes in the lines quoted can only be understood when one realizes the futility of what Montaigne terms pejoratively 'cette apparence de discours que chacun forge en soy,' that is, the speculative faculty of the mind which experience shows to be fallible and variable in the extreme.[81] And the comedy of such reasoning can, by the same token, only be perceived by the reason which perceives the absurdities of which reason is capable.

The reason of comedy here coincides with the reason of Le Vayer, which excludes from its scope what he terms 'les mystères' of religion. When such 'mystères' come under the purview of human reasoning, irreparable confusion is the inevitable result.[82] In its reaction to Orgon's confidence in his own power of reasoning, the wisdom of comedy comes into natural accord with the discreet ideal of *folle sagesse,* so central to sceptical thought and to Le Vayer in particular. In his *Dialogue sur la Divinité,* Le Vayer describes this paradoxical conception of reason as follows:

Saint-Paul ne se lasse point de nous faire appréhender toutes ces sciences, qui ne font que nous bouffir d'une vaine enflure, ces sagesses qui ne sont que folie devant Dieu, et ces prudences humaines desquelles il se déclare si capital ennemi, et cela pource que notre Religion étant toute fondée sur l'humilité, voire même sur une respectueuse abjection d'esprit, elle a promis le Royaume des Cieux expressément aux pauvres d'entendement.[83]

This notion of *folle sagesse* is naturally embedded in the comic texture of the play, enshrining the folly of reason, and the reason of folly, which is the true wisdom. Orgon is the supreme *sage* possessing his great revelation, to whom the wise fool Cléante can say with perfect truth 'Parbleu! vous êtes fou, mon frère, que je croi' (l. 311). In the comic framework of the play, Orgon becomes a hypocrite because he is the comic character, and he is the comic character because he is the Fool: his essential folly is not merely in contradicting what he professes, but rather in displaying that complete unawareness of human limitation and the frailty of human reasoning so characteristic of the *imaginaire*. How does *folle sagesse*, the comic and sceptical norm for human nature and religion, place the thought of the play, particularly with reference to religious belief in the century?

(4)

Cléante rejects the intrusion of Orgon's dogmatic reasoning in the domain of religion, and is content to oppose his more moderate idea of human wisdom, *la raison*. In his use of the term, he designates not a theoretical concept but a practical and empirical criterion of conduct, identifiable with *la juste nature*, and able therefore to take full account of human nature. It is evident that the *Lettre sur la Comédie* has the true *dévot* of the play in mind when it writes of religion as follows: 'Il est certain que la religion n'est que la perfection de la raison, du moins pour la morale, qu'elle la purifie, qu'elle l'élève, et qu'elle dissipe seulement les ténèbres que le péché d'origine a répandues dans le lieu de sa demeure, enfin que la religion n'est qu'une raison plus parfaite. . .'[84]

This conception of reason as the basis of religion places *Tartuffe* at the centre of the debate about man and his nature which occupies such a prominent part in the history of religious thought in the century. It is a debate embracing Jansenism and Molinism, the rigorist Ecole Française, and the Christian humanists and Deists. There is certainly no doubt that the author of *Tartuffe* was no stranger to the moral issues involved in this debate, for, as H. Busson has reminded us, '...les hommes du XVIIe siècle vivaient dans une atmosphère de théologie.'[85] If the writer of the *Lettre* and Cléante believe that religion consists principally in following one's natural reason, they implicitly accept man's ability to perform good works unaided by gifts of supernatural grace. Cléante, for example, is warm in his praise of those *dévots* who do not adopt a theological or dogmatic approach to human nature such as that of Orgon (and the *dévots* who criticized *Tartuffe*): rather 'On les voit, pour tous soins, se mêler de bien vivre' (l. 398). He considers the religion of such people as authentic principally on account of the good works produced by them, and the fact that they are not concerned with theological exactitude, but are content to allow others of differing opinions to live as they wish without interference (ll. 382 ff). It is significant that Le Vayer, in his *De la Vertu des Payens* (1642), written against the Jansenists, should make such requirements the essence of his religion. He pleads for the salvation of any pagan who has been virtuous, that is, who has followed his *lumière naturelle*, enabling him 'd'aimer Dieu...et son prochain comme soi-même.'[86] To the Jansenists, any indulgence towards human nature was heretical, good works being but the products of what Arnauld in reply to Le Vayer stigmatized as 'l'idolâtrie de soi-même, l'amour-propre, l'orgueil': to follow reason was still to leave intact 'ce vilain fond de l'homme, ce figmentum malum', which for Pascal rendered good works morally null and void.[87] Cléante, on the other hand, has as little room in his religion for dogmatic theological notions such as original sin as the writer of the *Lettre sur la Comédie* and Le Vayer. He extols especially those people who, unlike Orgon, are not prepared to attribute the faults of others to evil tendencies. On the contrary 'L'apparence du mal a chez eux peu d'appui' (l. 395). This is by no means to infer that Molière conceived of Cléante's views on human nature as a deliberate attack upon Port-Royal. In spite of the attack upon his theatre by the Jansenist B.A. Sieur de Rochemont, we do know that he was friendly with certain Jansenists, with whom he had arranged to read an early version of *Tartuffe*.[88] Nevertheless, the Jansenist view of man as corrupted and sinful is fundamentally at variance with the more tolerant cast of mind of Cléante. But it is in the portrayal of Orgon that we find a much more explicit refutation of Jansenism in particular and rigorist piety in general — a condemnation which also embraces Stoicism, and brings into sharp focus the play's conception of *folle sagesse* as an ethical and religious guide.

In spite of the obviously irreconcilable differences between Stoic moral philosophy and the Jansenist view of man — the Jansenists unequivocally condemned the Stoics for the primacy which they gave to unregenerate human reason and will[89] — it is nevertheless a fact that in the minds of seventeenth-century humanists such as the author of *Tartuffe* and La Mothe Le Vayer, the intransigent piety of rigorist devotion and Jansenism could seem to merge easily with the rigorous moral attitude of the Stoics. Le Vayer, for example, discovers and emphasizes subtly the common characteristic of moral austerity, and uses Stoicism as a means by which he can attack the strict piety of Jansenism and Christian devotion. In *De la Secte Stoïque* (1642), he writes that the Stoics display such a steadfast attitude to misfortune that they may be compared to the glorious martyrs of the Church. He notes carefully that the moral beliefs and practices of the most austere of all the Jewish sects (the Pharisees!) were practically the same as those of the Stoics. But his principal attack on the Stoics is intended specifically for the Jansenists, against whom he wrote his treatise in the first place:

> La morale des Stoïciens a été reprise par tout le reste des Philosophes, d'avoir rendu les vertus si inséparables les unes des autres, qu'il était impossible à leur dire, d'en posséder une sans les avoir toutes. Par le même raisonnement, il ne se pouvait faire qu'un homme vertueux eût le moindre vice, parce que celui qui se rendait coupable d'un seul, le devenait de toutes sortes de crimes . . . un seul défaut dans les moeurs rendait un homme tout à fait vicieux, nonobstant toutes les bonnes habitudes qu'il avait acquises auparavant.[90]

The doctrine of Jansenism is similarly absolute in its requirements: the actions of those people not solely motivated by love of God are sins, just as morally negligible as more heinous and intentional acts, even though good results from them. One is either in possession of divine grace, enabling one to perform truly virtuous actions, or bereft of it and capable only of sins. If an apparently virtuous action does not satisfy this condition, then it is no longer virtue, but merely sin in disguise.[91]

It is a criterion of such an absolute kind which the *sage* Orgon applies to others, and by which he claims to be able to judge their moral standing. The *honnêteté* of Cléante, which the more moderate members of the family and society regard as a positive moral attribute, is peremptorily dismissed as *libertinage* (Act I, Sc. 5, l. 314). Of Valère, whom he does not see frequenting church, he says 'Je le soupçonne encor d'être un peu libertin' (Act II, Sc. 2, l. 524). Once Tartuffe's machinations have been exposed, he begins to rain abuse on his erstwhile saint: 'te voilà, traître...' he exclaims before he is interrupted by Cléante (Act V, *Scène dernière*, l. 1947). Earlier, he announces that he will henceforth adopt an attitude of total mistrust towards *dévots* of whatever kind, as a result of Tartuffe's treachery:

> C'en est fait, je renonce à tous les gens de bien;
> J'en aurai désormais une horreur effroyable (Act V, Sc.1, ll. 1604-5)

It is left to the equitable Cléante to reiterate the lesson already spoken at the beginning of the play, but unheeded:

> Hé bien! ne voilà pas de vos emportements!
> Vous ne gardez en rien les doux tempéraments;
> Dans la droite raison jamais n'entre la vôtre,
> Et toujours d'un excès vous vous jetez dans l'autre. (ll. 1607-10)

The exercise of *la droite raison*, continues Cléante, consists in constant discrimination between imposture and authenticity. Such discrimination in turn leads to a balanced outlook on life, which is disrupted once the process of weighing up the good and the bad, the true and the false, is replaced by the systematic attitude of his brother-in-law. Rather than take his verbal revenge on Tartuffe, Orgon ought instead to hope that he may amend his nefarious way of living, according to Cléante. This seems to me to be more than a facile attempt on the part of Molière to introduce a harmonious note on which to terminate his play. These words are the very embodiment of Cléante's humanism, which, in contradiction to absolute doctrines such as Stoicism and Jansenism, perceives that ethics, no less than religion, is not an exact science, such as logic or mathematics, which do not admit inconsistency and change, but a sphere where relativism reigns supreme. Consequently men, even Tartuffe, are compounded of both good and bad qualities, and to quote Le Vayer, 'Les plus vertueux de ce monde sont simplement ceux qui ont le moins de vices.'[92]

The humanist outlook of the play attacks absolute divisions of *vice* and *vertu* on account of the absurdity which it sees in the application of moral absolutism to infirm human nature. The *Lettre sur la Comédie* provides an excellent commentary on the inevitable failure which ensues, in its description of Act IV, Sc. 3. Here the falsely authoritative Orgon is attempting to coerce his daughter Mariane into marriage with the hypocrite:

> D'abord Mariane se jette à ses genoux et le harangue si bien, qu'elle le touche. On voit cela dans la mine du pauvre homme; et c'est ce qui est un trait admirable de l'entêtement ordinaire aux bigots, pour montrer comme ils se défont de toutes les inclinations naturelles et raisonnables. Car celui-ci se sentant attendrir, se ravise tout d'un coup, et se disant à soi-même, croyant faire une chose fort héroïque: *Ferme, ferme, mon coeur, point de foiblesse humaine.*[93]

The pathetic failure of Orgon to maintain his Stoic-like pose of *apatheia,* or freedom from passion, is clearly attested by Molière's stage direction at this precise moment of the role: Orgon, *se sentant attendrir.* According to the Stoa, passion was a perturbation of the mind, contrary to right reason and nature.[94] Molière deliberately reverses the Stoic equation of freedom from passion with reason: an irrational movement of the soul against reason and nature becomes something natural and *raisonnable.* As seen in the second optic, Orgon the *sage* becomes comic, and therefore foolish in the deepest sense of the word, because he affects to despise human nature. Just as there can be no absolute division between *vice* and *vertu,* so there can be none between *sagesse* and *folie,* for the human condition is shown to be one of *folle sagesse* in the comic perspective. Because of the relative nature of man, he may represent both sides with the greatest unpredictability. Le Vayer puts the truth of *folle sagesse* into one of his more extreme paradoxes, when he writes that fools and wise men are sometimes scarcely to be distinguished from each other, so much so that '...comme faire le sage est quelquefois...une espèce de Folie...cette même folie passe en tel lieu, et en telle occasion, pour une grande sagesse.' There is no one, he adds, so penetrated by wisdom that he is not occasionally abandoned by it.[95] It is at such points in the role of Orgon in particular that the comedy of character and the philosophy behind the comedy are indissoluble.

Jansenism and Christian rigorism were not content to condemn human passions in the abstract, as did the Stoics, but linked their condemnation with an attack on the theatre, which, in their view, set out intentionally to excite them. The Jansenist Nicole may be quoted in this connexion, not only because his attitude represents that of the rigorist tradition of the Church (Bossuet in his *Maximes sur la Comédie* will say precisely the same), but because he seems to have intended his *Traité de la Comédie* (1667) as a specific attack upon Molière's theatre. In this treatise, he stigmatizes in particular the use which comedy makes of the passion of love:

> On doit toujours la regarder comme le honteux effet du péché, comme une source de poison capable de nous infecter à tous momens, si Dieu n'en arrêtoit les mauvais effets. Ainsi de quelque honnêteté apparente dont les Comédies . . . tâchent de la revêtir, on ne peut nier qu'en cela même ils ne soient contraires aux bonnes moeurs puisqu'ils impriment une idée agréable d'une passion vicieuse . . .[96]

Molière's *Préface* to *Tartuffe* of 1669 isolates this central objection of the *dévots* to his theatre, and is obviously couched in the form of a reply to Nicole:

> Je sais qu'il y a des esprits dont la délicatesse ne peut souffrir aucune comédie, qui disent que les plus honnêtes sont les plus dangereuses, que les passions que l'on y dépeint sont d'autant plus touchantes qu'elles sont pleines de vertu, et que les âmes sont attendries par ces sortes de représentations [cf. Nicole: cette passion y paraît avec honneur et d'une manière qui, au lieu de la rendre horrible, est capable au contraire de la faire aimer . . . On y fait gloire d'en être touché]. Je ne vois pas quel grand crime c'est que de s'attendrir à la vue d'une passion honnête; et c'est un haut étage de vertu que cette pleine insensibilité où ils veulent faire monter notre âme. Je doute qu'une si grande perfection soit dans les forces de la nature humaine; et je ne sais s'il n'est pas mieux de travailler à rectifier et adoucir les passions des hommes, que de vouloir les retrancher entièrement.[97]

This entire passage seems to designate Stoicism as well as all forms of austere piety such as Jansenism. The first is rejected because Molière holds that the extirpation of the passions, even if such a thing were possible, would not be compatible with the psychological structure of human nature. The second is also rejected by implication, for Molière confesses himself completely unable to grasp the position of those people who think that it is wrong to be moved by a 'passion honnête'. By admitting the nature and existence of such passions, he displays the same indulgence towards human nature as Cléante does, underlining how irreconcilable it is with Christian rigorism. Far from allowing the existence of *honnêtes* passions, Nicole insists forcefully that, however *honnêtes* they appear to be, they are nevertheless fundamentally 'vicieuses' and 'illégitimes' in so far as they do not originate from the creature's love of God. The human heart must not tolerate the sharing of any attachment whatsoever for the creature with the attachment due alone to the creator.[98]

He anticipates Bossuet when he conceives of the fixed gulf between comedy and piety as but one manifestation of that between the principle of the world ('concupiscence') and God.[99] Comedy cannot therefore on any account serve as a legitimate *divertissement* for the Christian: for, if loved for itself, it is sinful in that it usurps the rightful place of God, and if regarded as pure relaxation for the mind, it is equally so, since the Christian must always seek in his recreation activities which predispose him to a deeper piety and sanctity of life: that is, which intensify still more his love of God. Comedy, as Nicole makes explicit, does not equip one more fully for the Christian duties of prayer and holy living.[100] Molière's *Préface* makes another unmistakable reference to this part of the Jansenist's argument, by apparently conceding this point to him in theory. But he then proceeds to advance a view of man as observed by him in *reality* which opposes it all the more to the essence of Nicole's argument:

> J'avoue qu'il y a des lieux qu'il vaut mieux fréquenter que le théâtre, et si l'on veut blâmer toutes les choses qui ne regardent pas directement Dieu et notre salut, il est certain que la comédie en doit être, et je ne trouve point mauvais qu'elle soit condamnée avec le reste. Mais, supposé, comme il est vrai, que les exercices de la piété souffrent des intervalles et que les hommes aient besoin de divertissement, je soutiens qu'on ne leur en peut trouver un qui soit plus innocent que la comédie.[101]

Molière, in common with Le Vayer, bases his rejection of Stoicism, Jansenism and austere religious practice upon a concept of reason which takes full account of man with his manifest weakness and imperfection. Unlike both these teachings, they make no attempt to force human nature into the mould of absolute reason or absolute love of God, because they recognize it as incapable of attaining either. Man is neither a being of pure reason, or of complete spirituality, but is composed of both body and mind, both of which are equally and intrinsically essential to authentic humanity. Once this unity and equality have been accepted, the *raison d'être* for any duality of mind-body or any tension between a higher and lower order disappears, precisely because no duality or tension is seen. The reality of the human condition is, as Montaigne says, that 'Les hommes vont ainsin.' One must be guided by this empirical truth in establishing human principles, otherwise one incurs the risk of becoming unreasonable, that is rational and absolute, hence unnatural and, paradoxically, inhuman.[102]

Hence it is natural that Cléante should praise those *dévots* of whom he can say unreservedly that 'leur dévotion est humaine, est traitable' (Act 1, Sc. 5, 1. 390). Orgon, in extolling Tartuffe's piety to him, had sounded the note of Stoic-Jansenist tension between body and spirit when he had proclaimed

> Qui suit bien ses leçons goûte une paix profonde,
> Et comme du fumier regarde tout le monde.
> Oui, je deviens tout autre avec son entretien;
> Il m'enseigne à n'avoir affection pour rien,
> De toutes amitiés il détache mon âme;
> Et je verrois mourir frère, enfants, mère et femme,
> Que je m'en soucierois autant que de cela. (ll. 273-9)

Cléante replies ironically: 'Les sentiments humains, mon frère, que voilà' (l. 280). In one of his *Discours ou homilies académiques*, Le Vayer amplifies his criterion of 'humanité' and allows us to see the implications which it contains for religion. The homily, *Des Pères et des enfants,* is of the greatest relevance to this passage spoken by Orgon as regards both theme and, more importantly, the way in which it is treated. Noting the natural bond of affection which has existed since time immemorial between parent and child, he observes that it has been implanted by nature in all animals and human beings. Once he has established the sacred nature of this principle, he evokes, with feigned surprise, the tension between body and spirit which the Christian religion teaches. The passage of Scripture which he paraphrases to illustrate the apparent contradiction between such teaching and nature is the same one which Orgon has just adapted so clumsily to his own ends, and through which his inhumanity is comically revealed: 'Mais que dirons-nous à ce que l'Auteur de cette même nature, après tant de préceptes en faveur des Parents, ne laisse pas de prononcer par la bouche de ses Evangélistes, que celui qui ne hait pas son père et sa mère, n'est pas digne d'être son disciple?'[103]

He goes on to suggest that it is scarcely possible to believe that we are intended to become our own enemies by the same God who enjoins us to love our neighbour as ourselves. In the presence of a text which, although couched in dramatic language in order to emphasize the stern nature of Christian discipleship, nevertheless poses a tension, a discipline and a form of abnegation as a basic principle of the Christian religion, Le Vayer does not attempt to refute its meaning directly. Instead, he prefers to undermine its force by a process of studied exaggeration. He underlines, by the use of emotive terms, the inhuman and totally unreasonable nature of Christianity, were such a tension between life and religion taken seriously. The necessary consequences for us would be 'une aversion de notre propre vie, une haine criminelle' of our own selves. Once the caricature has been carefully evoked, it is shown to be so grotesque that the reader immediately acquiesces in Le Vayer's rejection of it. But the essential question of any tension between the temporal and the spiritual orders has, by the same token, been subtly avoided.[104]

Is this not somewhat akin to the procedure which Molière employs in *Tartuffe?* In Orgon he gives a caricature of piety which even religion itself is bound to reject as inhuman and unreasonable.[105] But the true problem is also dismissed, or rather not perceived, behind the subject of ridicule. The caricature of the conflict between the temporal and the spiritual cannot, however, be so lightly dismissed when Molière claimed at such great length that his play was in no way of an irreligious nature! Molière's claim becomes less credible when the conflict is seen as an integral part of the Christian attitude to life. For the contrast between the two orders is not a posterior version appended to the Christian faith by a rigorous form of piety. One need only quote several of the many passages of the Pauline writings to realize that from the inception of Christianity, this contrast formed an intrinsic part of its doctrine: 'Et même je regarde toutes choses comme une perte, à cause de l'excellence de Jésus-Christ mon Seigneur, pour lequel j'ai renoncé à tout, et je les regarde comme de la boue, afin de gagner Christ' (*Epître aux Philippiens*, Ch. III, v. 8 (Version L. Segond)) and 'Affectionnez-vous aux choses d'en haut, et non à celles qui sont sur la terre' (*Epître aux Colossiens*, Ch. III, v. 2).

Both Le Vayer and Molière show the extreme poverty of their understanding of Christianity here, less in any explicit hostility to it than in their obvious determination to show that no such tension need exist. It is true that Le Vayer does give an appearance of orthodoxy in the course of his interpretation of the passage from St Luke, when he writes that its lesson is that the love for our creator must be incomparably stronger than our love for his creatures. The exegesis is formally correct, but nowhere in his work does it impose itself with the semblance of a vital conviction.[106] Similarly, Cléante's devotion is impeccably orthodox in appearance, but like that of Le Vayer balks at the suggestion of any sacrifice imposed by a higher order on humanity, because for him humanity is the highest moral and spiritual order. That such a humanist attitude prevailed in the circle in which Molière is certainly known to have moved, is suggested by the similar reactions of two of his most intimate friends to the idea of religious discipline and penance. Chapelle, describing the austerity of a religious order at Saint-Lazare, displays in his humorous lines a total incomprehension of religious discipline: he watches cadaverous *dévots* who force themselves to penance day and night because they stand in dread of eternal torment, and who

> ...pour mieux surmonter la chair,
> Se donnent cent coups d'étrivières,
> Ce qui s'appelle en triompher.[107]

Bernier, in his travels in the Mogul empire, looks at the flagellations of the religious in a spirit of incredulous detachment, concluding '...et tout cela, ce semble, par dévotion comme j'ai dit, par motif de Religion, où on n'en saurait seulement découvrir l'ombre.'[108]

The deep gap between humanism and the rigorist piety of Jansenism, of the Ecole française of Bérulle and Condren, of Charpy de Sainte-Croix (for whom the Christian life consisted 'à mourir à la chair et aux choses du monde...et ne vivre qu'en Dieu avec luy'),[109] of Olier and Bossuet, does not in itself make any fusion of Christianity and humanism impossible in the seventeenth century, although it does tend to give an impoverished appearance to such a fusion. In spite of the fact that the century was one in which Christian rigorism flourished in many forms, it is nevertheless dangerous to overlook the extent to which humanism and Christianity apparently could and did merge harmoniously. As P. Bénichou has judiciously pointed out, the logical incompatibility between the natural wisdom of Molière and the folly of the Cross might well have posed no problem to the conscience of the *honnête dévot*, even though it was recognized keenly by Christians of more austere bent.[110] It is true that there was a more moderate form of religion which did not preach the mutually exclusive nature of *honnêteté* and piety, and H. Bremond has aptly termed this current of belief *l'humanisme dévot*. It accepts as one of its bases the antique formula of Terence 'nihil humani a se alienum putet', and attempts to synthesize the central aspects of humanism and Christianity. In this synthesis, emphasis is willingly placed upon the divinity of man's reason as well as upon his natural goodness, which grace can bring to perfection. Grace indeed is not parsimoniously bestowed on the chosen few alone, but generously on all men, for all are held capable of responding to it. Rigorism is anathematized because it offends against the definition of humanity accepted by *l'humanisme dévot*. Just as Le Vayer condemns the Augustinian doctrine which consigns children who die unbaptized to eternal torment, so too does Christian humanism.[111] A theology which stresses reason and humanity as worthy attributes lends itself easily to *honnêteté*, which draws its inspiration from the same humanist principles. It is therefore not surprising to hear the greatest and most representative of the *humanistes dévots*, St François de Sales, not only re-echoing the adage of Terence, but also apparently epitomizing the spirit of *folle sagesse* in his rejection of absolute moral doctrines as he exclaims 'Grande folie de vouloir être sage d'une sagesse impossible!'[112] His *Introduction à la vie dévote* (1608) is undertaken with the precise intention of demonstrating the possibility of being *honnête* and Christian at the same time. One finds here not the harsh absolute note of austerity, but an insistence that the Christian life need be neither rigorous nor separate from society, rather 'douce, heureuse et amiable'.[113] Devotion need not necessarily be the cheerless and exclusive exercise of an Orgon or a Mme Pernelle: 'C'est un vice sans doute, que d'être si rigoureux, agrestre et sauvage, qu'on ne veuille prendre pour soi ni permettre aux autres aucune sorte de récréation.'[114] Indeed, he seems to show complete indulgence to Philothée, the subject to whom he addresses himself, and permits her activities which to other *dévots* symbolize the pernicious spirit of the world: '. . . les jeux, les bals, les festins, les pompes, les comédies, en leur substance ne sont nullement choses mauvaises ains indifférentes, peuvent être bien ou mal exercées.'[115] He also extends his approval to attendance at fashionable gatherings, and Molière's ridicule of Mme Pernelle's condemnation of such innocent pleasures would seem to indicate substantial agreement:

> Ces visites, ces bals, ces conversations
> Sont du malin esprit toutes inventions,
> Là jamais on n'entend de pieuses paroles;
> Ce sont propos oisifs, chansons et fariboles. (Act I, Sc.1, ll.151-4)

But in fact Christian humanism is far from the humanism of *Tartuffe,* in spite of similar appearances. If St François permits Philothée to indulge in worldly activities freely, he continually warns her of the danger of attaching her affections to the temporal instead of the spiritual: 'Mais surtout prenez garde, Philothée, de ne point attacher votre affection à tout cela; car pour honnête que soit une récréation, c'est vice d'y mettre son coeur et son affection.' He accompanies this with an admonition to flee all forms of human vanity, and he devotes a chapter to reminding her that during the time spent in worldly pleasures, she could have been engaged in more spiritually profitable service.[116] In other words, he still retains, in modified form, the Pauline antithesis of the world and God. Although expressed in an attenuated way which is far from the denunciatory tones of a Bossuet or a Nicole, his concessions serve only to palliate what is a predominantly Christian rather than humanist attitude to life. In spite of 'la dévotion aisée' of Père Le Moyne, the naïve optimism about human nature displayed by Yves de Paris, and the casuistical attitude of the Jesuits in Pascal's *Lettres Provinciales* towards moral questions, Christian humanism is very different from the humanism which H. Bremond characterizes as *l'humanisme éternel,* in which no place is reserved for dogmatic concepts such as original sin and which reduces all religions to the same position.[117]

Both Christian humanism and Christian rigorism affirm in their characteristic ways man's need of and dependence upon his creator. Both thus display what one might term a Christian instinct, which leads them at different stages of their religious thought to introduce some standard other than a solely human one to their consideration of man. It is such a Christian instinct which *Tartuffe* seems to me to lack. I said above that implication tends to outstrip overt intention in the play. It is by implication rather than by intention that the thought of the play appears to me to relate more closely to the humanist *libertin érudit* of the century than to the Christian humanist. In the remainder of this chapter I should like to develop this line of thought in a more detailed way.

(5)

According to the dogma of the Church, man is formed in the image and likeness of God: consequently the ultimate motivation for all his actions is deemed to be an innate desire towards God, whether implicitly or explicitly expressed. This notion of innateness, based firmly upon the doctrine of St Augustine and St Thomas, forms the cornerstone of the arguments of seventeenth-century apologists for the Christian religion.[118] It is against people such as the humanist *libertins érudits*, who apparently have no innate desire for God, that Pascal formulates the famous argument of the *Pensées*, specifically designed to re-awaken the dormant 'sentiment de Dieu' in the unbeliever.[119] La Mothe Le Vayer was one of the most notable and intelligent of such *libertins érudits*, apparently devoid of all religious awareness. According to him '. . . si cette connaissance d'un Dieu dépendait de la lumière naturelle, personne n'en serait privé . . .' But since this is manifestly not the case, he concludes that 'On ne peut donc pas dire qu'elle soit née avec nous et que naturellement nous la possédions.'[120] With the demolition of the innate notion of God, the *libertin érudit* reduces it (though always by implication, never by rebuttal) to one more example of the aberrations of which the human mind is capable. In the same dialogue, Le Vayer writes that there is no other belief held by humans 'qui découvre davantage notre imbécillité . . . n'y ayant point de proportion du fini à l'infini, et du Créateur à la créature.'[121]

Tartuffe is written from a standpoint which seems to share something of this incredulous detachment with regard to man's faculty for credulous belief. The *Lettre sur la Comédie* lets us glimpse this, when the writer speaks of what he terms 'le pouvoir vraiment étrange de la religion sur les esprits des hommes'.[122] What is the source of this strange capacity for belief on the part of Orgon, of whom the *Lettre* is speaking? Simply what has been called by Fernandez 'l'instinct du salut au spirituel'.[123] He possesses, in hypertrophied form, of course, a Christian instinct which is nothing less than an innate aspiration towards God, which he deforms into worship of the god Tartuffe. The ultimate objective in his worship of the hypocrite is, as he himself confesses, 'Le Ciel'. It was the extreme ardour with which Tartuffe prayed to 'Le Ciel' which initially attracted his attention to him. And observing his acts of 'charity', it was 'Le Ciel' which impelled him to offer Tartuffe the hospitality of his home (ll. 281-310). It is noticeable that throughout the play Molière often avoids the use of such an undoubtedly emotive term as God, which is clearly the synonym of the euphemism 'Le Ciel'. Tartuffe, the presumed mediator of God's grace to Orgon, has become god himself in the eyes of the worshipper. For Orgon is throughout the play in a state of religious ecstasy. Dorine, if somewhat more earthy in her description of him, confirms this impression (ll. 195-8). L. Gossman has described Orgon's worship of Tartuffe so well that he is worth quoting in full at this point:

> Orgon does not demand that he should be the center of attention, he demands that Tartuffe should be; he does not put his health and well-being before that of his wife and children, but Tartuffe's; he does not require that his own innate superiority be recognised by his family, but that Tartuffe's should be. It is not he who is quasi-divine, but Tartuffe . . . Indeed, Orgon presents Tartuffe as a kind of Christ figure.[124]

The *Lettre sur la Comédie* underlines the holiness with which Orgon invests Tartuffe when it employs the former's habitual description of his idol as 'le saint homme', 'le saint personnage' in ironic vein. [125] There is of course nothing at all divine in the ribald impostor Tartuffe, but the manifest falsity of the idol ought not to blind us to the fact that in Orgon's worship of him, indeed in his *need* to worship him, comedy has laid bare, however unintentionally, a certain mechanism of belief shared by both fanatic and true *dévot,* but not by the hypocrite. Man must instinctively reduce God to finite proportions; he must, as Montaigne writes in his *Apologie,* '(le) compiler en certaine image à son modelle'.[126] Both Montaigne and Le Vayer show how religious belief originates in a naturally explicable way. In so doing, they are careful to distinguish between the idea which man forms of the existence of God, and the actual existence of God which they accept fideistically.[127] Both isolate anthropomorphism, or the ascription of human characteristics to God, as one of the ineradicable elements of human belief. Orgon's belief in the god Tartuffe also originates from his own autocratic temperament. All his actions are motivated by his temperamental desire to antagonize the family; as he tells Tartuffe, 'faire enrager le monde est ma plus grande joie' (Act III, Sc. 7, l. 1173). It is his natural perverseness which he willingly confuses with the will of heaven (in Act

I, Sc. 5 he rationalizes his procrastination with regard to the marriage of his daughter to Valère by invoking the will of heaven; in Act III, Sc. 6 he drives his son angrily from home for the same reason). In Tartuffe he perceives the means of imposing his perverse will on others, whilst giving this desire the highest possible motivation and justification. His god is one who only too readily allows him to indulge his whimsical bad humour — not, of course, for the reasons which Orgon ascribes to him. Tartuffe in fact is something more than Orgon's god; he becomes an intermediary in Orgon's worship of himself and his imagined domination over others. He is, without knowing it, his own god, just as Argan becomes his own doctor at the end of *Le Malade Imaginaire.*

Cléante, on whom the 'divinity' of Tartuffe makes no impact whatever, rejects Orgon's crude anthropomorphic form of religion, but has not the Christian instinct which his brother-in-law deforms. As far as his religion is concerned, perhaps he is closest to that select group of Deists whom one of Molière's friends, Dassoucy, wittily characterizes as '...des Esprits en qui la lumière naturelle est trop puissante pour laisser aucune entrée à la surnaturelle.'[128] They agree in regarding the natural credulity of man as the perpetual source of religious superstition and excess, which they equate with the supernatural aspects of religion. Le Vayer uses credulity as his means of classifying religions, of which '...la moins humaine et la plus surnaturelle, pour ne pas dire extravagante, sera d'autant plus opiniâtrement soutenue qu'elle tombera moins sous l'examen de notre raison.'[129] This is the main burden of Cléante's two lengthy speeches to Orgon in Act I, Sc. 5. He draws the clear distinction which he perceives between true and false piety: the *faux dévot* is characterized by a parade of religion at odds with reason and moderation. Reason is a value singularly overlooked in the behaviour of the *dévots* whom Cléante estimates as hypocrites. They display 'le dehors plâtré d'un zèle spécieux' (l. 360), they wear a 'trompeuse grimace' (l. 362), and achieve the desired effect upon the naïvely credulous 'à prix de faux clins d'yeux et d'élans affectés' (l. 368). The true *dévot*, on the other hand, is distinguished by a tranquil and reasonable piety which avoids all the inhuman and extravagant trappings of superstition. In Cléante and Orgon these two types of devotion are embodied: the former lives in harmony with himself and others, the latter is constantly a prey to agitation and intolerance. The way in which *Tartuffe* illustrates the theory of Cléante resembles closely the remarks of Pierre Charron on true and false religion. His treatise, *De la Sagesse* (1601), forms an important link between the *Essais* of Montaigne (from whom he borrows much) and the sceptical dialogues of Le Vayer (who quotes him frequently).[130] In a chapter entitled *Estudier à la vraye piété*, he begins by emphasizing the same argument which Cléante's speeches labour. In order to know truly what piety is, one must be able to distinguish it from spurious devotion. He ascribes the same qualities to each as Cléante does: '. . . les differences des deux, sont que la religion ayme et honore Dieu, met l'homme en paix et en repos, et loge en une ame libre, franche, et genereuse; la superstition trouble et effarouche l'homme et effray; se cacher et s'enfuir de luy s'il estoit possible, c'est maladie d'ame foible, vile et paoureuse.' He then gives a portrait of the superstitious *dévot*, which describes accurately the tetchy Orgon: 'Le superstitieux ne laisse vivre en paix ny Dieu, ny les hommes: il apprehende Dieu chagrin, despiteux, difficile à contenter, facile à se courroucer, long à s'appaiser . . . Il tremble de peur, il ne peust se fier ny s'asseurer, craignant n'avoir jamais assez bien fait, et avoir obmis quelque chose, pour laquelle omission tout peut-estre ne vaudra rien.'[131]

The same picture of the *superstitieux* is given in the anonymous *Quatrains du Déiste,* which at the beginning of the century summarized objections to the traditional conceptions of God as enshrined in the Judaic-Christian religions. The type of *dévot* which Orgon represents is qualified as an 'homme bigot', 'furieux', 'cruel', 'impitoyable', 'plein d'inquiétude'. This is because of the inborn fear which he nourishes of eternal retribution at the hands of a vindictive deity. The unconscious practice of anthropopathy by him in his ascription of human passions to God is naturally denounced and attributed to the two familiar faults of ignorance and superstition, in answer to which the Deist proposes his own superior form of religion.[132]

The belief of the true *dévot* is antithetical to such crude conceptualizing about God in material terms. Cléante does not make any precise statement about his belief in God (nor should he be expected to in what is, after all, a comedy and not a theological discourse): but it is evident that his God is believed in without any of the direct fervour and passionate attachment of Orgon. His attitude in this respect harmonizes singularly with the approach of the Deist, who is content that his worship should consist of admiration and contemplation of the greatness and majesty of the Supreme Being, and that it should be devoid of what Charron describes as 'grande declaration et determination . . . ou prescription de son service.' In other words, there is no religion or form of service which may be said to be more exclusively true than any other. The Deist transcends all human conceptions of religion, acknowledging God as 'la bonté, perfection et infinité du tout incomprehensible et incognoissable'.[133] As Montaigne writes in the *Apologie*, God is the ultimate effort which it is possible for the imagination to make in conceiving of perfection. Once one attempts to go farther than this spiritual conception of religion, one risks falling into the error of an Orgon, who worships a visible God, perceptible to the senses.[134]

One might well ask the 'petite question indiscrète' which Sainte-Beuve poses regarding Cléante: 'Ce Cléante fait-il encore ses Pâques?'[135]

How do the Deistic Cléantes lead their lives within the context of a predominantly Christian society? As one might expect, they will most assuredly not contradict or oppose openly the conventional forms of religious tradition. Charron defines their attitude in a way which is perfectly consistent with what Molière tells us of Cléante's moderate line of conduct (the observation of the *juste-milieu*): 'Ne faut toutesfois mespriser et desdaigner le service exterieur et public, auquel il se faut trouver, et assister avec moderation, sans vanité, sans ambition, ou hypocrisie . . .'

Although such a believer is fully aware that '. . . ce qui se fait au dehors est plus pour nous que pour Dieu, pour l'unité et edification humaine que pour la verité divine . . .', Charron is not guilty of contradiction in expressing the wish that such observation should be without hypocrisy.[136] For there is an authentic conviction underlying the difference between the religious theory of the Deist and his religious practice. On the one hand he knows as well as Montaigne that '...nous sommes Chrestiens à mesme titre que nous sommes ou Perigordins ou Alemans.'[137] But on the other hand, his public attitude results from his wish to maintain the established order in society. Any innovation in religious practice, such as the rigorism of Orgon and his friends, is regarded as a threat to private and public *tranquillité*. The principal advantage of religion is seen to reside not in its theological value, but in its importance as a restraining and stabilizing factor in society.

One can see now an additional significance in Cléante's warm praise of those *dévots* whose only concern is to live well, and one which is borne out by a scrutiny of their social conduct. Their most outstanding feature is that they neither do nor say anything which could possibly disturb the even surface of social existence. As exemplified in the true piety of Ariston, Périandre etc. (ll. 385 ff.), religion forms a powerful corollary to Cléante's desire for *tranquillité*, since it inculcates the social virtues of tolerance, mutual respect, restraint of passion, and respect for authority. But great care must be taken not to disassociate the secular from the religious virtues; otherwise one falls into the extremity of the iconoclastic Orgon, who allows his individual view of religion to determine his actions in society and in the family. It is scarcely surprising to find Pierre Charron laying great store on the same point. Piety in a purely religious sense must never be divorced from 'la vraie preud'hommie', a virtue which exists independently of religion, and which may be said to be social honesty and integrity. The pursuit of the first to the detriment of the second can only issue in 'superstition' or 'hypocrisie'. The true mainspring of conduct is simply the aspiration to be 'homme de bien', to follow 'cette équité et raison universelle qui esclaire et luit en un chascun de nous.'[138]

It is this balance between 'piété' and 'preud 'hommie' that Cléante's true *dévots* reflect so well:

Ils ne censurent point toutes nos actions;
Ils trouvent trop d'orgueil dans ces corrections,
Et laissant la fierté des paroles aux autres,
C'est par leurs actions qu'ils reprennent les nôtres.
L'apparence du mal a chez eux peu d'appui,
Et leur âme est portée à juger bien d'autrui. (ll. 391-6)

They refuse steadfastly to interfere with the opinions, beliefs and behaviour of others. They are 'hommes de bien' who practise constantly the ideal of charity which is the expression of the truly religious man. There is an invaluable commentary on this ideal in *Lettre sur les Observations d'une comédie du sieur Molière* (August 1665), which was written either by Molière or by one of his friends in defence of *Dom Juan*. It deals particularly with the accusation of impiety made by Rochemont against Molière's *Dom Juan*. Molière, Rochemont writes, is not well qualified to write about devotion, with which he is so little concerned, since he has never experienced it in theory or practice. The writer of the *Lettre* professes himself unable to believe that such a statement could have been made by a charitable person. How has he been able to make such an observation? Has he plumbed the depths of Molière's conscience or does he know him intimately enough to pass judgement on him? He then makes his essential argument clear by asking: 'Est-il enfin un homme qui puisse parler de la conscience d'un autre par conjecture, et qui puisse assurer que son prochain ne vaut rien et qu'il n'a jamais rien valu?' He goes on to quote the injunction of St Paul to the Romans that one should neither despise nor judge one's brother, and alleges that Rochemont has offended against the cardinal principle of religion, that is, charity: 'Mais ce qui regarde la religion perçant jusques à l'âme, il n'est pas permis d'en parler, ni d'accuser si publiquement son prochain.'[139]

The exercise of charity is, in the last analysis, determined by one's inability to judge the innermost spiritual state of one's neighbour. Whilst the deception of a Tartuffe is clear to most people, one must nevertheless accept the appearances which people present or choose to present. This is what Cléante must do himself. He has no proof other than that provided by appearances of the authenticity of the *dévots* whom he so much admires. Cléante's position is finally that of nominalist Sceptics such as Le Vayer, Gassendi and Montaigne , who accept that there must always be a separation between things as they appear and things as they are in reality. Orgon is totally unaware of the problem of 'real' appearances when he chooses to categorize people conveniently as saints or *libertins*. All Cléante can say of his own spiritual state is that 'Je sais comme je parle, et le Ciel voit mon coeur' (1. 324). Cléante's charitable refusal to judge others is primarily defensive and negative in its nature. Lacking something of the spontaneous altruistic character of personal sacrifice which religion demands of its adherents, it is adopted by him in order to preserve his own *tranquillité* from the curiosity of others, and imposed on him by the knowledge that he lives in a world where appearances offer the only truth. Outwardly he combines two attitudes which ultimately stand in direct opposition to each other — the Christian attitude of charity, and preoccupation with self-interest. This fusion of the sacred and profane, compatible for the moment in Cléante's *honnête* conduct, will reveal their deep incompatibility in the philosophy of his successor, Philinte of *Le Misanthrope*.

Nevertheless, the essentially sceptical perspective which Cléante has on society does lead to a positive attitude of tolerant open-mindedness. If one is convinced that appearances are truth, one is more likely to countenance divergent opinions than are the dogmatists of society. This is an important step towards that detachment from one's own opinion which enables Le Vayer to envisage all shades of opinion with sceptical moderation and equanimity. The most vital conviction behind the writing of *Tartuffe* seems to me to be that of the necessity of possessing such qualities in one's religious outlook. In one of his *Petits Traités*, Le Vayer stresses this in a way which is particularly germane to the subject of the play: '. . . on abuse souvent du mot d'impie, quand on l'attribue à tous ceux qui pensent autrement que nous des choses divines, encore qu'elles soient problématiques, et qu'ils s'en expliquent avec beaucoup de circonspection.' Often, adds the Sceptic, our categorical statements about what is or is not religious truth are founded on nothing more solid than our *amour-propre*, which induces us to defend them with obduracy '. . . n'en reconnaissant point d'autres pour orthodoxes'.[140] Cléante and the embattled author of *Tartuffe* would be in agreement with him most assuredly when he writes elsewhere that there is more than one way which leads to heaven, and that God probably takes as much delight in such variety as in the diversity of nature itself.[141]

(6)

The last word on religion in *Tartuffe* does not, however, rest with Cléante. The *dénouement,* which Molière certainly added to his play when victory over the intrigues of the *dévots* was secure, contains in idealized form his conception of the role which the monarch ought to play in the affairs of religion. It is left to Louis to re-establish order in the household and society, an order that the moderation of Cléante could never restore, by his punishment of the hypocrite and his acolytes. Molière thus makes the King the epitome of established authority both in the secular and religious spheres, and the play ends with the restoration of the *status quo* on both levels. Just as Cléante's conservatism in religious practice transcends the implications of his beliefs, so too the conclusion of the play transcends the idea, so fundamental to the conception of the subject, that the individual has a right to hold his own view of religion independently of any external authority or pressure. R. Pintard observes the same voluntary illogicality in the typical attitude of the *libertins érudits* towards absolutism. One would expect, he writes, of such independent thinkers in religious matters, a hostility to the very idea of constraint and dependence embodied in any concept of absolutism. Yet he observes that precisely the reverse is found to be true.[142] Le Vayer, for example, recognizes that the monarch must be an undisputed autocrat in matters of authority, whose primary duty is to dispense justice. He considers religion as a mere extension of his secular authority, as 'un acte de justice'.[143] As one of the cohesive elements in society it must be protected by the monarch, and his rule must exemplify this.[144] In common with Charron, Le Vayer encourages the monarch to conceive of himself as God's representative on earth in his discrimination between right and wrong and in his dispensation of justice. The conception of divine right invested in God's temporal representative confers authority upon all his decisions. But in no question will he have to display this authority more fully than in that involving the distinction of true from fraudulent piety: 'Comme il y a des zélés indiscrets, il s'en trouve aussi d'hypocrites, et l'on voit assez de personnes qui n'emploient la piété que comme un fard sur le visage, dont ils se tiendraient intéressés au dedans.'[145]

The theocratic conception of the monarch is embodied in the final Act of Molière's play, where the omniscient and omnipotent Prince is able to make this distinction with rare clarity of vision. As L'Exempt announces

> Nous vivons sous un prince ennemi de la fraude,
> Un prince dont les yeux se font jour dans les coeurs,
> Et que ne peut tromper tout l'art des imposteurs.
> D'un fin discernement sa grande âme pourvue
> Sur les choses toujours jette une droite vue;
> Chez elle jamais rien ne surprend trop d'accès,
> Et sa ferme raison ne tombe en nul excès. (Act V, Scène dernière
> ll. 1906-12)

Le Vayer's corollary to this ideal theodicy — that the monarch ought to be indulgent to individuals but ruthless whenever society is threatened — is illustrated by the King's pardon of Orgon (in gratitude for past services to the royal cause rendered during the Fronde, ll. 1937-44) and his punishment of Tartuffe. The exercise of unbiased judgement, Le Vayer stresses, is only possible whenever the monarch is acting independently of any particular religious influence or *cabale*.

There can be no possibility of sharing his secular and religious authority with anyone else. He alone is the divine representative, carrying out God's ordinance in both spheres.[146] The 'juste trait de l'équité suprême' (1. 1922), which ensures the happy *dénouement*, is logically at variance with the philosophic and religious vision of the play: yet the supreme act of the King does paradoxically reflect the ideal sceptical view of an ordered society, founded upon the unquestioned autocratic authority of the monarch.

4 Dom Juan[1]

The second play which Molière wrote during what I have termed the *Tartuffe* period was *Dom Juan ou Le Festin de Pierre*. Although it seems at first sight to treat a subject less complex than that of *Tartuffe*, it has proved nonetheless to be even more enigmatic: the nineteenth-century critic Jules Lemaître aptly described it as 'étrange . . . bizarre . . . hybride . . . obscure en diable'.[2] It was immediately attacked on its appearance at the Palais-Royal by the *dévots* who had reacted so violently to the satire of religious hypocrites in *Tartuffe*. Rochemont and the Prince de Conti in particular accused Molière of committing an outrage against decency and piety.[3] It was also defended by the well-meaning but ineffectual *Réponse aux Observations Touchant Le Festin de Pierre . . .* and the more stringently argued *Lettre sur les Observations d'une Comédie du Sieur Molière intitulée Le Festin de Pierre*, the author of which was certainly one of Molière's intimate friends, if not the playwright himself.[4] This initial division of opinion about the intention of the play persists today; it has either been regarded as not essentially subversive in design, or as thoroughly impious in intention.[5]

If Molière's intentions have been seen as obscure, his reasons for writing the play in the first place would appear to be vague and ill-defined. Most *Moliéristes* have tended to accept the traditional account of why Molière should have been attracted to the legend. According to this account, *Dom Juan* was hastily improvised as an *oeuvre d'occasion* after the unexpected interdiction of *Tartuffe*: in addition, Molière did not choose to treat the theme himself, but was persuaded by the members of his own troupe to write a play on the theme of the legend, in order to benefit from its current popularity in Paris.[6] At first sight this may appear acceptable, since the original theme of Tirso de Molina's *El Burlador de Sevilla* had been used by Dorimond in his *Le Festin de Pierre ou Le Fils Criminel* (performed in Paris in 1661, but published in 1659) and by Villiers in a play of the same title (performed in Paris in 1659 and published the following year). It was left to G. Michaut to point out the weakness of this assumption. He argued that when Molière wrote his own version of the legend, four and six years after other Parisian theatres had first performed the contemporary French versions, the theme of Don Juan could scarcely be said to be still in vogue.[7] It is highly improbable, to say the least, that Molière was unaware of this fact, or that he should have needed to rely on the suggestions of others for the choice of a play to succeed *Tartuffe*. As the successful *directeur* of a troupe of actors, he must have known that he needed a play in reserve to meet the contingency of the controversial *Tartuffe* being banned. The source of this traditional account was La Serre, writing not in 1665 but in 1734, in his *Mémoires Sur la Vie et les Ouvrages* de Molière. In fact, it is clear that he attributed the manner of origin of Villiers' play to Molière, for the former recounts in his preface how his actors encouraged him to write a French version of the legend, when they saw the popularity enjoyed by the current Italian scenarios of the *commedia dell'arte*.[8]

The reason why Molière chose to treat the legend of Don Juan at this particular time seems to me to be found elsewhere, and is bound up with the experience of *Tartuffe*. It is of the utmost importance to remember the context in which the play was written. *Dom Juan* was first performed in February 1665, and was most likely finished if not conceived during the period from September 1664 to January 1665, that is after the interdiction of the first *Tartuffe* and the *Premier Placet* to the King in August 1664. In other words, the play was cast in its final form, and performed, at a time when its author was profoundly and personally committed to his unrelenting struggle against the *dévots* who had secured the interdiction of *Tartuffe*, thereby threatening to ruin his theatrical career. To remember this is neither to read into the play an extraneous autobiographical meaning, nor to add a false dimension to a work of art, but merely to remember that whichever subject Molière turned to at this time would be treated by a man ruled by genuine indignation and bitter disappointment. One might of course deny this connexion between art and life: 'art is art . . . because it is not life.'[9] But in the case of *Dom Juan*, the contemporaries of Molière were fully aware of the connexion between his experiences after *Tartuffe* and the present play. There is a suggestive passage in the anonymous reply to Rochemont's strictures of *Dom Juan* which underlines the continuity of inspiration which they saw between the two plays: 'A quoi songiez-vous, Molière, quand vous fites dessein de jouer les tartufles? Si vous n'aviez jamais eu cette pensée, votre *Festin de Pierre* ne seroit pas si criminel.'[10] The experience of *Tartuffe* is at the origin of *Dom Juan*, shaping Molière's treatment of the legend's structure, and recasting it in its own terms. The continuity with *Tartuffe* accounts for the original manner in which Molière handles the theme of Don Juan, and in order to determine this more clearly, it will be necessary to consider very briefly the use made of the legend by the dramatists before Molière.[11]

The dramatic theme of Don Juan originated with Tirso de Molina's play *El Burlador de Sevilla* (1630), and was quickly taken up by both the *commedia sostenuta* and the *commedia dell'arte* in Italy, as is shown by Cicognini's *Il Convitato de pietra* (before 1650), and an extant scenario, *L'Ateista fulminato*, probably written about the same time as Tirso's play. It has been convincingly established, however, that Molière's version of the theme owes nothing to these plays, but rather draws for the material details of plot and character on the plays of Dorimond and Villiers.[12] These two authors used a common source — another Italian version of the legend by Giliberto, *Il Convitato de pietra*, written around 1652, but unfortunately not extant.[13]

The plays by Dorimond and Villiers are very similar in structure and in plot, and differ only occasionally with regard to the order and length of scenes. It will be helpful to give a concise summary of their versions.

Act I Dom Juan overhears Amarille expressing her love to Dom Philippe and immediately plans to supplant him by force. Before executing his plan, both dramatists give a lengthy discussion between the Dom's valet (in Dorimond he is called Briguelle, in Villiers Philipin) and his father about Dom Juan's *libertin* behaviour. The concluding scene of Act I consists of a confrontation between father and son. In both plays, Dom Juan behaves callously towards his father: in Dorimond he insults him, and in Villiers he strikes him.

Act II Dom Juan attempts to seduce Amarille, is discovered, and kills her father before escaping. Amarille's long lament is followed by Dom Philippe's resolve to avenge himself on his rival. The archers begin to search for Dom Pierre's murderer.

Act III This opens with a long soliloquy by a Pèlerin on the tranquillity of solitude. Dom Juan and his valet appear, each disguised in the other's clothes. The valet tells Dom Juan that he has been the cause of his father's death from grief. Dorimond's Dom Juan shows genuine remorse at this news, whereas Villiers' hero is content to reproach destiny which persecutes him. Dom Juan offers the Pèlerin money in exchange for his habit; when he refuses, he forces him to change clothes with him using threats of violence. Disguised as a pilgrim, Dom Juan meets his enemy Dom Philippe, and under the pretext that heaven forbids the wearing of arms in a holy place where they go to pray, he persuades Philippe to relinquish his sword and then reveals his true identity. In Dorimond, he merely humiliates his rival; in Villiers' play he kills him.

Act IV Master and valet are shipwrecked and rescued by villagers. Dom Juan seems to repent sincerely for his past misdeeds and gives thanks to providence for having saved him. But at the sight of a shepherdess, he promptly yields once again to his natural inclinations and seduces her. In Dorimond, after the seduction he glimpses a rustic wedding and abducts the bride. Act IV ends with Dom Juan and his valet coming to a tombstone, on top of which sits the shadow of the murdered Dom Pierre. Dom Juan insults the memory of his victim, and to provoke his superstitious valet, issues a cavalier invitation to supper which the shadow accepts.

Act V   This begins with the traditional supper scene. The shadow arrives, and in Dorimond delivers a lengthy moralizing tirade of forty-two lines. Dom Juan insults it, and accepts its invitation to supper that evening at the grotto where the Commander (Dom Pierre) is buried. In Dorimond there is a scene with Amarille and Dom Philippe, in Villiers this is replaced by the wedding scene where Dom Juan abducts the bride. The second appearance of the shadow follows the traditional pattern of the legend. Dom Juan draws his sword in order to kill it, and is struck down by divine vengeance.

It will be seen at once that Molière's play adheres to the basic structure of the legend, at least as it was transmitted to him by the two contemporary French versions. Apart from traditional features of the legend, such as the seduction of the fiancée and of the peasant girls, the humiliation of the poor pilgrim, the murder of Dom Pierre and the intervention of divine justice, Molière also accepts largely the traits of his hero from Dorimond and Villiers, although he does modify him slightly. The *libertin* of these plays, who nevertheless continues to believe in a supreme monarch of the universe, becomes in Molière's play a cavalier atheist, in the style of many contemporary French noblemen.[14] But the principal difference lies in the manner in which the plays are constructed. Although the two contemporary versions are diffuse and romanesque melodramas, full of excessive action and violence, their authors have endeavoured to make them into *pièces bien écrites* and to provide fairly logical motivation for the sequence of the plot. By comparison, Molière's schema is bare to the point of stark simplicity, with little or no emphasis on actions external to the minds of the protagonists. Dom Juan does not kill the Commander before our eyes; instead of two lengthy scenes at his tomb there is an extremely brief discussion at the tombstone between master and valet; and the intervention of the statue at the end is so rapid that it seems designed to have little or none of the theatrical effect which it is intended to produce in the other two French plays. Such differences in treatment probably account for the standard judgement that the play is incoherent, and that it gives the impression of a series of *tableaux* hastily strung together.[15]

In spite of this undeniable impression of incoherence, there is a recognizable unity in Molière's version of the legend, a unity which is provided not by the traditional and 'set' episodes of the theme as in Dorimond and Villiers, but by the developing relationship between Sganarelle and Dom Juan, who thereby acquire a complexity and depth not to be found in the other French versions. This structural and thematic innovation by Molière gives rise to important considerations which arise only with his treatment of the material. Who, for example, is to be taken as Molière's *porte-parole*, Sganarelle or Dom Juan? Or, as Michaut has suggested, does Molière convey his intention through the secondary characters of the play instead?[16] Bound up with this problem is the question of whether Dom Juan is a comic figure or immune from comedy.[17] The basic contention of this chapter will be that *Dom Juan* has an organic and thematic unity not to be found in the other versions, a unity which resides in the comic principle underlying the relationship of man and master, which at once sheds light on the questions raised above and roots the play firmly in the philosophic preoccupations of *Tartuffe*.

(2)

In my analysis of the play, I propose to devote as much attention to Sganarelle as to Dom Juan. It is probably true to say that most critics have concentrated largely on the eponym, doubtless because Molière's treatment of the *libertin* was considered to indicate clearly his intention in writing the play, and also because he seems at first sight to enjoy a manifest superiority over the other protagonists. But it is important to note that the role of the valet was played by Molière himself, whereas La Grange played the part of the hero;[18] and in many respects it is the valet who, like Orgon in *Tartuffe*, provides the key to Molière's attitude towards his *libertin*. As A. Simon has remarked perceptively '. . [Molière] a choisi le meilleur poste pour rester en vue de son héros; pour le voir et être vu de lui.'[19] It is also noteworthy that out of twenty-seven scenes in the play, Sganarelle is on stage for twenty-six of them. This represents the single greatest innovation by Molière in his treatment of the legend; in the other French versions, the valet appears merely as the stock character of farce, whose function is to add set pieces of comedy to the melodrama. At all times he is nothing more than an episodic and subservient type, whereas in Molière's play he has an importance at least equal to that of Dom Juan.

The role of Sganarelle is not only central to the comedy; in his opening speech on the virtues of 'tabac' (ll. 1–13) he illustrates the main theme of the play.[20] It is not just another proof of the play's incoherence, or merely 'un hors d'oeuvre d'actualité', as Arnavon supposed it to be;[21] the valet's burlesque reasoning exemplifies that subtle transmutation of trivial reality (here *tabac*) into an object worthy of veneration, which illustrates the basic paradox at the heart not only of the most elementary type of comedy (see Chapter I) but also of the philosophy of *Tartuffe*. Sganarelle has a natural penchant for argumentation, but what is even more important to note in this scene is the skilful manipulation of appearances and reality, which not only forms the basis of his nature, but also defines his paradoxical relationship with his master. For Sganarelle is simultaneously engaged in the service of Dom Juan *and* in satirizing him to others. After having told Gusman the unpleasant truth about his master, he then adds that 's'il fallait qu'il en vînt quelque chose à ses oreilles, je dirais hautement que tu aurais menti' (ll. 89–91). Dom Juan is the catalyst who provokes criticism and acquiescence, truthfulness and lying on Sganarelle's part, and the instantaneous conversion of the one into the other. Without having seen his master, we glimpse the element that links his valet to him; this is none other than Sganarelle's nature, which is grounded on the expedient conversion of appearances into reality and vice versa.

Their ambivalent relationship is fully illustrated in their first dialogue in the second scene, when Dom Juan tries to elicit his valet's reaction to the abandonment of Elvire: 'Que t'imagines-tu de cette affaire?' (ll. 106–7), he asks. When Sganarelle expresses his suspicion that some new infatuation has been responsible for the Dom's latest infidelity, he is asked again for his reaction to such a state of affairs: 'Et ne trouves-tu pas que j'ai raison d'en user de la sorte?' (l. 118). The truth is that Dom Juan is not at all interested in Sganarelle's answers as such, for his questions are more quizzical than purposive. He certainly does not envisage any possible change of his conduct depending on Sganarelle's response. The valet's answer is equally as paradoxical as his master's question — 'Assurément que vous avez raison, si vous le voulez; on ne peut pas aller là contre. Mais si vous ne le vouliez pas, ce serait peut-être une autre affaire' (ll. 121–3) — and is born of his instinctive fear of his master ('la crainte en moi fait l'office du zèle,' he had said to Gusman in the first scene, l. 84) and of the fundamental characteristic of his own nature, his predilection for argument, which was noted above. Right and wrong depend apparently for him not on any objective principle, but on his master's will. But Dom Juan sees the expediency of such an answer; nothing less than an unambiguous and *truthful* reply from Sganarelle will satisfy him. Thus liberated from his fear of reprisals for being honest, Sganarelle can now express his utter disapproval of the Dom's recent actions (ll. 126–8). The latter has now achieved what he planned in his initial question: having isolated for a brief moment the true Sganarelle, that is to say the valet too deeply steeped in traditional moral beliefs to share the libertine notions of his master, he can now afford himself his principal pleasure of overthrowing Sganarelle's absolute condemnation of his conduct. He achieves this by a brilliant rationalization of his own *libertinage*, and his argument proceeds in three successive stages: 'Quoi? Tu veux qu'on se lie à demeurer au premier objet qui nous prend . . .' (ll. 129 ff.). To be faithful to one's fiancée is to cut oneself off from all objects of beauty, to die in one's youth; constancy and fidelity are therefore only the prerogative of fools, who blind themselves to the fact that beauty has the right to charm us wherever we are (ll. 135–9); it is therefore unjust to refuse to recognize the beauty and merit of others by withholding one's affections (ll. 139 ff.).

Dom Juan is not at all concerned with a moral justification of his conduct, but is merely content to demonstrate to his bewildered valet that reasons can be effortlessly adduced against the traditional moral standards of fidelity, honour and chastity, which thereby lose that absolute character with which Sganarelle has invested them. He does not even trouble himself to set these reasons in opposition to those of his valet; they are incidental to his objective of creating doubt in the mind of Sganarelle about the moral code by which people are supposed to live. He is in fact so successful in his reasoning that Sganarelle can only say 'Ma foi, j'ai à dire, et je ne sais que dire; car vous tournez les choses d'une manière, qu'il semble que vous ayez raison; et cependant il est vrai que vous ne l'avez pas. J'avais les plus belles pensées du monde, et vos discours m'ont brouillé tout cela' (ll. 177–81).

Sganarelle cannot argue with him now on the plane of reason; all he can do is to point to the indubitable fact that his master has *not* succeeded in making the reality of evil evaporate: '. . . je conçois que cela est fort agréable et fort divertissant et je m'en accommoderais assez, moi, s'il n'y avait point de mal' (ll. 192–4); Dom Juan does not like to be reminded of this unpalatable fact, or of Sganarelle's warning 'que les libertins ne font jamais une bonne fin' (ll. 200–1). At this point in the play, he would seem to illustrate the principle of the comic, the *disconvenance* which, according to the *Lettre sur la Comédie*, can be seen in contradictory actions proceeding from the same source. It is therefore the dramatist's function to engineer scenes in which such *disconvenance* manifests itself to the spectator. But in the case of Tartuffe, the hypocrite has himself taken over the role of the dramatist as he exploits mischievously the contradictions in language and reason to an extent which threatens to afford him immunity from comedy. Dom Juan is also one of these superior characters whose behaviour is grounded on his ability to manipulate at will the principles by which society coheres. He has triumphantly 'proved' the basis of his morality to Sganarelle, at least in reason and in theory. But how profound is his assurance of the *rationale* of the code which he professes? Does it command complete assent from his will and emotions as well as from his theory of *libertinage*? His reply in this scene to Sganarelle's warning about the disastrous end of *libertins* is highly revelatory in this respect: 'Holà, maître sot, vous savez que je vous ai dit que je n'aime pas les faiseurs de remontrances' (ll. 202–3). This sharp reaction to his valet's homily is certainly proof that his self-assured impunity from traditional moral scruples is purely verbal, and not emotional. It is surely supremely comic that the *libertin* who prides himself on being able to persuade others that black is white and that white is black, should give the impression that he has so succumbed to his own verbal virtuosity as to affect disbelief in the supernatural, of which he seems nonetheless to have an emotional conviction! But he is doubly comic in this scene in his remonstrance to his valet; for has he not repeatedly asked Sganarelle to give him his true opinion about his conduct? (ll. 124–5). Now he says that he has previously warned Sganarelle of his dislike of 'les faiseurs de remontrances!' Does he then seek mere approval from his valet? No, because he has just refused the latter's compliant acquiescence (ll. 121–3). He can only threaten to impose silence on his valet by force, as Sganarelle is used to emphasize the one weakness in the *libertin* credo. Sganarelle manages however to prolong his satire of Dom Juan's disbelief, by deftly employing the tactic of the *libertin* against him. He does this by reverting to oblique condemnation:

> Je ne parle pas aussi à vous, Dieu m'en garde! Vous savez ce que vous faites, et si vous ne croyez rien, vous avez vos raisons; il y a de certains petits impertinents dans le monde, qui sont libertins sans savoir pourquoi, qui font les esprits forts, parce qu'ils croient que cela leur sied bien; et si j'avais un maître comme cela, je lui dirais fort nettement, le regardant en face: 'Osez-vous bien ainsi vous jouer du Ciel, et ne tremblez-vous point de vous moquer comme vous faites des choses les plus saintes?' (ll. 204–12)

The *libertin* who delights in providing specious reasoning to justify himself is the victim of Sganarelle's speech, which can always be defended on the grounds that it is concerned with others, and not with Dom Juan. *A bon entendeur salut.*

It is opportune then to raise the question of Molière's attitude to Dom Juan in this scene. It is obviously impossible to identify the author's views solely with one protagonist, since each makes use in turn of the comic principle which is the basis of Molière's comic art.[22] But the fact remains that Dom Juan, in spite of his self-assured appearances, fits into the same comic framework here as does Orgon; the latter is profoundly comic to the extent that he presumes to overstep the bounds of human nature by his overweening desire to know the unknowable. Dom Juan does precisely the same thing in this scene; the basis for his libertine behaviour can only be the absolute denial of divine retribution in an after-life, and it is such a denial which promises to free him from the scruples of traditional morality. Yet Dom Juan can never be absolutely freed from the weakness of human nature (i.e. those emotions and passions which combine to keep such belief in a supernatural after-life alive). If he could be assured in all equanimity of the truth of such a denial, it would be unnecessary for him to react so testily to Sganarelle's moralizing. Sganarelle's function in this scene and in the rest of the play is to bear out the impossibility of such a denial by provoking answers from his master which suggest a loss of libertine composure on his part.

Such an interpretation of the thought underlying this scene would seem to be confirmed in an interesting way by La Mothe Le Vayer's similar attitude to *libertins* such as Dom Juan. In discussing *Tartuffe*, I pointed out that both he and the dramatist share common conceptions of reason and humanity which they take as the bases of moral conduct. It is such a reasonable and humane ethic which prompts even the Sceptic to condemn *libertins* such as those described by Sganarelle in this scene, in one of his *Discours ou homilies académiques* (1664). In one homily, *Des Injures*, he writes '. . . y a-t-il rien de plus ordinaire aujourd'hui que les blasphèmes injurieux contre la Divinité, qui véritablement les souffre quelquefois impunément pour les punir en un autre temps avec plus de rigueur, ou plus exemplairement?' This corresponds exactly to the triple *avertissement* given by Sganarelle to his master in this scene about the inevitability of divine retribution for the *libertins* (see ll. 199–201, 210 ff., 222–4). Whilst it is highly improbable that Le Vayer and Molière believed in a supernatural retribution for the deeds and misdeeds of this life (both in fact seem to have considered the existence of evil as the most cogent argument against the idea of a providence controlling human destiny), their attitude to seventeenth-century *libertins* is to be found *behind* these ironic phrases, in their strong denunciation of such *poseurs*. Both arguments rest on the contradiction perceived between the *libertins'* belief in the superiority of their enlightened attitude and the real motivation for such *libertinage*, which is none other than the vainglorious wish to be distinguished from the common herd: hence Le Vayer's strong condemnation of such unnatural arrogance:

Mais n'est-ce pas une chose qui doit faire horreur, qu'on affecte de paraître impie, afin de passer pour esprit fort, dans la plus grande faiblesse d'entendement où l'on puisse tomber, qui est celle qui naît de l'irréligion? En effet il se trouve des gens qui n'ont point d'autre motif pour paraître libertins, pour se moquer de ce qu'il y a de plus Saint au-dessus des nues, et pour jeter insolemment des crachats contre le Ciel, qui leur retombent misérablement sur le visage; que cette folle pensée d'être plus hardis et plus clairvoyants que les autres . . . Certainement c'est être bien aveugle de sa vanité, c'est affecter une liberté bien esclave de sa passion, et ce n'est pas merveille qu'on rogne les ailes à des personnes qui ont le bec si pointu et si offensant, qu'ils ne font pas difficulté de le porter outrageusement contre l'auteur de tout bien, de leur propre Etre, et de toute la Nature.[23]

This passage bears comparison with Sganarelle's bold lesson to the *esprits forts*, part of which was quoted above: 'C'est bien à vous, petit ver de terre, petit myrmidon que vous êtes . . . c'est bien à vous à vouloir vous mêler de tourner en raillerie ce que tous les hommes révèrent. Pensez-vous que pour être de qualité . . . que tout vous soit permis . . . Apprenez . . . que le Ciel punit tôt ou tard les impies . . . (ll. 212–23).

The second scene of this Act is therefore of great significance, because it is what Sganarelle says and does here which seems to provide the best insight into Molière's attitude towards his *libertin's* actions in the rest of the play. It is the valet, with his apparently weak arguments and innate pusillanimity, who will best expose the libertine pose of Dom Juan. It is, I believe, a basic misunderstanding of the importance of the role of Sganarelle that has largely contributed towards confusion concerning Molière's intentions. We find, for example, that B. A. Sieur de Rochemont anticipates much later criticism when he objects that Molière ought to have entrusted the defence of morality and religion to a character equal in argument to Dom Juan.[24] The author of the *Lettre sur les Observations* answers this charge effectively by saying that had Molière replaced Sganarelle by someone more obviously suited to theological debate, the play would no longer be a comedy but a 'conférence sur le théâtre'.[25] Sganarelle has certainly much in common with his master, notably a remarkable dexterity in juggling with the values of appearances and reality. But to suggest, as recent criticism has done, that he is nothing more than a *coquin* enslaved by Dom Juan, is to confuse his use of the comic principle (the manipulation of appearances and reality which offers both the only way of escape from domination by his master and the triumph of the comic spirit over the *libertin*) with the morality of that principle. In other words, we are surely intended by Molière to enter into complicity with the comic hero (whether he be Sganarelle or Dom Juan), without stopping to consider the morality of his actions. The conclusion of such critics as A. Adam is that since neither protagonist is edifying, the intention of Molière must remain rather dubious.[26] But in fact Molière is merely using the apparent gross inferiority of the valet as a veil beneath which his satire of the *libertin* here is all the more complete and damning. There is no doubt that this satire gains in pointedness by astute deflection rather than by direct application. This is not to say that Sganarelle is the 'âme simple et pure' which J. Arnavon made him out to be, standing against the villainy of his master.[27] He is rather the character in the play who reflects *par excellence* the strength and ultimately the weakness of the *libertin* in the eyes of Molière, and not just 'ce rôle de conscience dérisoire et servile'.[28]

In the following scene (Sc. 3) Elvire arrives to confront Dom Juan with his act of infidelity towards her. His avowal of surprise at seeing her parallels the moments in *Tartuffe* whenever the mask of 'l'âme de toutes la mieux concertée' involuntarily falls to expose the real face behind it. The *libertin* is disconcerted here because Elvire has penetrated the aristocratic decorum surrounding his infidelity, and he can therefore only ask his valet to present the reasons for his departure to her. Sganarelle's garbled answer 'Madame, les conquérants, Alexandre et les autres mondes sont causes de notre départ' (ll. 313–14) exposes the comic side to the Dom in this scene. The *libertin* who prides himself on the coherence (whether simulated or real) of his actions, is dependent on the incoherence of his valet's inventiveness. Elvire underlines his manifest confusion, by suggesting to him the role he ought to play in such a situation (ll. 319–35). In order to re-establish in the eyes of others the myth of his coherence, a paradox of the most extreme kind is required to justify his confusion. This is duly supplied when we hear the sinner reply in saintly terms worthy of his great *confrère*, Tartuffe, '. . . que je n'ai point le talent de dissimuler, et que je porte un coeur sincère' (ll. 336–7). He is correct verbally, for he scrupulously refuses the role of the hypocritical *galant* which Elvire has suggested to him. Instead, he substitutes the higher, more intangible form of deception which consists precisely in telling the truth; the infidelity which Elvire has suspected is perfectly true (l. 340), but he gives the wrong reasons for it, rationalizing his action by pretexting 'un pur motif de conscience' (l. 342). He knows that she is not deceived by this stratagem, just as Tartuffe knows that Cléante has not succumbed to his casuistical reasons for appropriating Orgon's *donation*. But both also know that, objectively, their fictitious 'obedience' to the divine will nullifies for the moment the accusation of deceit brought against them. Such an intellectualization of their position gives them the necessary time and freedom to manoeuvre. Elvire, like Cléante, can do nothing against such consummate evasiveness, but as a last resort she imprecates divine retribution for his actions (ll. 360–2). Apparently the meeting with Elvire has ended in the Dom's victory; yet as she invokes heaven for a second time (ll. 374–5), Dom Juan can do no other than divert his thoughts from the possibility of punishment to his most recent project of seduction (ll. 378–9). In reality, however, there is here more than a hint of the loss of composure and self-assurance discernible in the previous scene, on which the comic aspect of the *libertin* is based.

In the scenes with the *paysannes*, (Act II, Sc 2, 3, 4) we see an illustration of the code elaborated by the Dom in Act I, the 'donjuanism' which he summarized in two points: 'la beauté me ravit partout où je la trouve' (ll. 139–40), and 'je ne puis refuser mon coeur à tout ce que je vois d'aimable' (ll. 146–7). To follow this instinctive desire to conquer each new beauty is the principle that governs his nature, and in each of his manifestations of passion the Dom is sincere, because he follows the imperious call of that nature. But in order to be sincere to such a credo, he must, by his very nature, be insincere to the

individual to whom he spontaneously avows his love, because his
sincerity has a purely relative value and is predestined to be transferred
continually to someone else.[29] The *paysanne* Charlotte, like Sganarelle
in Act I, illustrates the effect of this fundamental ambiguity in his
character when she says in answer to his blandishments that '. . . je ne
sais comment vous faites quand vous parlez. Ce que vous dites me fait
aise, et j'aurais toutes les envies du monde de vous croire . . . je ne sais si
vous dites vrai ou non, mais vous faites que l'on vous croit' (ll. 607–9,
ll. 641–2).

Dom Juan's enslavement to the senses has been seen as providing a
comic contrast with his self-confessed awareness of what he is doing.[30]
This is in fact yet another facet of the paradox of lucidity and cecity
which make up his nature; but whereas the contrast may be said to exist
in theory in this scene, in the theatre we have at this point an
overwhelming sense of his ability to appear simultaneously as what he is
and what he is not. It is this total paradox underlying his nature which is
emphasized here, rather than one particular aspect of it. For Dom Juan
is so much a prisoner of his paradoxical nature, that he must be sincere
and insincere at one and the same time. Sganarelle, in a mocking
comment, shows that he does indeed understand perfectly the truth of
his master's nature (as he had said to Gusman in Act I, Sc. 1): when the
Dom protests that he is different from all the other plausible courtiers
of whom the *paysannes* have heard, and that he will certainly marry
Charlotte, he unwisely invokes Sganarelle's testimony to him: the valet
confirms his affirmations whilst insinuating his discreet contradiction:
'Il se mariera avec vous tant que vous voudrez' (ll. 628–9). For
Charlotte, màrriage is the ultimate and unimpeachable proof of a
suitor's sincerity; to Sganarelle's practised eye, marriage is but the
culmination of the insincerity of a master whom he has described as 'un
épouseur à toutes mains' (l. 72). Sganarelle once again allows us to
glimpse momentarily his superiority over his master, as he indirectly
exposes for all to see (but not Charlotte!) that true side to the Dom's
nature which he is here at pains to hide.

The dialogue between the two *paysannes* and the Dom in Scene 4
provides an excellent example of the way in which the latter
manipulates appearances and reality. Called upon to declare
unequivocally his love for the one or the other (having promised
marriage to both), he extricates himself with a virtuosity which matches
perfectly the ballet-like sequence of *répliques*. He begins his defence
with a lie to each *paysanne*. To Mathurine he says that Charlotte wished
to marry him, but that he could not because of betrothal to her (ll.
725–7). He tells the corresponding lie to Charlotte (ll. 729–31). He
follows this with a second lie to each in turn, pretexting that 'no amount
of persuasion will convince her that she is wrong' (ll. 733–45). Having
convinced each of the blind obstinacy of the other in maintaining that
he promised to marry her, he can now afford to hazard the truth in jest.

He tells each in turn to wager that the other will maintain that he promised to marry her (ll. 749–52). He has succeeded in diverting attention temporarily from himself, as both now start to quarrel with each other, but the stratagem threatens to rebound on him as both coalesce in pressing him for a definite answer (ll. 768–88). Dom Juan once again escapes with a masterly *échappatoire*: each, he tells them, has an inner assurance either of the truth or of the error of the claim she makes. It is therefore superfluous for him to try to add to such certainty (ll. 789–808). He himself inadvertently sums up the principle which has governed the entire dialogue and which he has exemplified so well when he says that 'Tous les discours n'avancent point les choses' (l. 797). Words, he seems to tell the very people whom he has just deceived by his *belles paroles*, can only possess relative certainty, because their latent and unsuspected meanings can be exploited so easily.[31]

Once again Dom Juan has, to all appearances, secured a resounding triumph of resourcefulness and plausibility. But the last word in the *imbroglio* belongs again to Sganarelle, as he gives a kind of glossary of 'donjuanism' to the *paysannes* at the end of this scene. He profits from his master's momentary absence to tell them the truth about him, a truth which the Dom partially overhears as he comes back to fetch his valet:

> Mon maître est un fourbe; il n'a dessein que de vous abuser, et en a bien abusé d'autres; c'est l'épouseur du genre humain, et . . . [il aperçoit Dom Juan] Cela est faux; et quiconque vous dira cela, vous lui devez dire qu'il en a menti. Mon maître n'est point l'épouseur du genre humain; il n'est point fourbe, n'a pas dessein de vous tromper, et n'en a point abusé d'autres. Ah! tenez, le voilà; demandez-le plutôt à lui-même. (ll. 818–25)

Having instantaneously converted his negative criticism into positive attributes, Sganarelle can now explain carefully to his master that the world is full of calumny (ll. 827–31), and that the *paysannes* are to disbelieve everything adverse about him. The Dom's own technique of evasion by paradox has again been surreptitiously turned against him; and he, like his victims in this scene, has no means of redress against someone who can convert the unpleasant truth into its opposite with such impeccable ease. We admire Sganarelle for his irreproachable *tour de force*, and at the same time share the ironic perspective into which Molière has placed Dom Juan's frustrated attempt at seduction.

The discussion in Act III, Sc. 1, between master and valet on medicine and on the existence of heaven, hell and retribution in after-life, has been integrated by Molière into the framework of the legend, and gives the play a philosophical character quite out of keeping with the two French versions. Once again it is the role of the valet which seems to me to provide the key to the significance of this controversial scene. Tradition has viewed the credulity and *naïveté* of the valet as nothing more than a butt for the cynical atheism of his master. Once again it was probably Rochemont who first gave currency to this notion when he described Sganarelle in this scene as 'un extravagant qui raisonne crotesquement [sic] de Dieu, et qui, par une chute affectée, *casse le nez à ses arguments*; un valet infâme, fait au badinage de son maître, dont toute la créance aboutit au Moine bourru . . .'[32]

It is not difficult to see how such a view of the valet's role leads to the conclusion that this scene represents another disquieting triumph for the Dom's scepticism over the well-intentioned but hopelessly inadequate Sganarelle. But such an interpretation tends to overlook the fact that Sganarelle is made to express these naïve views first and foremost for the purpose of comic dialogue; it is important to take into account the extent to which this exigency influences the mode of expression of his ideas, before accepting them literally as a solemn formulation of his own creed. Just as he has previously argued in this scene, in an (unsuccessful) attempt to stimulate a response from his master, that doctors are effective because they manage to kill suffering patients more rapidly than the disease (ll. 903–11), so he now moves away from medicine to the one subject which he feels can be guaranteed to unloose his master's opinion, religion. Here, therefore, as elsewhere throughout the play, he acts primarily as an ironic and burlesque spectator of his master, both eliciting his opinions and sitting in comic judgement on them. When he has catechized Dom Juan, and has made the not unexpected discovery that the *libertin* professes disbelief in heaven, hell and immortality, (in Act I, Sc. 2, ll. 114–15 he tells us that 'je sais mon Dom Juan sur le bout du doigt'), he reacts with simulated and pious concern: 'Voilà un homme que j'aurai bien de la peine à convertir. Et dites-moi un peu, le moine bourru, qu'en croyez-vous, eh?' (ll. 928–30).

Of course he does not intend to convert him, any more than he intends to believe in the 'moine bourru'. But since he has exhausted his store of questions on orthodox matters of faith, he resorts to such traditional superstitions to provoke the Dom's exasperated reaction. Eventually he is successful in prompting a sceptical retort from his master: 'Je crois que deux et deux font quatre, Sganarelle, et que quatre et quatre font huit' (ll. 938–9). This *boutade* has been seen as furnishing one of the articles of Molière's own beliefs;[33] but it is surely impossible either to attribute this to Molière, given the comic context in which it occurs, or to see it as the formalized credo of the *libertin*. Dom Juan is both curiously amused and vaguely irritated by Sganarelle's buffoonery, and he takes the line of least resistance to the importunate questioning which his cavalier riposte offers to him. But hoping to silence the valet by this lapidary remark, he merely provides him with the pretext he has desired so avidly for his discourse on the harmony of man's being, which he takes as proof of his divine origin (ll. 940–63, ll. 965–73). The fact that part of his bizarre argument is probably a burlesque version of Pierre Gassendi's treatise on man can scarcely be taken as an indication that Molière shares the philosopher's view about the nature of things.[34] Nevertheless the central part of Sganarelle's argument does seem to indicate the verdict of comedy on the *libertin's* beliefs: 'Il faut avouer qu'il se met d'étranges folies dans la tête des hommes, et que, pour avoir étudié, on est bien moins sage le plus souvent' (ll. 942–4).

This is no less than a summary of that *folle sagesse* which was, in *Tartuffe*, comedy's conclusion on Orgon's futile attempt to pronounce dogmatically on things which elude the grasp of man. Dom Juan's conduct is based upon such a belief which, although diametrically opposed to that of Orgon, is rooted in the same kind of dogmatism which consists in asserting that a non-empirical proposition is absolutely true or untrue. Rather than dismiss peremptorily the existence of the supernatural, it is better, say Sganarelle and the so-called *raisonneurs*, to be wise within the bounds permitted by our human condition. This will therefore exclude any pretence to absolute knowledge, and will most certainly include a degree of *folie*, which is nothing else than the modest confession of one's own ignorance about such transcendent matters.[35] Sganarelle well illustrates such wisdom, by arguing empirically about the relationship between cause and effect, and then choosing to fall grotesquely on his face just as he reaches the climax of his argument for the harmonious functioning and interaction of the human organs. The burlesque *raisonneur's* self-contradicting 'method' of argument offers an interesting parallel with Le Vayer's *Petit discours chrétien sur l'Immortalité de l'âme* (1637), where he begins by promising, as confidently as Sganarelle, to prove irrefutably the immortal nature of the soul by no less than thirty-three syllogisms of 'apodeictic' value. His conclusion is predictably analogous to that of Molière's scene, namely that 'La grande connaissance fait souvent le même effet que l'extrême ignorance, d'où vient qu'on a toujours remarqué que les plus savants étaient ceux qui avouaient le plus franchement la faiblesse de l'esprit humain . . .'[36]

If Molière and Le Vayer appear to condemn those *libertins* like Dom Juan who fail to recognize this truth of human nature, they also show the absurdity of presuming to demonstrate beyond doubt such an obscure matter as that of the immortality of the soul. Sganarelle's deliberate fall is symbolic not only of his knowledge of what can and cannot be achieved by human wisdom, but also of the futility of trying to prove the improvable. And Le Vayer likewise condemns those Christian apologists (like Silhon, Cotin, Yves de Paris) who maintain the ability of natural reason to prove a belief such as that of the immortality of the soul:[37] 'Au lieu qu'on s'est promis de forcer les plus incrédules à la reconnaissance d'une vérité si importante, par la seule puissance de notre raison, je crois qu'il vaut mieux avouer ingénument sa faiblesse, et la captiver doucement sous l'obéissance de la Foi.'[38]

I do not believe that this scene, or indeed the play as a whole, allows us to say anything of a more specific nature than this about its treatment of religious beliefs. However, a belief such as that outlined above by Le Vayer is consonant with the ideas on religion expressed in *Tartuffe*, and would identify Molière's views in this scene neither solely with Sganarelle, nor with Dom Juan, although Sganarelle's views have more in common with *la docte ignorance* of scepticism than Dom Juan's presumption. This is confirmed by the fact that the valet, although apparently imbued with less intelligence than his free-thinking master, nevertheless glimpses the contradictory essence of man's nature, namely that it is compounded of reason and unreason at the same time. Seen in this light, is it not the *inhuman* Dom Juan who is comic in Molière's eyes in this scene, and not Sganarelle after all?

The following scene (Sc. 2), in which *Un Pauvre* plays a central role, is no less ambiguous than the previous one. Although the equivalent scene exists in Dorimond and Villiers (Dom Juan stops a *Pèlerin*, and forces him to forfeit his religious habit), there is a complete absence of the overtly tendentious features of Molière's scene, where Dom Juan commits sacrilege as he offers the hermit money on condition that he swears an oath. His Dom Juan is here no longer just the *libertin* whose independence of religion incites him to maltreat a religious. More obviously than hitherto in Molière's play, he assumes the role of evil incarnate, a Mephistopheles who issues an unequivocal challenge to the good man to recognize the supremacy of an ethic based on self-indulgence and expediency over self-abnegation and moral principle.[39] The hermit resists Dom Juan's temptation to swear in order to gain the proffered *louis d'or*, acceptance of which would imply dissatisfaction with the impoverished state that providence has allowed him. Does such a result represent the triumph of good over evil? G. Michaut at least thought so when he wrote that 'Le Pauvre reste invaincu, dédaigneux des railleries et des séductions . . .'[40] But the implications of the scene seem more complex than such a straightforward judgement would allow. The essence of the scene is contained in three questions, the first asked by the *Pauvre*, the others by Dom Juan. Having indicated to Sganarelle and his master the path to be taken through the forest the *Pauvre* asks:

> Si vous voulez me secourir, Monsieur, de quelque aumône?

Dom Juan   Ah! Ah! ton avis est intéressé, à ce que je vois.

Le Pauvre   Je suis un pauvre homme, Monsieur, retiré tout seul dans ce bois depuis plus de dix ans, et je ne manquerai pas de prier le Ciel qu'il vous donne toute sorte de biens.

Dom Juan   Eh! prie le Ciel qu'il te donne un habit, sans te mettre en peine des affaires des autres. (ll. 991–8)

Molière here crystallizes dramatically the general problem of the play, and also returns in a more forceful and insistent manner to one of the principal preoccupations of *Tartuffe*; to all appearances innocence, goodness and devoutness suffer on earth, whereas the *libertin* Dom Juan prospers with impunity. It is the questions of the *libertin* to the hermit which are used by Molière to bring this situation into even sharper focus:

Dom Juan   Quelle est ton occupation parmi ces arbres?
Le Pauvre   De prier le Ciel tout le jour pour la prospérité des gens de bien qui me donnent quelque chose.
Dom Juan   Il ne se peut donc pas que tu ne sois bien à ton aise?
Le Pauvre   Hélas! Monsieur, je suis dans la plus grande nécessité du monde.
Dom Juan   Tu te moques; un homme qui prie le Ciel tout le jour ne peut pas manquer d'être bien dans ses affaires.
Le Pauvre   Je vous assure, Monsieur, que le plus souvent je n'ai pas un morceau de pain à mettre sous les dents.
Dom Juan   Voilà qui est étrange, et tu es bien mal reconnu de tes soins . . . (ll. 1002–13)

I do not think that Molière's answer to the problem raised in this scene is to be found either in the faithful endurance of the *Pauvre* or the truculent incredulity of Dom Juan, but rather in the philosophical vision which imagines and dramatizes such an encounter. In their opposition, the two characters symbolize the kind of question and answer about providence that has always taken place in the minds of those people who have found it difficult, as the author of *Tartuffe* and *Dom Juan* apparently found it difficult, to accept the proposition that 'Just are the ways of God; and justifiable to Men.' Molière is raising such a question, and leaving it without a categorical answer, for such an answer appears to be unobtainable. This tentativeness on his part does not mean that we cannot discern the general tendency of his thought in the dramatic movement of the scene. It is clear that as the dramatist and spectator see this scene, the *Pauvre* is utterly defeated by the Dom's probing scepticism which points out the manifest discrepancy between his fervent praying and his abject state — he is defeated, that is to say, *objectively* and as far as human logic is concerned. He can only 'justify' this discrepancy between his faith and his penury by trusting blindly in the kind of subjective conviction which Milton's lines express so well:

All is best, though oft we doubt,
What th'unsearchable dispose
Of highest wisdom brings about. (*Samson Agonistes*, ll. 1745–7)

To what extent does Molière use Dom Juan to illustrate the problem behind the creation of the scene? There are sufficient indications throughout the play to show that his *libertin* posture is treated in a comic or an ironic way for us to know that Molière does not entirely approve of his ideas; certainly there is not the slightest sign that Molière approves in any way of his actions towards the *Pauvre*. But Molière has *permitted* Dom Juan to go with impunity to the furthest limits of provocative impiety and odious conduct towards the *Pauvre*, not presumably because he approves of his attitude, but because he wishes to place the more urgently before us the ineluctable fact that all too frequently those who live without due regard for sanctity or piety or humanity do indeed flourish, whereas those whose lives are spent in devotion and selflessness, although infinitely more admirable than the Dom Juans and Tartuffes of this world, are inexplicably exposed to suffer their ridicule.

The sceptical implications of this scene are close to one of Le Vayer's problems which he asks and 'answers' in his *Problèmes Sceptiques* (1666). To his question 'Y a-t-il des Prières désagréables à Dieu?' his first answer is 'Non', but he qualifies this by saying that one must always be careful not to attribute too much to prayerful intercessions. In his second answer, 'Oui', he quotes with irony the opinion of those who allege that it is ridiculous to pray to someone who knows what we desire even before we ask.[41] Dom Juan is used by Molière in a similar questioning way, as he, like Le Vayer, implies the objections in the path of a simple belief in the Christian theodicy of the *Pauvre*, whose faith and prayers are left unanswered by heaven. The scene ends with the same ironic implication that is found in a passage of Le Vayer's *De l'Ingratitude* where he points out that the sun shines on the wicked just as on the good: 'Tant s'en faut, que la main du Tout-puissant se raccourcisse sur le sacrilège et sur l'impie, que souvent il leur multiplie ses grâces, afin de donner mieux à connaître l'excellence de sa nature et l'immensité de sa bonté.'[42]

The attempt by Dom Juan to sow the seeds of doubt in the minds of others concerning what they hold as true or false, to provoke hesitation on their part with regard to moral issues, is illustrated still more explicitly in the following scene. There he goes to the rescue of Dom Carlos who has been attacked by thieves. Critics have found difficulty in reconciling the cynical and amoral Dom Juan of the previous scene with the 'aristocratic' hero who spontaneously hazards his life for an unknown person.[43] Once again, the entire conception of this episode is original to Molière's play: the brother of Dom Carlos recognizes the Dom as the seducer of their sister Elvire, and demands immediate vengeance to satisfy their honour (Sc. 4); Dom Carlos, who before this revelation of Dom Juan's identity had shown himself by his remarks equally as zealous as his brother Dom Alonse in his pursuit of the *libertin*, is now caught in a moral dilemma. He is torn between his 'reconnaissance de l'obligation' (ll. 1135–6) which he owes to the man who has just saved his life, and his legitimate 'ressentiment de l'injure' (ll. 1136–7). His eventual solution to the dilemma is of a temporizing nature; he puts off the opportunity to satisfy his family's honour, and is forced into the paradoxical position of having to defend his erstwhile enemy against his pragmatic brother Dom Alonse.

Once again the moral confusion into which Dom Juan throws others is used by Molière to illustrate dramatically one of the basic tenets of scepticism, which is that ethical codes can merely have a relative and not absolute value, because of the situational contingency to which they are exposed. Before Dom Alonse recognized Dom Juan, his brother was as absolute as he in his determination to apply the rigid aristocratic code to the case of Dom Juan: he could not have envisaged any possible circumstance which would change his mind (ll. 1066 ff.). The debate which ensues between the brothers is the conflict between the absolute nature of Alonse's conception of the aristocratic code — (circumstances such as one's enemy saving one's life do not change the eternal obligation of avenging one's honour; as honour is infinitely more precious than life, it follows that we owe nothing to an enemy who has saved a life which he has deprived of all honour) (ll. 1126 ff.) — and the willingness of Dom Carlos to take Dom Juan's bravery into account and modify the immediate demands of honour. In the same *opuscule* from which I have just quoted, Le Vayer illustrates the kind of morally ambiguous situations where it is impossible to apply a strict rule elaborated in advance. After having stated the traditional moral doctrine of the scholastics and Aristotle, which decrees the separate natures of *vice* and *vertu*, he advances cases where it is somewhat more difficult to distinguish between them. As 'une autre difficulté de Morale' he evokes the moral dilemma which underlies the scene in Molière's play, namely, 'si une injure postérieure peut tellement effacer le bien-fait précédent, que nous en demeurions quittes sans tomber dans l'Ingratitude.'[44] Like Dom Carlos, he is inclined to attribute a lower degree of moral value to an action based solely on expediency rather than on gratitude for the original service: '. . . vu que l'obligation est la plus ancienne, il y faut satisfaire, et puis on avisera au reste.'[45] This is in fact the compromise which Dom Carlos chooses: he will show his gratitude to the Dom by delaying his pursuit of vengeance, but will nonetheless carry out his duty ardently: he tells Dom Alonse that regarding his recent benefactor and ancient enemy '.. . . je lui ai une obligation dont il faut que je m'acquitte avant toute chose. (ll. 1167–8) . . . la reconnaissance de l'obligation n'efface point en moi le ressentiment de l'injure' (ll. 1135–7).

In Le Vayer's dialectic on moral paradoxes, as well as in Molière's dramatization of the practical difficulties to which they give rise, the kind of inflexible approach of a Dom Alonse is to be avoided in all situations (cf. ll. 1126–33) as he estimates whether the 'bienfait' is greater or not than the loss of honour occasioned by its author. Dom

Carlos, on the other hand, eschews such attempts to weigh and compare the respective moral values of actions and pleads above all for '. . . une valeur qui n'ait rien de farouche, et qui se porte aux choses par une pure délibération de notre raison, et non point par le mouvement d'une aveugle colère' (ll. 1163–6). So too does Le Vayer, in terms reminiscent of those used by Molière's character: 'C'est être ingrat et injuste tout ensemble, de vouloir user des compensations en des choses qui ne sont pas de même poids, et dont l'une doit toujours prévaloir sur l'autre, si nous ne donnons beaucoup plus à la passion qu'à ce que nous prescrit le droit usage de la raison.'[46]

Dom Carlos makes a 'right use of reason' in this scene which would certainly be acceptable to the Sceptic. Unlike his brother, he has not prejudged Dom Juan's moral character, and events confirm that no one, not even the *libertin*, is totally incapable of performing a good action. The juxtaposition of the Dom's heroism with his cynical temptation of the *Pauvre* is an extreme paradox which only serves to illustrate and confirm Le Vayer's conviction in his *opuscule De l'Ingratitude*, with which this scene has so much in common: '. . . le divorce du vice et de la vertu n'est pas si formel, que l'un et l'autre ne se puissent jamais rencontrer dans un même sujet.'[47]

In the scene with the *Pauvre* and in the encounter with Elvire's brothers, Dom Juan does not appear in a comic light; in those scenes he is exempt from comic irony within the universe of the play, as Molière uses him to demonstrate firstly the strong objections to a belief in a controlling providence operative in human affairs, and secondly, the indefinable nature of the *libertin*-hero which can elude facile attempts to situate it in a precise moral category. But in Scene 5 of this Act Dom Juan and Sganarelle only are on stage — an indication that the Dom's attitude will once more be put into an ironic perspective by his valet. As they find themselves in front of the tombstone of the *Commandeur* whom the Dom has killed, the statue lowers its head. The naïve valet is nevertheless sufficiently open-minded to admit that he *does* see the *Commandeur* move. It is only the stubborn preconception of the *libertin*, that he *will* not and therefore *cannot* permit the supernatural to have an objective existence, which makes him persist in denying the valet's observation. Above all, he is intent on keeping up the myth of his own superiority over the rest of humanity in Sganarelle's eyes. He is comic here because although he is convinced that he is superior to everybody, he cannot (because he will not) see what even the meanest creature can see plainly. He whose boast is that he lives by his senses will not accept the irrefutable evidence which they offer to him!

In the following scene (Act IV, Sc. 1), Sganarelle repeatedly stresses to Dom Juan the manifestation of the supernatural '. . . que nous avons vu des yeux que voilà' (ll. 1283–4). The comic aspect of Dom Juan refusing to assent to such a physical sign of the reality of the supernatural is now underlined in his reaction to Sganarelle's renewed warning about divine retribution. His threat to the valet is certainly the most violent and terse which he has yet uttered: 'Écoute. Si tu m'importunes davantage de tes sottes moralités, si tu me dis encore le moindre mot là-dessus, je vais appeler quelqu'un, demander un nerf de boeuf, te faire tenir par trois ou quatre, et te rouer de mille coups. M'entends-tu bien?' (ll. 1288–92). Once more the self-assured free-thinker can only have recourse to physical threats as he seeks to keep up his image in front of Sganarelle — and once more Sganarelle eludes adroitly his attempt to dominate him completely by a *réplique* which barely conceals its irony under its compliance: 'Fort bien, Monsieur, le mieux du monde. Vous vous expliquez clairement; c'est ce qu'il y a de bon en vous, que vous ne m'allez point chercher des tours; vous dites les choses avec une netteté admirable' (ll. 1293–6).

Dom Juan can only momentarily re-establish his former superiority in Scene 3, where he makes the most elementary use of polite appearances to conceal his impecunious state from M. Dimanche. Nevertheless his *tour de force* in making his *bourgeois* creditor wish to be his debtor for the obsequious way he has received him does elicit our admiration. But the juxtaposition of the confident Dom Juan in this scene, and the reflective and disconcerted *libertin* of Scene 1, underlines the brittle nature of his superiority, which now depends less on his ability to explain away the existence of the supernatural than on his mere cleverness in profiting from his aristocratic supremacy in order to dominate others.

Even this superior attribute is about to be removed from him in principle, if not in practice, as his father, Dom Louis, arrives to denounce and disown him (Sc. 4). This scene corresponds to the traditional scene in Dorimond and Villiers between Dom Alvaros and the hero in Act I. Nevertheless, there is a critical difference both in content and treatment of the confrontation of father and son in Molière's version. In the two other French plays, the scene is composed of the father's conventional moralizing and Dom Juan's filial recalcitrance, whereas in Molière's play this is reduced to an extended speech by the father on the nature of the difference between true and false nobility.

It is clear throughout the play that the Dom's actions are largely motivated by an overwhelming sense of personal superiority over others, which he believes is conferred on him by his aristocratic caste. The theme of this scene has been curiously prefigured in Act I, Sc.1: Gusman, Elvire's servant, retains the traditional idea about nobility when he says of Dom Juan's infidelity 'Un homme de sa qualité ferait une action si lâche?' Sganarelle's reply is worthy of note: 'Eh! oui, sa qualité! La raison en est belle, et c'est par là qu'il s'empêcherait des choses!' (ll. 37–9). The valet is here drawing attention to the paradoxical position of the *libertin,* which the latter exploits to the full: taking the social benefits belonging to nobility (prestige, esteem, etc.), his *libertinage* provokes him to contradict flagrantly the moral code which Dom Louis ascribes to it. In his lengthy speech on true and false nobility, Dom Louis stresses three basic points: it is not sufficient for a nobleman to lay claim to aristocratic origins if he has no *vertu* to accompany them (ll. 1448-55); we have a right to share in the *noblesse* of our ancestors only if we accept the obligation incumbent upon us to imitate their *vertu* (ll. 1455-62); judged by this criterion, Dom Juan falls lamentably short of the requisite behaviour and has no right whatever to call himself a nobleman (ll. 1462-73).

Once again Molière appears to draw on ideas similar to those of La Mothe Le Vayer for this scene and its underlying thought. In a letter entitled *Des Gentilshommes* (1660), the latter underlines Dom Louis' central preoccupation: any fault or merit is independent of one's social status and is one's personal responsibility: '...les belles actions de nos prédécesseurs ne servent guères à notre gloire si nous n'y coopérons...'[48] And Dom Louis dwells pointedly on the same truth when he asks his son '...qu'avez-vous fait dans le monde pour être gentilhomme?...nous n'avons part à la gloire de nos ancêtres qu'autant que nous nous efforçons de leur ressembler' (ll. 1451-2, ll. 1455-7). But often, continues Le Vayer, the noble actions of one's forefathers only throw into sharp relief the mediocrity of their successors:

...mais il n'arrive pas toujours, que ceux qui ont cette puissante recommendation du sang, possèdent le mérite personnel absolument requis pour se la conserver. Souvent au contraire l'on remarque qu'ils en sont tellement dépourvus, que les vertus de leurs ancêtres ne servent qu'à mieux faire reconnaître les défauts qu'ils ont, et combien ils sont dissemblables à ceux, dont ils se contentent de porter les armes et le nom...[49]

Similarly Dom Louis tells his son that the glory and honour of his ancestors only serve to illuminate the infamous nature of his actions (ll. 1465-7). Both Le Vayer and Dom Louis agree that the only sure foundation for true nobility is to be found in virtuous conduct on the part of those at present bearing an ancestral title.[50]

The common idea of *noblesse oblige* might seem to be a banal coincidence in thought between Molière and Le Vayer. That might well be the case, were not the same sceptical conclusion from this idea common to both, making mere coincidence highly improbable. In his *opuscule,* Le Vayer asks a question which relates pertinently to this scene in Molière's play: how does one explain the fact that a renowned hero may engender an infamous son? He answers by placing this problem in the wider context of natural development and also uses it to illustrate one of his perennial theses. Such a tendency towards irrational degeneration in the species is by no means uncommon in nature: 'Comme les meilleures viandes et les plus estimées, font les excréments qui ont le plus d'infection et de puanteur; les personnes les plus héroïques engendrent les plus vicieux et les plus méprisables de leur siècle.'[51] To the Sceptic, such an apparent aberration forms an intrinsic part of the unpredictable and irrational processes of nature, as well as a salutary corrective to man's presumption in trying to interfere with natural laws. Dom Louis has ardently attempted to mould nature into his own pattern: he has importuned heaven to give him an heroic son who would be the pride of his life, and he laments the result: 'Hélas! que nous savons peu ce que nous faisons quand nous ne laissons pas au Ciel le soin des choses qu'il nous donne, quand nous voulons être plus avisés que lui, et que nous venons à l'importuner par nos souhaits aveugles et nos demandes inconsidérées' (ll. 1433-7).

In so doing, he has inadvertently come close to that very *hubris* which impels Dom Juan to flout the laws of nature. J. Doolittle has commented on this point in a penetrating manner: 'He has presumed to tamper with the will of Heaven, to set himself, by means of the formal activity of prayer, above his human lot.'[52] It has been customary to regard Dom Louis as a serious character who expresses Molière's own opinion against Dom Juan's misconduct. It has always seemed natural to identify ourselves and therefore Molière against the filial ingratitude of Dom Juan — and thence it is but one step towards seeing the father as Molière's *porte-parole*. Yet it seems that Molière has insinuated an implicit level of irony into Dom Louis' speech which deprives him of the noble Cornelian status which has sometimes been assigned to him.[53] L. Gossman however has noted that although Dom Louis equates natural virtue with nobility — towards the end of his peroration he says that he would prefer the son of a porter whose conduct was *honnête* to the infamous son of a monarch — he does not nevertheless advance a moral code based on nature but rather 'a conventional social code designed to maintain the superiority of some members of society to other members of society.'[54] He lays down, in other words, standard signs by which a nobleman may be known and therefore estimated (imitation of the *gloire* of one's ancestors, etc.), all of which tend to elevate nobility by according to its members the special prerogative and obligation of being virtuous. One will always be able to distinguish a virtuous noble from a virtuous *roturier* by reason of the peculiar and ancestral *éclat* which underlines his excellence.

Molière, like his friend La Mothe Le Vayer, would seem to have been too independent a thinker not to grasp the intrinsic absurdity of such reasoning, which is certainly implicit in the attempt of Dom Louis to justify the separate social identity of the aristocratic class. Besides, his theatre is too full of satire against those who desire either to rise above their social station or to convince others of the intrinsic advantages of nobility for him not to assent to Le Vayer's opinion in *Des*

Gentilshommes that there is no such thing as the existence of nobility, because '...ne sommes-nous pas tous sortis d'un même principe? Y a-t-il vilain qui n'ait son extraction de quelque Patriarche? Ou Prince qui ne vienne d'un Planteur de Vigne?'[55] Dom Juan provides the *raison d'être* of this scene, as he provokes this speech on the nature of nobility from his father; he is therefore the agent used by Molière for the discreet exposure of archaic conventions to which even an essentially sympathetic character like Dom Louis clings, and thus remains true to his function in the play as a catalyst of truth and falsehood, appearances and reality.

From the end of Act IV onwards, the importance of the supernatural elements of the play is much more evident than hitherto: the first appearance of the Commander's statue at supper (Act IV, Sc. 8) follows closely on the warnings of imminent retribution given by Dom Louis and Elvire in Scenes 4 and 6. The reality of divine retribution becomes increasingly inevitable as the Dom appears more and more successful in inverting and perverting the basic human values of filial affection and fidelity; there is only one more step for him to take before he divests himself completely of every human attribute, and he crosses this when he feigns religious conversion to his father, in Act V, Sc.1. This paradox in his own behaviour is brought about not merely for sacriligious and libertine reasons, but rather because he knows that it corresponds to an objective inversion of moral values which has taken place in the world at large: '...l'hypocrisie est un vice privilégié, qui, de sa main, ferme la bouche à tout le monde, et jouit en repos d'une impunité souveraine' (ll. 1716-18). These lines crystallize the most extreme confusion of truth and falsehood within the character and the play; in fact they go beyond mere confusion and point to the more permanent paradox of the fusion of truth and error, symbolized by the deference shown to hypocrisy by those who are at the same time aware that it is grounded in falsehood. Formerly, whilst Dom Juan had been able to invest untruth with the appearance of truth, he had only been able to do it long enough to deceive Elvire, the *paysannes* and Sganarelle for a time: he could not do it permanently, because such a situation would automatically have meant the defeat of the forces of morality and good within the play, and the virtual end of the drama. But at this point of the play, no such conflict of good and evil is possible, according to the words of Dom Juan, because society at its worst is composed of hypocrites and scheming rogues, and at best, of those who acquiesce tacitly in the deceptions practised by the numerous Dom Juans in their midst, as well as of those who, like Dom Louis and Elvire and her brothers, penetrate the mask of deception but cannot ensure that its wearer is brought to justice. It is as though Dom Juan's specious inversion of values had been suddenly extended to embrace everyone, and all the moral values of society, neutralizing the forces of good. La Rochefoucauld might have summed up such a situation by saying that 'le monde n'est composé que de mines'[56]. But although everyone has suffered a morally adverse effect from their encounter with Dom Juan, forcing them to contradict in some degree the moral codes by which they profess to live, such a conclusion would be in direct contradiction with the dramatic situation of the play. Dom Juan has not, at this point, triumphed; he has just been denounced by Dom Louis, by Elvire, and is still being pursued by Dom Carlos and Dom Alonse. If human retributive justice fails, there is still the certainty of a dramatic conflict between the divine representative of goodness and truth, the statue, and Dom Juan, the hypocrite. The suspension of the human drama, so strongly implied in Dom Juan's words and actions here, in turn implies that his creator was himself brought to the point where he saw no real opposition to his *libertin.*

Molière has thus permitted Dom Juan to push his deception to its farthest limit (religious hypocrisy), and the *libertin,* like his predecessor Tartuffe, knows the impunity such hypocrisy affords him from human retribution. He illustrates this as he takes refuge in casuistry in front of Dom Carlos (Scene 3). The paradox of Dom Juan the unassailable *libertin-dévot* must therefore call forth a *dénouement* responsible for a still greater paradox — namely, that of the defeat of the *libertin,* who cannot be defeated from within the universe of the play. The supernatural *dénouement* implies the recognition by Molière of the Dom's invincibility (or rather the invincibility of his subterfuge), and is thus necessarily and logically motivated by the evolution of Dom Juan's character. This is confirmed by a comparison between Molière's *dénouement* and those of Dorimond and Villiers; whereas in these versions the *dénouement* retains its traditional character of a spectacular set piece which the audience has come to expect as of right, and which is superimposed without due regard for the evolution of the hero (so much so that one has the impression that the plays have largely been conceived as a corollary to the *dénouement*), Molière reverses this conception and the *dénouement* becomes both the only possible ending to the play and, in the vision of the playwright, at least the symbol of the re-affirmation of justice over falsehood if not of his actual belief in such a possibility.[57]

The fact that in Molière's play the evolution of the hero and the conception of the *dénouement* are essentially independent of the legend (although the general structure is loosely retained), means that Molière's condemnation of his *libertin* is based upon something other than a desire to emulate the traditional ending. That he does finally condemn and disapprove of the Dom's impenitent attitude has never been seriously doubted, except by critics so blinded by prejudice as the Sieur de Rochemont. It is equally clear that Molière does not condemn him for the sake of expediency, in an attempt to dispel some of the doubt that might have subsisted as to his religious orthodoxy after *Tartuffe*; had this been his central aim, he could surely have succeeded in doing it in such an unequivocal way that would have been understood by *dévots* and *honnêtes gens* alike. Henri Gouhier seems to have suggested an answer to this question when he writes that 'La déshumanisation du personnage s'accroît...à mesure que l'on approche du souper.'[58] Molière takes care to alienate the *libertin* progressively from the ties and responsibilities which bind him to his fellow-men: he has nothing but scorn for those in distress, like the *Pauvre:* he does not pay his debts to his social inferiors; he seduces and marries as he pleases; he abandons Elvire whom he has abducted from a convent; he rejects the natural bonds of filial affection; he puts religion to his own perverse ends. If he sets himself above the values by which his fellow human beings live, he seeks in his Promethean independence to reject their God in order to take his place himself. His refusal to admit God's existence (thereby admitting the existence of someone greater than himself) is a transposition onto the plane of myth of his refusal to consider his fellows as anything other than instruments to do his pleasure. By intensifying the moral flaw of the *libertin* in such a way, Molière has made his final attitude towards Dom Juan perfectly clear. To quote once more from Gouhier's excellent article: 'Le Commandeur a donc attendu que Don Juan soit Tartuffe pour le foudroyer: le Ciel punit ceux qui se moquent de lui. Mais Don Juan se moque du Ciel pour se moquer des hommes...Or la déshumanisation de Don Juan pose justement la question d'une religion de Molière fondée sur l'accord de la nature et du christianisme...'[59]

Gouhier's conclusion to his article is that in punishing Dom Juan, Molière was probably in agreement with Christian humanism, rather than with secular humanism divorced from Christianity. But whilst it is true that the Christian humanist's code of behaviour will certainly include man's humanity to man, he also shares this belief with the free-thinking humanist, in spite of the spiritual inspiration of the former's belief, and the purely human origin of the latter's. The Sceptic Le Vayer belongs completely in spirit, if not in profession, to the second of these groups, and it is interesting, in view of the deep similarities between his thought and that of Molière's play, to note the importance which he attaches to man's avoidance of ingratitude to his fellows. In *De l'Ingratitude*, which was quoted above, he writes that '...l'homme est un animal merveilleusement enclin à l'ingratitude, puisque les mêmes choses qui l'obligent le plus à la reconnaissance, opèrent si diversement sur son esprit, et font des effets si contraires.' This is all the more surprising, says the Sceptic, since gratitude is the one quality so deeply ingrained in humanity that all the diverse systems of ethics have agreed that it is fundamental to the preservation of the human race and of society. He evokes the examples of people like Dom Juan who fly defiantly in the face of this categorical imperative of humanity 'comme si tout le genre humain leur devait quelque hommage, et qu'ils ne fussent obligés à rien.' Such behaviour is condemned by all natural laws, and is, to the *libertin* Le Vayer, certainly the greatest sin against humanity and religion. In *Dom Juan* Molière illustrates that ingratitude to humanity which is the cardinal sin to the *libertin érudit*, by making it so heinous that only a supernatural intervention can provide an adequate retribution. Le Vayer adopts precisely the same mythical form of condemnation for it as Molière has done in his play: 'Mais lorsqu'on afflige sciemment ses Bien-faiteurs, qu'on ruine comme le lierre ce qui a servi d'appui, et qu'on fait périr ceux à qui l'on est redevable de sa conservation, c'est à l'heure qu'on encourt la malédiction divine . . .'[60] No condemnation is too extreme for those like Dom Juan who, by their wilful refusal to carry out their most basic obligations to their fellows, weaken the fabric of human society and fly in the face of all human and divine imperatives to duty. Molière thus fuses harmoniously humanist standards which ought to govern man's actions with the requirement of a supernatural *dénouement* demanded by the legend, and so accords it both a highly literal and a mythical significance.

In conclusion, it would seem that *Dom Juan* is a much less impious play than it has frequently been considered to be. Written during the fierce polemics surrounding *Tartuffe,* it has owed its impious reputation as much to the controversial circumstances of that play as to the sceptical aura of the legendary figure of Don Juan. Yet the view of W.G. Moore, on the other hand, to the effect that there is nothing in the conclusion of the play to show that Molière did not agree with Pascal in his condemnation of the *libertin* is arguable if in my view an overstatement.[61] Molière's last word on his subject would appear to be at once more ambiguous and nuanced than either of these views.

Nuanced and ambiguous, because the real hero of the play is Sganarelle and not, after all, Dom Juan, in spite of contrary appearances. It may well be said, as seventeenth-century critics did in fact say, that the opinions of the valet are equally if not more subversive from a religious point of view than those of his master — but this does not take into account the comic principle which underlies and shapes the attitude of the protagonists. All the burlesque and extravagant postures of Sganarelle are only of importance to the extent that they elicit or provoke some kind of response from Dom Juan. Their *raison d'être* is, therefore, dramatic before it is moral. Sganarelle provides Molière with a means of acquiring distance from the *libertin,* in a way that would make identification with what the latter says and does totally impossible. How could the author of the defiant postures which

Dom Juan strikes accept them seriously, and without reservation, when they are inevitably satirized almost simultaneously by the unassailable irony of Sganarelle? Even though Molière may conceivably have assented mentally to some of Dom Juan's opinions, how could he ever divorce them from the caustic corrective supplied instantaneously by the comic vision? The converse is also true — if he is detached sufficiently from his *libertin* to view him in Sganarelle's ironic perspective, he is also sufficiently detached from the valet to see him as a character playing a part in a comedy assigned to him by his creator. And as the creator of the play, he sees the individual comedies which they play consciously or unconsciously, as well as the comedy of their mutual relationship. In his creative detachment he perceives the manifest inability of the Dom to disprove or to refute definitively the existence of the supernatural: his every reaction to its intimations betokens a man who would like to dogmatize about it, and who does indeed in a certain limited way, but who lacks that ultimate rational proof to secure his assumption and his existence as a *libertin*. Sganarelle also seeks to ground his existence rationally, attempting to prove the immortality of the soul and the existence of God. The *folie* of the first issues in inhumanity, and he comes to grief. The *folie* of the second issues in extreme humanity in all its ignorance of metaphysical matters, and survives. He does survive because the comic vision springs from the refusal to accept one's strictly finite and creaturely nature, and emphasizes man's need to disabuse himself about the limitations of humanity.

'Il nous faut abestir pour nous assagir' writes Montaigne in his *Apologie;* the survival of the fool and the destruction of the wise man is not only a theatrically spectacular endorsement of his maxim, but also an extremely searching comment upon the significance and resilience of the comic vision.[62]

5　Le Misanthrope

A. Adam has rightly written that if *Le Misanthrope* is to be classed without doubt among Molière's masterpieces, it is nonetheless 'l'une de ses créations les plus mystérieuses, la plus mystérieuse sans doute'.[1] Its mysteriousness is reflected in the variety of interpretations to which it has given rise in the last fifty years; it has been regarded as the apex of the philosophy of the *juste-milieu* which Molière preached continuously throughout his plays;[2] as a means of coming to terms with his private misfortunes and his own temperamental incompatibilities;[3] as 'un des chefs-d'oeuvre de la littérature personnelle';[4] as being a reflection of his own emotions, yet not strictly autobiographical;[5] as essentially a satire of contemporary social customs and fashions;[6] as a critique of aristocratic and courtly values;[7] and, in recent criticism, as a play to be studied according to its own internal principles, without recourse to external information.[8]

The source of much of the play's traditional difficulty — both for those critics who believe in a literary approach to the play and for those whose approach is that of the new criticism — lies chiefly in Molière's attitude to his principal protagonist. All, or nearly all, the problems confronting any interpretation of the play are subordinate to, and clarified by, one fundamental question: namely, whether Molière intended Alceste to be either tragic, or comic, or both alternately.[9] The most important contemporary document on the play, Donneau de Visé's *Lettre écrite sur la Comédie du Misanthrope,* which appeared with the first edition of the play in 1667, is fairly ambiguous in this respect: 'le héros en est le plaisant sans être trop ridicule.'[10] If modern critics have rejected as equally extreme Rousseau's view that the play represented 'le ridicule de la vertu' and the Romantic notion of Alceste as sombre and sad, they have nonetheless continued to emphasize the serious aspect of his character.[11] R. Kemp, writing in *Le Monde* in 1958, probably expresses the most characteristic attitude of the twentieth century towards Alceste: 'Alceste a pu être comique, mais le monde s'est beaucoup attristé depuis deux siècles trois quarts.'[12]

Besides the difference in outlook to which R. Kemp alludes, such an attitude towards Alceste stems chiefly from the traditional and therefore hallowed view of *Le Misanthrope* as the play in which Molière reveals most directly his more sombre view of life. It is true that the autobiographical approach to the play has a veritable plethora of information here. The play was written at a time when Molière was beset by troubles on every hand; during the period 1664-6 he was engaged in a lawsuit, his son died in 1664, his health began to deteriorate, and Armande's infidelity probably dates from these years.[13] In particular, three texts, one of which is contemporary, and one written some sixteen years after the composition of the play, can be quoted to support the autobiographical position. The first is Le Boulanger de Chalussay's satire of Molière, *Elomire Hypocondre* (1670), where the author writes in his *Préface*: 'il y a long-temps qu'il (Molière) a dit en particulier et en public, qu'il s'alloit jouer luy-mesme...'[14] The second reference occurs in the 1682 edition of Molière's works, edited by La Grange and Vivot: the *Préface* says that Molière '. . . a joué tout le monde, puisqu'il s'y est joué le premier en plusieurs endroits sur des affaires de sa famille et qui regardoient ce qui se passoit dans son domestique.'[15] The third text, that of Grimarest writing in 1705, relates the origin of *Le Misanthrope* to the quarrel of *Tartuffe:* 'Les Hypocrites avaient été tellement irrités par *Le Tartuffe*, que l'on fit courir dans Paris un livre terrible, que l'on mettait sur le compte de Molière pour le perdre. C'est à cette occasion qu'il mit dans *Le Misanthrope* les vers suivants' (he then quotes lines 1500-7 of the play, where Alceste makes mention of 'un livre abominable', which has been maliciously attributed to him.)[16]

But in spite of the apparently cogent reasons for adopting an autobiographical approach to the play, I believe that such a method can only succeed in falsifying our view because it is not the correct criterion to apply to drama. Using it, one risks interpreting as tragic something which in a given dramatic context may be inexpressibly comic, but which may seem deeply moving or tragic when seen from the viewpoint of autobiography. This is not to suggest that biographical details are without value regarding an interpretation of the play. On the contrary, providing they are subordinated to the play's dramatic principle, they may well serve to confirm the interpretation which it suggests of the author's vision of life. In any work of literature, where the biographical and aesthetic criteria overlap so closely, the author is at once intensely absorbed by his personal preoccupations and at the same time sufficiently detached from them to write about them. But this creative paradox is most clearly underlined by the nature of drama itself. Louis Jouvet has expressed this in the following terms: 'Une pièce, une pièce véritable, n'est rien d'autre d'abord qu'une nécessité interne pour celui qui l'écrit, une impérieuse délivrance pour celui qui est soudain hanté par une idée ou un sentiment dramatique'.[17]

As the author of the play, Molière experiences both the inner necessity and the deliverance from this necessity, to use Jouvet's terms, in the contradictory characters of the irascible Alceste and the phlegmatic Philinte. As their creator, he shares their opinions not only on an intellectual level, but also on an emotional level. There is an abundance of evidence to show that Molière was a melancholy, hypochondriacal and jealous man — the extraordinarily well-informed De Chalussay makes Elomire refer to his 'trop jalouse humeur', and Grimarest points to the preponderantly serious side of his nature.[18] But it is an equally objective fact that as a comic playwright he had sufficient detachment from himself and life to deliver himself from the morbid introspection to which he was prone. He is at once Alceste, who feels the need to speak against the injustice and the abuses of society, *and* Philinte, who sees his friend with the detachment of the audience.[19] The dramatization of these conflicting natural tendencies must not be confused with the literal expression of such tendencies in real life; indeed, it is necessary to know nothing at all about them to appreciate the play. But the fact that the author shares the personal characteristics of Alceste and Philinte to such an extent gives the play the profoundly human resonance which accounts for its position as a universally recognized masterpiece.

In the fullest sense, therefore, it is his own views which each of his comic protagonists embodies, by virtue of the fact that he, as their creator, endows them with his own life and thought in poetic expression. Of *L'Ecole des Maris*, a play which can justly be termed a microcosm of *Le Misanthrope*, R. Fernandez writes:

> On sent, entre Molière et Sganarelle, des affinités réelles, quoique déguisées...il vivra de la vie de Molière, de ses muscles, de son sang, de son élan...[Molière] s'abandonnera à l'exquise et funeste paresse d'être absolument tout ce qu'il veut être, tout en sachant qu'il n'est rien de ce qu'il veut être. Sans doute Molière n'est pas Sganarelle, mais dans le sang de Sganarelle passe beaucoup du sang de Molière. Il me semble que qui ne comprend cet abandon de soi sous le couvert d'une sagesse concertée ne comprend pas tout Molière, ni tout le sens ni toute la force de son comique . . . [la pièce] représentait surtout pour lui une expression de soi dans une vision absolue où ses tendances incompatibles se composaient dans l'harmonie comique.[20]

Such poetic truth however is not, as W.G. Moore and R. Bray have so rightly stressed, the truth of everyday life and conduct, and because of this dichotomy, the question of which ideas the author of *Le Misanthrope* accepted in reality seems to me to have no essential value, no definitive answer being possible. It is not therefore my concern here to try, as R. Jasinski has done, to codify his presumed teaching in *Le Misanthrope*. Rather I wish to show how the dramatic principle underlying the play and the contradictory characters of Alceste and Philinte (whose ideas are simultaneously shared and not shared by their creator) finally identifies itself with the sceptical principle on which Le Vayer's philosophy is based. Consequently, the main contention of this chapter will be that *Le Misanthrope* is neither a tragedy nor a sombre drama, but the most profoundly and constantly comic of all Molière's plays because of the sceptical vision which conceives and sustains it. In the play in which Fernandez saw the virtual disappearance of the comic principle, I see its triumphant re-emergence as the principle behind the philosophy of Molière's comedy — scepticism.[21]

(2)

R. Jasinski has shown the importance of Le Vayer's *Prose Chagrine* (1661) as a literary source of *Le Misanthrope*;[22] but the weakness in his attribution of Le Vayer's philosophy to Molière seems to me to lie precisely in this literary approach, which tends to overlook the fundamental fact that *Le Misanthrope* is first and foremost a drama, even before it becomes literature. The importance of the play does not therefore lie in textual similarities which it may offer with the philosopher's works (Molière could very well have used Le Vayer's sceptical treatises purely as sources for his comic situations and ideas, without in any way sharing the same sceptical vision as his friend), but rather in the sceptical inspiration which animates the dramatic dialogue between Alceste and Philinte. The views which Molière shares alternately and simultaneously with his characters, because of the 'double vision' which he possesses as the dramatist, are also an integral part of Le Vayer's scepticism. The first of these views which forms part of this 'double vision' of the playwright is that of Alceste, and it issues in a stern condemnation of contemporary society:

> J'entre en une humeur noire, en un chagrin profond,
> Quand je vois vivre entre eux les hommes comme ils font;
> Je ne trouve partout que lâche flatterie,
> Qu'injustice, intérêt, trahison, fourberie;
> Je n'y puis plus tenir, j'enrage, et mon dessein
> Est de rompre en visière à tout le genre humain (Act I, Sc.1, ll. 91-6)

This 'misanthropic' theory of Alceste is confirmed by society's incomprehensible deference to someone who is commonly acknowledged as being morally devious in his ways:

> Nommez-le fourbe, infâme et scélérat maudit,
> Tout le monde en convient, et nul n'y contredit.
> Cependant sa grimace est partout bienvenue:
> On l'accueille, on lui rit, partout il s'insinue;
> Et s'il est, par la brigue, un rang à disputer,
> Sur le plus honnête homme on le voit l'emporter. (ll. 135-40)

In *Prose Chagrine* Le Vayer begins with the same total indictment of humanity which characterizes Alceste here. It is scandalous, he proclaims, that men of the utmost probity and honour are deprived of the social recognition which is their due; all domains of administration, particularly those of Justice and Finances are thoroughly corrupt.[23] Such general condemnations of society form but one *part* of Le Vayer's scepticism, in the same way that they form just a *part* of Molière's dramatic vision. In *De la Vie Solitaire,* Le Vayer provides a restatement of such grievances, which correspond in detail to those mentioned in Alceste's tirades above:

> Mais quand je vins à examiner la vie des Courtisans, ou de ceux qui pensent composer ce qu'on nomme le grand monde, je ne pus m'empêcher de conclure, que c'est celle de toutes, qui était la plus capable de jetter un esprit clairvoyant et Philosophique dans une parfaite misanthropie, ou totale aversion du genre humain: parce qu'il n'y voit presque rien qui ne choque sa raison, et où souvent la folie, l'injustice, ou quelque violente cabale ne l'emporte sur l'intégrité, sur le bon sens, et sur la plus haute Vertu.[24]

It seems legitimate to assume that Molière is using Alceste in a similar satirical intention to that of Le Vayer; but the play is not merely conceived as a satire, as Donneau de Visé supposed in his letter on the play, for the satire of Alceste is used by Molière to point towards the same sceptical 'conclusion' on humanity as that of Le Vayer.[25] According to Alceste, iniquity and perversity have increased to the extent that the moral values of right and wrong have not merely been confused, but inverted: honour is no longer the prerogative of the virtuous man, but of his enemy, the man who wears the mask of virtue. He thus expresses dramatically the same moral paradox which is central to scepticism, namely that 'Le vice et la vertu ne sont presque plus reconnaissables, et les cas de conscience ont quelquefois tellement sophistiqué le bien et le mal, qu'il est très difficile de les discerner.'[26]

This permanent state of moral ambiguity which Alceste has just discovered in society represents the last phase of the evolution of Molière's thought from *Tartuffe* and *Dom Juan.* In both these plays, such a paradoxical conversion of falsehood into its opposite was undertaken by scheming hypocrites for their own ends. They nearly achieved such an inversion of moral values — Tartuffe within the localized *milieu* of a family, Dom Juan in the wider context of society. But such a situation was in each case averted by the intrusion of the *deus ex machina,* contravening the laws of the dramatic universe to secure a non-tragic *dénouement.* In spite of the apparently inexorable extension of falsehood, the norms of justice and order (represented by the family and the King) triumph and preserve themselves essentially from corruption. In *Dom Juan,* perversity still meets resistance from the forces of justice, but towards the end of the play (ll. 1716 ff) the author apparently suspends the moral conflict as though he were using Dom Juan here to proclaim that hypocrisy had become the moral rule of society. In *Le Misanthrope* however it is no longer a religious hypocrite who announces the normality of such a situation, but Alceste who claims to stand against such corruption.

This is not to say, as did Rousseau, that Alceste is the representative of absolute virtue and integrity in the play. Whether he does or does not remain true to his profession (a question which will be considered below) is not important in this connexion. But it is important to note that his theory that complete honesty ought to reign supreme among men is morally irreproachable, and is eventually rejected by the world in which he preaches it. He is, in the first instance, perfectly correct in his diagnosis of the ills of society; the basic premise of the play, which Philinte accepts as readily as Alceste, is that society is undermined by corruption and hypocrisy (ll. 145 ff.). The fact that this state of things is posited as the accepted norm of the play, against which Alceste rebels, will help to answer the problem of whether or not he is tragic in his rebellion against society, typifying the Alceste whom Macaulay saw as a 'Vertueux et noble esprit, qu'a douloureusement blessé le spectacle de la perfidie et de la malveillance...'[27]

The first view of Molière's 'double vision' of things in the play, that of Alceste aspiring to truth, justice, and sincerity, and stating to Philinte that he cannot find these values in society, could appear to be tragic if one were led to imagine that such virtues are practically desirable as well as attainable within the play. In such a perspective, failure on the part of the protagonist to reach what is judged to be the *summum bonum* within the universe of the play will appear tragic when measured in terms of the knowledge that such a worthwhile objective ought to, and could have been, attained. But such a perspective is not that in which *Le Misanthrope* was conceived: from the first Act, the play accepts the doubtless regrettable but nonetheless objective situation that corruption *abounds* and cannot be changed. In this perspective, and only within such a perspective, the position of Alceste is theoretically as comic as that of the *imaginaires* who undertake vainly to revolt against the established order of things. Consequently, Alceste's position as a comic character within the play is not essentially modified by the fact that he claims, unlike the other *imaginaires*, to fight for the cause of virtue and honesty:

> The spectacle of man seeking, in despite of all the odds, to fulfil an ideal, to live up to his own best intentions, may be a deeply moving and ennobling one; but there comes a point at which the pity that we feel for the embattled idealist gives way to amusement at one who steadfastly refuses to recognize the conditions of his all too human frailty. Tears turn to laughter as the tragic struggle ends in a rather grotesque effort to transcend the limits of mortality.[28]

Molière succeeds in placing Alceste in such a comic perspective, because although he shares Alceste's satirical views on men and society, he also shares simultaneously with Philinte the sceptical notion that no ultimate source of perfection or truth can be known to man, and that all those who, like Orgon and Dom Juan and Alceste, strive for absolute knowledge, power and justice, are profoundly comic in that they illustrate the greatest possible comic *disconvenance* — that of overstepping the limits of the human condition. Le Vayer experiences continually the powerful urge for a more perfect and a more sincere world that Molière shares with Alceste; yet like Philinte and the creator of Philinte, his scepticism detaches him sufficiently from such absolute aspirations to enable him to examine them with a degree of objectivity. Just as he is, in *Prose Chagrine,* aware of his dissatisfaction, which stems from the absolute nature of his condemnation of society, so too he is aware that much of this comes not so much from lofty moral principles, as he is at first tempted to believe, as from purely individual and therefore relative considerations, such as his own temperament and humour, which detract implicitly from his absolute indictment. Sometimes, he says, we take a perverse delight in seeing our obdurate temperament set us in total opposition to society:

> ...les dégoûts de la vie, dont je veux m'entretenir, ont leurs charmes aussi bien que les satisfactions qui leur sont opposées. La diversité des esprits, que donne le tempérament, fait que les uns trouvent leur joie dans ce qui cause l'affliction des autres; de sorte qu'il n'y a pas moins de différentes sortes d'ennuis et de plaisirs, qu'il y a de diverses sortes d'inclinations et de raisonnements.[29]

One's absolute demand for integrity and justice in society, even if highly laudable in theory, is nevertheless for the Sceptic both the proof and the product of an individual temperament which makes the person in question take a particular view of life, a view which is certainly not shared unanimously by others. Hence Le Vayer, from the first page of his *opuscule,* enjoys a double vision of himself which is closely related to that of Molière in *Le Misanthrope*; on the one hand, he indulges in the pleasure of a diatribe against the 'slings and arrows of outrageous fortune', whilst on the other never losing sight of the basic contradiction in this position, which scepticism leads him to perceive.[30] It is no mere coincidence that having placed at the heart of his play the sceptical notion that perfection is unobtainable by mortals, Molière should take pains to show us the comedy of Alceste in terms similar to those used by his friend Le Vayer. In the first scene, the connexion between Alceste's misanthropic outlook and his temperament is unmistakably emphasized by the comic hero himself as he says to Philinte

> Mes yeux sont trop blessés, et la cour et la ville
> Ne m'offrent rien qu'objets à m'échauffer *la bile;*
> J'entre en une *humeur noire,* en un *chagrin profond,*
> Quand je vois vivre entre eux les hommes comme ils font . . .
>
> (ll. 89-92)[31]

It is such *humeur noire* which occasions his intemperate outbursts against humanity, making him take a secret delectation in them. We need only remember some of his first words in the play to realize this; when Philinte tries to elicit from him the reason for his abrasive attitude, he retorts petulantly: 'Moi, je *veux* me fâcher, et ne *veux* point entendre' (1. 5).[32] He will not, he insists, visit his judges before the examination of his lawsuit, but will lose with sublime equanimity. If it is scarcely possible to believe that he is provoked to such an extremity by genuine moral indignation, there is no room for doubt in the spectator's mind about his motive in adopting such an attitude when he proclaims defiantly for all to hear: 'J'aurai le plaisir de perdre mon procès' (1. 196). And he reiterates the same challenge to the justice of the day in more bombastic terms several lines later:

Je voudrois, m'en coûtât-il grand'chose,
Pour la beauté du fait avoir perdu ma cause. (ll. 201-2)

But physiological disposition does not only account for the contradiction between Alceste's absolute theory and the contingent factors from which such lofty theorizing proceeds: it also determines the dramatic conflict in the first scene between Alceste and Philinte. The latter draws attention to the different type of humour which rules his own conduct:

Ce chagrin philosophe est un peu trop sauvage,
Je ris des noirs accès où je vous envisage,
Et crois voir en nous deux, sous mêmes soins nourris,
Ces deux frères que peint *l'Ecole des Maris*...(ll. 97-100)

Je prends tout doucement les hommes comme ils sont,
J'accoutume mon âme à souffrir ce qu'ils font;
Et je crois qu'à la cour, de même qu'à la ville,
Mon flegme est philosophe autant que votre bile. (ll. 163-6)

His *flegme* helps him to put the temperamental rodomontades of Alceste into the same perspective as that of Le Vayer and Molière, that is, of a comedy (see ll. 105-8, ll. 203-4). Both protagonists are predestined to act throughout the rest of the play in strict accordance with their temperament. But why should Philinte's *flegme* react in a totally different way to Alceste's *bile* when both are confronted with the same spectacle of duplicity and insincerity? (Cf. ll. 173-8). Le Vayer once again gives an invaluable commentary on this source of the dramatic conflict in the play when he writes in *Prose Chagrine* that

un estomac débauché ne sauroit faire son profit des meilleures viandes, qu'il corrompt au lieu de les tourner en bonne nourriture; l'esprit chagrin agit de même sur tous les événements de la vie, dont il augmente sa mauvaise humeur, ne se passant rien de si indifférent, ni même de favorable, qui ne multiplie ses ennuis...Tant il se trouve vrai que l'homme est la mesure de toutes choses, qui deviennent telles qu'il se les représente; et tant il est constant que nos biens et nos maux croissent ou multiplient selon notre constitution intérieure, et selon que nous voulons les considérer.[33]

There is no difference, he continues, in the letters which go to make up a comedy or a tragedy. Our attitude towards the human condition is conditioned not by external reality, but depends on whether our temperament inclines us towards sceptical detachment or impassioned involvement. It is such sceptical detachment from the serious Alceste which Philinte shares with Molière, which enables him to draw attention to the contradiction between the absolute theory which Alceste preaches, and the course of action to which he will eventually be reduced by the contingency of human nature and reality. In my discussion of the play, I wish to show the ways in which Molière exploits this contradiction in his hero to keep him constantly comic, in spite of the apparently serious aspect of his character.

The sub-title of the play, *l'Atrabilaire amoureux,* was included in the *privilège* taken for the play on 21 June 1666, and although Molière seems to have omitted this from the play's title for reasons of convenience, it nevertheless gives the clearest indication of one way in which he renders Alceste comic.[34] In answer to Philinte's ironic query, as to whether his condemnation of *le genre humain* should be taken to include everyone, Alceste issues his most trenchant denunciation of humanity's failings (ll. 118-44). But Philinte, who obviously fulfils the role of *provocateur* in the first scene, points out that if Alceste desires truthfulness among mortals, he has chosen to pay court to someone diametrically opposed to his own principles (ll. 205 ff). He who has just told Philinte that 'l'ami du genre humain n'est point du tout mon fait' (l. 64) will soon make the same reproach to his *coquette médisante*: '. . . tout l'univers est bien reçu de vous' (Act II, Sc. 1, l. 496). It is immediately evident that he is comic because he finds himself in such flagrant contradiction with the principles of conduct which he has just laid down for others; but he is still more comic when viewed within the sceptical framework of the play. Philinte draws attention to the fact that the most logical choice for him to make would have been either that of *la sincère Eliante* (l. 215) or that of *la prude Arsinoé* (l. 216). In Eliante he would have chosen someone with his own concern for truthfulness, who will say later of him that

...la sincérité dont son âme se pique
A quelque chose, en soi, de noble et d'héroïque.
C'est une vertu rare au siècle d'aujourd'hui,
Et je la voudrois voir partout, comme chez lui.
(Act IV, Sc. 1, ll. 1165-8)

And when Célimène, pressed by her suitors for her true opinion of them, turns for help to Eliante, the latter ripostes in terms which Alceste would not disavow:

> N'allez point là-dessus me consulter ici;
> Peut-être y pourriez-vous être mal adressée,
> Et je suis pour les gens qui disent leur pensée.

> (Act V, Sc. 3, ll. 1660–2)

In the acerbic Arsinoé he has likewise someone who is not only admirably suited to his contradictory humour and puritanical attitude towards society, but who is also favourably disposed towards him. By choosing either Eliante or Arsinoé he would therefore be exempt from any contradiction between his avowed principles and his practice; in short, he would have remained true to the one principle by which he professes to live and by which he proclaims that others ought to live, namely reason. He has not followed such reason which he preaches as the one absolute guide to conduct, but has succumbed instead to his own individual inclination for the *coquette:* 'Je confesse mon foible, elle a l'art de me plaire' (l. 230). By contradicting his theory, he has fallen into a mode of behaviour at least as illogical as that which he has just criticized in Philinte, whom he castigated for bestowing profuse greetings on someone whom he scarcely knew (ll. 17-28). Some commentators, notably Jasinski, have thought that Molière was condemning Alceste for being *unreasonable* in his choice of Célimène: 'Alceste a tort d'aimer une coquette...elle (Célimène) ne lui convient pas. Elle n'est pas la femme qu'il lui faut. Peut-être siérait-il de chercher en amour un certain rapport d'humeurs.'[35]

But such a banal lesson of *bon sens* is certainly out of harmony with the basic *leitmotif* of the play, which is precisely that of the vindication of individuality and diversity at the expense of theory and reason. In affirming the irrational nature of man and of life in the misanthrope's choice of a *coquette,* Molière underlines that diversity in human actions which constantly belies reason and good sense, and which Le Vayer sees most fully exemplified in the friendships men contract; in one of his *Homilies Académiques,* he writes that

> ...nous prenons plaisir souvent à rechercher la correspondance de certaines personnes d'inclinations assez contraires aux nôtres,...en quoi on peut soutenir, que nous ne faisons qu'imiter la Nature, puisqu'en effet la contrariété des Eléments n'empêche pas, qu'ils ne s'unissent pour composer ce beau Tout de l'Univers. La Terre comme sèche n'aime rien tant que l'humidité de L'Eau, cette diversité, au lieu d'y mettre la discorde, les portant à une jonction très étroite...[36]

Just as Le Vayer remarks on the irrational basis for human friendships, so too Alceste perceives the incongruity of his friendship with Célimène (ll. 225 ff.); but unlike Le Vayer and Molière, he does not see that such incongruity is nonetheless in perfect accord with the contradictory and relative nature of men, which results from the inability of reason to exercise infallible control over human judgement.[37] On the contrary, he still hopes fervently to change Célimène into someone who will be exempt from 'ces vices du temps' (l. 234) against which he vituperates. By so doing, he will eventually harmonize his choice of a beloved with his claim to see life through the eyes of reason. Molière thus makes him supremely comic at this point for two closely related reasons; firstly, he is not at all blind to his own contradiction between his love for Célimène and his profession of absolute sincerity, but is confident that he will be able to resolve it satisfactorily (that is, by marrying a reformed Célimène and so obtaining both her hand and her conversion from coquetry); and secondly, Molière makes the point as clearly as Le Vayer, that in order to resolve this contradiction, Alceste will have to do away with that irreducible diversity of humour, temperament, and personality which go to form human beings. In his attempt to transform Célimène into his image of what she should be, he is engaging in the same unequal 'gigantomachy' which has defeated previous *imaginaires* such as Arnolphe *(L'Ecole des Femmes)* and Sganarelle *(L'Ecole des Maris).* To be successful, he would have to change Célimène's coquettish nature; but if he changed her nature, she would no longer have any power of attraction for him, for it is precisely to Célimène the *coquette médisante* that he is attracted, in preference to Arsinoé and Eliante.

In *De l'Amitié,* Le Vayer foreshadows the eventual outcome of Alceste's unequal struggle against nature and life, when he writes that as a young man he sought avidly the ideal quality of friendship which the moralists of antiquity extolled as the highest good. In such friendship one would be perfectly truthful and devoid of egoism at all times. But experience of life leads him to adopt the more realistic view of Philinte: '...si nous voulons quitter les idées pour suivre la réalité des choses, et considérer l'Amitié selon la portée de notre humanité, plutôt que par abstraction...nous trouverons qu'il n'y en a point qui n'ait ses intérêts, et qui sous ce beau prétexte de l'honnêteté, ne s'entretienne principalement par les considérations de l'utilité ou du plaisir.'[38]

It is precisely because Alceste provides the clearest example of the truth of Le Vayer's remark that he is so comic in the first scene of the play. He stigmatizes the conventional protestations of friendship which are obviously founded on self-interest. True friendship, he says, must be honest and disinterested:

Je veux qu'on soit sincère, et qu'en homme d'honneur,
On ne lâche aucun mot qui ne parte du coeur. (ll. 35-6)

When Philinte asks him discreetly if Célimène has given him good reason to believe that she loves him, his reply is somewhat less disinterested:

. . . Oui, parbleu!
Je ne l'aimerois pas, si je ne croyois l'être. (ll. 236-7)

The comic discrepancies in the first scene between Alceste's profession and his actions originate from his ability to see all too clearly the faults of others and from his total inability to see his own. In his treatise on friendship from which I have quoted above, Le Vayer foreshadows the way in which Molière will put his hero into sceptical perspective, when he describes such cecity as that from which Alceste suffers:

A peine sommes-nous capables de répondre de notre propre fait; et souvent nous ne savons pas bien si nous-mêmes nous aimons de la bonne sorte, à cause de la difficulté naturelle de rentrer en soi, et de se connaître suffisamment . . . Que sera-ce si nous sortons au dehors? N'est-ce pas une grande vanité, et une extrême témérité ensemble, de se croire plus clairvoyant chez autrui, que l'on n'est chez soi?[39]

Aspiring towards the absolute and universal, Alceste will merely confirm by his failure the relative nature of man and life. In such a sceptical framework, the principal comic paradox of Alceste stands out clearly; it is from this basic paradox that all his manifold incongruities and foibles derive.

(3)

The scene which follows provides Alceste with the opportunity to exemplify his profession of absolute honesty not only in front of Philinte, but also in front of Oronte, the very epitome of the *honnêteté* which he has professed to despise. Oronte couches his esteem for Alceste in exclusive terms:

...j'ai conçu pour vous une estime incroyable,
...depuis longtemps, cette estime m'a mis
Dans un ardent désir d'être de vos amis.
Oui, mon coeur au mérite aime à rendre justice,
Et je brûle qu'un noeud d'amitié nous unisse. (ll. 254-8)

In the previous scene, Alceste had said that he wished to be singled out from the common herd and given special esteem (ll. 63-4). One of the principal reasons for his anger with Philinte in that scene was the latter's custom of lavishing praise on chance acquaintances, whilst claiming to be Alceste's friend (ll. 41-62). Now he is given what he so ardently desires and he refuses to listen to Oronte! In this scene Molière has placed his hero on the horns of a dilemma, and exploits consummately all the latent as well as the obvious comic aspects in Alceste's position. He receives from Oronte the excessive protestations of respect which he regards as his due, and, although he is certain that these compliments are basically insincere, he nevertheless hears what his megalomania demands that he should hear. He is therefore torn between what he knows to be his right, and his temperamental need to refuse all such compliments, in order to afford himself the pleasure of satirizing the duplicity of polite society in withholding its recognition from him. Yet if he vents his misanthropic spleen on a representative of *honnête* society, he cannot then expect to receive recognition from that society. He is caught in a vicious circle, formed partly by his vanity, and partly by his atrabilious temperament. His temporizing 'Monsieur...' (ll. 267, 269, 271, 276) reflects the tension set up in his mind by these two irreconcilable temptations. Eventually he does speak words of moderation and discretion (ll. 277-84), but even here he contradicts his promise enunciated in the first scene to express his own opinion unvarnished and without hesitation (ll. 35-6). His reply to Oronte, to the effect that friendship demands mutual knowledge of each other's nature, temperament and humour, sounds eminently reasonable until we realize that he has not heeded precisely the same argument advanced by Philinte in the previous scene with regard to Alceste's love for Célimène (ll. 213-24).[40] Alceste, so intransigent towards *honnête* society in the first scene of the play, here is forced to adopt the flexibility in attitude for which he has already castigated Philinte.

The central part of this scene is undoubtedly the reading by Oronte of his poem, and Alceste's consequent condemnation of it. It is highly interesting to study the way in which Molière uses the sonnet to crystallize the basic issue of the play, the conflict produced by the absolute demands of Alceste on the one hand, and the relative nature of life on the other. By replacing Alceste in the same sceptical perspective in which he was viewed in Scene 1, Molière lets us glimpse something of his attitude towards his comic hero and the explanation of one of the most perplexing parts of the play.

A paragraph in Donneau de Visé's letter on the play has accounted for much of the traditional hesitation of critics with regard to the standpoint of the author in this scene: 'Le sonnet n'est pas méchant, selon la manière d'écrire d'aujourd'hui;...J'en vis même, à la première représentation de cette pièce, qui se firent jouer pendant qu'on représentoit cette scène; car ils crièrent que le sonnet étoit bon, avant que le Misanthrope en fît la critique, et demeurèrent ensuite tout confus.'[41] More recently, A. Adam has taken Alceste's denunciation of the sonnet as being that of Molière too.[42] But this is to overlook the fact that any absolute identification of Molière with one of his characters only is always dangerous. Although Molière is the creator of Alceste's tirades against the sonnet, it cannot be asserted that he shares his character's viewpoint at this or at any other point in the play. But what one can say with certainty is that Molière *is* the creator of the situation into which he has placed his character for the purpose of exploiting Alceste's reaction dramatically. The dramatic situation here is that of the misanthrope who has earlier exposed to us at considerable length the theory by which he claims to live, and who is now unexpectedly called on by the dramatist to put that theory into practice. In short, Molière is principally concerned in the sonnet scene with depicting the misanthrope in action, and not primarily with any criticism of the sonnet or the literary *genre* to which it belongs.[43]

The misanthrope of the previous scene is now revealed as hesitating and tentative in his reply to Oronte. Why does Molière make him contradict his previous decision to give his true opinion whatever the consequences, by making him delay his tirade against the sonnet and *précieux* poetry? It may well be the case, as H. Bergson has pointed out, that the ideas of *honnêteté* are too deeply inbred in Alceste to be jettisoned at a moment's notice.[44] But there is a deeper reason for this hesitation, which is both at the dramatic and philosophic centre of the play. Alceste tries to escape from the dilemma by saying to Oronte:

...j'ai le défaut
D'être un peu plus sincère en cela qu'il ne faut. (ll. 299-300)

What exactly, one wonders, does sincerity mean whenever it is used, as it is here by Alceste, as a pretext? To Oronte, it is merely synonymous with the normal usage of *honnête* language, according to which the user assures his interlocutor that he is being perfectly frank with him even when he has not expressed his true opinion. Therefore Oronte replies

C'est ce que je demande, et j'aurois lieu de plainte,
Si, m'exposant à vous pour me parler sans feinte,
Vous alliez me trahir, et me déguiser rien. (ll. 301-3)

It is evident that whenever he speaks of sincerity, he refers to polite and diplomatic ways of keeping intact the other person's self-esteem, 'ce grand aveuglement où chacun est pour soi' (l. 968), as Célimène will describe it. Alceste's interpretation of sincerity, however, is somewhat different. By it he means that uncompromising determination to express what is in one's mind at the moment in question, without pausing to make allowances for the susceptibility of others. Alceste is doubtless sincere in saying this; but one must not confuse the language of sincerity in which Alceste believes, with the possibility of his being sincere in this or in succeeding scenes. It seems quite evident that he involuntarily subscribes to a definition of sincerity which is at least as subjective and as self-interested, and therefore as relative in its meaning, as that of Oronte. For the truth is that to him total sincerity *must* be equated with total opposition to the customs and fashions of *honnête* society. In Scene 1 he had already made up his mind about this: as regards speaking the truth '...je vais n'épargner personne sur ce point' (1.88). One is surely justified in asking whether the indiscriminate expression of such determined bias against *honnête* company can be termed sincerity by any stretch of the imagination? It cannot, and this scene of the sonnet strips from Alceste the mask of sincerity, as well as the language and forms of sincerity which he delights to use, revealing to us precisely what he does mean by it.

The impossibility of absolute sincerity on Alceste's part is further stressed in this scene by the fact that Oronte is one of Célimène's suitors and his sonnet is certainly addressed to her.[45] Alceste is bound to know, or at the very least strongly to suspect (given his jealous temperament) that one of his rivals is asking him for his opinion on a sonnet addressed to the woman he loves. The presence of Oronte in Célimène's *salon* suffices as proof of his intentions. In Act II, Sc. 1, Alceste reproaches Célimène for the encouragement which she gives to his rivals and makes mention of 'Le trop riant espoir que vous leur présentez' (l. 471). His words here remind us ironically of Oronte's preamble to his sonnet:

> *Sonnet*...C'est un sonnet. *L'espoir*...C'est une dame
> Qui de quelque espérance avoit flatté ma flamme (ll. 305-6)

Alceste is therefore supremely comic here when he talks of his sincerity in appraising Oronte's sonnet. He believes that the opinion he will eventually express will be unbiased and given on his estimation of the sonnet's intrinsic worth. But his knowledge, or his suspicions, that Oronte has come to Célimène's *salon* in order to read his poem to her arouses his jealous temperament and renders him totally incapable of giving a balanced, disinterested judgement. His claim to be sincere is, however, even more deeply comic when one realizes that even if the sonnet seemed to him to be well written, and were *not* addressed to Célimène, he would still be unable to bring himself to praise it because of his determination to criticize everything of a contemporary (which is to him synonymous with decadent) nature. Any possibility of equanimous judgement is nullified by the fact that his powers of discernment are so completely a prey to his uncontrollable *humeur* which opposes him in his use of language, dress, as well as in literary taste, to *honnête* society.[46]

It is not therefore essential to know Molière's opinion of the sonnet in order to see that the dramatic conception of this scene is based on ambiguity of language, of intention and of life itself, a conception which we, as spectators, are forced to re-create as we enjoy all the different dilemmas confronting Alceste. Both Alceste and Oronte, we can see, understand very different things by the terms 'amitié' and 'sincérité'.

Alceste ultimately *does* remain faithful in this scene to his fixed intention of criticizing everything contemporary, but also compromises it in his prevarications. The scene principally illustrates the ambiguous nature of life, upon which no absolute schema may be foisted: life will continue to thwart Alceste's pertinacious attempts to make it fit into his set theory that 'la vérité est toujours bonne à dire'. He is more comic still in these attempts to regulate life since absolute sincerity, which he elevates into an objective criterion of human conduct, is impossible to attain. For the realization of such absolute honesty is dependent on many contingent factors: either the circumstances attending it will differ radically from those imagined in theory, or else one's judgement will be conditioned by such relative things as temperament and taste.

The sonnet scene has emphasized the obvious as well as the latent difficulties confronting Alceste's grandiose design. But Alceste does not pause to reflect on such difficulties; as a true *imaginaire,* he possesses the natural faculty of excluding from his vision every detail which does not exactly square with it. His inerrable theory cannot be wrong, and therefore in the following scene he attempts petulantly to put the blame for his quarrel with Oronte onto Philinte. He is comic in his reaction to the previous scene, in that he tries, consciously or unconsciously, to divert attention from his own failure to live up to his own standards of absolute sincerity. If Philinte has been politely hypocritical in his approval of the sonnet, Alceste has surely been at least as hypocritical not only in belying his theory, but also in his wilful confusion of sincerity with his desire to be impolite towards an *honnête homme.*[47]

(4)

Alceste's first meeting in the play with Célimène reveals more clearly still the comic discrepancy between his absolute theory and the relative nature of his conduct when we measure it by the ideas exposed in the first scene of Act I. Molière immediately stresses his comic aspect as Alceste remonstrates with Célimène:

De vos façons d'agir je suis mal satisfait;
Contre elles dans mon coeur trop de bile s'assemble (ll. 448-9)

His *humeur* makes him adopt an unequivocal and pompous tone, characterized by his predilection for formulae such as 'tôt ou tard' and 'indubitablement' (l. 452). Yet he will belie such commanding postures by being more emotionally committed to Célimène at the end of this scene than hitherto in the play.

In this scene Molière develops the contradiction which Philinte has noted earlier between Alceste's desire to follow reason and his choice of Célimène. Alceste can see plainly that the *coquette* is directly opposed to his way of thinking (cf. ll. 517-20). But he is comic not merely on account of the straightforward contradiction between reason and passion; as J. D. Hubert has pointed out, the case of Alceste is somewhat more complex: 'In previous plays, Molière had exploited the humor of psychological and intellectual blindness...but until *Le Misanthrope* he had not attempted to combine systematically within a single character lucidity with blindness...'[48] Alceste is sufficiently perspicacious to be able to take Célimène's faults (or rather what he deems to be faults) into consideration, and to wish to reform her. Yet he is so rhapsodic in expressing the hope of winning her hand that it is evident that his commitment to her at this point is deeper than that to his reason and theory (cf. ll. 514 ff.). Seeing what he ought to do, he is powerless to do it. But it is enough for Alceste to *think* that he is aware of the incongruity of his position; not for a moment does he imagine himself incapable of reforming Célimène. On the contrary, he possesses such a boundless 'adolescent' faith in his own reason and will-power that mention of the disparity between himself and Célimène is for the moment tantamount to a solution of his problem.[49] Having paid lip-service to his theory by his importunate reminder to her that she will have to reform her ways, he can now, in all good conscience, give free course to his passion for her.

He falls comically short of his own principles in his jealous demands to Célimène that she ought to distinguish him from all her other suitors; when he complains that she devotes too much attention to Clitandre, she replies that she needs his influence to favour her lawsuit. Alceste's advice to her reveals once again his monstrous egocentricity:

Perdez votre procès, Madame, avec constance,
Et ne ménagez point un rival qui m'offense. (ll. 493-4)

Earlier he has condemned those people like Philinte who strive in social life to avoid undermining the *amour-propre* of others: and in the sonnet scene he has also shown that he has scant regard for their opinion of themselves. The reason for this is that his high-sounding idealism is founded on nothing more than an intense and passionate concern with the maintenance of his own *amour-propre*. And he can only maintain and affirm it by destroying the *amour-propre* of others, that is, of both the *honnêtes hommes* who withhold the recognition from him to which he feels entitled, and of his rivals for Célimène's hand.

Alceste's continual preoccupation with his own ego and its maintenance provides the key to the problem of a misanthrope being attracted to a *coquette*. It was suggested above that his passion for her was proof of the irrationality of life, which attracts individuals of contrary temperament and inclination to each other. But from the evidence which this scene gives about the nature of Alceste's passion, it is possible to be more explicit about the nature of his attraction for her. At the end of the scene, he proclaims that his ardour for Célimène is so great that '...je puis là-dessus défier tout le monde' (l. 522). He is attracted to her because, as a *coquette,* she is surrounded by the praise, adulation and esteem of *honnête* society, the very things which he wishes to attain for himself. Society having refused to accord him its recognition, he turns his attention to the person who symbolizes the conquest of its recognition and prestige. In addition, she provides him with the opportunity of confronting *honnête* society — and his aggressive temperament rejoices in such a confrontation. His *humeur* incites him therefore to prove his superiority over society by attempting to reform Célimène (thus depriving society of its idol) and also to defeat the *honnête* suitors who are his rivals. All his apparently sincere protestations of love for her ought not to blind us to the fact that they are fundamentally motivated by his powerful desire for self-aggrandisement.[50]

Célimène's attitude towards Alceste in this scene is no less ambiguous than his own. When pressed by him to give a direct answer to the question of whether or not she prefers him to her other suitors, she replies that he has the privilege of possessing 'Le bonheur de savoir que vous êtes aimé' (l. 503). The ambiguity of this remark is, as I hope to show later, of critical importance in the light of Alceste's accusation that he has been betrayed by Célimène's favours to his rivals (Act IV, Sc. 3). If one takes her words as a solemn pledge of fidelity towards Alceste, then her future actions will seem to justify his accusation, and he will appear as a character who has suffered at the hands of an insincere social adventuress. But this is to place a construction on these words which violates the context and the psychology of a *coquette* in the seventeenth century. Such a promise as that given to Alceste contains nothing exclusive or absolute whenever spoken by a *coquette.* What she plainly means is that she does not find his company disagreeable. She can only retain her influence and social position if she remains the central figure in this *honnête* society, and she enjoys the attention and adulation of her many suitors, to each of whom she is careful to distribute the same insignificant favours, which are sufficient to retain them, but sufficiently uncompromising to encourage their rivals. She typifies Saint-Evremond's remark on the *coquette* who 'va chercher à qui plaire, et non pas qui lui plaît'.[51] It is certainly not her fault if Alceste, in the context of a *coquette's salon,* should seize upon a banal *précieux* utterance as tantamount to an avowal of love for him. But that is precisely what the literal-minded Alceste will do, for his whole attitude towards society stems from his belief that words ought not to be mere approximations of the ideas they are supposed to represent, but that they should be identical with them. This is the reason for his refusal to adopt the fashionable method of complimenting one's friends in profuse and unreal language, because the form is out of all proportion to its content. He is therefore not prepared to play the *honnête* game according to which language is tacitly understood by both parties to be primarily a polite end in itself, without having as its function the direct conveyance of one's thoughts.

Alceste's contradicting temperament sets him in voluntary opposition to society; but in opposing it he is also brought to oppose himself involuntarily. When Célimène informs him that she is about to receive the fashionable *habitués* of her *salon,* (Sc. 3) he makes up his mind to leave forthwith (see stage-note at l. 552). When she entreats him to stay, he answers that this is impossible: once she has told him flatly to leave (l. 558), his jealous temperament masters his will (ll. 561-2). He can rationalize the spontaneous effects of his *humeur* by telling Célimène that if he has decided to stay, it is only because he wishes her to choose between himself and his rivals.

The same comic principle of internal opposition brought about by temperament also underlies his intervention in the *salon* scene against the *honnête* company. Here, Molière makes use of a similar comic device to that employed in the sonnet scene. Alceste does not start directly to inveigh against the satirical conversation in which the group indulges. In fact, he listens to nearly one hundred lines of fashionable gossip before interrupting, just after Célimène's witty *portrait* of Damis (ll. 634-48). Why, one may ask, does he intervene at this particular point? Is his motive for doing so disinterested generosity, as J. Arnavon has supposed it to be?[52] The contrary is perhaps nearer to the truth. The foppish Damis does in fact share Alceste's principal characteristics.[53] He is eternally finical in his judgements, has never been known to praise anyone, and is steadfastly convinced that nothing can have value if it is modern. He is also, like Alceste, persuaded of his own innate superiority over others. Consequently, Alceste's eventual intervention after the *coquette's* description of Damis is his typical reaction to *salon* conversation, but here a reaction made more vehement still by the fact that he has recognized his own *portrait* painted by Célimène. His similarity with Damis is underlined in his reply to Clitandre, who stresses that it is Célimène whom he ought to criticize for her satirical humour, and not the others. But Alceste refuses to deviate from his *idée fixe*: if Célimène delights in such criticism, it is entirely due to the pernicious influence of her admirers over her, and, ultimately, to the general moral climate of *honnête* society. (Let it be noted that Célimène, without her *honnête* suitors, reveals the same censorious bent of mind in her encounter with Arsinoé in Act III, Sc. 4). Alceste's own individual bias has once again rendered him purblind to the manifest faults of his *coquette*, and enables him to seize the opportunity to attack the *marquis* for reasons of personal rivalry and animosity (ll. 659-66).

At this point of the play, Alceste unwittingly provides an excellent example of the sceptical principle underlying his actions and the actions of others in the play: for none of his decisions and acts can be entirely free of personal prejudice, however much he may attempt to disguise his motives from himself and from others. He would like to hide this truth from us, a truth which he perhaps feels instinctively, and consequently uses a universally acknowledged maxim to mask his personal antipathy towards *honnête* society:

C'est ainsi qu'aux flatteurs on doit partout se prendre
Des vices où l'on voit les humains se répandre. (ll. 665-6)

In order to sustain his role as a misanthrope, Alceste must give the illusion to himself and to others that the motivation behind his words and actions is morally more noble than those of his fellows. Molière takes care that we should not overlook this false basis of his actions, for Alceste, who has just issued a trenchant condemnation of the personal criticism which passes for polite conversation, has been just as acrimonious as Célimène in his *portrait* of Clitandre (ll. 475-88).

It is therefore appropriate that Célimène should now give a *portrait* of Alceste, the enemy of such *divertissement* except whenever he makes use of it for his own lofty ends. Her *portrait* of him not only provides us with an insight into the misanthrope's nature: more important still, it allows us to see that Molière, the creator of Célimène as well as of Alceste, can understand, in terms of *honnête* society, the comic aspect of his misanthrope. By pointing out that the deep-seated law of Alceste's nature is the contradiction which he feels bound to oppose to everything and everyone, Célimène supplies the comic theory behind the character, which Molière exploits dramatically. Alceste is, she says, predestined by his very nature to contradict, and to follow 'l'esprit contrariant qu'il a reçu des Cieux' (l. 672). Célimène offers Molière the means of acquiring the same kind of detachment with regard to Alceste that Le Vayer achieves in analysing his own disposition towards contrariness in *Prose Chagrine*, where he asks himself '...d'où vient que le chagrin me fait aujourd'hui trouver à redire à presque tout, et qu'il se passe peu de choses...où je ne trouve beaucoup à reprendre?' Elsewhere, Le Vayer gives an example of such self-contradiction which is very similar to that of Alceste, when he condemns someone who '...nommait flateurs ceux, qui acquiesçaient doucement à ses sentiments, et d'un autre côté...haïssait cruellement tous ceux qui lui contredisaient.'[54] And through Philinte, Molière sees Alceste in a more indulgent way, but essentially in the same perspective, as his friend tells him

Mais il est véritable aussi que votre esprit
Se gendarme toujours contre tout ce qu'on dit,
Et que, par un chagrin que lui-même il avoue,
Il ne sauroit souffrir qu'on blâme, ni qu'on loue (ll. 683-6)

Alceste does not delay in providing comic confirmation of what Célimène and Philinte have just said about him. When the *marquis* assert with banal flattery that the *coquette* is devoid of faults, Alceste's riposte is both immediate and consistent with her *portrait* of him. He must not only contradict but must also show to all the world the superior judgement by which he is ruled: accordingly, true love for him is not compatible with flattery or self-deception, and makes no indulgent allowance for faults (ll. 699-706). By his claim to see Célimène as she really is, Alceste once again succumbs to what can perhaps best be termed within the context of the play 'the myth of objectivity'. Does he perceive faults in Célimène which the *marquis* accept as qualities of a *salon* figure? In reality, his judgement of her proceeds purely and simply from his *humeur,* his temperament and outlook on life. A fault to one person is virtue in the eyes of another. To Alceste, her *esprit médisant* symbolizes the corruption of his age: to Philinte and Eliante, she is neither corrupt nor virtuous, but merely reflects what is good and bad in society, whilst to the *marquis* she is the very epitome of *honnêteté,* the social code by which they profess to live.

The speech by Eliante on the essentially subjective notions which constitute definitions of beauty (ll. 711-30), which Molière probably took from Lucretius, is in this respect not the turgid set piece which it could appear to be, but rather reinforces the sceptical principle of the play. When seen through the optic of love, she says, negative attributes are transformed into positive qualities, for 'beauty is in the eye of the beholder.'[55] The characteristic of the true lover is to love 'jusqu'aux défauts des personnes qu'il aime' (l. 730). Alceste immediately tries to contradict this view, and at first sight it scarcely seems to apply to his feelings for Célimène, since he makes no attempt to minimize her failings. Nevertheless Eliante's words are strikingly apposite in his connexion, for although he continually says that he wishes to reform her ways, it has been seen that he also enjoys his role as a critic of Célimène and of society. So much so, in fact, that he uses Célimène's censoriousness as nothing less than a 'spring-board' for his posturing as the sole representative of virtue and sincerity. As long as she remains a *coquette médisante* he can persuade himself of the need to reform her, whilst allowing her satirical humour to gratify his own misanthropy.

Alceste has been consistently and subtly comic throughout the scene with the *petits marquis,* and Act II ends with Molière emphasizing one of the more straightforwardly comic aspects of his behaviour. At the end of the *salon* scene, he says to his rivals 'Nous verrons si c'est moi que vous voudrez qui sorte' (l. 742). At the beginning of this scene, the presence of his rivals made him wish to leave; now it makes him wish to stay. His premature exit to answer the summons from the *Cour des Maréchaux* (Sc.7) underlines the truth of the play that life is unpredictable and will continue to escape from the rigid pattern he is determined to impose on it.

In the last scene of this Act, Alceste intensifies his attitude towards Oronte's sonnet. He will not apologize or seek a compromise with the offended sonneteer before the *Cour des Maréchaux*. His extreme language ('lâche complaisance', l. 758; 'Je ne me dédis point de ce que j'en ai dit', l.763; 'Je n'en démordrai point', l.765) contrasts comically with Philinte's indifference. The latter attempts to minimize the importance of the episode (he dismisses the quarrel as 'la ridicule affaire' (l. 754) and refers discreetly to 'certains petits vers' (l. 756)). Molière uses Philinte's well-intentioned advice to increase beyond all measure the comic obstinacy of Alceste: the more Philinte counsels him to be flexible and to treat the affair with indifference, the more the tetchy Alceste becomes inflexible and prepared to see the sonnet as the ultimate test for his high moral principle of absolute sincerity.

Alceste does not reappear until Act III, Sc. 5. From this point onwards, he is generally held to be increasingly less ridiculous. A modern critic has expressed this widespread opinion as follows: 'From now on, Alceste enjoys the sympathies of the audience more than previously. His ridiculous side still appears occasionally, but it is attenuated, not stressed.'[56] This view sees the grounds for Alceste's jealousy (the *marquis* unite in mutual interest against him in Act III, Sc.1) as making him more sympathetic to the audience. Once again, such a judgement seems to illustrate the fallacy of judging Alceste according to one's own subjective notion of whether he is or is not funny or ridiculous, whilst overlooking the fact that it is possible for him to become more deeply comic still although he may not make us laugh more than previously. It is true perhaps that some of the more extravagant and burlesque language has disappeared, and has been replaced by more sober reflection, at any rate in the scene with Arsinoé. Nevertheless, the real comedy of Alceste is not dependent on external aspects such as language, but is deeply rooted in his own nature. As his nature does not alter radically throughout the second half of the play (like that of the true *imaginaire* who remains firmly imprisoned in his obsession), Alceste continues to be at least as comic, if not more so, in the later Acts as he was at the beginning of the play.

One fact must be underlined in order to appreciate the rich comic aspect of Alceste in his meeting with Arsinoé. She is ideally suited to him. Of this there is no doubt, for not only have such perspicacious observers of society as Philinte and Célimène remarked on this (ll. 216 ff., ll. 1033 ff.), but Arsinoé has just proved this herself by emulating Alceste's criticism of Célimène's conduct (Act III, Sc. 4). There is perhaps one slight difference in the method, if not in the content, of their social criticism: Arsinoé is ready to use the formulae of *honnêteté* for her own devious purposes, whereas Alceste deliberately eschews them. But she shares in full measure the same prudish attitude of the misanthrope towards society. Célimène, in the previous scene, has mentioned her 'pruderie' and her 'éclats de zèle' (l. 925), her 'discours éternels de sagesse et d'honneur' (l. 928), her conviction that she is superior to everyone else ('Cette hauteur d'estime où vous êtes de vous' (l. 931)), her 'fréquentes leçons', and the 'aigres censures' (l. 933) with which she is so prodigal. Her apparent concern for the moral principle and practice of others leads the *coquette* to formulate a maxim which is equally applicable to Alceste:

Qu'on doit se regarder soi-même un fort long temps,
Avant que de songer à condamner les gens (ll. 951-2)[57]

All these faults and characteristics are shared in abundance by Alceste, and in both cases they stem from the same source. Arsinoé is so critical of Célimène because the *coquette* is in possession of that recognition from society to which she, like Alceste, aspires, but which she cannot have. Knowing how fundamental such a grievance is to Alceste's cast of mind, she tells him of his intrinsic merits which ought to be universally recognized (ll. 1045 ff.). But society is unjust in its distribution of favours and does nothing for him! As in the sonnet scene, Molière pushes his misanthrope into an impossibly comic position. He hears what he wishes to hear, but cannot divest himself of his natural 'esprit contrariant' which instinctively supersedes his vanity. But the *prude* Arsinoé goes much further than Oronte, who merely limited himself to a panegyric of Alceste's virtues. In this scene, Arsinoé gives him not only praise, but something which is of more importance to him — namely the sympathy and pity to which he feels entitled, and which serve to authenticate his position as a martyr in his own eyes even more fully than hitherto (ll. 1051-2).

The fact that Alceste hears what he craves to hear and yet cannot assent because his nature predestines him to contradict even his own opinions whenever he hears them uttered by others, helps us to see his refusal of Arsinoé's influence as something radically different from the disinterestedness, self-knowledge, and modesty which have been frequently ascribed to him at this point of the play.[58] His attempt at self-criticism, to the effect that he has performed no service for the Court which would merit recognition by it, is closer to false modesty than to self-knowledge (ll. 1053-6). He is proud to parade the fact that he has no record of service as courtier to his credit for two reasons. Has he not boasted earlier that he would be angry if society accounted him as one of their conformist members (ll. 109-12)? To have accepted the conventions of the Court would be to forfeit his position as the wronged outsider, and this is the basis of the role which he likes to play. And if he says that he does not wish for a post at Court, it is not, as he would have us believe, on account of his stand for principles, but simply because he would be reduced to the mundane rank occupied by others:

Ce n'est plus un honneur que de se voir loué;
D'éloges on regorge, à la tête on les jette,
Et mon valet de chambre est mis dans la Gazette (ll. 1072-4)

It is true that he does seem to display a certain insight into his nature in the central speech of this scene, in which he tells Arsinoé that fortune has given him a humour which is incompatible with Court life (ll. 1081-4). But on closer examination, one will see that the description of himself upon which he embarks is merely another pretext for his superior indictment of the Court. He invokes incessantly his sincerity and frankness (l. 1087), not as qualities in themselves, but in order to throw into relief the insincerity and truthlessness of his fellows. A personal trait is elevated to the stature of a universal maxim, with objective validity for all:

> Je ne sais point jouer les hommes en parlant;
> Et qui n'a pas le don de cacher ce qu'il pense
> Doit faire en ce pays fort peu de résidence. (ll. 1088-90)

If he says with apparent modesty that he does not possess the gift of concealing his thoughts, he has proclaimed two lines earlier that sincerity is his greatest talent! Apart from the enormous vanity behind these words, it is impossible to overlook the peculiarly subjective notion which Alceste insists on giving to sincerity here as in previous scenes.

The same psychological combination of apparent lucidity and real cecity about his motives can be discerned in his reaction to Arsinoé's subtle suggestion that Célimène's affection for him is simulated. His reply is that this may well be so, but he rebukes her for trying to sow the seeds of doubt in his mind (ll. 1116-18). Yet such is the power of his temperament over his reason that Arsinoé has merely to threaten not to tell him anything of Célimène's 'treachery' towards him for his attitude to alter from cold indifference to the most jealous and morbid curiosity (ll. 1121-4). He attempts to rationalize his sudden interest in what Arsinoé is about to reveal concerning Célimène by placing it on the level of permissible curiosity. The comic truth is, however, the reverse of what he claims; in reality, he seizes with alacrity the slightest opportunity for examining Célimène's conduct towards him, with the sole hope and intention of discovering that she has in fact betrayed him. Already he has told her that sooner or later he is going to break off his relationship with her (l. 452), and to Arsinoé he says that he desires proof of the clearest kind (ll. 1123-4). To have objective validation of such infidelity would justify all the criticisms which he has made of her and at the same time provide him with a supreme opportunity for self-pity and righteous self-exaltation.

Alceste does not appear in the first scene of Act IV, but on the strength of Eliante's favourable opinion of him (ll. 1165-8) an established view is that he is more sympathetic and therefore less comic than hitherto.[59] Confirmation of this has traditionally been seen in the following scene, where Alceste enters in a state of anguished rage, claiming that Célimène has betrayed his faith in her. He demands justice against someone who has misused his 'constance' (l. 1218). If what Alceste asserts here is literally true, then it is highly probable that he will appear as a more serious character than the extravagant misanthrope of the earlier Acts. But as observed in previous scenes, it is extremely misleading to accept Alceste at his word, without pausing to consider the premise from which he argues, which is usually founded upon his imaginary obsessions. Has Alceste in fact been constant in his attitude towards Célimène? It has been seen that he has accepted with alacrity the slightest hint from Arsinoé that Célimène might have betrayed him. A suitor who is prepared to embrace the most extreme conclusions on mere suspicion alone (suspicion fed by nothing more than Arsinoé's gossip), cannot by any stretch of the imagination be qualified as 'constant'. Alceste exaggerates the incongruity between his vaunted constancy and his eternal suspiciousness by his use of hyperbolic language to describe his 'betrayal' (ll. 1220-3). Philinte and Eliante unite vainly to impress upon him the deceptiveness of appearances. The former, in particular, draws attention to the central comic aspect of Alceste's behaviour in this scene when he tells him 'Et votre esprit jaloux prend parfois des chimères...' (l. 1233). He echoes here the cryptic advice which Célimène has already dispensed to her jealous suitor, to the effect that '...rien ne sauroit plus vous tromper que vous-même' (Act II, Sc.1, l. 513).

The ironic truth of these statements is fully and comically borne out by his behaviour in this scene. He is supremely comic here because he imagines that he has been able to draw such an absolute and objective conclusion from the letter which Célimène has written and which Arsinoé has procured for him. But in fact, not only is it true that Alceste has no ultimate proof of his betrayal by the *coquette* (nothing either in this scene or in the following one leads us to suppose that it is a question of anything more than an innocuous *billet doux* written by a *coquette* to one of her many admirers), but it is also true that Alceste is entirely responsible for such a conclusion. I have said that Alceste ardently desires concrete evidence of Célimène's infidelity towards him in order to justify his criticism of her; now he imagines that he has achieved this goal by claiming to have discovered nothing more important than a fact which the presence of Célimène's suitors in her *salon* has amply indicated to all. This 'discovery' leads him to still more comic aberrations; on the basis of such fragile 'evidence' as that provided by the letter, he implores Eliante to avenge the outrage he has suffered by accepting his proposal of marriage (ll. 1251-8)! He has never previously revealed such abysmal depths of hypersensitive egoism and puerile vanity: not only does he expect Eliante to share as personally as he does his sense of dishonour, but also wishes to use Célimène's cousin as a mere foil in order to induce in the *coquette* feelings of guilt at having betrayed his trust. The man who is so outraged by insincerity envisages for a moment a subterfuge of the most elementary and ridiculous kind, in order to satisfy his wounded vanity and his vindictive desire for revenge.

Perhaps the most important scene in any consideration of Alceste's character is that between himself and Célimène in Act IV, Sc. 3. The earliest commentary on it, by Donneau de Visé, has served to perpetuate doubt about Alceste's comic status at this critical stage of the play: 'Je ne crois pas qu'on puisse rien voir de plus beau que cette scène: elle est toute sérieuse; et cependant il y en a peu dans la pièce qui divertissent davantage.'[60] Critics have consequently been inclined to view Alceste in this scene as a predominantly serious and tragic figure, experiencing what one of them terms 'ce calvaire de la passion'.[61] Yet it scarcely seems possible to see him as a figure of tragedy if due attention is paid to Molière's treatment of him at this juncture of the play. Molière loses no time in fixing our attention on the grotesque nature of Alceste's blustering behaviour, as Célimène remarks on

...ces soupirs poussés
Et ces sombres regards que sur moi vous lancez. (ll. 1279-80)

Such an abrupt diversion of attention from the potentially serious subject of infidelity would seem to exemplify one of Bergson's laws of the comic: 'Est comique tout incident qui appelle notre attention sur le physique d'une personne alors que le moral est en cause.'[62] Molière sustains his caricature of Alceste by giving him a hyperbolic form of expression: his tirade of indictment abounds in such absolute terms as 'trahison' (l. 1288, 1306), 'perfidie' (l. 1306), 'châtiments' (l. 1307), 'ressentiments' (l. 1308), 'outrage' (l. 1309), 'rage' (l. 1310), and in the lofty vocabulary of a Cornelian hero (ll. 1311-14, 1371-90). And there is the most glaring comic discrepancy between such an intemperate diatribe, and the simple fact that he has not yet explained to Célimène the reason for it! When Célimène weathers the storm of his abuse and asks him innocently

D'où vient donc, je vous prie, un tel emportement?
Avez-vous, dites-moi, perdu le jugement? (ll. 1315-16)

any sense of involvement on the part of the spectator with Alceste's suffering is irretrievably banished in the theatre by such calm deflation on the part of the *coquette.*

Throughout this scene, Alceste, the plain-spoken man who abhors the subtle and figurative language of *galanterie,* lapses comically into a form of language more *précieux* by far than any which Oronte would ever dream of using. *Précieux* and *galant* metaphors abound and jostle each other, one succeeding the other with such rapidity that an impression of irreparable confusion is produced in the spectator's mind. The hater of all things *précieux* speaks passionately of 'les troubles de mon âme' (1. 1289), 'ma flamme' (1. 1290, 1. 1305, 1. 1354, etc.), of each heart being able to choose its conqueror (1. 1300), of 'ce fatal amour né de vos traîtres yeux' (1. 1384). But comedy of a sort transcending mere form of expression lies surely in the fact that Alceste, although despising such figurative vocabulary to the extent that it is conventional and therefore in his eyes hypocritical, is himself driven involuntarily to use it: words such as 'cruel', 'flamme', 'feu', which magnify and personify normal human emotions, are the *only* ones which suffice to translate literally the abnormal passion which he feels. The language of hypocritical and effete *galanterie* is after all capable of expressing the truth and directness of Alceste's emotions! So long as Alceste remains Alceste, that is the possessor of a 'seismographic' sensitivity, he will be condemned to his own inverted and comic use of *précieux* language.

If Alceste utters language ridiculous even by the standards of *préciosité*, he nevertheless remains true to his character by virtue of his unrelenting and morbid gravity. At the beginning of this scene he says in answer to Célimène's frivolity 'Ah! ne plaisantez point, il n'est pas temps de rire' (1. 1286), just as he had earlier told the *marquis* that

> ...je ne croyois pas être
> Si plaisant que je suis. (ll. 773-4)

By reminding us at a highly dramatic moment of the simple but fundamental fact that Alceste is totally devoid of anything approaching a sense of humour with regard to himself, Molière issues a certain invitation to the spectator to put his 'tragic' tirades into comic detachment. To take Alceste seriously here is to succumb to the logic which his misanthropic nature and *humeur* make him follow: he needs people to take seriously his accusations against Célimène as well as against society, in order to confirm his jaundiced view of life and so be enabled to prolong his role of the morally irreproachable man oppressed by the treachery of his fellows.

Alceste is at last convinced that he has secured irrefutable proof of Célimène's infidelity. In his instinctive need to bolster up his judgement with such proof we see the same trait which dominates Harpagon — 'Il faut bien que je touche quelque chose' (*L'Avare*, Act II, Sc. 5). Possession of the letter is to him a tangible symbol of the fact that he was, after all, right about Célimène's fickleness. The most comic aspect of this scene lies in the complete reversal of this certainty by the *coquette,* who demonstrates to him that his 'proof' lacks by far the character of indubitable evidence which he claims for it. On the hearsay evidence of Arsinoé, he states categorically that the letter has been written by Célimène to Oronte (ll. 1337-8). But it is equally possible, as Célimène points out, that the letter has been written by her to a woman (ll. 1344-5). Célimène is content merely to suggest this obliquely, for she knows from her experience of Alceste the effect of suggestion upon the powerful imagination of her jealous suitor. Is Célimène guilty of deceiving Alceste in this scene? If she is, then Alceste will undoubtedly appear as a more serious character, meriting our sympathy. Such is a well known view of this part of the play.[63] To one critic in particular, Molière's failure to answer unequivocally the question of the identity of the person to whom the letter is addressed constitutes the principal flaw of the play.[64] But it seems to me that the question of whether or not Célimène does deceive Alceste is as unimportant as Molière's opinion of Oronte's sonnet. We may be assured that had Molière thought that failure to tell us the identity of the recipient of the letter was a dramatic defect, he would certainly have supplied an answer forthwith — he was too much a man of the theatre to make such a fundamental blunder. Far from being a defect in the play, the ambiguity surrounding the letter would appear to be an incontestable dramatic advantage, as we see Alceste's irrefragable certainty gradually dissolve into doubt and eventually transform itself into reluctant acceptance of the ambiguous explanation offered by Célimène — surely a most radical peripeteia within the limits of one scene! Alceste, who is guided by reason and who believes only what is proved to him, ends by craving voluntarily to participate in an illusion:

> Efforcez-vous ici de paroître fidèle,
> Et je m'efforcerai, moi, de vous croire telle. (ll. 1389-90)[65]

The dramatic change of fortune in the scene points naturally to the sceptical conclusion which underlies the comic vision of the play: Alceste has persistently tried to scrutinize Célimène's thoughts, to interpret her favourable or unfavourable disposition towards him from her most insignificant action. To this vision, such an urge for knowledge into the precise nature of one's relationship with others can only issue in perverse self-affliction; if one wishes to maintain any degree of happiness, it is advisable to limit one's glance to appearances only, accepting them for what they are worth, and controlling morbid desires to satisfy inordinate curiosity. Alceste is paradoxically brought to the point where he chooses the incuriosity against which his nature and temperament rebel, through his fear of possible revelations by Célimène which might dispel what she has described earlier in the play as 'Ce grand aveuglement où chacun est pour soi' (l. 968). In his struggle to protect his *amour-propre* from the possible ravages of reality, Alceste bears out Le Vayer's admonition not to probe too keenly into such delicate matters: '...s'il nous était possible de voir ce que nos amis mêmes, ou ceux, qui se disent tels, ont souvent dans le coeur, nous en serions mortifiés au dernier point.'[66]

The dramatic change from curiosity to self-delusion on Alceste's part heightens the fundamental contradiction between his declared intention to break at once with the *coquette* and his increasing emotional dependence on her. When he tells her in grandiloquent terms that he knows she is deceiving him but wishes to see to what extent she is prepared to betray him, he is, once more, giving a clever rationalization of his true motives (ll. 1415-20). He is disappointed that his accusations against her have not produced the effect which he ardently desired — that is, of reducing Célimène to a state of contrite docility by inducing guilt in her for her 'treachery' towards him. More than anything else, he aspires to bring Célimène to the point where she will plead with him to forgive her and take her back on his own conditions, so that her utter dependence on him may be made manifest.

In attempting to reduce Célimène to such a dependent state he is brought to comic excesses in this scene more by his combination of lucidity and cecity of judgement than by the *coquette* herself. On the one hand, he utters words of eminent reasonableness, when he tells her that love must not be born of dependence or coercion and that its essential value lies in its freedom to choose what it desires (ll. 1297 ff,); and on the other, he inevitably belies such moderation by succumbing to his wish to remake Célimène in his own image: he would like to deprive her of her social position and advantages

Afin que de mon coeur l'éclatant sacrifice
Vous pût d'un pareil sort réparer l'injustice,
Et que j'eusse la joie et la gloire, en ce jour,
De vous voir tenir tout des mains de mon amour. (ll. 1429-32)

If any doubt subsisted about the intrinsic comedy of Alceste, Molière surely dispels it in this scene, where his hero's resolve to remake the world is most clearly focused in his attempt to reform the worldly Célimène. In order to be able to achieve such a reform, he must bring her to full dependence on him, and in order to do this, he must allow himself to be completely and satisfyingly betrayed by Célimène. If he does this, he will at once advance his plan for Célimène and indulge to the full his masochistic complex, which affords him the supreme pleasure of posturing as the persecuted representative of true values. In the light of such motives, which were previously discernible but are now most glaringly revealed by his belief in Célimène's infidelity, one may well ask whether or not he can be said to love her. Of course he hopes eventually to win Célimène — but only to affirm his superiority over his fashionable rivals and her coquetry. His main preoccupation is not the conquest of Célimène's love as such, but rather the conquest of her, the *coquette,* to illustrate and prove his challenge to society's ways; thus he would enjoy objective confirmation of his own worth from one of society's erstwhile idols, and his ultimate revenge on that society.

The final Act has always seemed difficult to explain in terms of comedy. R. Jasinski, for instance, speaks of it as constituting the final phase of Alceste's *folie* and *maladie*, and P.J. Yarrow sees him here as being 'almost wholly *sympathique*'.[67] It is true, as the latter has pointed out, that the satire of justice of which Alceste delivers himself is scarcely comic: Alceste is unequivocally right in his *procès* and the court is wrong in dismissing his case. Philinte has no doubt or hesitation in agreeing with the valid grievance of his friend (ll. 1555 ff.). Yet in the light of the basic moral principle upon which Molière has built his comedy, Alceste remains permanently comic. At the beginning of this chapter it was seen that Alceste and Philinte were in fundamental agreement about the morally ambiguous nature of contemporary life; perversity, insincerity and untruthfulness in all forms abound, and they are to be taken as some of man's normal attributes. Such faults are by no means 'tragically' discovered by Alceste in the last Act; they constitute the unalterable terms of reference within which humanity as well as Alceste are to be judged. Not to take this into account, or to apply other more ideal and desirable terms of reference to the play can only result in flagrant deformation of its vision of things. It may be highly regrettable that a man of Alceste's probity should lose his lawsuit; but within the sceptical framework of the play, it is scarcely surprising that such a miscarriage of justice should arise, in view of the fact that everyone, including Alceste, knows that falsehood is a prerogative of justice. Alceste's astonishment at such occurrences could only seem tragic if we were totally unaware of the moral assumptions which underlie the play. If it were assumed that true justice did in fact exist, then the loss of Alceste's lawsuit would appear as a tragic injustice. But Alceste does not assume this, nor indeed is he blind to the habitual machinations of justice. He deliberately *chooses* not to solicit his judges, thus forfeiting in advance the opportunity of winning his lawsuit. By refusing to participate in the normal course of justice, he is caught in his own vicious circle: convinced of the innate perversity of humanity, he nevertheless insists on demanding perfect justice from human institutions.

Alceste is too lucid not to see the impossibility of such a demand, which makes the loss of his lawsuit inevitable. This is precisely what he desires, for he is not at all interested in winning it, but is prepared to use it for the sake of his 'theory' about life in general. This is borne out amply by the first scene of this Act; when Philinte suggests a pragmatic course of action which may reverse the result of the lawsuit, Alceste refuses petulantly to countenance any possible change of verdict:

> Philinte: Et pour votre procès, dont vous pouvez vous plaindre,
> Il vous est en justice aisé d'y revenir,
> Et contre cet arrêt...
> Alceste: Non, je *veux* m'y tenir (ll. 1538-40) (my italics)

It is immediately apparent that Alceste's pursuit of justice is similar to his pursuit of Célimène; whilst he would like in each case to defeat his rivals (the *scélérat* with whom he litigates, and the *honnête* suitors) to prove his superiority, he secretly hopes that he will lose both his lawsuit and Célimène in order to parade before all the validity of his 'misanthropy'. The loss of his lawsuit, he tells us, must forever stand as

...un fameux témoignage
De la méchanceté des hommes de notre âge.
Ce sont vingt mille francs qu'il m'en pourra coûter;
Mais, pour vingt mille francs, j'aurai droit de pester
Contre l'iniquité de la nature humaine,
Et de nourrir pour elle une immortelle haine. (ll. 1545-50)

Never before has he been able to luxuriate in such self-flagellation and vituperation, because never before has he had such an apparently reasonable basis for these attitudes. His words bear out the comic truth of Le Vayer's observation in *Prose Chagrine,* that whenever we imagine ourselves to be persecuted by events and people '...Souvent nous n'avons point de plus grand adversaire que nous-mêmes.'[68] The fact that justice may be erratic and even corrupt is as nothing when compared to the monstrous nature of Alceste's pose here. As in the first scene of the play, he utters his condemnation of humanity and its institutions in lofty, universally applicable terms, giving the impression that innocence has been betrayed by a century of perversity, whilst obscuring the mundane truth that one of his principal motives in undertaking his lawsuit is nothing more than a vendetta against his opponent (cf. ll. 123 ff., ll. 1493 ff.). In fact, the principal source of his massive indictment of humanity is to be found in this personal and temperamental antipathy. In using abstract concepts such as 'justice', 'truth', etc. as a pretext to give added weight to a temperamental dislike, he is surely behaving in a puerile and patently dishonest fashion. He does not deviate from such tactics throughout the play; at the beginning, his 'misanthropy' is quick to allege 'le franc scélérat' as its justification (l. 124); in the present scene, the absolute statement that 'Trop de perversité règne au siècle où nous sommes' (l. 1485) is seen to depend on the relative fact that

Un traître, dont on sait la scandaleuse histoire,
Est sorti triomphant d'une fausseté noire! (ll. 1493-4)

Having used humanity in general and the *scélérat* in particular to justify his perverse outlook on life, he is quite content to maintain his *status quo.* He thus finds a way of ascribing the highest possible motive to his misanthropic pose, that of wronged innocence. By refusing to appeal, he can continue to use this pose as a defensive mechanism to cover up his temperamental inadaptability and insecurity.

In the following scene, Oronte and Alceste join forces to make

Célimène choose between them. Their expedient pact is not without its comic incongruity, when one realises that the person responsible for bringing them together, the *coquette,* was the ultimate cause of their quarrel over the sonnet in Célimène's *salon.* In addition, the enemy of all things *honnête* is himself cast in the role of an *honnête* suitor, pleading for her favour in the *galant* language of his fashionable rival.

The *dénouement* in Scene 4, with its revelation that Célimène's feelings for her admirers are merely on the level of those of a *coquette* enjoying their attentions, completes admirably Molière's comic portrayal of Alceste. The impetuous suitor who in the first scene of the play demanded that

> Je veux qu'on me distingue; et pour le trancher net,
> L'ami du genre humain n'est point du tout mon fait. (ll. 63-4)

now discovers the truth of which he has had many presentiments, but which his vanity has served to conceal from him. He has no more claim to the favours of 'l'amie du genre humain' than any other of her admirers. His long silence throughout the reading of the letters and the resigned tone of his eventual reaction (ll. 1733 ff.) are due to his wounded vanity at having been 'betrayed' by Célimène. But Célimène has never at any time disguised the fact that other suitors were paying their attentions to her, or indicated that she was averse to this! Her coquetry is, at any rate, so deeply rooted in her nature that to disguise it would be to become someone other than Célimène.

After the reading of Célimène's mordant lines about Alceste, he appears 'calm of mind all passion spent' in his speech from l. 1747 onwards, but he has now achieved the objective to which all his emotion and fury were directed, that of acquiring proof for all to see of Célimène's treachery towards him. In fact, Célimène obliges him with an apparent confession of guilt on her part: '...je tombe d'accord de mon crime envers vous' (l. 1742). It seems, however, questionable to take these words to mean a recognition of her deception of Alceste. The basis for her social role lies in her ability to project herself convincingly into the thoughts and words of her admirers, in order to retain their interest in her. Now, for the first time, she realizes that she is in danger of being abandoned by the last of her suitors, and she must avoid at all costs the awful solitude with which she taunted Arsinoé previously. Hence her voluntary use of terms such as 'crime', 'trahir', 'haïr', which will convey adequately to Alceste's jealous imagination the magnitude of guilt which Célimène cannot experience so long as she remains true to her own coquettish nature.

Alceste has now heard from Célimène the avowal of her 'infidelity' towards him which he has desired to hear from the beginning of the play. But, as Célimène herself said earlier, Alceste is never completely satisfied with the opinions of others, even when they are his own. To create for himself the Célimène he desires, he must make her go beyond her confession and espouse his great design of going to live with him in his *désert*. His forgiveness of her misdeeds, and his love for her, are conditional upon her acceptance of his resolve (ll. 1757-68). If she acquiesces, he tells her that 'Il peut m'être permis de vous aimer encore' (l. 1768). When Célimène hesitates and eventually refuses such an invitation, Alceste speaks lines which indicate the depth of the comic paradox in his nature:

Puisque vous n'êtes point, en des liens si doux,
Pour trouver tout en moi, comme moi tout en vous,
Allez, je vous refuse...(ll. 1781-3)

There can surely be no more flagrant misinterpretation, even by a comic hero in Molière's theatre, of his own motives than this. Whatever else he may have found in Célimène, Alceste has certainly not found everything in her. He has merely found in her nature many characteristics which he aspired to change, and the possibility of reforming society's idol to his own misanthropic way of thinking. He has attempted to gain his supreme revenge on society by transforming her into a female version of himself. To find his all in her would automatically imply not merely his formal acceptance of Célimène the *coquette,* but also his active wish that she retain her individual characteristics of coquetry, censoriousness and gregariousness — in short, her right to exist as the Célimène who originally attracted him. By so doing, he would thus have remained true to the first irrational movement of his nature which attracted him to someone diametrically opposed to himself.

Alceste appears to manifest the superiority of his motives in his haughty refusal of her. But the motives of both protagonists seem ironically similar in nature if not in degree. To Célimène, leaving society would be synonymous with deprivation of the adulation to which *salon* life has accustomed her; to Alceste, it is merely a pretext for organizing his life around those things in which society is not interested, that is, his own *chagrin* and introspection. In their very different universes, both nevertheless aspire to the same absolute position, in which they are the unique dispensers of rank, favour and importance.

Does Alceste come to the end of the play with more self-knowledge than at the beginning? I find it difficult to agree with G. Rudler when he writes that 'Alceste commence à se connaître son épreuve n'a pas été vaine.'[69] It is true that he appears to display commendable lucidity and humility when he admits to Eliante that '...le Ciel, pour ce noeud, ne m'avoit point fait naître' (l. 1792), thus disengaging himself from a rash commitment which he had made earlier to her. But apart from these words, there is no evidence in the last Act to show that he is any less imbued with his intrinsic worth and self-righteousness than he was at the beginning of the play. At that point, he was already contemplating with relish his misanthropic vision of fleeing society (ll. 143-4) and looked forward to losing his *procès* (ll. 196 ff.), which he regarded even then as his crucial moral test for society. Having duly lost his lawsuit, his initial vision of his *désert* has now acquired a greater attraction for his misanthropic tendencies (ll. 1573 ff.). It is with this design firmly fixed in his mind that he made his grandiose offer to Célimène to accompany him. Now that he has fully formulated it, he cannot and will not on any account renounce it or allow his promise to Eliante to interfere with his *idée fixe*. False humility is a tactic in the use of which Alceste has proved himself convincingly adept. His *désert* stands as a symbol of his increased self-absorption and self-pity.

The misanthropic pose of Alceste has now fully and convincingly evolved. He has, on objective testimony, suffered harshly at the hands of justice and of Célimène; he has also been seen to extend a generous pardon to the guilty *coquette*, who has misused his good faith, and he has selflessly withdrawn his offer of marriage to Eliante, thus allowing Philinte to propose to her instead. His grandiloquent nuptial benediction to Philinte and Eliante conveys so well the martyred status that he has given himself that critics have discerned true and noble pathos in its expression:

> Puissiez-vous, pour goûter de vrais contentements,
> L'un pour l'autre à jamais garder ces sentiments!
> Trahi de toutes parts, accablé d'injustices,
> Je vais sortir d'un gouffre où triomphent les vices,
> Et chercher sur la terre un endroit écarté,
> Où d'être homme d'honneur on ait la liberté. (ll. 1801-6)[70]

It is perhaps not fruitless to speculate upon what Alceste will do in his *désert,* since the psychology of the *imaginaire* is rigid in its permanence. He departs with the firm intention of indulging his 'misanthropy' to the full in his solitude. But in order to derive any satisfaction from his 'misanthropy', he must have a sympathetic audience to recognize the justice of his grievances. Without them, he cannot possibly nourish his martyr's complex which makes up the basis of his nature. His need of society therefore is, paradoxically, greater than his misanthropic quest for solitude. Alceste, obeying the fixity of the true comic hero in Molière's theatre, will not deviate from his own nature, and will return to the society for which he professes such profound contempt as soon as he sees that the fires of his 'misanthropy' are burning low in his *désert.*

(5)

At the centre of the vision of life in *Le Misanthrope* lies the paradox of the creator of Alceste and Philinte expressing their ideas simultaneously through dramatic conflict. The inevitably paradoxical position of the creator of a play, although universal in its applicability, has nevertheless an important and no less paradoxical consequence for *Le Misanthrope* in particular. This is that Alceste and Philinte both share the same fundamental ideas on man and life. They may be, and are, different from each other in the attitudes which they adopt towards society: in reality both agree closely on the moral premises of the play. That justice when practised gives rise to such an example of injustice as that experienced by Alceste, that the poison of hypocrisy has penetrated into all levels of society, that honourable men of moral principle must forgo the social esteem which is their due — both share to some degree such sceptical views of man. Indeed, the dialogue between Alceste and Philinte which opens the play *could* only take place if both accepted this common premise. It is because Alceste is so personally aware of such a situation that he experiences the overwhelming desire to change it — and it is because he is so outraged by Philinte's apathetic acquiescence in it that he proceeds with renewed determination.[71]

This concordance between the two friends is therefore not in the nature of an arbitrary coincidence, but rather indicates the invariable element in the sceptical vision of the play — as though Alceste and Philinte were permitted a certain choice of attitude situated anywhere outside the area of common agreement. It may be noted here that such identity of view between the so-called *raisonneur* and his counterpart, the *ridicule,* is by no means exceptional in Molière's theatre. In an earlier comedy, *L'Ecole des Maris* (1661), a more banal debate on the excesses of fashion between Ariste and his brother Sganarelle reveals a similar ambiguity — both agreeing in opinion and differing in attitude.[72] In both these plays, it is as though Molière were proclaiming that his traditional comic character (Sganarelle, Alceste, etc.) is fundamentally correct in his theory of society and of man (thus detaching himself from the corpus of *honnête* opinion which condemns social eccentricity) while simultaneously proclaiming that this character is wrong in the ridiculous extent to which he carries his theory (thus detaching himself from the comic character by seeing him through the eyes of his *honnête* audience). Because of this 'double vision' which he enjoys throughout the play, Molière can at all times sympathize with the essential grievances of his *ridicule* whilst viewing him continually in an objective light. There is one character in *Le Misanthrope* who shares to a remarkable degree this paradoxical position with Molière throughout, and that is Philinte. (It may be objected that Eliante shares the same vision as Philinte. It is true that she does echo his opinion of Alceste when she describes the misanthrope as *singulier* but nonetheless sincere and admirable (ll. 1163-8). Yet I think that she is altogether too episodic a character — she speaks not more than seventy lines in all — to be said to be in possession of an overall vision of the play.)

On the other hand, Philinte continually shares with Molière a double vision of Alceste, although the dramatist automatically enjoys the superior detachment of the creator from his character which renders total identification with Philinte impossible. Nevertheless Philinte shares the vision of the comic dramatist to the extent of being able to detach himself from Alceste and to put his extreme behaviour into the perspective of a comedy:

> Je ris des noirs accès où je vous envisage,
> Et crois voir en nous deux, sous mêmes soins nourris,
> Ces deux frères que peint *L'Ecole des Maris* (ll. 98-100)

Philinte repeatedly returns to the comic aspect of Alceste's behaviour:

> Je vous dirai tout franc que cette maladie,
> Partout où vous allez, donne la comédie (ll. 105-6)

> On se riroit de vous, Alceste, tout de bon,
> Si l'on vous entendoit parler de la façon. (ll. 203-4)

But Philinte does more than share an essential part of the author's comic vision; he also shares the philosophic basis for this vision, namely scepticism. The scepticism of Philinte may be seen from an elucidation of his concept of reason. It is a common-place among Molière scholars that his most famous *raisonneur* shares with his creator the view that men ought to be guided in their affairs by reason, the practice of which enables Philinte to avoid the unreasonable conduct of Alceste.[73] Such a view of Philinte is certainly encouraged by Alceste when he says to him in the first scene of the play:

> Mais ce flegme, Monsieur, qui raisonne si bien,
> Ce flegme pourra-t-il ne s'échauffer de rien? (ll. 167-8)

> . . . Morbleu! je ne veux point parler,
> Tant ce raisonnement est plein d'impertinence. (ll. 180-1)

He comes back to this theme in the final Act in his objurgations to Philinte:

> Non: vous avez beau faire et beau me raisonner . . .
> En beaux raisonnements vous abondez toujours; (ll. 1483, 1571)

Nevertheless, it is clear on examination of Philinte's role that he most certainly cannot be said to argue in the name of reason. When Alceste castigates him in Act I, Sc. 1 for bestowing profuse greetings on a stranger, he does not attempt to reason with him, nor does he try to rationalize his action. He merely contents himself with an answer couched in axiomatic terms of social expediency (see ll. 37-40, 65-6, 73-80). His replies to his irascible friend are much less a considered and reasoned examination of Alceste's indictment against society than a mechanical attitude, fabricated in advance, rather in the nature of an instrument kept in readiness for appropriate application. Hence the preponderance of such irrational formulae as 'Il faut bien' (l. 38, l. 65), 'Il est bon de' (l.76), 'Encore en est-il bien...' (l. 117), in his speeches. The detached attitude typified by such phrases is only possible because he refuses steadfastly to do what Alceste insists on doing, that is, to question the intrinsic merit of social usage by demanding that there be a rational connexion between a person's worth and the social distinction which he enjoys. Like his predecessors Ariste and Chrysalde of *L'Ecole des Maris* and *L'Ecole des Femmes* respectively, his detachment with regard to the events he witnesses in society can only be maintained as long as he recognizes the futility of applying a rational criterion to the subject in question; but unlike them, he is prepared to extend this detachment beyond the limited areas of fashion and marriage, making it the foundation of his moral outlook on humanity:

A force de sagesse, on peut être blâmable;
La parfaite raison fuit toute extrémité,
Et veut que l'on soit sage avec sobriété. (ll. 150-2)[74]

These gnomic lines, which have traditionally been taken as containing the quintessence of Molière's philosophy of reason, merely conceal Philinte's *opposition* to Alceste's determined attempts to follow reason at all costs. He characterizes Alceste's intention to follow the dictates of his reason as 'une folie à nulle autre seconde' (l. 157). Such paradoxical treatment of reason is fully in line with the moderation of Cléante in *Tartuffe* (who controls his reason by recognizing that it cannot go beyond the world of appearances), and with the burlesque *folle sagesse* of Sganarelle in *Dom Juan*. But in those plays, such 'wisdom', although providing an appropriate commentary on the comic character's actions, was not set at the dramatic heart of the action. In the case of Cléante, such advice was given from the periphery of the play, and in that of Sganarelle it was reduced to the level of a valet's buffoonery in front of his master. For the first time in Molière's theatre this 'wisdom' spoken by Philinte to the theorist of reason forms the explicit theme of the play, enunciated at the beginning and illustrated throughout in the contrasting actions of the two protagonists. The famous words which Philinte speaks to Alceste are not to be seen merely as a shrewd comment on the action of the play — they both lead to the action and illustrate it, as Alceste sets the course of his conduct in a direction diametrically opposed to that which his friend has advised him to take. It is because Philinte thinks that it is *foolish* to tell the truth about themselves to such *salon* figures as the aging Emilie or the boastful Dorilas that Alceste deems it *wise* to do so (ll. 81-8). In fact, it is because of Philinte's worldly foolishness that Alceste is the more determined to be wise in his misanthropy in the final Act (Sc. 1) by withdrawing from society.

Philinte's paradoxical view that the application of reason to life is tantamount to foolishness must, in a general conclusive sense, be that of Molière the dramatist, who, like his *raisonneur*, was able to put Alceste's struggle against the unreason of life into the perspective of a play. Philinte's standpoint is the only one in the play from which Alceste is viewed as being *right* and *comic* at the same time. And this paradoxical view of Alceste rests upon the basic conviction that folly and reason are one and the same thing. A consideration of the philosophy from which his notion of reason originates will therefore shed some light upon the comic vision of Molière's play.

If some of Alceste's opinions concerning men tended towards scepticism, those of Philinte are completely sceptical in inspiration. His view of human reason, which is so central to his opinion of man, is scepticism in its purest form. One need only compare La Mothe Le Vayer's attitude to it with that of Philinte to confirm this. Le Vayer gives the most extensive treatment to the principal theme of his scepticism, *folie,* in his *Petit Traité Sceptique sur cette Commune Façon de parler N'Avoir Pas le Sens Commun* (1646)[75] Following Erasmus' *Encomium Moriae* (1511), to which he explicitly acknowledges his debt, his *Petit Traité* is written in the first instance against the philosophy of the Stoics, whose wise man claims to lead a life perfectly controlled by wisdom and therefore free of the limitations attending common humanity.[76] Philinte, at the outset of the play, seems also to be thinking of those people who make such grandiose pretensions to wisdom, when he condemns

Cette grande roideur des vertus des vieux âges...
[qui] veut aux mortels trop de perfection (ll. 153, 155)

Molière's play is only possible because of Alceste's dogmatic claim that he alone sees life steadily and sees it whole. That he claims a monopoly of good sense and reason is seen from his unequivocal condemnation of everything that does not please him. Le Vayer shares Molière's detachment from those, like Alceste, who display such boundless confidence in their own opinion and reason, and to illustrate their folly he sets out to examine a proverb 'N'avoir pas le Sens Commun'. This axiom is normally used, he writes, whenever we judge that the opinions of others have offended against our own conception of what is reasonable in speech, custom and behaviour. We therefore come to the natural conclusion that something which has appeared unreasonable to us must in fact be unreasonable, because each of us believes in the inherent superiority of his own judgement. Opinions which are in reality no more than subjective thus acquire in our own eyes a kind of certainty which predisposes us to express them dogmatically, as though no other conflicting opinions could possibly be tenable. Le Vayer, in a passage which may be seen as an appropriate commentary on Alceste's rigid *sagesse*, cannot but admire the temerity of the human mind which effects so uncritically the transition from subjective judgement to entrenched dogmatism, as he describes

... l'arrogance et la témérité de l'esprit humain, lorsqu'elles lui font condamner pour être irrégulier, tout ce qui lui est nouveau, comme s'il pouvait être la règle de toutes choses...comme si la Nature n'avait point d'autre étendue que sa connaissance; et qui sont cause qu'il croit qu'on n'a pas le Sens Commun, aussitôt qu'on s'écarte de sa façon de concevoir, comme si sa sphère d'activité n'avait point d'autres limites que celles du globe intellectuel, et qu'il eût tenu registre de toutes les opinions humaines, dont il ne sait pas la millième partie. Car s'il ne possède qu'à grande peine quelque légère connaissance de la façon dont raisonnent les hommes de notre Europe...que sera-ce quand on lui fera voir, qu'il reste plus de Terres à découvrir...a-t-il supputé les pensées de tant de Peuples et de Cosmopolites, comme il le faudrait avoir fait, pour déterminer quel est le Sens Commun?[77]

The Sceptic's method of proving the absurdity of such an absolute claim consists in accumulating evidence to show its relative nature: he has recourse to his beloved sceptical tropes, which illustrate, in devastating fashion, the contingency of customs, laws and knowledge, which all vary incessantly from country to country, generation to generation, and person to person.[78] For Le Vayer, the most convincing argument for such contingency lies in the infinite variety of ways in which the human mind reacts to the same phenomena. The relativity of our opinions and sense impressions may be seen most clearly in the differences of humour and mood which characterize man's behaviour:

Car comme il y a des hommes qui sont tellement dans l'usage de la raison, qu'ils ne se laissent presque jamais transporter de colère pour quoi que ce soit, l'on en voit d'autres qui s'offensent de rien, et que la fougue prend sur les moindres sujets qui se présentent...et il se trouve des esprits si délicats, qu'ils se troublent et s'irritent pour des choses dont d'autres qu'eux ne feraient que rire...[79]

Molière, in terms similar to those used by the Sceptic, acquires the same detached outlook on the claims of reason and dogmatism by making different reactions to life into the dramatic opposition of the equitable and imperturbable Philinte, and the irascible Alceste. In the opening scene he shows that since the diverse nature of life may account for two totally different attitudes to the same experiences, no one interpretation of reality may claim to be entirely reasonable or sensible. If reason admits of no fixed interpretation, it is because it is as diverse a concept as men themselves. Alceste's reason, on the other hand, leads him to trust in 'La raison, mon bon droit, l'équité' (l. 187), absolute moral categories which stand in irrevocable opposition to injustice and falsehood. Le Vayer, having invoked such an absolute distinction between truth and falsehood, finds it easy to contradict it with a paradox which is also at the centre of Philinte's thought, when he approves the argument of the philosopher Chrysippus, namely that

> ...le vice n'était aucunement vice selon sa Nature, et qu'il ne pouvait pas être dit du tout inutile à l'égard de l'Univers, vu qu'autrement le bien ne s'y rencontrerait pas. Cela se prend de la raison des contraires, qui ne sauraient subsister l'un sans l'autre...comme les excréments et les mauvaises humeurs ne servent pas moins à l'entretien du corps humain que les bonnes, on voit aussi que les hommes vicieux ne laissent pas de servir au public, et que le mal particulier qu'ils font, se tourne en bien dans l'ordre général du monde...[80]

When Alceste's absolute moral categories have been thrown into confusion by the loss of his lawsuit, Philinte has recourse to substantially the same argument as that employed by Le Vayer, as he attempts to point out to his friend that there is still a blind order operative in the apparent moral chaos of life, invariably extracting virtue from deceit:

> Tous ces défauts humains nous donnent dans la vie
> Des moyens d'exercer notre philosophie:
> C'est le plus bel emploi que trouve la vertu;
> Et si de probité tout étoit revêtu,
> Si tous les coeurs étoient francs, justes et dociles,
> La plupart des vertus nous seroient inutiles, (Act V, Sc. 1, ll. 1561-6).

Alceste instinctively rejects this argument as being yet another of Philinte's 'beaux raisonnements' (l. 1571). In his mind, reason cannot countenance such an illogicality, and admits of only one solution: 'La raison, pour mon bien, veut que je me retire' (l. 1573). His unequivocal attitude to the advice of the sceptical Philinte follows that of the Stoics who assert that there is no intermediate state between good and evil. His indignation at all those who refuse to make such a mathematical division between *vice* and *vertu* is the logical outcome of this Stoic notion:

> ...ce me sont de mortelles blessures,
> De voir qu'avec le vice on garde des mesures. (Act I, Sc. 1, ll. 141-2)

he has already told Philinte. If he judges his friend as harshly as the 'franc scélérat' who has calumniated him, it is because he accepts fully the logical conclusion which follows from this moral premise of the Stoics, that there cannot be any degree in falsehood, just as there cannot be any degree in virtue. All faults are equally heinous in nature, and he who is guilty of one is necessarily guilty of all.[81] This belief accounts for his extreme condemnation of Philinte's mild social flattery, a crime for which the only retribution is hanging (ll. 14-28). One is either completely sincere in word, thought and deed, or else an odious hypocrite. The same categorical attitude makes Alceste adopt an intransigent position with regard to his lawsuit: 'J'ai tort, ou j'ai raison' (l. 192), he tells Philinte. In Act V the latter says that the unfavourable decision of the judges can be reversed, by reopening the case. But even if this were so, it would still be unacceptable to Alceste, since even the momentary tarnishing of his perfect 'bon droit' would be sufficient proof to him of the proximity of *vice* and *vertu* which reduces justice (i.e. reason according to Alceste), to that irrational moral disorder which characterizes everyday life. And the morally absolute (the rational) cannot temporize with the morally relative (the irrational).

The scepticism of Philinte, by its fatalistic acceptance of the disordered sequence of events which make up life, at once refuses to impose its own rigid pattern on life and implicitly rejects the possibility of a discernible pattern which a controlling providence imposes. If there is any constant element in human experience, it can only be inherent in the paradoxical scheme of things, operating through the irrational interaction of *vice* and *vertu*. In spite of Philinte's more optimistic tone in comparison to Alceste at the end of the play, he does not believe in the maxim that 'all is for the best in the best of all possible worlds.' But by making of the moral disorder of life the impetus towards perseverance in the face of adversity, he does believe that 'all may be made to work for the best in the best of all possible worlds' on one condition: that one recognize the fundamental irrationality of life and use it as a basis for one's personal philosophy.

Alceste of course refuses to do this, and the irrational 'order' of life confounds hopelessly his presumption in seeking to mould it into the pattern of his reason. His defeat represents a final sceptical comment on the value of man's distinctive quality, his speculative faculty, and runs counter to the buoyant humanism epitomized in Hamlet's famous lines: 'What a piece of work is a man! How noble in reason! How infinite in faculty!...in apprehension how like a god!...the paragon of animals!' (Act II, Sc. 2.). In fact, it brings us close to the conclusion of Le Vayer, that perhaps reason is not after all the divine gift which men imagine it to be; if the gods had wished to mock at our earthly struggles, they could not have chosen a better way of doing so than to give us such an overweening sense of confidence in its power. Hence the philosopher's approval of the laughter to which Democritus gave expression each time that he considered '... qu'un animal si faible de corps et d'esprit comme est l'homme, se trouvait néanmoins rempli d'une si sotte vanité.'[82]

Le Vayer now draws together the practical conclusions from this view of man's reason, and they illuminate the sceptical vision of *Le Misanthrope*. In his *Petit Traité* he answers the objection that if every man possessed in the same degree the gift of reason the affairs of the world would be managed more smoothly, by saying 'Cependant, si l'on veut prendre garde un peu plus près, on reconnaîtra bientôt le contraire; et que tant s'en faut, c'est la folie qui fait subsister le monde, lequel apparemment périrait sans son entremise.'[83] To Le Vayer, all the activities of life take place under the aegis of *folie,* which offers to its followers an agreeable illusion under the spell of which they pass their days. It embraces all the occupations and festivities of mankind, and all the pomp and ceremony which go to make up the fiction of social life. It is the *raison d'être* of public functions and imbues magistrates, financiers and courtiers with the illusive conviction that what they are doing is important and that they themselves occupy such positions on account of their intrinsic worth. The condition of *folie,* which is universal in its scope, arises from the discrepancy between the contingent nature of human enterprises and the absolute character with which they are invested by their practitioners. The Sceptic, detached from the spectacle of life, and at the same time engaged in it, is acutely aware of what a modern writer has described as being 'Ce divorce entre l'homme et sa vie, l'acteur et son décor, [qui est] proprement le sentiment de l'absurdité.'[84] But although Le Vayer is fully aware of the folly and absurdity of life which escape the mass of humanity, he will not seek to lift the veil of illusion which conceals the truth from them. On the contrary, he is convinced that *folie* has an indispensable and positive function in society:

> Ainsi, il est aisé de conclure que la folie, considérée de ce côté, est aussi utile au monde que la sagesse y mettrait de confusions irréparables. Si l'on dit que les hommes étant sages, se donneraient aisément d'autres meilleures occupations; on répond, qu'ôtant les guerres, les meurtres, les voluptés de toutes les mauvaises actions que la sagesse ne peut souffrir; la terre n'aurait pas à demi de quoi nourrir le genre humain, à cause de sa trop grande multitude...Mais grâce à Dieu, nous n'avons pas beaucoup à craindre de cet inconvénient. Pendant qu'il y aura de l'humanité dans le monde, la folie n'y manquera pas pour lui fournir d'entretien.[85]

One may thus safely dispense with the impossible suggestions made by the Alcestes of this world, that reason be adopted as the sole criterion of judgement. In any case, says Le Vayer, it is a truth verified by daily experience that although the wise may propose, it is still the foolish who dispose in the end. But his principal reason for not wishing to interfere with the *folie* of the world is to be found in the simple fact that everyone concerned appears to be entirely satisfied with his or her condition as it is at present: 'Le bon est que personne ne se plaint de ce côté-là, et que...chacun se plaît à jouir de sa marotte.'[86] The truth of this statement is abundantly confirmed by the *salon* figures against whom Alceste's *sagesse* is directed. The importunate Dorilas, who boasts eternally about his aristocratic pedigree, the aged crone Emilie, who cuts a ridiculous figure as a *coquette,* the fatuous Clitandre and Acaste, who preen themselves on their intelligence and good appearance, are all blissfully content with the illusory image of themselves which they have come to accept as truth. Hence Philinte's total disapproval of Alceste's determination to shatter such illusions by telling them of the real impression which they give to society, an impression of which society is fully aware but which it agrees to connive at, because all its members participate to some extent in similar illusions. To enter into the game of social life is to understand something of the lesser and individually practised illusions which go to make up the collective illusion, society. For there are as many different kinds of *folie* as there are people willing to act them. People who indulge their own private *marotte* under the guise of a grave exterior, who derive subtle pleasure from their role as public moralisers, all succumb to the spirit of *folie* no less than those whom their reason leads them to despise: 'Il y en a d'(folies) étudiées comme de naturelles; il y en a d'austères, et de sérieuses, comme de gaies et d'enjouées.'[87]

Molière and Le Vayer leave us in no doubt that in the comic hierarchy of *folie* the spectacle of the Alcestes of this world occupies the highest position. If the *petits marquis* and the other *salon* figures are comic because they are supremely unaware of their own *folie,* Alceste is doubly so, because he seeks to reform the unchangeable condition of his fellows with a *folie* all the more irremediable in nature: for although he is fully aware of the *folie* of others (as aware as Philinte), he is totally unaware of the mask of *sagesse* which is merely one of the many forms which protean-like *folie* may assume. Le Vayer expresses this 'paradox of paradoxes' in the most memorable and epigrammatic passage of his *traité:*

En effet, comme le premier degré de folie est de s'estimer sage, le second est de faire profession de sagesse, et le troisième de vouloir en conséquence réformer le Monde, et guérir la folie des autres. La raison de cela se prend de ce que...la folie est une maladie dont on ne guérit jamais...Ainsi la témérité de ceux, qui osent entreprendre de rendre sages leurs voisins en dépit qu'ils en aient, a fait dire aux Italiens, que pour guérir un fou, il en fallait un et demi...Il semble donc bien à propos de laisser le monde comme il est, et un chacun dans la libre profession de sa marotte, que souvent il ne changerait pas pour un Sceptre.[88]

We recall that Philinte also considers the reforming zeal of Alceste as the epitome of *folie* when he tells him that

...c'est une folie à nulle autre seconde
De vouloir se mêler de corriger le monde. (ll. 157-8)

(6)

Although Philinte is the spectator of mankind's folly and imperfection, he does not forget that he himself partakes of that folly and imperfection. The misanthropic perfectionism of Alceste cuts him off from his fellows: the scepticism of Philinte resembles that of Le Vayer, in that it avoids what the latter considers as the arch-enemy of scepticism, 'cette haine du genre humain qu'on nomme Misanthropie'.[89] It enables him to view the flaws of others as 'vices unis à l'humaine nature' (l. 174). Philinte may differ from his contemporaries in degree, but not in kind. His *morale* is therefore a profoundly humanist one in practice, since it seeks to display comprehension and indulgence towards others, characteristics which imply a dimension of self-knowledge lacking in Alceste, to whom he says

Mon Dieu, des moeurs du temps mettons-nous moins en peine,
Et faisons un peu grâce à la nature humaine;
Ne l'examinons point dans la grande rigueur,
Et voyons ses défauts avec quelque douceur. (ll. 145-8)[90]

Le Vayer lays particular stress on the connexion between self-knowledge and one's attitude to others: only those people who have observed their own failings without connivance exemplify that lenience towards the weakness of their fellows which is to him, as to Philinte, of the highest importance in one's dealings with others.[91] This practical wisdom of scepticism is firmly rooted in a knowledge of man's limitations, which renders any idea of perfectibility superfluous. It is not explicitly hostile to a Christian view of man, but the observation of Sainte-Beuve on the *morale* of one of Molière's contemporaries is entirely apposite here. The *morale* of La Rochefoucauld, he wrote, in no way contradicts the Christian religion: it dispenses with it.[92] Philinte does not experience the need to improve any of humanity's inherent imperfections, but feels content to live within the existing moral framework in which he found, and finds, himself. He is alien to the Christian idea of man as a creature who ultimately needs moral and spiritual assistance from a source outside himself and his fellows. His *morale* derives rather from the antique humanism rediscovered in the Renaissance, of which the Socratic precept, Know Thyself, forms the cornerstone.

But Philinte's code of self-knowledge is not merely elaborated as a self-sufficient end. Since no higher life can be sought for man than that which develops in his present social context, his wisdom is first and foremost a socially orientated ethic, far removed from the 'dehumanized' and abstract *sagesse* which recent commentators have made it out to be.[93] In the first scene, he underlines the importance of bringing one's conduct into line with the manners of *honnête* society: 'Il faut, parmi le monde, une vertu traitable' (l. 149). Society demands that one should prove *disponible* in one's approach to *honnête* company. Any form of mental rigidity, displayed in clinging obstinately to attitudes and beliefs not in vogue, is seen by this society as ridiculous and therefore must be eschewed. The practice of *honnêteté*, which one of its leading exponents in the seventeenth century, the Chevalier de Méré, describes as being 'la quintessence de toutes les vertus', demands what the same writer terms 'une disposition à la souplesse' in the conduct and converse of the *honnête homme*. Similarly Faret, in *L'Honneste Homme,* had already emphasized the importance of flexibility on the part of the *honnête homme:* '...[il] saura prendre son temps, presser et différer à propos, se ployer et s'accommoder aux occasions...il saura feindre, il saura déguiser, et lorsqu'un expédient viendra à lui manquer, il se trouvera toujours d'un esprit assez tranquille et assez ouvert pour en inventer mille autres capables de terminer ce qu'il poursuit.'[94]

When Philinte urges Alceste to be tractable in his attitude in society, he echoes the advice of another of Molière's *raisonneurs* — Cléante of *Tartuffe.* Both illustrate the extent to which the individual must be willing to let society mould even his deepest convictions. Philinte exemplifies, in the purely secular order, that compliance in outlook which must also guide one's attitude in religion. Cléante's recommendation to Orgon that he follow '(une) dévotion...traitable' (l. 390) asserts, as much as does Philinte's ideal of a 'vertu traitable', the primacy of secular ideals (*honnêteté*) over any systematized form of idealism, whether it be personal or religious in inspiration.[95] It is paradoxical but true to say that the *honnête homme* may only be born at the expense of his own individual nature: of all the theoreticians of *honnêteté* Méré in particular stresses repeatedly that true *honnêteté* is 'un art consommé', and may only be acquired after long practice and study. And Faret makes precisely the same point in the opening pages of his treatise, when he recommends his readers 'd'user partout d'une certaine négligence qui cache l'artifice, (qui) témoigne que l'on ne fait rien que comme sans y penser, et sans aucune sorte de peine.'[96]

If Philinte may be regarded as the epitome of an *honnête homme* (and contemporaries such as Donneau de Visé were not slow to recognize this), it is on account of his indifferent sceptical nature which enables him effortlessly to sacrifice his individual opinions and tastes to the social ideal. As La Rochefoucauld shows, individual *amour-propre* is the natural motivation which may set the individual at odds with *honnête* society: according to him 'c'est ce qui trouble et ce qui détruit la société.'[97] And Le Vayer gives an example, particularly appropriate in the case of Alceste, of the way in which such *amour-propre* may disrupt the social harmony: 'Nous devenons presque insociables et incapables de conversation par cet amour-propre qui maîtrise presque tous les Dogmatiques.'[98] Excessive faith in one's own reason is linked in Le Vayer's mind with a failure to control one's *amour-propre* which can only result in the negation of polite conversation. The role of Alceste amply illustrates the truth of this statement, as his tirades against society are rendered almost inarticulate by his refusal and inability to detach himself from his personal point of view. Hence the preponderance of explosive exclamations such as 'Morbleu', 'Parbleu', 'Têtebleu', which offer his temperament the only satisfactory means of self-expression.

If Philinte is freed from the socially harmful effects of *amour-propre,* he cannot of course be entirely free from its influence, as it forms an ineradicable part of human nature. He can only follow the advice of La Rochefoucauld, that one recognize the omnipotence of *amour-propre* in one's actions, and then make discreet and enlightened use of it by harnessing it to one's own and to society's ends.[99] This is precisely what Philinte does, as he tries to create for himself that quietude of mind to which his indifferent nature aspires, and he pursues this ideal no less ardently than Alceste pursues his.

There are two points in the play which illustrate the way in which the sceptical Philinte makes his own satisfaction coincide with that of *honnête* society. They also shed light on the vexed question of the motivation for his actions. The first is in the scene of Oronte's sonnet. As Oronte reads each verse of his poem to the truculent Alceste and the indifferent Philinte, the latter intervenes with laudatory comments:

Je suis déjà charmé de ce petit morceau...
Ah! qu'en termes galants ces choses-là sont mises!...
La chute en est jolie, amoureuse, admirable. (ll. 319, 325, 333)

When Oronte replies that 'Vous me flattez, et vous croyez peut-être...' (l. 337) Philinte comments unequivocally 'Non, je ne flatte point' (l. 338). Yet in the following scene he explains his action in praising the sonnet to the exasperated Alceste: 'Et j'ai bien vu qu'Oronte, afin d'être flatté...' (l. 441). It is obvious that, even if he does not share Alceste's drastic view of the sonnet, Philinte has spoken less than the thought in his mind to Oronte. What is however less clear to the spectator or reader is the reason for his polite insincerity. For G. Michaut, Philinte intervenes not principally from a desire to flatter Oronte, but because he sees that Alceste is inevitably going to offend him and wishes to forestall and possibly avert his indignation.[100] E. Faguet, on the other hand, sees Philinte as an *agent provocateur* who praises the sonnet only in order to provoke Alceste.[101] Neither of these interpretations of his motives in this scene seems to me to be satisfactory. If he wishes to stem the tide of Alceste's anger, as Michaut suggested, he has recourse to the singularly inept tactic of showering upon Oronte precisely the kind of fashionable compliments which he knows are bound to infuriate Alceste beyond all measure. Yet he does not seem to try to provoke Alceste deliberately here; having involuntarily incurred his wrath in the opening scene, he was then manifestly at pains to placate his irascible friend. His principal argument against Alceste then was that his unfashionable honesty will only serve to make him look ridiculous in the eyes of society. Philinte's chief preoccupation in the sonnet scene is neither with Alceste nor with Oronte — it is with fulfilling the appropriate code of *bienséances* which will help to maintain both the harmony of society and his own *repos*.[102] He knows not only that no absolute principle is at stake in one's disapproval or approval of such a trifle, but more importantly that by his approval he will maintain Oronte's fond opinion of himself as a poet, his favourable opinion of Philinte, and the social harmony which his own *flegme* desires. If Philinte has preserved his standing as an *honnête homme* in Oronte's eyes, there is nevertheless one important difference between their positions. Philinte is acutely aware of the role which his *flegme* and society lead him to play in this scene and throughout the play; he is the superior and ironic spectator of Oronte who is allowed to play out blissfully his role of a poet thus enjoying what Le Vayer terms 'la libre profession de sa marotte'.

It is chiefly Philinte's very human sense of refined pleasure in being simultaneously detached from and a part of the comedy of social life which saves him from the extremes of generous disinterestedness and abstract inhumanity. It is because he enjoys his role of sceptical observer that he can submit with equanimity to customs which might displease him personally. In one of his letters, Le Vayer writes that although there is nothing so patently unreasonable in society as the extravagant misuse of compliments, yet 'il faut...se rire de mille choses pareilles, qu'on y trouve autorisées par la coutume.'[103] Even whenever there is no good reason for bestowing profuse compliments, one must do so because it is the social custom, and because you, as dispenser, will have a share in the euphoria which they engender. Le Vayer echoes Faret here, for the latter had written some years earlier that '...les louanges que l'on donne à autrui ont encore cet avantage, qu'elles nous acquièrent les acclamations et les louanges de ceux que les nôtres ont obligés. Obligeons donc autant de personnes que nous pourrons par de bonnes paroles...' Dubosc, having regretfully stated that he is living in a century of flattery, has no other solution to offer than that of Le Vayer and Faret: one must try not to lie, but one must often embellish: without complaisance, society would be unpleasant to live in.[104]

The second point in the play which illustrates the way in which the

sceptical Philinte accommodates himself to *honnête* company is
provided by the scene in which Célimène receives her suitors in her
salon (Act II, Sc. 4). Throughout the entire scene, Philinte is
conspicuous by his detachment and silence, only intervening at two
stages of the conversation in order to make banal remarks. His longest
speech is one of four lines, addressed to Alceste. Throughout, he
observes what Le Vayer recommends as the most prudent attitude in
company — 'un silence approchant du Pythagorique'.[105] Philinte's
silence here is of course directed towards the same end as that envisaged
by his praise of Oronte's sonnet — that is, the maintenance of his own
tranquillity and the outward harmony of the social group. But there are
nevertheless several points in this scene where his behaviour has given
rise to ambiguity as to his precise motivation. During Célimène's series
of satirical *portraits* of *salon habitués*, he intervenes with an apparently
innocuous question concerning one of Cléon's relatives:

> On fait assez de cas de son oncle Damis;
> Qu'en dites-vous, Madame? (ll. 631-2)

When Célimène replies that 'Il est de mes amis' Philinte immediately
answers 'Je le trouve honnête homme, et d'un air assez sage' (ll. 632-3).
By such diplomacy he will not risk contradiction by an adverse or
favourable opinion on Damis given by Célimène. Is Philinte once more
attempting to spare Alceste further cause for embarrassment as has
sometimes been thought?[106] If this be so, it is difficult to understand
why such a penetrating observer of the *salon* types as Philinte
undoubtedly is should fail to see that the mention of a well-known
figure such as Damis will merely serve to encourage the censorious
Célimène and not silence her. And in fact she promptly adds a *portrait*
of Damis to her list! By delaying his opinion of Damis until he has heard
Célimène's reaction, he reveals his adroit *disponibilité,* which enables
him to accommodate his opinions effortlessly to those of the company.
He belongs to those people whom Le Vayer describes as being '...des
personnes si clairvoyantes, qu'elles ne manquent guère à s'avantager
de tous les moments favorables qui se présentent. L'excellence de leur
esprit se manifeste à prendre parti sur le champ, et à tourner
adroitement la voile selon le changement des vents.'[107]

His next intervention comes in response to Alceste's denunciation of
the group's delectation in insidious criticism of its own members.
Although they have unanimously joined in the game of satirical
portraits, says Alceste, they will still continue to greet the subjects of
their satire as effusively as ever (ll. 651-6). Philinte's intervention is in
the form of a question to Alceste:

> Mais pourquoi pour ces gens un intérêt si grand,
> Vous qui condamneriez ce qu'en eux on reprend? (ll. 667-8)

Philinte neither justifies the social hypocrisy of the group's criticism,
nor criticizes Alceste's principle that one ought not to gossip about

one's 'friends'. But he does draw attention to the explicit contradiction between Alceste's own condemnation of such people, and his disapproval of criticism of them as expressed by the group. Since he is at pains to point this out to Alceste, he aligns himself automatically with the group against his friend. Does he not lay himself open to the charge of having deserted his friend in public?[108] Such a view of Philinte is surely only defensible if Alceste's behaviour in this scene is not open to the criticism which the former brings against him; and Alceste, as it was pointed out above, is at no time during the play exempt from contradiction between his ideal and the way in which he illustrates it in practice. Philinte is perfectly justified in his criticism of such practice here, when he asks Alceste why he is so interested in defending the *salon* figures whom the group has satirized, when he himself continually criticizes them. It may be objected that Alceste's criticism of them does not spring from the same sources of interest and hypocrisy as does that of the group. But to believe this is to believe what Alceste *wishes* us to believe, that the motivation for his censure of society is beyond all reproach. And that is to be deceived by the most persuasive of all Molière's comic heroes. In fact, his censure of society springs from his vanity, self-interest, and an extremely vulnerable ego. By refusing implicitly to differentiate between Alceste's censoriousness and that of the group, Philinte performs the invaluable function of exploding the self-created myth of Alceste's moral superiority, and allows us to glimpse the common human motivation which he shares with those whom he affects to despise.

There is another and perhaps less apparent reason for Philinte's intervention on the side of the group against Alceste, one which is not directly concerned with his own opinion of his friend, but which undoubtedly influences his reaction to Alceste's interruptions. As an *honnête homme,* he is supremely aware of the fact that what one says and does in society must bear the imprint of *bienséance.* Whilst Alceste may well be correct in theory in reproving the pernicious habit of satirizing one's 'friends', he is scarcely advancing the cause of sincerity or of polite conversation by choosing such an inopportune time for his moralizing. If such advice is going to bear fruit, it must be given at a more seasonable time. Otherwise, Alceste will only incur the ridicule of the *honnête* company, as Philinte had predicted in the opening scene. Le Vayer too is just as conscious as Philinte of the humiliating way in which well-intentioned but indiscreet moralisers such as Alceste will be received by society, and of the inevitable failure which attends their efforts:

...jamais ils ne s'acquiteront bien de leur charge, s'ils ne l'exercent en temps et lieu, lorsqu'ils trouvent de la disposition en ceux, qu'ils veulent reprendre, à bien recevoir les corrections qui leur doivent apparemment être utiles...Il n'y a rien aussi d'odieux à l'égal de ces personnes, qui font profession de censurer tout le monde, et qui recherchent avec importunité les occasions . . . et de semblables affectations sont toujours mal reçues, et l'usage trop fréquent de cette manière de mortification . . . les rend infructueuses, comme nous expérimentons, qe les meilleurs remèdes ne servent de rien, quand on les réitère trop souvent.[109]

In *Du Temps et de l'Occasion* he says that time may alter radically even the most sensible statements: put the most cogent truth into the mouth of someone who expresses it in the wrong context, and it will immediately become ridiculous.[110] As Célimène will point out caustically to the prude Arsinoé, it is better to vouchsafe the responsibility for the moral reprehension of others 'A ceux à qui le Ciel en a commis le soin' (l. 956).

A further difficulty in Philinte's role concerns his motives towards Alceste with regard to their mutual friend, Eliante. Philinte, at the beginning of the play, tells Alceste that she would appear to be a much more suitable partner for him than Célimène, and he goes on to say that if he were to choose a wife, she would be his choice (ll. 243-4). In Act IV Sc. 1 Eliante tells Philinte that if Alceste were not Célimène's suitor, and offered her his hand, she would consent to marry him (ll. 1191-1202); Philinte replies that he would not oppose her intention, but if she were not able to marry Alceste, he himself would be glad to become her suitor (ll. 1203-12). In the following scene, Alceste, in order to avenge himself on Célimène for her 'infidelity' towards him, offers his hand to Eliante. In the final scene of the play, he declares to her that he is unable to marry her, since he intends to go off alone to his *désert*. It is at this point that she turns to Philinte, and offers him her hand in marriage.

Michaut and Jasinski see in Philinte's attitude towards Eliante the ultimate proof of his altruism. It is true that he does advise Alceste to choose Eliante instead of Célimène; and it is also true that he waits until Alceste makes his final choice not to marry Eliante before doing anything to promote his own interests. If it is true, as Jasinski asserts, that '[Philinte] est passionnément épris d'Eliante', then we may have no hesitation in agreeing with Michaut that there is a rare quality of self-abnegation in his action.[111] But can one really maintain that Philinte is passionately in love with Eliante? Such an interpretation of an aspect of his role is fundamentally at variance with the psychological and physiological elements of his character. It is surely no accident that Molière should have put such stress on his phlegmatic humour, which provides the great dramatic contrast with Alceste's choleric temperament. And it would be pointless to do this if his actions were not intended to symbolize this basic characteristic. His indifference towards love shows itself in his detachment from Alceste's passion in the opening scene, where he wishes to point out the ironic discrepancy between Alceste's theory that reason ought to be applied universally, and the singularly illogical choice which he has made in not choosing Eliante. He brings the same detached outlook to bear on his own relationship with Eliante. All his professions of interest in her are couched in remarkably dispassionate terms:

Pour moi, si je n'avois qu'à former des désirs,
La cousine Éliante auroit tous mes soupirs. (ll. 243-4)

In Act IV Sc. 1 he is sufficiently free from passion to see that his love for Eliante depends on contingencies outside his control. In fact he formulates his proposal of marriage in undogmatic, almost negative terms (ll. 1203-12). The practice of such indifference even in love is an essential part of Philinte's principal concern — that of protecting his ego and his *amour-propre*. Indeed, one may say that it is a mechanism which has become a second nature, and which shields him from the vagaries of capricious Fortune. He knows that whenever one formulates a rash design or ambition, Fortune invariably intervenes to thwart one's purpose. He is therefore content to practise his detached fatalism, hoping discreetly that Eliante will be enabled by circumstances to marry him, but prepared to resign himself without recrimination or regrets to her possible marriage with Alceste. This seems to me to account for the fact that he can wait until Alceste has made his final decision about marriage before consenting to marry Eliante. Such an attitude is certainly in line with the fatalism and firm control over their will which his predecessors, Ariste and Chrysalde, display in the *Ecoles*. It is also in harmony with the advice given by La Mothe Le Vayer in his *Dialogue sur le Mariage* (1631), as he makes Eleus say: 'qu'il était à peu près du mariage comme des autres conditions de la vie, qui nous réussissent faciles, ou importunent, selon que la fortune, ou notre adresse et bonne conduite nous permet d'en bien ou mal user...'[112] Whichever marital fate is reserved for Philinte by the gods, we may be sure that he will meet all contingencies with the same sceptically attuned attitude which underlies his actions in the play.

(7)

Finally one must ask the question: how is Philinte's attitude towards life and society to be evaluated within the moral framework of the play? What position does he occupy in *Le Misanthrope's* scale of moral values? Alceste's answer to such questions is that Philinte is nothing less than a base hypocrite, who practises the deceptions which form the basis of society. But Alceste's judgement of him as a hypocrite is over-simplified in the extreme, and ignores completely the moral dilemma with which the play confronts us. This dilemma is the following one: is it in fact possible to be sincere in a world where absolute sincerity and truthfulness do not and cannot exist? They cannot exist because each character's interpretation of them is motivated by his *amour-propre* and formulated in terms of his own self-interest. Absolute sincerity and honesty must, by their very definition, strip away all pretence and illusion from the object upon which they are brought to bear; in *Le Misanthrope,* a definition of sincerity and honesty is only acceptable if it is based upon illusion. Even Alceste, the man who claims to strip away pretence and vanity which hide the truth from men, fails to uncover and to deal with the monstrous egoism which underlies his 'mission'. Célimène, on the other hand, does not seek to destroy the illusions with which her suitors nourish their *amour-propre.* Her social role as a *coquette* is based upon her ability to flatter the self-interest of each of her suitors in turn, whilst enjoying the adulation which they give her. Yet with all her knowledge of society, she too is blinded by her own *amour-propre* into accepting as quasi-permanent a precariously balanced situation which rests on the continuing illusions of her suitors. For although *amour-propre* gratefully accepts the illusion that it is an object of love, it can confound all logic and calculation by demanding that its illusions be based upon solid reality. Arsinoé, as Célimène clearly demonstrates, is acting out the part of a virtuous and truthful friend and adviser; in reality she is a vindictive spinster, who schemes to deprive Célimène of Alceste's attentions. In the cases of Acaste, Clitandre and Oronte, the self-delusion and reality are one, as they are fully convinced that their self-adulation and pride are founded upon reality. Only once is their illusion threatened, when Célimène is seen to dispense to others the same banal favours which she accords to them. But such is the persistence of their invincible illusion that their reversal is immediately forgotten in their indignation that such merit could be treated in this fashion.

It is against this background that Philinte and Éliante must be viewed in their dual roles of actors and spectators of the social comedy. Their roles are created by their need to maintain their *tranquillité* by protecting their ego from possible injury. Nevertheless, they do practise an enlightened self-interest, which leads them consciously to contribute to the surrounding social euphoria. Philinte in particular does not dissociate private and public aims — the need to maintain his own *tranquillité* is intimately bound up with maintaining the harmony of society. Although he is supremely aware of the necessity for cultivating what the Chevalier de Méré terms 'ce talent d'être bon acteur', he does not seek unduly to exploit his superior knowledge (as, for example, does Célimène).[113] Since the role and the mask symbolize *honnête* society and ultimately the human condition, it is not paradoxical to say that Philinte is the most honest and the most lucid of all the characters in the play, because he recognizes the necessity of playing a role, and because he uses this knowledge to fulfil himself within the existing social conventions.

When we view the character of Philinte in a wider perspective than that of the play, it does not behove us to condemn him, for he is surely one of the two souls which inhabit us all. In *Le Misanthrope* Molière does no less than dramatize the duality of the absolute and the relative, the ideal and the realistic, which confronts everyone. We all share, to some extent, the idealist vision of an Alceste, and we are all constantly forced to accommodate our idealism to more mundane reality. If it is true, as Gilbert Norwood asserts, that 'tragedy is found not only in the death of the body but in the death of ideals', then it is just as true to say that most of us have at least understood that the course of the world runs counter to such idealism.[114] At the end of *Le Misanthrope,* an alternative outlook on life to that of Alceste is suggested, one which is at once more mature and more profound than his superficial idealism. This is, of course, the outlook which finds dramatic expression in Philinte's role, which takes fully into account the inevitable failure of absolute idealism when applied to the stuff of human nature, and regrets that this should be so, but which finds no merit in vain recrimination against humanity or in withdrawal from it. The reality which is conducive to 'the death of ideals' remains and cannot be altered or explained away, but this by no means signifies that tears cannot be changed to laughter. 'A change of lighting suffices to make one into the other.'[115] A change of lighting which is only possible if one acquires sufficient detachment from self and life to see that both are composed of the same mixture of good and bad and that to pit oneself against the injustice and imperfections of life is to forget that one is part of the unchanging picture oneself. It is such detachment which can herald the re-emergence of the comic spirit, not as a facile refusal to countenance reality, but as offering a means whereby one can look reality squarely in the face and yet make it more bearable by passing from a tragic view of things to a philosophic smile at the vagaries of the human condition. La Mothe Le Vayer shares with Molière this ability to 'rire philosophiquement' at life, and in a passage from *Prose Chagrine*, which might serve as an epigraph to the play, he describes his transition from the view of life of an Alceste to that of a Philinte, a transition which must also have been effected by the author of *Le Misanthrope:* '...je ne sai si je ne ferais point mieux de congédier tant de chagrins inutiles...et passant d'une extrémité à l'autre, m'abandonner aux ris de Démocrite, qui dans un égal mépris des choses de ce monde, me donneront du moins une humeur beaucoup plus supportable. En effet, il vaut bien mieux, selon le sentiment commun, rire que pleurer.'[116]

6　Amphitryon

(1)

Amphitryon was performed in January 1668, and was favourably received by the audiences at Palais-Royal. In spite of this, Grimarest mentions the criticism of a pedantic contemporary to the effect that Molière 'a tout pris sur Rotrou, et Rotrou sur Plaute. Je ne vois pas pourquoi on applaudit à des Plagiaires.'[1] It is probably true to say that *Amphitryon* has a longer and richer literary history than any other of Molière's plays. Its theme, the usurpation of Amphitryon's identity and that of his servant Sosie by Jupiter and Mercure, had been frequently used in antiquity both in poetry and drama. Plautus dramatized the fable in *Amphitryo,* and Jean Rotrou wrote a French version entitled *Les Sosies* (1637), which relies heavily on the Latin original. It is not my purpose in this chapter either to contest the antagonistic generalization quoted from Grimarest (each dramatist, whatever the quality of his inspiration, brings his own method of composition to identical material), nor to make an exhaustive comparative study of the three plays.[2] What I intend to do is rather to isolate the central differences between Molière's conception of the subject and that of Rotrou and Plautus, without impugning the originality proper to those plays, in order to see how the theme and the manner in which Molière treats it are integrated into his comic vision.

(2)

It is apparent from the beginning that Molière adheres rigidly to the formal structure of the fable as handled by the two previous versions: the prologue, the mutual deception of Sosie and his master, and the appearance of Jupiter at the end of the comedy, form the essential structural pillars, and all are to be found in Molière. In addition, he has also retained the basic plot, which may be outlined very briefly as follows.

Sosie is sent by Amphitryon to Amphitryon's wife, Alcmène, to announce the victory of the Thebans over the Teleboians. Rehearsing the story of his valorous exploits, he is intercepted by Mercure, who, by astute application of physical force, compels him to abdicate the name Sosie, which he himself assumes. Sosie flees in disarray. Jupiter, who has retarded the appearance of dawn in order to prolong his stay with

Alcmène, ardently takes his leave from her. Sosie recounts his adventure to his incredulous master, who has returned. The latter goes into his home and is told by a surprised Alcmène that she cannot understand why he has returned so unexpectedly. His questioning gives rise to mutual suspicion. Alcmène, to prove that she is telling the truth, shows Amphitryon the present which he has just given to her — and Amphitryon discovers that the present which he had intended to give her has disappeared from its box. Questioned by her husband, Alcmène reveals that she has just spent the night with him. He leaves in jealous anger; Jupiter returns to Alcmène to apologize for what he has just said to her, and at length succeeds in mollifying her. Amphitryon returns alone, having been unable to find the relative of Alcmène who can explain the situation to him. He meets Mercure in the guise of his valet and discovers that he has been refused admission to his house. Amphitryon returns with his captains to force entrance but Jupiter appears, and no one can distinguish between the true and the false Amphitryon. Amphitryon returns yet again with different friends, and it is at this extreme point of his confusion that Jupiter appears, announces his identity and the imminent birth of his son to Alcmène, and departs.

Whilst all these events are common to the three plays, Molière treats them with great originality. Thus he introduces a completely new character, Cléanthis, the garrulous wife of Sosie, and creates comic dialogues between them which employ his frequently used device of allowing the servants to parallel, on a much lower and less eloquent level, the situation of their master and mistress (Act I, Sc. 4; Act II, Sc. 3; Act II, Sc. 5; Act II, Sc. 7). This innovation allows Molière to duplicate the Jupiter – Amphitryon – Alcmène situation with the confusion of Mercure – Sosie – Cléanthis. Although he lengthens the dialogues between Alcmène and Jupiter, making the latter a true *précieux* hero (Act I, Sc. 3; Act II, Sc. 6), in general he accelerates the action (Amphitryon, after Jupiter's first appearance to him, goes away and returns almost immediately), the comic dialogue becomes much more rapid than in Rotrou, and the sense of bewilderment of the participants is consequently doubled. But the key to his completely different conception of the subject lies less in such typically *moliéresque* additions than in the Prologue. It will be profitable to compare his Prologue with those of Plautus and Rotrou.[3]

The Prologue in Plautus is typical of his fusion of formal proclamation with witty asides, and is above all expository in nature. Mercury, dressed as a young slave, announces that he is here at Jupiter's command. After giving the audience several details about his master's parentage, he informs them that the play is going to be neither a tragedy nor a comedy, but, since Jupiter is appearing, it must at least be a tragi-comedy. He asks the audience to look out for any *cabales* which might show a biased attitude towards the performance. Addressing the actors, he tells them that they must act their parts well since Jupiter himself is joining them. Then he narrates briefly the argument of the play — Amphitryo is away from home, leading the Theban army. In his absence Alcmena has been made pregnant by Jupiter, appearing as her husband, and now expects both Amphitryo's child and that of Jupiter. As Sosia approaches, Mercury continues his vigil outside Amphitryo's house, to make sure that no one disturbs his master inside.

In Rotrou's play, the Prologue, which is in alexandrines, is lofty in tone and is spoken by Junon, Jupiter's wife, who recounts her history. Abandoned by her immortal husband, her place is occupied by the beautiful mortal Alcmène. She laments at length on the sorry pass to which virtue has been reduced, and announces the imminent birth of Alcide to Alcmène, who is going to eclipse her fame and reign in her place. She laments the duration of the night, in which Jupiter's son is to be born, and imprecates him. His son is going to be attacked by serpents and bulls, and will even triumph over hell. Eventually he will destroy himself, which will be Junon's supreme act of vengeance upon Jupiter.

Molière's Prologue is vastly different in design, and is doubtless the most thoroughly original part of his play. The opening dialogue between Mercure and La Nuit sets the tone for what is to follow; far distant from the witty urbanity of Plautus or the formal dignity of Rotrou, the two 'gods' speak together in an extremely human tone. Mercure leads off lightly by referring in the most offhand way to his divine commission with which he has been entrusted by his master:

> ...j'ai deux mots à vous dire
> De la part de Jupiter. (ll. 3-4)

His casual remark ('Ma foi! me trouvant las'..l. 7) earns him reproof from the more serious La Nuit: 'Sied-il bien à des Dieux de dire qu'ils sont las?' (l. 12). To Mercure's irreverent question as to whether or not the gods are made of iron, she replies in rather staid fashion:

> Non; mais il faut sans cesse
> Garder le *décorum* de la divinité. (ll. 13-14)

And the emphasis is ostensibly placed upon *décorum*. The level of language here is more akin to that of Rotrou's play, where the mythological background serves to sustain the noble and solemn tone which prevails throughout. Here, Molière's intention is quite clearly to demythologize the lofty language and *grandeur* which conventional mythology confers on the theme, and through Mercure he debunks from the beginning the status of the gods in an irreverent and ironic way which is totally lacking in Rotrou or Plautus. In Plautus the gods remain only discreetly personalized, to the extent that they appear in the guise of mortals. One looks in vain in both plays for the complaints of Mercure that, although he is supposed to be the messenger of the gods, yet he must needs carry out his divine errands on foot: the quixotic conventions of the poets, he says, are to blame for this. La Nuit obliges her disquietingly independent colleague to come to the point of his request, and he tells her that Jupiter wishes her to prolong the duration of night. The reason is given in highly ironic and disrespectful terms:

...vous n'ignorez pas que ce maître des Dieux
Aime à s'humaniser pour des beautés mortelles. (ll. 55-6)

This witty *jeu de mots* provides the pretext for his succinct and *piquant résumé* of the argument. Whilst Amphitryon, the new husband of Alcmène, is away, Jupiter is going to visit her in the form of her husband. Normally this tactic would be unworthy of Jupiter's ingenuity, since husbands do not generally find favour in the eyes of his conquests, but here is a favourable opportunity for its application.

In Plautus and Rotrou the birth of Jupiter's son to Alcmène is already announced in the Prologue (in Plautus she is expecting both her husband's child and Jupiter's), whereas in Molière's Prologue all mention of this is omitted, and is relegated to the last scene of the play, where Jupiter announces it himself. The effect of this significant omission here is to reduce the mythological figure of Jupiter further to the dimensions of an earthly Tartuffe, engaged, albeit by more ingenious means, in the business of seducing Alcmène. Freed from the trappings of the mythological convention which poses the miraculous birth of Jupiter's son as the prior condition of the legend, Molière can now complete the process of humanization begun by Mercure by showing Jupiter in the role of Alcmène's ardent and persuasive suitor, whose success depends upon his ability to harmonize his use of language with his appearances as Amphitryon. We recognize immediately that not only Mercure but also Jupiter are essentially no different from the rest of Molière's comic characters who attempt to conceal their true nature from other people. Tartuffe, Alceste, Armande, all prefer to act a part in society — the part of a *dévot*, a martyr to justice, or a coldly intellectual woman spurning mere physical pursuits. In each case love is the catalyst which brings to the surface their latent humanity (which they hide from the other actors).[4]

Mercure touches here upon one of the most important differences in Molière's treatment of the theme. In Plautus and Rotrou, Jupiter's descent from Olympian heights to disport himself at the expense of mortals is heralded in triumphant style by his servant. In both plays, the imposture practised upon man and master has the character of pure 'jouissance', as Mercure says in Rotrou (Act I, Sc. 1), and nothing more than that. The commerce of Molière's Jupiter with humanity springs from a more fundamental urge in his nature: as Mercure tells us

Il veut goûter par là toutes sortes d'états,
Et c'est agir en Dieu qui n'est pas bête.
Dans quelque rang qu'il soit des mortels regardé
Je le tiendrois fort misérable,
S'il ne quittoit jamais sa mine redoutable,
Et qu'au faîte des cieux il fût toujours guindé.
Il n'est point, à mon gré, de plus sotte méthode
Que d'être emprisonné toujours dans sa grandeur;
Et surtout aux transports de l'amoureuse ardeur
La haute qualité devient fort incommode.
Jupiter, qui sans doute en plaisirs se connaît
Sait descendre du haut de sa gloire suprême;
Et pour entrer dans tout ce qu'il lui plaît
Il sort tout à fait de lui-même,
Et ce n'est plus alors Jupiter qui paraît. (ll. 78-92)

In the guise of Amphitryon, the omnipotent actor will introduce the comic confusion of identities into the world of men; but the comedy can only take place because he is subject to the same passions which move common mortals. He is the author of the comedy which is about to be performed at his command and for his benefit, but he is also an actor in it as well as the subject of it. For the divinity of Jupiter has, paradoxically, acquired in Molière's play a mythical meaning not attaching to his two dramatic predecessors, even though he himself has been thoroughly humanized. He stands as the supreme symbol of the man who, by virtue of the rank which he occupies and enables himself to occupy in the public imagination, has so perfected the wearing of a mask that people cannot pierce it, whatever guise he may choose to appear in. On a superior and public level, he is an Alceste or a Tartuffe, imagining that his actions are exempt from contradiction in the eyes of others — and whilst this is true in the perspective of the play, nothing could be further from the truth for the spectators of his comedy. Acting out his divine role, he needs to relinquish this mask occasionally because his basic nature and instincts are dissatisfied with it and seek an outlet. Unlike the usual comic characters in Molière's theatre, he is aware of the necessity of both playing his habitual role and leaving it: like Tartuffe, he is a superior comic character who exemplifies the deep paradox that the true self can only be revealed as an extension of one's essential role. Tartuffe stretches his role of *dévot* to its uttermost limit, allowing it to embrace seduction: Jupiter apparently abandons his 'mine redoutable' of a god, but changes this role instead to that of a *galant,* in other words to one which expresses the essence of his real person. Comedy is the activity which separates, as nothing else can, the true from the false Jupiter, revealing the true self not only through a role but as being synonymous with the role. The role itself symbolizes, as Mercure makes clear in the passage quoted, man's need to liberate himself from absolute pretensions to power or wisdom or, as in *Tartuffe,* inhuman devotion, and affirms the primacy of *folie* over *sagesse,* of contradiction over the well-knitted appearances of rationality which he likes to give to his actions. Le Vayer points to the same basic idea of comedy which Mercure here expresses, when he writes '. . . qu'il n'y a point d'homme si confirmé dans la sagesse, qui n'ait quelques moments où elle semble l'abandonner.'[5]

La Nuit, with her attachment to the decorum of the gods which Jupiter is momentarily relinquishing, professes astonishment at his formal request for the dubious kind of service which he requires from her (that she should prolong the duration of night). Mercure chides her for her old-fashioned scruples; he has adopted a more critical and cynical attitude to Jupiter's activities:

> Lorsque dans un haut rang on a l'heur de paroître,
> Tout ce qu'on fait est toujours bel et bon;
> Et suivant ce qu'on peut être,
> Les choses changent de nom. (ll. 128-31)

Everything that Jupiter does appears correct, because like Tartuffe, he knows that people need to look up to the absolute standards of the idol which they deify. Jupiter is, like Tartuffe and Dom Juan, the supreme manipulator of appearances and reality: but just as it attains the supreme point of development which these comic impostors brilliantly exemplify, comedy creates its own dilemma. Grounded as it is on the discrepancy which it perceives and manifests between man's ideal and his reality, its *raison d'être* is effaced once the ideal has apparently been converted into reality. The comic metamorphosis has been so convincingly performed by its authors that the comic vision can only maintain itself by accepting both the metamorphosis at its face value and the premise of its authors. So absolute does the supreme comedy of appearances appear, that the comic vision must enter into its game of complicity by accepting these appearances more absolutely than absolutely — only then can the absolute appearances be undermined in spirit, if not in fact, by comic irony. Mercure's admiration for his master's dexterity does not conceal the ironic perspective into which, like Sganarelle in *Dom Juan*, he has succeeded in placing Jupiter. In fact, Mercure employs his irony so penetratingly that La Nuit must re-emphasize how important it is for the gods not to show the slightest discrepancy between what they are and what people imagine them to be. The *persona* must be maintained at all costs, otherwise the comedy of the gods laughing at men would be reversed:

> N'apprêtons point à rire aux hommes
> En nous disant nos vérités. (ll. 146-7)

The ironic Mercure must now engage in the execution of a double paradox. He must continue to play the part of a god consistently, as well as the role which Jupiter's caprice has imposed upon him. He prepares to go onto the stage

Pour y vêtir la figure
Du valet d'Amphitryon. (ll. 150-1)

As in *L'Impromptu de Versailles,* we see the actors preparing to play their roles, but here the comic vision is heightened both by the number of parts which they play and by the hierarchy of comedies visible to the authors in 'heavenly' and terrestrial spheres. (Jupiter is the author of the human comedy, but is reduced to the position of an actor in Molière's perspective of the play.) Mercure and Jupiter attempt to keep up the appearances of gods; and now they attempt to keep up the appearances of humanity as well. Comedy fulfils the same function for the truculent messenger of the gods as it does for Jupiter. He longs to escape from the comedy of the immortals, which he sees through, and acting the part of Sosie will restore temporarily his true self by giving freer course to his ironic spirit. The comic vision of Molière, usually concerned with the comedy of man aspiring to be God in his own right, attempting to eradicate the traces of his human nature, is now neatly reversed as the gods aspire to nothing more than common mortality.

The Prologue of Molière's play allows us to glimpse the extent to which his *Amphitryon* differs initially from those of the two other dramatists. They accept the convention of mythology as their basic dramatic premise, and the gods appear as imposing and superior figures in the background. They are actors in the plays, but unlike Molière's gods, they do not act the part of gods, nor do they aspire to realize themselves in their human roles. As mythological characters, they remain unquestioned, providing a stable position from which to see the comedy of the master and his servant. In Molière's play, on the other hand, the Prologue provides the divine comedy which it is necessary to see in order to understand the human comedy which results from it, and even the divine sustainer of both comedies, Jupiter, plays his role, and changes incessantly. The description by Scudéry of his *Comédie des Comédiens* could form an appropriate epigraph for Molière's play: 'le sujet de la comédie. . .fut la comédie même.'[6] Theatre within the theatre, a role within a role, these are the elements which are everywhere discernible: the only things which are constant and irreducible are appearances and illusions, which provide the basis of the comic characters' existence and of the comedy itself.[7]

(3)

Before the intrusion of Jupiter into the world of men dissolves all established truths and values into illusions, Sosie provides an interlude between the higher comedy of the Prologue and the lower comedy in which the gods are going to act. It is a fitting link between the two comedies, for we see Sosie engaged in acting out his own private comedy alone. In fact he is continually condemned by circumstances to play a role. We hear him complain bitterly about his master who has sent him on a dangerous mission — he must proceed to Alcmène's house with her husband's message of greeting at dead of night. His whole life has been sacrificed to the capricious bidding of his master: he has not received the gratitude which he feels he deserves. Yet he realizes that he protests in vain, for his ingrained habits of service and obedience will inevitably overcome his wishful thinking:

> . . . la moindre faveur d'un coup d'oeil caressant
> Nous rengage de plus belle. (Act I, Sc. 1, ll. 186-7)

Appearances have only to smile upon him and he will return to play his time-honoured role as Amphitryon's willing inferior. But there is a deeper reason for Sosie's role as subservient than that of his mere willingness to act as an inferior. The truth is that there is something of the artist's vocation in Sosie's continued attachment to his master *malgré lui* — a vocation of *comédien,* which enables Sosie to affirm his superiority over his master whilst ostensibly retaining the position of a valet. When Sosie recounts the fantastic story of his encounter with Sosie (his double) to Amphitryon, he is promised his usual *bastonnade* as reward for his lies, and he immediately strikes another tone:

> Si vous le prenez sur ce ton,
> Monsieur, je n'ai plus rien à dire,
> Et vous aurez toujours raison. (Act II, Sc. 1, ll. 693-5)

The exasperated Amphitryon insists flatly that Sosie begin at the beginning of his garbled story about his visit to Amphitryon's home, and that he answer truthfully each question put to him. The valet however must first establish the premises of his narration:

> Parlerai-je, Monsieur, selon ma conscience,
> Ou comme auprès des grands on le voit usité?
> Faut-il dire la vérité,
> Ou bien user de complaisance? (ll. 709-12)

Amphitryon is explicit: he merely wishes to hear 'un compte fort sincère' (l. 714) of the entire episode. Sosie begins by retracing minutely all his actions:

> Je suis parti, les cieux d'un noir crêpe voilés
> Pestant fort contre vous dans ce fâcheux martyre,
> Et maudissant vingt fois l'ordre dont vous parlez. (ll. 718-20)

To Amphitryon's enraged reaction, Sosie replies with a feigned *naïveté* which conceals marvellously a whole philosophic outlook on superiors, language, and human relationships in general:

Monsieur, vous n'avez rien qu'à dire,
Je mentirai, si vous voulez. (ll. 721-2)

What is truth and what is sincerity? Are the two compatible? Once more
we are confronted with the question which is so fundamental to
relationships between Molière's comic characters, and was previously
illustrated in the dialogues of Dom Juan and Sganarelle, and focused
most sharply in the sonnet scene in *Le Misanthrope* between Oronte
and Alceste. Amphitryon desires above all sincerity, which he
automatically equates with truth, as does his predecessor, Alceste. But
he unconsciously deceives himself, since his irascible reply to Sosie is
adequate proof that truth and sincerity for him can only coincide in
what he wishes to hear. For the enlightened Sosie, truth and sincerity
are variable quantities, solely dependent upon the value which a
superior's *amour-propre* confers on them. His art consists in so
manipulating these variables that the unconscious self-deception of
Amphitryon comes to the surface; by absolving himself obsequiously
from all appearances of blame by the instantaneous metamorphosis of
black into white, he can savour fully the consequent confusion of his
master. There is an immeasurable gap between the valet of Molière and
those of his two predecessors, as even the most cursory glance will
reveal. In Rotrou's play, Sosie is nothing more than the stereotyped
figure of the cowardly valet, imprisoned within his *état civil*, completely
lacking the dexterity and wit with which Molière's Sosie converts
appearances into their opposites. In the scene in which Rotrou's Sosie
tells Amphitryon how he was chased from the house by Mercure, he
restates laboriously the whole story, and at the end of the scene is still
protesting vainly that he is telling the truth; and the same *dialogue de
sourds* ensues in Plautus. It is obvious that this aspect of Molière's Sosie
is completely original and fully in line with the Sganarelle of *Dom Juan*
and earlier plays.[8]

It is clear that from the beginning of the play Sosie shares with
Mercure the double vision of the masters they serve, as well as the
double vision of themselves as servants and as spectators of their
masters. In the Prologue, Mercure had grumbled about the fatigue
which Jupiter's service occasioned him, and had remarked to the
subservient La Nuit that it was merely the name and reputation of his
master which lent a colouring of respectability to his deeds (ll. 127 ff.).
When Amphitryon finally dismisses his valet's ludicrous story, Sosie
similarly says

Tous les discours sont des sottises,
Partant d'un homme sans éclat,
Ce seroit paroles exquises
Si c'étoit un grand qui parlât. (ll. 839-42)

They stand in a special relationship to each other by virtue of the ironic perspective in which they see the attitudes of others, and especially the deeds and words of their masters — a relationship which will make duplication of Sosie's identity by Mercure, if not more logical or probable, at least strikingly appropriate. In spite of their protestations about their superiors, both take a secret delight in their exploits. Mercure will try to imitate the elegant amorality of Jupiter by saying to the prudish Cléanthis

> J'aime mieux un vice commode
> Qu'une fatigante vertu. (Act I, Sc. 4, ll. 681-2)

P. Bénichou has commented appositely on the master-man kind of relationship to one another in which Jupiter–Mercure, Amphitryon–Sosie and Mercure–Sosie may be said to stand, and on the valets in particular: '. . . ils sont comme des doubles dégradés de ceux à qui ils appartiennent, et qu'ils singent plus souvent qu'ils ne les maudissent . . . Le double, par son caractère de surnaturelle puissance, incarne les ambitions du moi. . . '[9] Sosie will return to Amphitryon and proudly tell him of 'ce moi plus robuste que moi . . . ce moi vaillant' which forced him to abdicate his identity (ll. 810-20). This 'moi' pre-exists in Sosie, before he encounters its physical manifestation in Mercure, but only on the level of imagination. It is precisely the role of the ideal 'moi' which the real Sosie assumes as he prepares to recount the story of the battle to Alcmène in the opening scene (unaware that the real 'moi vaillant' Mercure is watching). Molière here adds another dimension to his valet's role, which is neither in Rotrou nor Plautus. It is true that the Sosie of Rotrou tells the imaginary story of the battle to himself before he encounters Mercure, as he does in the Latin version:

> N'omettons rien pourtant dont on puisse juger
> Que j'aie été présent au plus pressant danger (Act I, Sc. 3)

The scenario of Molière's Sosie is however a solo theatrical performance, a play before the play, and not just a narrative account as in the other French version. His performance is necessitated, like that of Jupiter, by the astute awareness of the *comédien* of what others invariably expect him to do, even though such fictitious actions do not correspond to reality as he experiences it:

> Il me faudroit, pour l'ambassade,
> Quelque discours prémédité.
> Je dois aux yeux d'Alcmène un portrait militaire
> Du grand combat. . . (ll. 190-3)

He also experiences a sense of urgency to perform, which has nothing to do with others, or with what they wish to hear, but springs from his perpetual need to fulfil himself by playing a role: the role which he now proceeds to rehearse is but an extension of the real Sosie:

Pour jouer mon rôle sans peine,
Je le veux un peu repasser. (ll. 200-1)

His professional execution of it bears this out. After his ceremonious form of address to his 'lanterne' (which he takes as Alcmène), he supplies not only her observations, questions and reactions to his story, but also intermittent critical comments: 'Bon! beau début!' (l. 206), 'Bien répondu' (l. 214), 'Fort bien! Belle conception!' (l. 217), and his warmest tribute to his acting ability: 'Peste! où prend mon esprit toutes ces gentillesses?' (l. 226). Actor, critic, stage-manager, and public at the same time, he plays all his parts to perfection.[10]

He continues to play his role as the valorous Sosie as the aggressive Mercure approaches, whom he will later aspire to resemble. But his acting is also accompanied by knowledge of his real self underneath his many masks: 'Si je ne suis hardi, tâchons de le paroître' (l. 305). In order to play his roles he must have an awareness of what he is, and consequently of what he is not. He accepts, apparently with regret, the knowledge of what he is, but actually enjoys creating and playing his heroic role all the more, since it is diametrically opposed to his real pusillanimous self. The further his role differs from his real self, the better does he play it, and the more comic does our comic vision of him become, as we glimpse simultaneously the pseudo-heroic and the real in precarious comic co-existence. He can only remain a conscious actor so long as his awareness of his real self is not removed from him. But if his true identity is put into doubt, then he becomes unaware of his real self and so is unable to play his role as Sosie, the valet of Amphitryon. The loss of his role in the comedy paradoxically increases our appreciation of it, as the *comédien* who dominates the stage brilliantly in his solo performance as Amphitryon's valet is in his turn dominated by Mercure. The usurpation of his identity by Mercure will erase the double vision of himself (the 'moi poltron' and the 'moi vaillant') which he delights to exploit, whilst creating a new double vision of himself which we share with Mercure (the knowledge that he is still Sosie, but that the appearances of the true and false Sosie are absolutely identical) and which is immeasurably more comic. In the problem of identity which Sosie is about to be confronted with, Molière raises his comedy to a hypothetical level of intensity, hitherto unexploited in his theatre, a level at which he discovers the unlimited possibilities of the comic vision, as it may transcend itself and be transcended *ad infinitum*.

(4)

Molière's comedy is usually concerned with showing up the comic paradox within the nature of a character — whether it is that of the inhuman *dévot,* the *esprit faible* behind the pretence of the *esprit fort,* or the atrabilious suitor. His comic character resists the elimination of his paradox because it is by maintaining what others (i.e. the comic vision) see as contradictions that he assures himself of his own separate existence from them. He replaces the 'Je pense donc je suis' of Descartes by 'je me maintiens donc je suis'; as long as Dom Juan can keep up his *libertin* exterior, he refuses to grant existence to the supernatural, and thereby affirms his own. Orgon is happiest when imposing his own *fiat* on others. The opinions of others do not and cannot exist because they are seen as a threat to the comic character's own existence. His reaction to opposition to his design is therefore that of Orgon, when the family confront him with the possibility that Tartuffe may be an impostor — 'cela ne se peut'. His total refusal to realize that others may, after all, be correct, can only produce one logical consequence — the irreparable confusion of Orgon, the flight of Alceste to his *désert,* the spectacular punishment of Dom Juan. The frenetic reaction of Harpagon to the loss of his 'cassette' may well be an aberration, but it expresses the truth of the comic character who suddenly finds himself deprived of his *raison d'être:* 'Mon esprit est troublé, et j'ignore où je suis, qui je suis, et ce que je fais . . . tout est fini pour moi, et je n'ai plus que faire au monde: sans toi, il m'est impossible de vivre.'[11]

Molière now enlarges the domain of his comic vision from the struggle of a character to preserve his existence intact (which he concentrates in the object of his fixation) to include the struggle of characters to preserve their own existence *tout court.* The disproportion which comedy shows up between the true nature of the fixation and the total dependence of the comic character on it now disappears, and the comic struggle becomes more intense as he struggles to affirm his existence not against tangible opposition (i.e. others), but against the elusive author of the comedy (Mercure, Jupiter) in the guise of himself.

The intervention of Mercure into the world of men, which adds a higher dimension to the comic vision, is of course a hypothetical fiction provided by Molière himself, who stands behind and above the 'divine' authors of the comedy; yet it is necessary even though hypothetical, since it is the only fiction capable of containing the comedy of man's existence being usurped. The fiction of the gods is invested with literal truth by Sosie, who does no less than ground his existence upon it. When Mercure asks him for the first time about his name, Sosie affirms that he is indeed Sosie. Mercure accuses him of having wilfully arrogated to himself the name, and this causes Sosie to invoke the highest authority known to him:

Fort bien; je le soutiens, par la grande raison
Qu'ainsi l'a fait des Dieux la puissance suprême,
Et qu'il n'est pas en moi de pouvoir dire non,
Et d'être un autre que moi-même. (Act I, Sc. 2, ll. 359-62)

The affirmation of his existence as Sosie rests on his belief in a Cartesian-like ordering of the world into separate and recognizable categories and identities by the immutable decrees of the gods. This assures him of his existence as Sosie, and allows him to be what he imagines that he alone is and can be — namely Sosie, the actor of many parts and the wearer of many masks. Ironically, he is unaware that the same authority which assures him of his objective existence is involved, but at a higher level, in the perpetual activity which is the ground not merely of his being, but of all being — that is, comedy.[12] If the basis for what one takes as the ultimate guarantee of reality is no basis at all, everything might be true, and anything might be wrong. The only basis for reality is appearances, and one is thus engaged in a perpetual comedy of errors where the comedy may be truth and the errors may likewise be truth.[13] One simply has no means of distinguishing appearances from (apparent) reality and is submerged in a morass of doubt about oneself and the reality of external events. The dilemma of Sosie is precisely that which Descartes envisaged at the end of his *Première Méditation Des Choses que l'on peut révoquer en doute*: 'Je supposerai donc qu'il y a, non point un vrai Dieu, qui est la souveraine source de vérité, mais un certain mauvais génie, non moins rusé et trompeur que puissant, qui a employé toute son industrie à me tromper.'[14]

It might seem possible that Molière was not thinking of Descartes' *Méditations* at all when writing the scene between Sosie and Mercure. Was it not possible that he was only working within the framework of conventional seventeenth-century themes? I do not think so, even though J. Rousset has shown that doubt, the oscillation between illusion and reality, and disguise of one's true nature were recurrent motifs in the tragi-comedies of Scudéry, Du Ryer, Boisrobert and others, not to mention Rotrou.[15] One of his observations in particular is extremely pertinent when one considers the doubt of the characters in Molière's *Amphitryon* and the conventional expressions of it in contemporary drama: 'Est-ce une illusion? Quel démon nous enchante? Dormons-nous? rêvons-nous? Cette interrogation, plus émerveillée qu'inquiète, retentit partout, tant la tragi-comédie semble le lieu privilégié des charmes et des sortilèges qui changent la réalité'.[16] When Rousset describes the question behind the doubts of the characters in these plays as 'plus émerveillée qu'inquiète', we see clearly what distinguishes the doubts of Molière's Sosie from those of Rotrou and others. The Sosie of Rotrou tells his master that

> Quelque savant démon, en la magie expert,
> Fait qu'ainsi tout se change, et se double, et se perd. (Act II, Sc. 3)

Consequently, as Rousset notes, in his borrowings from Plautus Rotrou amplifies rhetorically the doubt of the characters about their own existence for the mere theatrical effects of bewilderment and confusion.[17] Rotrou seeks deliberately to produce this impression even before Sosie has encountered Mercure, and he makes him say

J'ignore qui je suis
En l'état malheureux où mes jours sont réduits; (Act I, Sc. 3)

Molière's characters, on the other hand, are not merely passive creatures, willing prey to confusion. Both Sosie and especially Amphitryon cling to their identities as fiercely as the *imaginaire* clings to his idol, as I hope to show presently. The *malus genius* induces in them not just 'émerveillement', the stock reaction of the characters in a theatre which specializes and delights in illusion, fantasy and bewilderment, but an 'inquiétude' which relates their dilemma, whether consciously or not on the part of Molière, to Descartes' sceptical hypothesis. This relationship to Descartes' supposition may be seen firstly in the continuity of the play's vision with the conclusion of *Le Misanthrope,* and secondly in the attitude of Sosie to Mercure.

Descartes' demon hypothesis is just at one remove from the sceptical vision of *Le Misanthrope,* where Alceste seeks in theory at least a rational order of things and is instead assiduously frustrated and deceived — he finds his 'mauvais génie, non moins rusé et trompeur que puissant' in the form of his legal adversary, who at each moment is able to turn appearances against him by 'le poids de sa grimace, où brille l'artifice' (ll. 1483-1524). Philinte had come to terms with the 'mauvais génie' at large in the world, who turns all truth and logic upside-down, by making appearances the basis of his being — accepting the ways in which people and things appear to him and replying in kind by acting the role of an *honnête homme.* In *Prose Chagrine,* which contains so many analogies with that play, we find La Mothe Le Vayer coming extremely close to Descartes' hypothesis when he writes that 'Je trouve tous les jours moins étrange l'opinion de ceux qui faisaient les mauvais démons auteurs de ce monde, vu ce qui s'y pratique.'[18] Pascal saw the implication of the 'mauvais génie' hypothesis in scepticism, and attributed it in his *Entretien avec M. de Saci* to Montaigne.[19] The hypothesis of the 'mauvais génie', although latent in scepticism, was of course put to completely non-sceptical ends by Descartes. He was concerned not with doubt as the only certainty of his philosophy, but with the use of a 'super-scepticism' which employs doubt in a hyperbolic way in order to defeat doubt. He knew that only when scepticism had been pursued to its extreme conclusion could it be completely defeated, and this could only be achieved by carrying doubt to its logical end. In the passage which precedes the *Cogito* in his *Discours de la Méthode,* he had already evolved a mild form of the 'mauvais démon' hypothesis which led to his discovery that

... pendant que je voulais ainsi penser que tout était faux, il fallait nécessairement que moi, qui le pensais, fusse quelque chose. Et remarquant que cette vérité: Je pense, donc je suis, était si ferme et si assurée que toutes les plus extravagantes suppositions des sceptiques n'étaient pas capables de l'ébranler, je jugeai que je pouvais la recevoir sans scrupule pour le premier principe de la philosophie que je cherchais.[20]

Amphitryon marks a singular coincidence between the philosophy of Descartes and the comic vision of Molière. Cartesian doubt had to contain the demon hypothesis if doubt were to be taken to its logical and ultimate conclusion and be defeated. The comic vision of Molière, seeing the comedy of deception and self-deception at work in everyone, had also to be taken to its logical and ultimate conclusion of the divine *comédies* responsible for human confusion, in order to achieve its most profoundly comic expression.

Of course there is a world of difference between the ways in which Molière and Descartes treat the hypothesis of the 'mauvais génie'. Molière envisages the hypothesis as a means of taking his characters into deeper and more inextricable comic difficulties than hitherto exploited as they struggle with questions of identity and existence, non-identity and non-existence. Descartes, on the other hand, was above all concerned to emerge from his hypothesis and to found an objective metaphysical point of reference which would serve as an unimpeachable source of further truth.[21] At first sight it might appear that Molière had seized upon the hypothesis for the possible comic value which it might yield, without concerning himself overmuch about the conclusion. Yet the progression of the 'mauvais génie' in the form of Mercure goes through several stages in his confrontation with Sosie, at each of which the probability that he (Mercure) is Sosie is intensified and the doubts of Sosie about his identity are increased. The conclusion is much more ambiguous than that produced by Descartes' *malus genius*, which led him to the certainty of his existence and the triumph of reason over doubt. For Sosie, the doubt cast upon his existence will result in both the triumph and the defeat of his reason; the scene would appear to be a rather ironic comment by Molière upon the strict application to which Descartes puts reason, a faculty which in his plays is susceptible to many uses and abuses, being, as Le Vayer describes it, 'un jouet à toutes mains que le mensonge manie comme il veut . . .'[22]

When Sosie receives his first *bastonnade* from Mercure for having dared to affirm his identity, the latter asks him 'Hé bien! es-tu Sosie à présent? qu'en dis-tu?' (Act I, Sc. 2, l. 379); the bemused Sosie replies

Tes coups n'ont point en moi fait de métamorphose;
Et tout le changement que je trouve à la chose,
C'est d'être Sosie battu. (ll. 380-2)

The first onslaught upon his identity and person has, paradoxically, only served to make him all the more certain that he still is Sosie, the valet perpetually condemned to be the inferior on account of his cowardice (cf. ll. 369-78). Questioned again by the threatening Mercure, the tone of his reply changes subtly:

> Il est vrai, jusqu'ici j'ai cru la chose claire;
> Mais ton bâton, sur cette affaire,
> M'a fait voir que je m'abusois. (ll. 393-5)

He still does not entertain the slightest doubt about his real identity, but chooses to make a politic abdication of it, employing the familiar weapon of irony which assures him of a momentary 'moral' superiority over superiors. The first change in his attitude occurs when Mercure affirms for the first time that he and he alone is Sosie, the valet of Amphitryon — woe betide anyone who takes it upon himself to play the role of Sosie! (ll. 396-9). For Sosie, who sees himself reduced to playing the role of himself instead of his habitual roles, which he can enjoy because he knows only too well what he is in reality, this is too much: 'Ciel! me faut-il ainsi renoncer à moi-même' (l. 400). But in the very act of imagining such an enormity, he once again spontaneously affirms his true nature:

> Que son bonheur est extrême
> De ce que je suis poltron!
> Sans cela, par la mort . . .(ll. 402-4)

The aspiration to be his 'moi vaillant' is however just as much a permanent part of his nature as the real 'moi poltron': the real Sosie is not conceivable without his ideal role and the cowardice which co-exist and maintain each other. The two 'mois' are so closely bound up that one cannot distinguish one from the other; is it his 'moi poltron' or his 'moi vaillant' which makes him wax bold enough to say incredulously to the *malus genius*

> Qui te jette, dis-moi, dans cette fantaisie?
> Que te reviendra-t-il de m'enlever mon nom?
> Et peux-tu faire enfin, quand tu serois démon,
> Que je ne sois pas moi? que je ne sois Sosie? (ll. 412-15)

Mercure's claim to be Sosie appears too far-fetched when submitted to normal standards of reason and sense-perception: to the question which he poses to himself 'Rêvé-je? est-ce que je sommeille?' (l. 430), he gives a reply based on empirical evidence:

> Ne sens-je pas bien que je veille?
> Ne suis-je pas dans mon bon sens? (ll. 432-3)

He is aware of the reasons which motivated him to come to

Amphitryon's house with his message, of the cowardice which prevented him from trying to force an entry, and, most of all, of the blows which he has just received from Mercure.[23] He describes these sense impressions as 'cent indices pressants' (l. 429), which combine to refute 'un discours si loin de l'apparence'. (l. 425)

Up to this point Sosie has been able to maintain his identity intact, in spite of Mercure's pressure. He has, so far, relied successfully upon his reason, which affords him subjective and intuitive certainty both of his identity and his separate existence as Sosie. But Mercure too can give proofs of his identity and his origins, which not only parallel those which Sosie has just adduced but have the formal appearances of objective validity which those of Sosie cannot have. Mercure is able to tell him whence and why he has come, that he is the long-suffering husband of the prudish Cléanthis, and of an incident in Thebes which Sosie would prefer to forget (ll. 450-67). Sosie's initial doubt about his identity begins as he admits that no one, apart from himself, could know so much about him: 'Je commence, à mon tour, à le croire un petit' (l. 471). This doubt is reinforced by the physical resemblance of Mercure to the real Sosie, which the *amour-propre* of the latter finds impressive. Yet he still doubts, and poses the question which he imagines that he alone (i.e. the real Sosie) can answer. What did Amphitryon obtain as booty from the battle, and to whom did he intend to give it? Mercure's impeccable answer elicits much more serious doubts from Sosie than hitherto expressed: 'Et de moi je commence à douter tout de bon' (l. 485). Sosie, so dogmatic about his identity earlier, is now brought to a complete state of suspension of judgement about himself and Mercure, and is precisely half-way towards his great *volte-face:*

> Près de moi, par la force, il est déjà Sosie;
> Il pourroit bien encor l'être par la raison. (ll. 486-7)

He has not yet renounced all the empirical evidence which his reason and senses afford him of his identity: they still appear to convince him that he is Sosie:

> . . . quand je me tâte, et que je me rappelle,
> Il me semble que je suis moi. (ll. 488-9)

What is now different is that the appearances of Mercure as Sosie are also convincing, since they are founded upon proofs of identity at least as cogent as those which he experiences intuitively. Rationally, that is according to the appearances which are offered to his reason and senses, he cannot deny that Mercure is Sosie or that he himself is not Sosie. The third and culminating stage of his doubt is reached when Mercure is able to tell him precisely that he (Sosie) spent his time in a tent satisfying his gluttony while the battle continued (ll. 498-512); for

Sosie, this is the most indubitable as well as the most impressive proof
that his double is indeed himself:

Cette preuve sans pareille
En sa faveur conclut bien;
Et l'on n'y peut dire rien, (ll. 505-7)
Je ne saurois nier, aux preuves qu'on m'expose,
Que tu ne sois Sosie, et j'y donne ma voix. (ll. 509-10)

He has still a fundamental question to ask Mercure, in spite of the
double's apparent victory over him:

Mais si tu l'es, dis-moi qui tu veux que je sois?
Car encor faut-il bien que je sois quelque chose. (ll. 511-12)

Sosie has finally been brought to the stage where he goes beyond
doubting his own identity. He must rationally and formally concede
that Mercure is Sosie (or appears to be, that is, for throughout the scene
Sosie rigorously limits his judgement to appearances) and that,
conversely, he is not (does not appear to be, that is) Sosie. Yet he is still
conscious of his own existence, and knows that he must be something,
even if he cannot be Sosie, the valet of Amphitryon. Once again Molière
is without doubt making comic use of an important element in
Descartes' epistemology. In the part of the *Discours* which immediately
precedes the *Cogito,* Descartes agreed to accept as true the supposition
that everything he experienced by means of reason and the senses might
be nothing more than pure illusion. Nevertheless, thinking that every
perception of phenomena might well be deceptive *(faux)*, he perceived
intuitively an unshakeable truth, namely that '. . . il fallait
nécessairement que moi qui le pensais, fusse quelque chose.'[24] In the
second of his *Méditations Métaphysiques,* he intensifies his doubt
about the deception of reason and the senses, in order to be able to
intensify his eventual affirmation of subjective consciousness. He
admits the possibility of some alien and malicious power creating his
thoughts as well as himself. Yet one certainty withstands the onslaught
of his doubt:

Moi donc à tout le moins ne suis-je point quelque chose?. . . Mais il y
a un je ne sais quel trompeur très puissant et rusé, qui emploie toute
son industrie à me tromper toujours. Il n'y a donc point de doute que
je suis, s'il me trompe; et qu'il me trompe tant qu'il voudra, il ne saura
jamais faire que je ne sois rien, tant que je penserai être quelque
chose.[25]

Although overwhelmed with doubt concerning what he actually
conceives himself to be, Descartes cannot doubt his existence as a
conscious being, since the process of doubt carries with it the implicit
assurance of the existence of something which may be doubted.

Similarly, Mercure can suppress Sosie's identity, but cannot do away with his consciousness that he exists (ll. 513-16). Like Descartes, Sosie finds himself imprisoned in a world where he exists with subjective certainty; but, unlike the philosopher, he finds it impossible for him to validate his existence objectively. He is left by Mercure and by Molière at the stage of certainty which for Descartes was purely transitional. It is as though Molière had decided to truncate Descartes' second *Méditation* and his entire system of thought at the point where it seemed to hold out the greatest promise for comedy; ironically, Descartes himself provides a potentially comic summary of the progress of his thought, at the time when it is still suspended between the certainty of the *Cogito* and the uncertainty which engulfs it:

> Mais je ne connais pas encore assez clairement ce que je suis, moi qui suis certain que je suis; de sorte que désormais il faut que je prenne soigneusement garde de ne prendre pas imprudemment quelque autre chose pour moi, et ainsi de ne me point méprendre dans cette connaissance, que je soutiens être plus certaine et plus évidente que toutes celles que j'ai eues auparavant.[26]

The scene between Sosie and Mercure ends with Sosie still in this condition of uncertainty and doubt — but although he has conceded that Mercure must indeed be Sosie, he has not been entirely defeated by Mercure's imposture. Confused though he is, he has still sufficient lucidity to see something of the complex nature of his problem. On the one hand he is aware that 'la raison à ce qu'on voit s'oppose' (l. 518); in the light of what has appeared to him to be reasonable in the past, the episode is wholly fantastic and improbable. On the other hand, he knows that the appearances of reason are also against him, and that he cannot for ever remain suspended between the equal but contradictory appearances which confront him. He must terminate the bizarre encounter, and, in the best tradition of Molière's valets, chooses acquiescence in the will of the stronger as the better part of valour.[27]

In spite of the coincidence of Sosie's dilemma with the self-imposed difficulty of Descartes, it is the 'suspension de jugement' induced in Sosie by the double nature of appearances which relates the comic vision of this scene more closely to the position held by Descartes' opponents, the Sceptics. Gassendi in particular, in his *Disquisitio Metaphysica* (1642-4), presented lengthy and cogent sceptical objections to Descartes' metaphysical system.[28] Although there is disagreement about the extent of Gassendi's scepticism, there is no doubt that his *Disquisitio* is impeccably sceptical in the nature of his objections to Descartes' new method of doubting.[29]

Gassendi stresses again and again that his disagreement with Descartes rests not on the truth of the matter in question — that is, the existence of God, a belief which he accepts fideistically — but on the methods employed by Descartes to prove God's existence.[30] In particular, he disagrees with the principle of Descartes' hyperbolic doubt and its dramatic expression in the hypothesis of the *malus genius*. Nearly thirty years before Molière's play, Gassendi writes that it is a fiction which is truly theatrical in its conception. He cannot understand why Descartes should find it necessary to elaborate such an extreme hypothesis in order to confirm his *Cogito* — perhaps the reason lies in what Gassendi calls 'votre excessive confiance en vous-même', which makes Descartes conceive of his grand design *(hallucinatum)* in the first place. Gassendi demythologizes the grandiose hypothesis and at the same time the faith in reason which sustains it: '. . . pour vous donner à vous-même une telle assurance, il a été nécessaire d'imaginer un Dieu trompeur ou je ne sais quel malin Génie qui se joue de vous, alors qu'il semblait suffire de mettre en cause le peu de lumière de l'esprit humain et la seule faiblesse de notre nature.'[31]

Gassendi's ironic demythologizing of the *malus genius* harmonizes perfectly with Molière's dramatic treatment of it: as the Prologue reveals, his 'malin génie' in the form of Mercure owes his existence, as do the gods in the first place, not to mere mythological convention as utilized by Rotrou, but rather to human error and weakness, which means that man is continually unable to pierce to the essential meaning of phenomena. Throughout this important scene with Mercure, Sosie has not only illustrated such limitations, but has also been content to remain within them. He has reacted to Mercure's arguments according to their increasingly apparent cogency; initially refusing to countenance such a preposterous pretension (ll. 424-5), he has shown a readiness to accept the appearances of proof offered (ll. 468 ff., ll. 484 ff.) before agreeing to acknowledge them as true (ll. 517 ff.). His acknowledgement that Mercure must indeed be Sosie has nothing definitive or essential about it; the fact that he is prepared to do so is implicit recognition of the weakness of human reason, the unreliability of his judgement and his capacity to err — and these are all factors which serve to undermine any dogmatic opinion which one may hold of oneself or of others.

This acceptance of appearances by Sosie would appear to illustrate comically the sceptical attitude to doubt, as opposed to that of Descartes. As Gassendi writes in his *Disquisitio,* sceptical doubt applies only to those things which are 'réellement incertaines', but not to things which are 'effectivement apparentes': the object of the Sceptic's doubt is therefore 'la nature profonde de chacune de ces apparences', and not the 'apparences' themselves.[32] Likewise Le Vayer opts for a modest acquiescence in appearances, and consigns those who refuse to accept them to the province of comedy.[33] Sosie chooses not to resist appearances by abdicating his identity, but his master Amphitryon resists appearances by obstinately clinging to his identity. In the sceptical perspective of the play, the fool will appear once more as the wise man, and the wise man as the fool.

(5)

It is this sceptical perspective which is responsible for the Amphitryon of Molière, who turns out to be quite different from his two predecessors. The corresponding character in Rotrou is still the bemused Amphitryon of the Latin play, who is, *malgré lui,* a fairly passive spectator of his own conjugal misfortune. In *Les Sosies* he appears in particular as a less choleric and more vacillating character than his counterpart in Molière's play. When Sosie tells him of his encounter with Mercure, he can only exclaim

> Quelle confusion à la mienne est pareille,
> Et combien justement douté-je si je veille! (Act II, Sc. 1)

In his first meeting with Alcmène, who tells him of his sudden and recent visit to her, he says 'Je ne me connais plus: moi-même je m'ignore' (Act II, Sc. 3). The frequent repetition of such doubts by his Amphitryon is, as was noted above, a special characteristic of Rotrou's play and of the dramatic framework within which he was working. One looks in vain for the expression of similarly fundamental doubts about his own nature by Molière's Amphitryon. He could not say that he does not know who he is, because he is supremely aware of his identity and reputation as the victorious general of the Theban army, and the husband of the beautiful Alcmène, and he does not for a moment doubt that reality corresponds to his *persona*. The world for him is ordered in a firm and stable fashion, just as it was for Sosie prior to the arrival of Mercure upon the human scene.[34] Reality is not and cannot be problematic for him, and he therefore does not fall into confusion when Sosie recounts to him his bizarre adventure with Mercure (as did Rotrou's Amphitryon). To his mind, the story is merely just another role acted by his mendacious valet — and he dismisses it contemptuously as 'contes . . . d'extravagance outrés' (Act II, Sc. 1, l. 697). He, on the other hand, maintains a completely rational attitude, which Sosie also shared when he first listened to Mercure:

> Au mystère nouveau que tu me viens conter
> Est-il quelque ombre d'apparence? (ll. 769-70)

Sosie knows only too well how absurd his story must appear to the eye of reason, but since his encounter with Mercure he also knows something more of the power of appearances:

> Cela choque le sens commun;
> Mais cela ne laisse pas d'être. (ll. 775-6)

His formerly narrow understanding of what constituted common sense has now been enlarged by the paradoxical appearances of Mercure in the form of Sosie. Amphitryon, however, remains stubbornly fixed in his conception of what 'le bon sens' may be: 'Le moyen d'en rien croire, à moins qu'être insensé?' (l. 777). Since Sosie's account appears to him to be unreasonable, it simply cannot be, and there is no further problem. His dogmatic attitude to the opinions of others is easily recognizable as that of the Molière *imaginaire,* but he is in fact doubly dogmatic because of the apparently absurd *coq-à-l'âne* which Sosie tells him. Unlike the normal *imaginaire,* however, he passes for an ostensibly reasonable person in the eyes of others. In his reaction to Sosie and to subsequent events, Molière illustrates a favourite sceptical theme — what do we mean when we invoke the criterion of 'le bon sens' as a standard of reference for ourselves and others? Le Vayer devotes his *Petit Traité Sceptique sur cette commune Façon de parler, N'Avoir Pas le Sens Commun* to this very problem:

> ...le plus ordinaire emploi de notre proverbe est à l'égard de ceux que nous croyons avoir des opinions extravagantes, quand elles ne s'accordent pas aux nôtres: parce que cet Amour de nous-mêmes est si puissant, que nous ne considérons nos pensées que comme une partie de notre être, sans les examiner davantage . . . De là vient cette animosité ordinaire contre ceux qui nous contrarient, et qu'aussitôt que quelqu'un s'écarte de notre sens, pris pour notre jugement, nous disons qu'il a perdu le Sens Commun, c'est-à-dire qu'il ne raisonne ni ne juge comme le reste des hommes raisonnables.[35]

Le Vayer disposes of such narrow-minded *sagesse* by means of his beloved series of sceptical tropes which oppose reason to reason and *folie* to *sagesse,* until nothing is left of the notion that 'le bon sens' exists — apart from the certainty that it cannot exist objectively as a criterion of behaviour.[36] Molière achieves the same result by placing Amphitryon in a series of increasingly paradoxical positions which culminate in the recognition by his friends in the final Act that he is — the wrong Amphitryon! It will be profitable to follow the evolution of Amphitryon from his encounter with Sosie until Act III.

Having rejected utterly the fantastic story told by his valet, he goes in to see Alcmène. He receives her account of his supposed visit with incredulity, but she can produce evidence for the visit in the form of the present which he (i.e. Jupiter) gave her. He sees the diamonds in front of him, which he has brought in a sealed box. He himself admits that 'le cachet est entier' (Act II, Sc. 2, l. 964), and he now finds himself in a position similar to that of Sosie in Act I. But Sosie was prepared to accept the testimony of appearances for what they were worth, however intrinsically absurd they might seem to be. It is true that Amphitryon declares 'Je vois des incidents qui passent la nature' (l. 981), but he is not prepared to concede the intrusion of the irrational into his ordered world, in spite of Alcmène's assurance that he did visit her, and the story which Sosie has already recounted to him in the previous scene. On the contrary, the conclusion to which he hastily comes is one which by its very nature rules out the irrational. His honour is endangered, and he must quickly seek out his rival in order to avenge himself: 'Le déshonneur est sûr, mon malheur m'est visible' (l. 1052). He will find her brother who will explain everything to him:

> Après, nous percerons jusqu'au fond d'un mystère
> Jusques à présent inouï,
> Et dans les mouvements d'une juste colère,
> Malheur à qui m'aura trahi! (ll. 1060-3)

Once he has avenged himself, there will be no further problem for him. It is not the irrational nature of the occurrence with which he is concerned, but the outward gesture: he lives on the surface, taking surface for depth, appearance for reality, and the safeguarding of his reputation as his essential task.

Rotrou's Amphitryon, when he returns from his search for his brother-in-law, admits already that he must truly have a double: 'On s'y perd, on s'y double, on ne s'y connaît plus.' He even considers the double to be a kind of irrational manifestation of himself: 'Quand notre état premier nous sera-t-il rendu?' (Act IV, Sc.1). At the corresponding stage of Molière's play, his Amphitryon still has made no concession to the irrational, and believes himself to be in perfect self-possession in spite of his disquieting experiences. He is still preoccupied not with what he considers to be the mere theft of the diamonds by his rival, but with the loss of his honour:

> Le vol des diamants n'est pas ce qui m'étonne:
> On lève les cachets, qu'on ne l'aperçoit pas; (Act III, Sc. 1, ll. 1466-7)

He attempts instead to rationalize his supposed visit to Alcmène:

> La nature parfois produit des ressemblances
> Dont quelques imposteurs ont pris droit d'abuser;
> Mais il est hors de sens que sous ces apparences
> Un homme pour époux se puisse supposer,
> Et dans tous ces rapports sont mille différences
> Dont se peut une femme aisément aviser.
> Des charmes de la Thessalie
> On vante de tout temps les merveilleux effets;
> Mais les contes fameux qui partout en sont faits,
> Dans mon esprit toujours ont passé pour folie; (ll. 1470-9)

In other words, he is still as dogmatically rational as he was when he first listened to Sosie. He still insists on rationalizing his position after his bewilderment at the hands of Mercure (in the guise of Sosie) in the following scene, asking himself

> A quel parti me doit résoudre ma raison?
> Ai-je l'éclat ou le secret à prendre? (Act III, Sc. 3, ll. 1563-4)

His reason is still firmly under the sway of his natural impulse to safeguard his honour, and whatever happens to him cannot divert him in the slightest from that course. Even when Naucratès is able to assure Amphitryon in the following scene that Sosie has not left them and could not therefore have been responsible for the trick which Mercure has played on him, he still does not see, or refuses to see, that it may be a less straightforward matter than avenging his marital honour (Act III, Sc. 4, ll. 1612-14). The climax to his intransigence comes with the first appearance of Jupiter to him in Act III, Sc. 5. Once again a contrast with the attitude of Rotrou's Amphitryon is illuminating. There Jupiter and Amphitryon vie with each other to give proofs of their identities as the true Amphitryon. The real Amphitryon is so disconcerted at the sight of his double that he confesses

> Je doute qui je suis, je me perds, je m'ignore;
> Moi-même je m'oublie et ne me connais plus. (Act IV, Sc. 4)

and he therefore shows a certain understanding of the inability of his friends to distinguish the true Amphitryon from the false one:

> A peine me connais-je en ce désordre extrême;
> Me rencontrant en lui, je me cherche en moi-même,
> Mais cette ressemblance est assez confirmée
> Par le récent abus des chefs de notre armée;
> L'incertain jugement que ces gens ont rendu
> Laisse encore à présent leur esprit suspendu;
> Cette distinction ne leur est pas possible. (Act V, Sc. 4)

Molière's Amphitryon, on the other hand, remains rigidly true to his character, showing neither doubt of his own identity nor appreciation of the complex problem which confronts his friends. He and he alone is the true Amphitryon, and this ought to be immediately and objectively obvious to all, since it is to himself. Subjective certainty, as the opponents of Descartes' *Méditations Métaphysiques* continue to object, is no guarantee of objective certainty; and, as Gassendi points out to him in his objections to the *Ve Méditation*, to say that you perceive something clearly and distinctly yourself, as Descartes says he perceives the *Cogito* and the existence of God which guarantees it, is no guarantee that it is equally clear and distinct to others. The question of clear and certain knowledge, continues Gassendi, is further complicated by the fact that '. . . pas un seul de ceux qui pensent le contraire de vous ne manque de croire qu'il a une connaissance aussi claire et aussi distincte que la vôtre.'[37]

Amphitryon ignores the problem of the nature of reality completely, even though Sosie proclaims Jupiter to be the true Amphitryon (ll. 1625-6). Polidas, however, chooses to suspend judgement prudently:

Certes, ce rapport admirable
Suspend ici mon jugement. (ll. 1627-8)

And Naucratès re-emphasizes to the infuriated Amphitryon the reason for their hesitation in acting:

Nous voyons bien en vous Amphitryon paroître,
Du salut des Thébains le glorieux appui;
Mais nous le voyons tous aussi paroître en lui,
Et ne saurions juger dans lequel il peut être. (ll. 1656-9)

It is left to Jupiter to conclude that the problem of the true and false Amphitryon is ostensibly — and therefore definitively — insoluble, either by Amphitryon's violent methods or the more patient research of Naucratès:

L'un de nous est Amphitryon;
Et tous deux à vos yeux nous le pouvons paroître. (ll. 1679-80)

Ironically, he confirms the impossibility of a solution by his calm dispassionate attitude which favours his claim to be Amphitryon: the real Amphitryon's attitude is outward proof that he is the impostor:

Et lorsque de la sorte on se met en colère,
On fait croire qu'on a de mauvaises raisons. (ll. 1634-5)[38]

The final ironic thrust comes from the balanced Naucratès, who has weighed up carefully the respective claims of each aspirant, as he says with reference to Jupiter

Je ne sais pas s'il s'impose;
Mais il parle sur la chose
Comme s'il avoit raison. (ll. 1713-15)

The withdrawal of the disconsolate Amphitryon bears out the tenet of the Sceptics, that one can only doubt the things which are 'réellement incertaines' and not the things which are 'effectivement apparentes'. And since in this case Jupiter and Amphitryon are outwardly indistinguishable, the supreme paradox that the first is more apparently Amphitryon than the second appears as the most reasonable solution to the problem.

In the final scene Jupiter gives his promised explanation to Amphitryon, but unlike the corresponding scene in Plautus and Rotrou, Amphitryon is just a silent spectator. In Plautus Amphitryo says that he is content to share his happiness with Jupiter, and in Rotrou he deems himself honoured to have the god as his rival.[39] Molière cleverly transposes the remarks of their characters into

Jupiter's speech, as the latter proudly tells Amphitryon that he must take a shared rivalry with the master of the gods as a great personal compliment (ll. 1898-1901). However, the glorious cuckold's exasperated silence is proof, if proof were needed, of his ambiguous attitude to Jupiter's praise, and this is ironically underlined by Sosie. He proposes that all the actors in the event put an end to commentary and analysis of it, and that a discreet silence be henceforth maintained thereon.[40]

Jupiter had blandly claimed that he would be able to demonstrate to all that Alcmène's virtue was unsullied (ll. 1691 ff.), and that after his 'explanation' of events all would be well. All that Jupiter and Sosie suggest, however, is that the participants should act as though nothing at all had happened. The acceptance of this illusion might well be possible: Posiclès, after all, had ventured to suggest something of the kind to Amphitryon when he said

Si cette ressemblance est telle que l'on dit,
Alcmène, sans être coupable . . . (ll. 1818-9)

The supreme irony of the situation is that this occurrence has happened to the man most unlikely to adopt such an attitude. He must by his very nature probe as far as a mortal can into even the most delicate of matters for the sake of his honour:

Hélas! je brûle de l'apprendre,
Et je le crains plus que la mort. (Act III, Sc. 4, ll. 1613-14)

is the way he describes his urge to discover his marital fate. Like one of his predecessors, Dom Garcie, with whom he has so much in common, he is perpetually mastered by his jealous temperament, which is not easily given to forgiveness and forgetfulness. To accept an illusion involves fostering the belief that one's attitude to something or someone is the only opinion which really matters in spite of what others may say. But Amphitryon is far too dependent upon the image which he wishes others to have of him to be able to control his will to that extent. As he says himself, the re-establishment of one's reputation and honour is a consideration too important to be rationalized (Act III, Sc. 7, ll. 1823-6). Even the *pince-sans-rire* Sosie, who glibly proposes this solution, had illustrated its inherent difficulty when he confessed before his meeting with Cléanthis that

La foiblesse humaine est d'avoir
Des curiosités d'apprendre
Ce qu'on ne voudroit pas savoir. (Act II, Sc. 3, ll. 1083-5)[41]

The advent of Jupiter into the world makes men into unwitting actors in his comedy. His withdrawal from it leaves them with the new consciousness that henceforth only self-deception and illusion are suitable attitudes for them to adopt. Everyone must, willingly or not, play his own role in this imposed comedy. Amphitryon and Alcmène are the characters who fare worst because they did not play a part previously (the virtuous appearances of Alcmène corresponded to her real self, and the valorous image of Amphitryon was completely at one with its heroic creator). Only those who perpetually play a role are in harmony with the comic vision of Jupiter, and that of Molière above that. Such characters escape with impunity the comic fate which the two comic creators decree shall befall those who, too seriously and too concertedly, believe that their real essence can and does coincide with their outer gestures, their *persona*.

7 Les Femmes Savantes

(1)

Unlike *Tartuffe, Dom Juan* and *Le Misanthrope, Les Femmes Savantes* offers no comparable difficulty with regard to the interpretation of the principal characters. If there is ambiguity in the play, and this chapter will argue that there is, then it lies not in the comic or non-comic aspect of the characters, but in the ideas which they express. A well-established view of the play would have us believe that there is no semblance of ambiguity in those ideas, which are generally held to be prosaic in the extreme.[1] Henriette is usually seen as the character who expresses ideas which her author approves of, and as having a well-balanced outlook on life; yet those who view her thus frequently cannot refrain from wishing that the playwright had couched her *sagesse* in somewhat less mundane terms.[2]

But considered in the wider context of Molière's plays, Henriette presents difficulties to the point of view mentioned above. In previous plays, such as *L'Ecole des Maris* (1661) and particularly *L'Ecole des Femmes* (1662), Molière had seemed to be unfavourable to characters such as Sganarelle and Arnolphe, who attempted to inculcate ignorance of life in the minds of their wards. In *Les Femmes Savantes,* however, he would appear to be favouring the ideas of Henriette (if we accept her as being justified against the *femmes savantes*), who is, on her own admission, willing to be ignorant of everything to the exclusion of marriage and children. Such a girl would doubtless have appealed very much to Arnolphe, who reads with reverence the *Maximes du Mariage,* which prohibit to the married woman attendance at those 'belles assemblées' at which enlightened feminists expatiate.[3] Chrysale concurs wholeheartedly with the traditional view about the role of woman, which his youngest daughter expounds.

There is certainly a contradiction in logic between the fate met by the views of the *barbons* of the *Ecoles* and the apparent triumph here of Henriette's views. Indeed, examples of such illogicality in Molière's conclusions could be multiplied regarding other characters in his plays.[4] But the seemingly contradictory *dénouements* are perfectly acceptable as such when it is remembered that the mainspring of comedy does not lie directly in logical processes of thought. Molière himself saw the first principle of comedy as being *disconvenance* or *contrariété.* Contradiction and conflict are of the essence of his comedies, and point to the truth that his comic vision is, by its very nature, bound to transcend the rigid categories into which reason and logic would order thought. So, as with the rest of Molière's plays, the question we must ask is not 'Which ideas appear most reasonable in themselves or are least in contradiction with previous comic conclusions?' but rather 'How best can we understand the comic principle and its vision as illustrated within a certain thematic framework?'

(2)

As in so many of Molière's plays, the principle underlying the vision of the play is enunciated within the opening scene. Here the dramatist by way of the *raisonneur* indicates to the spectator the angle from which the comedy may be most fully enjoyed. In *Le Misanthrope*, for example, Philinte had warned Alceste that it was an act of folly to attempt to remould the world to his specifications, and the rest of the play is an illustration of this principle. We are not asked to provide our own subjective definition of comedy, but to interpret the play in the light of a given notion about what is ridiculous in human nature. The opening dialogue between Henriette and Armande is likewise of immense importance. From the beginning, the initiative is firmly grasped by the acerbic Armande. Depreciating her sister's desire for domestic contentment, she adjures her to leave marriage and all its mundane concomitants to people of low breeding and vulgar taste. Her argument is neatly summed up in the lofty injunction:

> Laissez aux gens grossiers, aux personnes vulgaires,
> Les bas amusements de ces sortes d'affaires;
> A de plus hauts objets élevez vos désirs.
> Songez à prendre un goût des plus nobles plaisirs,
> Et traitant de mépris les sens et la matière,
> A l'esprit comme nous, donnez-vous toute entière. (ll. 31-6)

Choosing to embrace such a high ideal and disparaging banal reality, Armande embarks upon the course of all the *imaginaires*. But she differs from them in the manner in which she speaks of her ideal. She does not merely assert the superiority of her own wisdom over that of others, as do Orgon and Alceste, for example. The ideal which she propounds to her sister gains additional elevation in her eyes because it involves the duality of ethereal, rarified pleasures of the intellect, and vulgar, sensual and "low" experience. Like the other *raisonneurs,* Henriette presents the more down-to-earth view of things which dramatic opposition makes necessary. Just as her sister goes further than any other comic character in the spiritualized form of her ideal, so too Henriette goes beyond the usual counter-answer of the *raisonneur* by expounding her exceptionally mundane version of her ideal:

> . . . tout esprit n'est pas composé d'une étoffe
> Qui se trouve taillée à faire un philosophe.
> Si le vôtre est né propre aux élévations
> Où montent des savants les spéculations,
> Le mien est fait, ma soeur, pour aller terre à terre,
> Et dans les petits soins son foible se resserre. (ll. 55-60)

The *raison d'être* for what Henriette says does not lie in any inherent merit which Molière attached to her views, or any profound didactic wisdom contained in them (although both may well be present), but in the necessity of providing a counteraction to the movement away from reality initiated by the comic idealist. The tone and content of her remarks about women's education and domestic duties are conditioned by the idea behind the comic situation. It therefore seems beside the point to argue that her ideas are somewhat parochial. She is just as much a character of comedy as Armande, complementing the comic idealist as well as provoking her into reactions which are increasingly more inflexible and comic.[5] A *juste-milieu* must be created between the two extremities of comic idealism and comic realism, in order that the spectator should enjoy a superior perspective on the play to that of the protagonist; it cannot necessarily be equated with the ideas of Henriette, the dramatic opponent of Armande. There is in fact a difference between the theory of *juste-milieu* which Henriette outlines --

> . . . tout esprit n'est pas composé d'une étoffe
> Qui se trouve taillée à faire un philosophe (ll. 55-6)

-- and the role of opposition given to her. This is clearly the fundamental principle which Armande has transgressed and from which the comedy of *Les Femmes Savantes* derives. For it is obvious that they are pedantic impostors, and the role which Armande plays cannot hide her nature, which is of all things *not* 'taillée à faire un philosophe'. But if this theory of the *juste-milieu* is a framework in which to view the comedy of the idealist, Henriette voluntarily assumes the role of *ignorante* in the play. The thought of the comedy does not reside in the literal acceptance of all Henriette's ideas, which are suitably exaggerated for the comic conflict, but in the way in which comedy accommodates the principle of *juste-milieu* to its own ends.

It will be profitable to amplify the principle which Henriette states explicitly but necessarily contradicts herself to some degree. The view of life which it enshrines takes full account of the diversity and individuality of human nature. If Armande's mind is born 'propre aux élévations', that of Henriette is designed to 'aller terre à terre'. Everyone who acts in harmony with his own instinct finds his personal *juste-milieu,* different to that of his neighbour. La Mothe Le Vayer outlines this view in terms strongly reminiscent of those used by Henriette, when he draws an analogy between the various levels of 'esprits' and the ways in which different kinds of birds fly: 'Les uns se plaisent à s'élancer jusqu'au plus haut de l'air; d'autres ne s'élèvent que fort peu de la terre, ou ne sautent que de branche en branche; et la troisième espèce est de ceux, qui volent dans le milieu que les premiers abandonnent, et où les seconds ne peuvent arriver.'[6]

Both Le Vayer's comparison and Molière's character proclaim that the only true basis for personal fulfilment is the maintenance of one's individuality. Henriette advances this justification for her refusal to follow the example of others, and in so doing astutely places her attitude beyond the reach of Armande's generalizing. The *juste-milieu* of which she speaks can neither be acquired by, nor imposed upon one's nature if this occurs, natural temperament and inclination will, however unconsciously, rebel against superimposed attitudes. At first sight, her view appears to be nothing more original than a summary of *honnête* principles. We find the Chevalier de Méré insisting on the importance of an affinity between one's actions and one's natural instinct: '. . . il faut consulter son inclination et ne la pas contrarier . . . on a peu de grâce quand on va contre son génie . . .'[7] La Rochefoucauld may also be quoted, to show how much of a commonplace such an observation would seem in the seventeenth century: '. . . il faut savoir discerner . . . ce qui nous est propre, et suivre alors avec raison la pente naturelle qui nous porte vers les choses qui nous plaisent.'[8] In the same maxim, La Rochefoucauld poses the question of individual authenticity in terms which are especially applicable to Molière's comedy: 'Une femme peut aimer les sciences mais toutes les sciences ne lui conviennent pas toujours et l'entêtement de certaines sciences ne lui convient jamais, et est toujours faux.'[9]

The ideas of *honnêteté* thus expressed do not go beyond the general principle of *juste-milieu*. Indeed, to become more specific, to lay down precepts for individual cases would undermine the belief in the diversity of human beings which is so basic to *honnêteté*. In Méré's descriptions of *honnête* behaviour, words such as 'subtil', 'imperceptible', 'je ne sais quoi' recur regularly, and it is clear that he is quite content that the intangible essence of *juste-milieu* should forever elude him.[10] But the comic vision is much less abstract and more adjacent to life than the detached *moraliste* could afford to be. There the *juste-milieu* is not couched in vague terms of reasonable injunction, golden mean, or avoidance of excessive behaviour, but is rather focused sharply in the extreme comic opposition between Henriette and Armande. The comic principle, enunciated by Henriette, was that behaviour and instinct must be in harmony with each other. Consequently comedy results from reason imposing on nature an attitude which is in disharmony with instinct, and in practical terms this is translated into Armande's refusal of marriage for the sake of philosophy. The paradox is that Henriette appears in the guise of the *raisonneur,* proclaiming, with every appearance of moderation and reasonableness, the unalterable supremacy of instinct over reason, a view which runs diametrically counter to such appearances! The corollary of this is even more paradoxical, but fully consistent with the *folle sagesse* which Henriette's smilingly enigmatic predecessors have expounded. Only if reason accepts the supremacy of instinct can it be accounted 'reasonable' (but not necessarily rational or logical); reason, on the other hand, if it does not accept this paradox, is unreasonable and comic (but not necessarily irrational or illogical).

If the touchstone of the comic vision of *Les Femmes Savantes* is provided by the sceptical notion of *folle sagesse* applied here to marriage, then one would expect to find a resemblance between that comic vision and the ideas of La Mothe Le Vayer on the subject. In fact it is surprising to find not only a remarkable similarity between Le Vayer and *Les Femmes Savantes,* but also to hear the same burlesque tone which characterizes the comic treatment of the *femme savante* in the play. In his *Promenades en Neuf Dialogues* (1662-4), Le Vayer devotes the fourth dialogue between Tubertus and Xilinus to a consideration of those people who seem to wish to repress their natural instincts. Xilinus reproaches Tubertus for his austere love of solitude and his misanthropic inclinations; he finds this attitude totally unreasonable and unacceptable, and bases his point of view upon one cardinal principle: 'Déjà, je m'étonnais qu'il y eût des humeurs assez austères, pour résister à des sentiments que Dieu et la Nature semblent avoir donnés également à tous les Animaux, et qui à l'égard de l'homme sont tels que les plus grands Législateurs n'ont rien trouvé de plus propre à les faire vivre heureusement que l'union conjugale.'[11]

In spite of his melancholy humour, Tubertus cannot but agree with him: those people who resist or are impervious to the call of nature and love involve themselves unwittingly in a kind of *gigantomachie,* a hopelessly unequal struggle against natural desires and instincts, which are destined to triumph over reason and will in the end.[12]

The Sceptic rests his ideas, not only of marriage but of life in general, upon this principle: the indisputable primacy of instinct over reason. And this is not only the principle behind the comedy of Molière, but also almost the sole principle which may be attributed to him with any degree of certainty, for it is the unvarying constant in every comedy and in every comic character. A comic character in his theatre becomes comic to the extent that he attempts to escape from his own nature, trying to eradicate his natural characteristics, which nevertheless remain all the more firmly rooted.[13] Hence the *gigantomachie* of the comic hero, who is doomed to failure because his true self can never be completely suppressed. Nowhere is this theory more apt than in the cases of women who, like the *précieuses ridicules*, are revolted by 'la pensée de coucher contre un homme vraiment nu' *(Les Précieuses Ridicules,* Sc. 4). Armande is one of the most ardent of such 'Jansénistes de l'Amour', as Ninon de Lenclos wittily described them.[14] In the opening scene of the play she advised Henriette 'Mariez-vous, ma soeur, à la philosophie' (l. 44), and later she outlines to Clitandre her lofty theory of a spiritualized love, purified from sensual commerce, in which 'l'on ne s'aperçoit jamais qu'on ait un corps' (Act IV, Sc. 2, l. 1212).

Molière takes great care not only to point out the manifest absurdity and discrepancies in such a platonic philosophy, but especially to underline the multiple hypocrisies latent in it. At four stages of the play the comic vision expresses itself without equivocation on this attitude. In Act I, Sc. 2, Armande attempts forcefully to prevent Clitandre from declaring his preference for herself or for Henriette. When he nevertheless states his love for the latter, Armande attempts immediately to rationalize her wounded pride by saying that Clitandre is unbearably conceited to imagine Armande concerned for him, and that Henriette cannot marry Clitandre without her parents' consent (ll. 155-68). The vehemence of her double reaction is ample proof, if proof were needed, both of the depth of her passion for Clitandre, and her determination to conceal it at all costs. In Act III, Sc. 5 she lauds Philaminte's choice of Trissotin as a husband for Henriette; when Henriette ripostes by asking why she herself does not accept such a learned and therefore eminently suitable husband, she again extricates herself, on the pretext that a maternal decree cannot legitimately be resisted. In Act IV, Sc. 1 she informs Philaminte of Henriette's continued disobedience to the projected marriage with Trissotin (and by so doing discloses to her Henriette's true position); but she succeeds in exacerbating Philaminte beyond all measure by announcing her news in carefully chosen terms — Henriette, she says,

> . . . sembloit suivre moins les volontés d'un père,
> Qu'affecter de braver les ordres d'une mère. (ll. 1125-6)

The fourth stage in Armande's attitude is found in Act IV, Sc. 2, and marks an involuntary deviation from the concerted rationalizing mentioned above. This final stage consists of three movements: she first of all accuses Clitandre of infidelity towards her in declaring his love for her sister (ll. 1167-74); when Clitandre rejects her charge, she reiterates her platonic ideal (ll. 1189 ff.); and when Clitandre emphasizes that his conception of love takes fully into account physical desire, she relents in the hope of regaining him: the fact that she still attempts to rationalize her radically changed attitude — marriage of the kind Clitandre favours will be grudgingly accepted by her as a concession to the baser part of human nature (ll. 1235 ff.) — cannot obscure one truth: the comic vision has remorselessly driven Armande from implicitly contradicting her ideal to voluntarily contradicting it by capitulation to Clitandre's point of view.

A. Adam has commented most perceptively on the *gigantomachie* waged by Armande throughout the play:

> On devine l'exaspération de Molière, l'antipathie instinctive, l'horreur. Ce faux idéalisme n'est à ses yeux que mensonge. Armande était belle, faite pour aimer et être aimée. Elle s'est installée dans l'imposture. Elle se ment à elle-même plus encore qu'elle ne ment aux autres. Elle s'enivre d'un orgueil chimérique, d'un idéal absurde. Il n'est de santé et de vérité que dans l'obéissance aux lois de la nature.[15]

The views expressed in this scene by Clitandre are fully in harmony with the principle of the comic vision ('l'obéissance aux lois de la nature'), of which marriage is not only a symbol but a literal expression. He possesses 'un corps tout comme une âme' (l. 1214), and cannot discriminate between the importance of each: '. . . mon âme et mon corps marchent de compagnie' (l. 1218). Platonic ideals are consequently 'trop subtilisés' (l. 1223) for him: just as he loves 'avec tout moi-même' (l. 1225) (i.e. with instinct and reason) so too he is attracted both intellectually and physically to Henriette (l. 1226). So the second cardinal principle of comedy is worked out dramatically in this scene, with, as Adam indicated, potentially tragic implications for Armande. That it is decidedly *not* tragic is entirely due to the forcefulness with which comedy is intent on exposing at all costs the imposture of Armande and the injustice done by her to human nature. The sceptical view of the human duality of mind and matter is identical to that which Clitandre has expressed burlesquely. In one of his *Homilies Académiques (Du Corps Humain)*, Le Vayer writes: 'Car de présupposer qu'en contemplation de l'excellence de l'âme, et des avantages qu'elle a comme divine sur le corps, il n'y ait nulle mesure à garder entre l'une et l'autre; ce serait être peu équitable et peu judicieux, à les considérer non pas séparément, mais dans l'union où ils sont constitués pour faire un seul composé.'[16]

The comic vision re-establishes the worth of this *composé* of body and mind in apparently straightforward terms — Armande is defeated, Clitandre triumphs. But the implication of the vision goes further than this — for in the culminating stages of Armande's self-deception her true nature has, however hesitatingly, re-emerged. There is another *précieuse* in Molière's theatre who stands side by side with Armande in her opposition to marriage, but in whom the optimism of the comic vision is more apparent. In *La Princesse d'Elide, comédie galante* (1664) — which was contemporary with Le Vayer's *Promenades* — the Princess has sworn never to let herself be enslaved by the chains of marriage; like Armande, she is able to rationalize her attitude so well to her servants that she betrays her underlying obsessions:

> . . . ne devez-vous pas rougir d'appuyer une passion qui n'est qu'er-
> reur, que foiblesse et qu'emportement, et dont tous les désordres ont
> tant de répugnance avec la gloire de notre sexe? J'en prétends sout-
> enir l'honneur jusqu'au dernier moment de ma vie . . . je ne puis souf-
> frir qu'une âme qui fait profession d'un peu de fierté ne trouve pas
> une honte horrible à de telles foiblesses. (Act II, Sc. 1)

Her two servants take a more down-to-earth view of things: do not
treat love arrogantly, they advise her, or else it may choose to revenge
itself upon you. But the Princess has no use for such prudence: the
legendary power which love is supposed to have is only invoked by
mortals as a concession to their own infirm nature. Yet the servants are
still sceptical about her vaunted resistance to love: '. . . toute la terre
reconnoît sa puissance, et vous voyez que les dieux même sont assujettis
à son empire.' In his fourth *Promenade* Tubertus likewise speaks
jocularly of '[le] pouvoir despotique et presque incompréhensible de
l'Amour'.[17] For the Princess, as for her more illustrious successor, love
is the natural force which strips away artifice and sophistication. Soon
she will be forced to concede defeat, as she succumbs to the attraction of
the Prince d'Ithaque. Tubertus once more could provide the perfect
epigraph for such a situation, based as it is upon the comic antithesis of
love and reason: '. . . toutes les maximes de la raison (sont) autant
d'hérésies dans l'École de cet enfant Aveugle . . . le premier soupir qu'il
nous (fait) jeter (est) ordinairement le dernier de la sagesse.'[18] Better to
resist the temptation to submit life to one's own ordered scheme, and to
make ample allowance for the unpredictable intrusion of one's own
nature and circumstances — in other words, of *folie* itself.

For both dramatist and Sceptic marriage is then both symbol and
literal expression of nature: but in both cases, it would also seem to
contain a hidden dimension of meaning. In Le Vayer, this dimension is
concealed in the discreet conclusion with which he chooses to terminate
the *Promenade,* and in *Les Femmes Savantes,* in the sheer implication
of the play. A comparison will reveal an interesting similarity of mind.
Le Vayer proceeds to give abundant examples for his thesis that
marriage is the state which is most closely in harmony with human
instinct. He adduces the presence of Christ at the wedding-feast of Cana
as 'proof', and skilfully extracts passages from Fathers of the Church in
such a way that they appear indeed to forbid celibacy: he even makes St
Ambrose responsible for the facetious observation that if marriage
populates the earth, then virginity does precisely the same for heaven!
By means of such adroit insinuation, he manages to create in the
reader's mind the impression that celibacy, whatever the motive behind
it may be, is nothing other than a form of *gigantomachie.*[19]

It would of course be totally futile to suppose that the author of *Les
Femmes Savantes* wrote his play with such a tendentious idea in mind.

But can we not glimpse something of his attitude in the impatience with which comedy unmasks Armande's views on marriage? If Armande is guilty in his eyes of a hypocritical prudishness which induces her to oppose marriage, it is nevertheless clear that Molière makes her utter statements which would come naturally to someone engaged in a vocation which did not admit of marriage. Her *idée fixe* is expressed most fully in her maxim 'A de plus hauts objets élevez vos désirs' (l. 33), which is somewhat reminiscent of St Paul's famous injunction: 'Affectionnez-vous aux choses d'en haut, et non à celles qui sont sur la terre.'[20] Armande is quite obviously not a religious, nor is she talking here of religion. The point I wish to underline, however, is that in so far as Molière seems to deny the possibility that one can have a more spiritual life than one centred upon marriage, one may conclude that religious celibacy, or celibacy of any kind, would also appear to him as an ideal incommensurate with the strength of human nature. For the man to whom Armande's ideas are so totally antipathetic, as for Le Vayer, marriage is principally the legalization of the deepest human instinct, and whenever the conjugal state harmonizes with this tendency, it can create the best basis for human happiness.

The reassertion by the comic principle of the importance of instinct whenever mind and intellect refuse to recognize its existence and its legitimate claim on human nature, helps to clarify Molière's attitude to *préciosité*. A long established view holds that Molière was in no way hostile to the ideas of Mlle de Scudéry, and the evidence is drawn from their apparently convergent views on many topics.[21] Indeed it is not difficult to discover similarities of expression between Sapho and Molière's comedies. He and the *précieuse* may very well agree in satirizing pedants and women who affect fine manners, but this can in no way be taken to imply fundamental agreement on his part with the essential spirit of *préciosité*. Conversely, it seems equally questionable to ask whether or not Molière was thinking of Mlle de Scudéry or Mme de Rambouillet when ridiculing Cathos or Magdelon, or Armande or Philaminte. The definitive answer to such questions would call for documentation of a kind that we do not, and are not likely to, have. But in the light of what has been said above about the comic vision in *Les Femmes Savantes,* it may be more meaningful to ask whether or not that vision is compatible with *précieux* ideas concerning marriage.

As Mornet has shown, there is no single monolithic form of *préciosité* in the seventeenth century. The *préciosité* satirized by Molière in 1659 was, according to him, the old *préciosité* of thirty years earlier, no longer in vogue in the *salons* around the middle of the century.[22] Even if one allows for such a distinction, it is still possible for us to isolate the *précieux* characteristic *par excellence,* present to varying degrees in all forms of seventeenth-century *préciosité*. Mornet himself sums up its essential attribute when discussing specifically the *précieux* understanding of love as revealed in novels from the time of *L'Astrée* to *Le Grand Cyrus:* 'l'esprit tout pur y apparaît fort souvent comme l'âme même du véritable amour.' Mlle de Scudéry places a spiritualized love above all other values of friendship, and extols it as being '. . . si spirituelle, si agréable, et si innocente tout ensemble, qu'elle ne choquerait ni la bienséance, ni la vertu.'[23] Such doctrine doubtless offers an attractive alternative to the imposed *mariage de raison* in the seventeenth century, and a kind of escape from restrictions of husband and children. And in practice the platonic conception of love is often translated into *précieux* repugnance for all forms of marriage which do not conform to the ideal. Marriage, in the conventional sense, is seen as a tyranny which moulds the lofty ideal into mundane reality, 'un scandale à ma raison', as Didascale proclaims in *La Prétieuse* (1656-8). The *précieuse* Eulalie stigmatizes the custom still more virulently, as she contrasts it with the minor matters about which her *précieuses* friends worry: it is '. . . un tyran bien différent de tous les vostres, et que je crois estre le seul véritable, le seul redoutable, le seul insupportable . . . celuy du mariage.'[24] Guéridie, once married, can only utter one reflection: 'Hélas! je suis mariée!' and Mlle de Scudéry confesses that she never witnessed the marriage of one of her friends without giving way to unconsolable grief.[25] Not all *précieuses* were as absolute in their opposition to marriage: many without doubt followed Sapho's example less rigorously, and were able to accommodate themselves to 'des noeuds de chair, des chaînes corporelles' to quote Armande's description of marriage (l. 1238). But in that case Sapho would have viewed such actions as falling short of the *précieux* ideal, and Molière would not have satirized them to the extent that he satirizes Armande. Both would have regarded them as defective *précieuses*.

It is perfectly clear from Molière's theatre that there are certain convergences of thought with *préciosité:* but it is equally clear where the limits of those convergences are to be situated. When the *précieuse* Armande declares that, according to platonic marriage, '. . . l'on ne s'aperçoit jamais qu'on ait un corps' (l. 1212), or when Saint-Sorlin makes his *précieuse* Sestiane say 'Le corps en nos amours ne prend aucune part' (*Les Visionnaires*, Act IV, Sc. 4, l. 1446), such utterances are flagrant deformations of anything a *précieuse* might be expected to say. Nevertheless, there is no deformation without a real impression capable of being deformed, and these lines are exaggerations of a real tendency in *préciosité*. It is at this point that Molière would seem to agree with Saint-Evremond's own penetrating assessment of the *précieux* ideas of marriage: 'Ces fausses délicates ont ôté à l'amour ce qu'il a de plus naturel, pensant lui donner quelque chose de plus précieux. Elles ont tiré une passion toute sensible du coeur à l'esprit, et converti des mouvements en idées.'[26] Saint-Evremond finds the *précieuse* ridiculous because of her tendency to solidify movement in ideas, or, in other words, to subsume life to thought. 'Du mécanique plaqué sur du vivant', the Bergsonian formula of the comic, is not then just a commentary upon the comic of the *précieuses:* it is inherent in their basic ideas. Comedy, to the extent that it symbolizes the constant triumph of the 'vivant' over the 'mécanique', the 'mouvement' over the 'idée', of instinct over reason, contains in its essence the dissolution of the *précieux* ideal, which invariably seeks to refine, subtilize, spiritualize its subject, whether that subject be language, literature or marriage.

(3)

Clitandre shares with Henriette the function of attacking the *précieux* conception of marriage, which is the cornerstone of their pursuit of learning. For it is by revolting against the baseness of physical nature that they derive the impulse towards the world of the spirit, that is, philosophy. It is Clitandre, much more than Henriette, who is entrusted with the function of stripping away the accretions of learning with which the *femme savante* invests herself. He has usually been viewed not only as the dramatic partner of Henriette, but also as the enunciator of the same moderate and reasonable views which she is supposed to express.[27] But the *juste-milieu* which Clitandre apparently expounds is subject (and indeed more clearly so) to the same paradox which underlies Henriette's expression of it. Both expose at considerable length complementary theories of moderate behaviour, calculated to avoid all excess, and both thus strike the familiar note of the Molière *raisonneur*. But both are overtaken by the dramatic role in which they have been cast by the author, that of the comic realist, extreme in his absolute opposition to the comic idealism of *la femme savante*. The consequence of this is that they are predestined to take a much less detached and balanced view of things than we might be led to think at first glance.

The contradiction in Clitandre between the role which he plays and the way in which he expresses himself may be glimpsed in Act I, Sc. 3, where he gives a lengthy exposition of his views on the education of women. He begins with a general statement which is also an outright affirmation of principle: '. . . les femmes docteurs ne sont point de mon goût' (l. 217). But immediately the general applicability of this is attenuated by an apparent concession: 'Je consens qu'une femme ait des clartés de tout' (l. 218). The important phrase in this line is obviously 'des clartés de tout'. Clitandre is willing to allow women to have knowledge of a general unspecialized character on a range of topics, but this is contrasted with and opposed to

   . . . la passion choquante
De se rendre savante afin d'être savante; (ll. 219-20)

which is, to Clitandre's mind, the essential characteristic of the *femme savante*.[28] This description qualifies both the previously mentioned Armande (l. 216) and 'Madame votre mère' (l. 227). The 'glossary' which Clitandre appends to the *genre* of woman originally described by him as *femme docteur* now explains the precise connotation of that term for him — it is a description which says plainly that such a woman is animated by a vainglorious desire to distinguish herself in learning. This is of the utmost importance in the context of Clitandre's speech, because it is now clear that for this *raisonneur* at least, there is no balanced *juste-milieu* between women who have general ideas about certain subjects and the pedantic specialist, the *femme docteur*. The corollary to this is that any woman who is anxious to instruct herself in a particular discipline finds herself in danger of being assimilated without reflection by Clitandre into the category of egotistical *femmes docteurs,* even though she may well be genuinely interested in her subject, and not intend or aspire in the slightest to enter that category. This is the first implication of immoderation in the *raisonneur's* speech, and it is further reinforced by what he goes on to say in the subsequent lines.

Having defined *femme docteur* or *femme savante* to his own satisfaction, he now makes more explicit the meaning which he attaches to the 'clartés de tout' which a woman may acquire without incurring his disapproval, that is, without becoming a *femme docteur*. The woman he approves of should frequently know how and when to appear ignorant of subjects and ideas with which she is nevertheless fully conversant; in addition, she should not display openly her knowledge of a subject, but be content with the inner knowledge that she does know about matters which she is hearing about in discussion. She must be unwilling to convey the impression that she is at all familiar with them. Although she may be informed about certain topics of conversation, she must be continually aware of what other people might possibly think of her if she entered into discussion about them. Her apparent modesty and deference in discussion, which Clitandre finds so praiseworthy, derive, not from true humility and insight into one's nature, but from a lively fear of 'le qu'en-dira-t-on' — a fear adroitly insinuated in the feminine mind by such people as Clitandre in the interest of traditional masculine domination. The equitable manner and moderate form in which he delivers his speech (we note above the respectful references to Armande and Philaminte), conceal not just the paradox of Socratic or learned ignorance but a much more surprising and fundamental one. For is not the suave *raisonneur* basically no different in his outlook on the education of women than Chrysale?

At first sight, the discreet views of Clitandre could not be further removed from the extremely direct ideas of Chrysale: for the latter

Former aux bonnes moeurs l'esprit de ses enfants,
Faire aller son ménage, avoir l'oeil sur ses gens,
Et régler la dépense avec économie,
Doit être son étude et sa philosophie. (Act II, Sc. 7, ll. 573-6)

Such are the tasks which ought to consume a woman's time, energy and talents.[29] It is true that in the theatre we tend to laugh more at the burlesque and excessive views of Chrysale than at those of Clitandre; the latter does not after all say or imply that women should be confined to the execution of menial duties. But he is firmly at one with the *barbon* as regards the undesirability of women receiving education. For if Clitandre's ideal woman ought to feign ignorance by not conversing about matters familiar to her, then there is no apparent reason why she should study at all, since the degree of education which Clitandre is prepared in theory to concede to her is bound not to make the slightest difference in practice.

The paradoxical form and content of Clitandre's views on the *femme savante*, and his intangible conclusion, have much in common with Le Vayer's treatment of this question, which was of such paramount interest to the seventeenth century, and perhaps give some indication as to what Molière's position may well have been with regard to it. In his fourth *Promenade*, which was quoted in the preceding section, Le Vayer is just as ironic about the parochial views which the *barbon* holds on this question as Molière so often seems to be: 'Car tout le monde n'est pas de l'humeur de ceux qui trouvent une femme assez savante, quand elle sait discerner le haut-de-chausse du pourpoint de son mari.' Chrysale, who is the quintessence of the *bourgeois* mentality which Le Vayer derides here, is precisely one of those people who does live by such a maxim:

Nos pères sur ce point étoient gens bien sensés,
Qui disoient qu'une femme en sait toujours assez
Quand la capacité de son esprit se hausse
A connoître un pourpoint d'avec un haut de chausse.

(Act II, Sc. 7, ll. 577-80)[30]

Through the medium of his beloved Tubertus, Le Vayer goes on to say that in his opinion the feminine mind is as capable of assimilating learning as the masculine one.[31] But his readers need not hope to find an unambiguous statement of principle, for the Sceptic, as though embarrassed by the possibility of committing himself, appends his usual self-contradictory qualification. He quotes with obvious approval the paradoxical opinion of one of his friends, who is, I believe, none other than the author of *Les Femmes Savantes*: '. . . je ne puis m'empêcher de vous rapporter ici la pensée d'un de nos amis communs, que celles dont nous parlons, qui veulent passer pour savantes, ignorent ordinairement tout ce qu'elles pensent savoir, et qu'elles ne sont véritablement savantes qu'en ce qu'elles feignent d'ignorer.'[32] We recall the enigmatic utterance of Clitandre:

> . . . j'aime que souvent, aux questions qu'on fait,
> Elle sache ignorer les choses qu'elle sait;
> De son étude enfin je veux qu'elle se cache,
> Et qu'elle ait du savoir sans vouloir qu'on le sache. (ll. 221-4)

The paradoxical mode and content of this speech have the salutary effect of making it as impossible to attribute Clitandre's views literally to Molière (even though we accept Molière as the 'ami commun' of Le Vayer's quotation) as it would be to attribute those of Tubertus to the Sceptic: for in Le Vayer's case, the burlesque detachment with which he envisages the whole question enables him to evoke contradictory facets of it, and then to dissolve them in paradox: in Molière's case, the necessary detachment of the dramatist who animates the contradictory attitudes of his characters is further accentuated by the paradoxical thesis which he gives to Clitandre to defend. Paradox is the formula by which both are able to evoke objection and counter-objection in exaggerated form, whilst retaining a detached and flexible position as ironic observers of the question of women and learning.

It seems necessary then to underline the detachment of Molière with respect to Clitandre on account of a double conclusion which is frequently drawn about the views of this character. The first is that Clitandre is Molière's *porte-parole* regarding the education of women; and the second is that since a parallel can be established between the opinions of the *raisonneur* and Mlle de Scudéry's views on this topic, Molière must therefore be in fundamental agreement with the feminist. In *Le Grand Cyrus* (1649-53), for instance, she declares herself hostile to all women who try to be *savantes* as well as to those who go to the opposite extremity; she wishes to establish a *juste-milieu* between what she terms 'une suffisance impertinente' and a 'stupidité ennuyeuse'.[33] She does not exclude learning for women, but says they must take care to avoid the terrible title of *femme savante:*

> Je veux donc bien qu'on puisse dire d'une personne de mon sexe, qu'elle sait cent choses dont elle ne se vante pas, qu'elle a l'esprit fort éclairé, qu'elle connoît finement les beaux ouvrages, qu'elle parle bien, qu'elle écrit juste, et qu'elle sait le monde; mais je ne veux pas qu'on puisse dire d'elle: c'est une femme savante, car ces deux caractères sont si différents qu'ils ne se ressemblent point.[34]

But on reflection, it will be seen that there is something of a gap between Sapho's ideal of an educated woman and Clitandre's thoughts on that subject. The kind of woman whom Sapho imagines as being far removed from the *femme savante* is nothing less than the *femme docteur* who displeases Clitandre so much. For if Sapho presumes to speak in company, however modestly, about philosophy, literature or the arts in general, she will automatically incur his reproach that she is indulging in a vain display of knowledge. What for her are merely judicious and finely chosen observations on the part of a woman would be instinctively attributed by Clitandre (not to speak of Chrysale!) to feminine ambition seeking to usurp the rightful place of man as the recognized head of the household.

(4)

One factor which does away with all semblance of moderation on Clitandre's part is his extreme antipathy for Trissotin. In the speech examined above, he connects his criticism of Philaminte directly to the ascendency which the pseudo-*savant* has gained over her, and her 'héros d'esprit' is the target for several lines of incisive satire (ll. 228 ff.). But the *raisonneur* reserves his heaviest attack on the pedant for Act IV, Sc. 3. At this stage of the action he learns that Trissotin is also his rival for Henriette's hand. In the scene between the two rivals, Molière makes Clitandre enlarge the paradoxical argument of Act I, Sc. 3 to include the general question of the desirability of knowledge. The increased acerbity of Clitandre is matched by a far more devastating use of paradox than in the earlier scene.

Trissotin's announcement of an important scientific event (the apparition of a shooting star) is interrupted by Philaminte, for whom Clitandre's presence introduces an improper element:

(Monsieur) fait profession de chérir l'ignorance,
Et de haïr surtout l'esprit et la science (ll. 1273-4)

Clitandre feigns to retreat in order to advance: knowledge is an excellent thing in itself, but becomes intolerable for him whenever it spoils the natural qualities of a person. In such a case

. . . j'aimerois mieux être au rang des ignorants,
Que de me voir savant comme certaines gens. (ll. 1279-80)

and 'La science est sujette à faire de grands sots' (l. 1284). To Trissotin this is mere paradoxical absurdity:

J'ai cru jusques ici que c'étoit l'ignorance
Qui faisoit les grands sots, et non pas la science. (ll. 1293-4)

Clitandre obliges by refining his paradox in epigrammatic form: '. . . un sot savant est sot plus qu'un sot ignorant' (l. 1296). The paradoxes of Clitandre, however, are far from being empty words. They serve an immediate dramatic function, and also have a wider application. The rationalization of linguistic absurdities mystifies Trissotin, thus fulfilling one of the important aspects of the role of the so-called *raisonneur;* and, by contrast the narrow literalness and rigidity of the pedantic mentality is conveyed to the audience through the ironic and flexible usage of language.

Both these aspects of the role would seem to be worth stressing, since they reflect an attitude towards the question of knowledge which may be compared to Le Vayer's treatment of the same subject. The paradoxical form and content of Clitandre's argument are to be found in one of the Sceptic's early dialogues, *De L'Ignorance Louable* (1631).[35] In the dialogue Le Vayer seems to amuse himself by arguing almost simultaneously through his various interlocutors both for and against knowledge, enjoying the detachment which the sceptical perspective affords him on the question. Remaining consistent to his sceptical mode of non-dogmatic argument, he refuses to embrace any less ambiguous conclusion than that implied by the title of the dialogue. Is this not akin to the treatment of the subject in this scene of Molière's play? He is both the author of Trissotin *and* of Clitandre, enjoying at all times the double vision of opposite views conflicting, and harmonizing them to form a comedy of opposites. As in the dialogue, there is no straightforward conclusion on the question of knowledge.

In the dialogue, Télamon assumes the role of Trissotin, which consists in defending the time-honoured veneration of *la science* and the *savants*. He defends both against the Sceptic Orasius just as confidently as Trissotin does in the play: '. . . aussi ne puis-je m'empêcher de m'opposer aux injustes et extravagantes pensées de votre Sceptique, principalement lorsqu'elle se rend injurieuse envers les sciences, les accusant d'impertinence, voire de nullité, ce que j'estime un blasphème insupportable.'

Orasius now provides the devastating counter-argument: if one studies all the erudite treatises and philosophies without prejudice one is forced '. . . de donner dans le panneau de notre Acatalepsie ou incompréhensibilité, et d'avouer ingénuement que toutes ces sciences prétendues n'auront servi qu'à nous faire mieux reconnaître les titres de notre ignorance, et les mauvais fondements de notre présomptueuse suffisance.'[36]

One recognizes in both arguments and counter-arguments the same dual movement which was also seen to characterize the first scene of Molière's play: the lofty theory of Trissotin and Télamon is exactly balanced by the earthy and paradoxical maxims of Clitandre and Orasius. The former unite in proclaiming that knowledge is the most distinctive mark of a person's moral excellence — for Télamon it is the *summum bonum*, and if not possessed of it one is necessarily assimilated to '. . . ces âmes ignorantes et dépourvues de ce caractère d'humanité . . .' One thus becomes '. . . un homme d'esprit défectueux,

ignorant et brutal . . . un animal extrêmement imparfait'.[37] The basis
for these views lies in his belief in the Stoic notion that knowledge is to
be fully equated with virtue, and ignorance with vice.[38] Philaminte is
likewise infatuated by the high-flown Stoic doctrine of the *sage* who
exemplifies all the divine wisdom and virtue of their philosophy (Act
III, Sc. 2, ll. 895-8). Stoicism has indeed an overriding influence on her
judgement of character. Clitandre, for example, is deemed to be
completely ignorant and is therefore appropriately qualified by her as
'sot', 'brutal', and 'impertinent'(ll. 1153-7). But all the moral worth which
he lacks in her eyes is embodied in Trissotin, who is invested with all the
virtues which, she imagines, are conferred by *les sciences*. She therefore
defends him against the attacks of Clitandre (Act IV, Sc. 3) and against
the import of the calumnious note sent to her by Vadius in the following
scene, in which she proudly vindicates his exemplary character.

It is interesting to note that Orasius and Clitandre take care to qualify
what could at first sight appear to be negative generalizations about
knowledge. Orasius is careful to point out that he does not condemn *in
toto* the various branches of learning: 'Sachez que nous ne condamnons
point la connaissance des lettres et des Sciences . . . mais nous en
blâmons seulement l'arrogance, et nous nous contentons d'en modérer
l'opiniâtreté.'[39] And Clitandre concedes that 'la science et l'esprit . . .
sont choses de soi qui sont belles et bonnes' (ll. 1277-8). It is not
knowledge itself which they both impugn, but a certain attitude to
knowledge which makes people like the *femmes savantes* or the pedant
transgress the limits of propriety in such matters. The former are so
unaware of what is and what is not within the compass of human
powers that the monstrous flattery of Trissotin quite eludes them when
he says '. . . pour vous la nature a peu d'obscurités' (ll. 888). Nothing
can deflect them from their supreme ambition to plumb the hidden
depths of nature, as Philaminte asserts (l. 874). In fact it is flattery such
as that practised by Trissotin which renders them purblind to the
ignorance suggested by Clitandre, which is the beginning of true
wisdom. The comic vision would seem to be essentially in agreement
with Orasius, as he takes care to point out that the ignorance which he
favours so much is '. . . une ignorance honorable, et vraiment
philosophique, laquelle s'accommodant à l'obscurité de la Nature, et se
mesurant à la portée de l'esprit humain, ne promet rien au-delà de ses
forces . . .'[40] It is an ignorance which inculcates in its proponents a
salutary modesty with regard to what one knows and what one is ever
likely to know, prophylactic against belief in one's own omniscience.

Blind to the limitations of knowledge in general, it is to be expected
that the *femme savante* should also be blind as regards the appropriate
branches of knowledge in which she ought, or ought not, to interest
herself. She does not ask whether or not she is drawn by inclination
towards a particular subject: she lets herself be guided by her belief that

anyone who does not share her ardent passion for learning must have a totally unnatural outlook on life. Consequently Clitandre places the possible artificiality of knowledge in opposition to one's nature (l. 1277), laborious study to natural knowledge or ignorance: 'Et l'étude dans l'autre [le pédant] ajoute à la nature' (l. 1302). It is against the kind of inverted reasoning which characterizes the *femme savante* that Orasius argues, when he poses the question of whether knowledge is natural to man, as the pedants like to claim. The argument is decided for him by evidence of the empirical kind that Clitandre has adduced in the verse quoted above: 'Car si ainsi était que la science nous fût propre et naturelle, il y a grande apparence que nous l'acquerrions sans beaucoup de peine, et la posséderions avec plaisir et volupté. Or je me rapporte aux Savants combien cette acquisition leur a été laborieuse . . .'

Neither sound common-sense nor good judgement are the necessary consequences of much laborious learning, according to Orasius, and he sees as examples of this truth pedants who persist in speaking in Latin to one another in the streets.[41] Clitandre's satire of such pedants is similar in content, but much more caustic in tone. Those people who have wasted

. . . neuf ou dix mille veilles
A se bien barbouiller de grec et de latin(ll. 1374-5)

are peremptorily dismissed as 'inhabiles à tout, vuides de sens commun' (l. 1380). 'Sens commun' for Clitandre denotes the opposite of what the *femmes savantes* do, and is simply a harmony between one's natural inclination and the way one chooses to fulfil it. When he professes his aversion for 'la science et l'esprit qui gâtent les personnes' (l. 1277), and emphasizes to Trissotin the discrepancy between self-imposed learning and natural instinct, he is saying something which Le Vayer never tires of repeating whenever he writes of a proper attitude to study. In *De L'Ignorance* (1664-6) he takes up again the argument of Orasius, and outlines his usual criterion to those who would study: '. . . je tiens qu'il serait plus avantageux à plusieurs personnes studieuses de suivre leur instinct . . . que de se laisser gourmander par des sciences qui les asservissent, et qui leur sont comme un bâton trop pesant dans la main, plus propre à donner la Loi au bras qui le tient, qu'à la recevoir de lui'.[42]

Learned ignorance would seem then to reside in an imperceptible blend of acquisition, inclination and awareness of one's limitations, and to be characterized by an individual, undogmatic and unself-conscious manner. Montaigne gathers up all these notions epigrammatically when he writes that we should not at all be concerned to ask who is 'plus sçavant' but rather who is 'mieux sçavant'.[43]

(5)

Les Femmes Savantes offers certain other similarities with the works of Le Vayer which at first sight may seem much less important than those described in preceding sections, but which should be quoted to illustrate the extent and depth of affinity between the comic vision and the Sceptic's outlook on various subjects, such as the motivation of *salon* poets and reasonable and unreasonable attitudes to literature and language. *Les Femmes Savantes,* more perhaps than any other of Molière's plays, provides examples of memorably comic episodes for which Le Vayer can provide the appropriate commentary.

In Molière's theatre the omnipresent motive behind the actions of his comic characters is *amour-propre*. But in this play there are almost as many conscious and unconscious levels of *amour-propre* as in La Rochefoucauld's well-known maxim about it.[44] On the most obvious level are characters such as *les femmes savantes* who believe in the illusory vision of themselves as viewed by their *amour-propre*. Characters like Vadius and Trissotin appear to move on a higher and more conscious level: they exploit the vanity of others for self-advancement, but they too can become mere tools of *amour-propre,* since its extreme sensitivity is, paradoxically, shown to be commensurate with its extreme subtlety. The *salon* scenes in particular (Act III, Sc. 2 and 3) are penetrating illustrations of the multiple disguises in which *amour-propre* may appear. In the first part of the *salon* scene, we have the total euphoria of *amour-propre* displayed by the *femmes savantes* and manipulated by Trissotin. When he judges them to have vied sufficiently with each other for superlative terms with which to describe his *Sonnet à la Princesse Uranie*, he underlines with unction the code of mutual admiration to which they variously adhere:

Si vous vouliez de vous nous montrer quelque chose,
A notre tour aussi nous pourrions admirer (ll. 842-3)

Le Vayer, in his *opuscule Du bon et du mauvais usage des récitations* (1643) had already discerned the many private and public comedies to which such *doctes assemblées* could give rise. The *raison d'être* of such gatherings is the eclectic one of *la femme savante* and of Cathos and Magdelon: 'pour ouïr réciter quelque pièce qui n'a point encore vu le jour . . .'[45] The prime disadvantage in such schemes lies, as one may see from Molière's scene, less in the *assemblée* as such than in the inevitable influence which an audience exerts over one's *amour-propre*. Le Vayer describes quaintly this besetting sin of the *salon* poetaster: 'ceux qui récitaient étaient transportés d'une si étrange passion de se voir écoutés par un si grand nombre d'auditeurs . . .' A *salon* poet like Trissotin or Vadius sets the tone of the gathering, and it is one which his listeners readily adopt. In reality they offer to recite their latest poems only because they know too well that dissentient voices will not be heard. The exaggerated image which such poets have of their poetic ability will be amply confirmed by the unanimous approval of what Le Vayer terms '. . . ces assemblées où l'on récite (qui) ne sont guère composées que de personnes qui veulent obliger celui qui parle . . . En effet, on n'est guère appellé en de semblables réduits que pour y apporter son approbation.'[46] He quotes the complaint of a friend who attended a gathering at which a poem was recited so unexpectedly that he was unable to compliment the author, since he had not received sufficient notice to prepare his eulogy. In more serious vein, Le Vayer's principal criticism is that it is impossible within the context of a *salon* to discriminate good writing from bad. One ought to be particularly critical of approval conferred on a poem in such circumstances because the dangers of self-deception are legion:

> . . . on doit bien prendre garde surtout, de ne s'assurer jamais de la valeur d'une pièce prononcée dans une ruelle de lit, ou dans un cabinet d'ami, sur les louanges suspectes qui s'y distribuent, ni sur les applaudissements de quelques personnes, qui ne sauraient pour lors, quand ils en auraient le dessein, remarquer suffisamment tout ce qu'elle a de bon, ou de blâmable. Car j'ai toujours souffert avec impatience l'humeur de ceux qui ne pouvaient permettre qu'on trouvât à dire la moindre chose en leurs ouvrages, sur ce mauvais prétexte qu'ils les avaient fait voir en fort bonne compagnie.[47]

Le Vayer by no means overestimates such dangers, for even the most cunning of *salon* authors may succumb to such heady intoxication, as Trissotin illustrates. When Vadius makes the devastating observation that, in plain terms, the sonnet on the Princess Uranie is absolutely worthless, Trissotin invokes the adulation with which the *femmes savantes* have greeted it: 'Beaucoup de gens pourtant le trouvent admirable' (1. 993)[48] That Molière should allow an ostensibly lucid *salon* adventurer such as Trissotin to fall victim to his *amour-propre* even when the character is aware that he is being flattered by the fatuity of the *femmes savantes* is a measure of the impossibility of resisting its all-powerful ascendancy.

The quarrel of the poet with the pedant Vadius is indeed an excellent example of the way in which *amour-propre* may manifest itself with subtlety and even modest lucidity. When Vadius makes his entrance into the *salon,* Trissotin bestows fulsome praise upon his fellow-poet, as he intimates to the *femmes savantes:*

> Au reste, il fait merveille en vers ainsi qu'en prose,
> Et pourroit, s'il vouloit, vous montrer quelque chose. (ll. 953-4)

Modestly, Vadius defers and, like Oronte in the second scene of *Le Misanthrope* who talks with apparent lucidity about sincerity, he utters very sensible strictures on those *salon* authors who habitually bore their listeners with their own mediocre works;[49] he, on the other hand, is going to follow the example of a wise Greek, who expressly forbad authors to rush indecently into a public reading of their works. He then promptly announces that he is going to read his 'petits vers' on a romantic theme. Before he can read his poem, however, Trissotin begins to praise his poetry anew. True to the *salon* rules of *politesse* and *bel esprit,* Vadius responds in kind, and their mutual compliments rise into a crashing crescendo of false praise. Trissotin must divert attention from Vadius' poem to his own sonnet, and consequently interjects to ask for his opinion on it. Vadius obliges by finding it execrable, the more so since it comes between his audience and the imminent glory of his poem. The alternating compliments now turn to alternating defence of his poem by Trissotin and furious attack on it by Vadius. Trissotin in his turn begins to attack the poetry of his rival, which he has just lauded to the skies — and Vadius, having previously praised Trissotin's poetry, now demolishes it at one fell swoop (ll. 955-1044). The predictable symmetry of the comic situation serves to emphasize all the more the fragile and unreliable nature of judgement, especially whenever it is concerned with one's own creations to which one is so attached that any attack upon them is immediately construed by *amour-propre* as an attack on one's person. Le Vayer, in *De L'Ignorance,* stresses the extreme difficulty of giving an unprejudiced opinion of one's own literary achievements and on those of others: for him, as in Molière's play, the impossibility of doing so seems inevitable: 'Car si nous devenons incapables de juger raisonnablement de nos propres compositions, que ne ferons-nous point . . . de celles des autres?'[50] In *De la Censure des Livres* he goes further than this, and in isolating the vanity of writers from that of common mortals takes up an important theme of Molière's play: '. . . c'est le défaut ordinaire de la plupart des hommes savants, non seulement de préférer leurs lumières et leurs connaissances à toutes celles des autres, mais encore d'être fièrement persuadés que rien n'échappe à leur vue . . .'

Elsewhere he speaks of those who write as imagining that they have merely to put pen to paper in order to change the course of history.[51] No one, he adds, could be further estranged from the true humanism which reading and study ought to inculcate. Literary criticism ought above all to be characterized by a sense of one's humanity, since one is aware that the extreme diversity of books is only equalled by the extreme diversity of opinions, and that no single opinion can possibly claim to be the true one. Knowing this, one should commend what one finds pleasing and to one's own taste, and excuse without undue acrimony what one does not like or appreciate. One should be indulgent towards the writings of others if one hopes that one's own achievements will be received favourably.[52] But Le Vayer was far too familiar with the kind of *habitué* of the *salon* to apply such ideal criteria to him. Fatalistically he admits (as fatalistically as the pedants of *Les Femmes Savantes* will quarrel over their poems!) that '. . . tous les discours et tous les raisonnements des hommes de cette profession, seront presque toujours accompagnés de beaucoup de contestation, et d'une extrême animosité.'[53]

The attitude which Le Vayer adopts in *salons* is both critical and discreet. He does not become uncritical towards an author because of his reputation, nor does he succumb to the idea that without a sophisticated and glib vocabulary one need be uncultivated or unintelligent. Henriette, the comic realist, exhibits some of these qualities at least when confronted with the fashionably intelligent Trissotin. She displays scant respect for his reputation as a poet, telling him that his poem is in no way importuning her: 'Je n'écoute pas' (l. 824). Invited to the feast of learning by her mother, her answer is starkly simple: 'Je sais peu les beautés de tout ce qu'on écrit' (l. 729). But her behaviour throughout the *salon* scene illustrates most completely one rule which Le Vayer recommends for particular application in those circumstances, which consists in simply knowing that 'on se peut taire éloquemment'. One does not need to opine verbally in order to give an opinion — for silence is, of all opinions, the most tacit as well as the most damning.[54]

The climax of the quarrel between Vadius and Trissotin is reached in the mutual accusations of plagiarism which they hurl at each other. Trissotin advises the Greek scholar thus:

Va, va restituer tous les honteux larcins
Que réclament sur toi les Grecs et les Latins.

and Vadius makes the same charge:

Va, va-t'en faire amende honorable au Parnasse
D'avoir fait à tes vers estropier Horace. (ll. 1019-22)

Clitandre satirizes virulently those scholars whose knowledge has been acquired by simply remembering slavishly what others have said and written before them (ll. 1371 ff). Literary imposture is but a natural supplement to the disguise of learning which they put on in the *salon*. It seems reasonable to assume from the sharpness of the satire against the plagiarists that Molière considered their duplicity in no way different to that of Tartuffe or Dom Juan or other comic impostors in his theatre. Indeed, a similarity between an aspect of the roles of Trissotin and of Tartuffe has often been noted by critics.[55] Even Le Vayer, normally so benevolent in his criticism of his fellow authors, scornfully speaks of those '. . . qui ne parlent jamais de leur chef, mais toujours par l'organe d'autrui . . .' Such writers may be said to 'transcrire' but certainly not to 'écrire'.[56] One must resist the temptation to bury one's own thoughts under an avalanche of quotation, and writers whose books could be reduced to a 'carte blanche' if one decided to extract their borrowed references are severely criticized. Yet he does show an awareness of the difficulty confronting writers when he says that it is virtually impossible to be original, and would doubtless have agreed with La Bruyère to the extent that 'tout est dit, et l'on vient trop tard . . .'[57] Nevertheless, if the thought cannot be original, at least the use made of it can be: '. . . encore faut-il contribuer quelque chose du sien, et assaisonner ce qu'on tient d'autrui de telle sorte, qu'on lui donne une grâce, qui ait quelque air de nouveauté.'[58]

It is outside the scope of this chapter to speculate on what the attitude of the author of *Les Femmes Savantes* might or might not have been to the point raised here by Le Vayer. But it seems reasonable to suggest that the lack of rigidity displayed by the latter is not far removed from the realism practised by Molière in regard to his own borrowings. The remark attributed to him by Grimarest — 'il m'est permis . . . de reprendre mon bien où je le trouve' — may well indeed be apocryphal, but the truth behind it is borne out by a study of the numerous 'sources' of *Les Femmes Savantes* in particular.[59] The cataloguing of such 'sources', however, tells us little or nothing about the working of his comic genius, since it is the peculiar use which he makes of his derived material which makes this play one of his more original creations[60].

There are certain stylistic features of *salon* writing reproved by Le Vayer which are prominent in the literary gatherings in Molière's play. He particularly dislikes 'fausse éloquence', which is inevitably present in what is read there: '. . . j'appréhende toujours qu'on ne m'impose en prononçant avec trop d'affectation, et d'emphase, ce qu'on veut faire passer pour excellent . . . Les prononciations pompeuses et ampoulées sont bonnes pour le théâtre . . .'[61] Eloquence of this specious kind is invariably accompanied by an ornate style, and presents a plethora of convoluted figures of speech: 'Les figures, qui doivent être autant de lumières d'un discours, et y briller comme les étoiles dans leur Ciel, n'y [sont] attachées qu'en forme de noeuds, obscurs, et raboteux, plus capables d'écorcher une oreille tant soit peu délicate, que de lui donner la moindre satisfaction.'[62]

Molière was, as F. Baumal and D. Mornet have well reminded us, too much a man of his time to avoid the influence of the *salon* and *précieux* type of expression. Indeed, in his *comédies galantes* it is particularly obvious that he was able to write *précieux* verse as well as Tristan, Benserade, Saint-Amant and other *habitués* of the salon.[63] Yet if this is true, it is also equally true that he could detach himself sufficiently from the language of the *salon* in order to incorporate it into a play, and to make a comedy of it. In Trissotin's poem, he obviously intends to ridicule the grandiloquent and sonorous choice of words which the poet has erected upon the flimsiest and most ludicrous of themes, but which nevertheless did in fact form part of the poetic works of l'Abbé Cotin.

The grotesque richness of the language ('magnifiquement', 'superbement', etc.) scarcely conceals the insipid banality of its subject. With Oronte's sonnet in *Le Misanthrope*, Molière can enjoy the spectacle of the self-appointed custodian of common-sense and naturalness (Alceste) delivering himself of his irate opinion of *précieux* poetry:

Ce style figuré, dont on fait vanité,
Sort du bon caractère et de la vérité:
Ce n'est que jeu de mots, qu'affectation pure,
Et ce n'est point ainsi que parle la nature (Act I, Sc. 2, ll. 385-8)

The *pointe* which terminates Oronte's poem — 'Belle Philis, on désespère, Alors qu'on espère toujours' — is doubtless preferable in taste to Trissotin's *jeu de mots* in his poem *Sur Un Carrosse de Couleur Amarante:*

Ne dis plus qu'il est amarante;
Dis plutôt qu'il est de ma rente.

Yet such poetry finds no more favour in the eyes of Alceste than in those of Le Vayer. For the former, it is quite simply 'bon à mettre au cabinet' (l. 376), since it relies for its effect on unnatural manipulation of language; for the second, all 'allusions puériles', 'antithèses ridicules' and 'métaphores exorbitantes au dernier point' are profoundly distasteful. But even more so is the cultivation of paradox as a stylistic device, which he dismisses as summarily as Alceste: 'En effet les Paradoxes, selon moi, ne sont bons que pour le Cabinet'.[64]

A second aspect of language with which Molière deals comically is introduced by Martine, the *servante*, whom Philaminte dismisses for the heinous crime of offending the canons of proper linguistic usage: she has, alleges Philaminte,

. . . insulté mon oreille
Par l'impropriété d'un mot sauvage et bas,
Qu'en termes décisifs condamne Vaugelas. (Act II, Sc. 6, ll. 460-2)

Whether or not Molière is formally condemning Vaugelas here (and the occasion would seem to be too burlesque to draw such a solemn conclusion from it), he is certainly showing us the ridiculous excesses to which regulations governing language and grammar may be taken. The growth of the *Académie littéraire* or *cercles* was a phenomenon of the first part of the century; founded initially by individuals interested in the reform of the French language, such as Mme des Loges or Charlotte des Ursins, they culminated in the foundation of the *Académie française* in 1634, of which Richelieu, Séguier and Louis XIV were the successive protectors.[65] As Molière pointed out in his *Préface* to *Tartuffe* in 1669, there is nothing so praiseworthy in the world that cannot be made ridiculous by men, and language is one subject so evidently exposed to this danger. Indeed, the fixity of grammatical rules which threaten to impose themselves upon a living thing such as language is an ideal subject for comedy, as Saint-Evremond well saw as early as 1638. In his *Comédie des Académistes,* he satirizes those pedants like Godeau and Chapelain who wish to expunge from the French language the *tournures* of Montaigne, and spend two years together in solemn conclave in order to reform six words. Similarly the grandiose *académie* which the *femmes savantes* intend to found is going to proscribe a certain number of words which are repellent to them; against these vocables, says Armande,

> . . . nous préparons de mortelles sentences,
> Et nous devons ouvrir nos doctes conférences
> Par les proscriptions de tous ces mots divers
> Dont nous voulons purger et la prose et les vers. (ll. 905-8)

When this has been accomplished, the ideal state will have been achieved and people will 'parler Vaugelas' according to the dictates of the purists. Comedy is no more indulgent towards what it takes as a misguided zeal for linguistic perfection (a perfection made synonymous in the play, rightly or wrongly, with Vaugelas) than was La Mothe Le Vayer. Vaugelas' *Remarques* appeared in 1647, and by 1654 Le Vayer had published his first *petit traité* against the former's strictures on correct and incorrect use of language, entitled ironically *Des nouvelles remarques sur la langue française.* He objects to the dogmatism underlying Vaugelas' approach to language, and to the assertion that one injudiciously chosen word could ruin the reputation of an author. There is no need, Le Vayer protests, to quarrel over the value of one syllable, and instead he invokes, as does Alceste, what seems to him to be an objective norm in language, *le bon sens.* This criterion opposes to linguistic theory the evidence of experience and recognized usage. His wish for a natural and flexible style provokes his principal criticism of Vaugelas: 'Comment se pourrait-il faire qu'un style fût naïf dans la gêne où il le met, et parmi tant de contraintes qu'il lui donne? . . . La rudesse d'un terme, la négligence d'une phrase, donnent quelquefois du goût, et plaisent par cela même, qui est le plus près du vice . . .'[66] Language must be allowed to evolve naturally, whilst observing the rules generally accepted as being essential to grammatical accuracy.[67]

From Le Vayer's attitude to Vaugelas, it will be seen that he shares with the comic vision a healthy disregard for linguistic perfection and purity. By refusing to allow words and concepts, however intrinsically valuable they may be, to dominate and become reality, he displays a practical scepticism for that theoretical approach to life which is grist to the mill of Molière's comedy. Words exist to be used by people, and not vice versa. In the case of the *femme savante,* she conceives of reality chiefly in terms of words to be approved of or proscribed, and consequently for her people exist not as beings in themselves, but to the extent that the words they use place them into one or other of her verbal categories.[68]

The principle which underlies Le Vayer's scepticism in this respect is, as I have attempted to show, fully consonant with the comic vision of the play as expressed on a number of subjects. According to this principle, it is as futile to endeavour to impose a rigid course upon the development of the spoken or written word as it is to conceive of human beings solely in terms of platonic relationships, Cartesian meta-physics, or pure reason. Whenever the comic character threatens to reduce the irregular and unpredictable nature of life to conformity with his *idée fixe,* then this principle comes into play and comedy demonstrates the unreasonableness of the *idée,* even though it be couched in the literal terms of pure unadulterated reason, as it claims to be in the play. It is on account of the nature of the fixation that *Les Femmes Savantes,* more than any other play by Molière, has to defend the reason of comic sanity against the ravages of reason *toute pure.* That is perhaps its most cogent justification against the widespread view, quoted at the beginning of this chapter, that it is more pedestrian and prosaic than most of Molière's plays.

Conclusion

What emerges from the preceding pages is, I hope, a renewed realization of the forms and the resources of Molière's comic vision. Although richly varied in form and content, this vision possesses an internal coherent structure, which is rationally ordered and designed to illustrate its superiority over those serious and self-conscious intruders onto the comic stage, reason and logic. Of the long line of such intruders into Molière's theatre, the reasoner Alceste offers the most sustained challenge to the comic vision as he attempts to impose his humourless view of life on the other members of Célimène's *salon*. When Philinte endeavours to divert his friend from his chagrined philosophy with a little drollery, reminding him of their similarity to the two brothers in *L'Ecole des Maris*, he answers testily 'Que la plaisanterie est de mauvaise grâce!' (Act I, Sc. 1, l. 33). Faced with the fatuous laughter of the *petits marquis*, he provides them with the best justification for it, by trying ponderously to suppress it:

Par le sangbleu! Messieurs, je ne croyois pas être
Si plaisant que je suis. (Act II, Sc. 6, ll. 773-4)

More intensely still, he commands Célimène to forfeit instantly her sense of humour: '. . . ne plaisantez point, il n'est pas temps de rire' (Act IV, Sc. 3, l. 1286). His self-enforced withdrawal at the end of the play is, with the survival of the fool Sganarelle and the annihilation of the wise Dom Juan, the most impressive symbol in Molière's theatre of the resounding victory which *folie* secures over reason at every level, be it on the level of the simple verbal joke, or that of a potentially dramatic and tragic situation.

In this comic vision, it is possible to discern three dominant elements which Molière combines to repeatedly reinforce this conclusion. They may best be seen at work in the three principal types which people his theatre — in the Fool, the *fourbe*, and the Wise Fool. His comedy invariably originates with the Fool, the *imaginaire* who assumes himself to be more reasonable than anyone else. Sganarelle of *L'Ecole des Maris*, Arnolphe, Orgon, Alceste, Amphitryon, the *femmes savantes*, Argan, all aspire to the beatific vision of a world in harmony with their fixation. To have reached the stage of Monsieur Jourdain and to be able to say: 'voilà tout le monde raisonnable' (*Le Bourgeois Gentilhomme*, Act V, Scène Dernière) is to consummate their ideal. These *sages*, standing alone against the tide of society, present to

Molière a vantage point from which he can survey with impunity its abuses, follies, and absurdities. But the creator of these unconscious *comédiens* is also the spectator of the comedy of their exclusive pretence to reason. In particular, the *fourbe* and the Wise Fool offer him privileged vantage points from which this comedy may be fully enjoyed.

The *fourbe* occupies in the comic hierarchy of Molière an intermediate position between the Fool and the Wise Fool. He is above all a conscious *comédien*, acting a part in order to impose himself on his dupe. Tartuffe, Dom Juan, Trissotin, the Doctors, all come into this group. They are adept at using appearances to adapt their designs to the particular reasoning of their dupe. But the comic vision can require that they themselves become dupes, as they succumb to excessive confidence in their power to manipulate appearances. Tartuffe can manipulate everything except Orgon's good opinion of himself. Dom Juan is able to metamorphose every value except divine retribution. The creator of the comedy shares their perspective on human vanity and credulity, just as he has shared that of his Fool on society. Yet he can see what the Fool cannot see, and what the *fourbe* partially sees, but is prevented by his cleverness from grasping ultimately — that they too are part of the comic picture, and not after all the authors or the spectators of the comedy.

The third vantage point from which the supreme *comédien* can overlook the comic scene is a still more comprehensive one, for it survives intact the deflation of the *imaginaire's* scheme, and the ruse of the *fourbe*. It is that of the Wise Fool, of Ariste, Chrysalde, Cléante, Philinte, Béralde, Sganarelle and Sosie. Their role is much more complex than that of straightforward opposition to the *imaginaire* or the *fourbe*, with each of whom they have an element in common. Very frequently they agree in theory if not in practice with the first, and their conduct can superficially be seen to resemble that of the second, to the extent that both are conscious *comédiens*. Ariste can agree with Sganarelle that current fashion is intrinsically absurd, Chrysalde with Arnolphe that there is nothing so comic as the spectacle of *le mari trompé*, Philinte with Alceste that the ways of the world are unjust and illogical, Béralde with Argan that nothing could be more desirable than the certainty of health, Sganarelle with Dom Juan's unanswerable arguments against traditional values, Sosie with Amphitryon to the effect that his story of someone usurping his identity is totally incredible.

They transcend, of course, the rigid reasoning which imprisons their comic counterparts. It is surely one of the most admirable and perhaps the most inconspicuous of Molière's achievements in comedy that they should be used with such freshness and originality to illustrate variations on the major theme of his plays. Life, they suggest, with mock solemnity or an all too simple buffoonery that eludes analysis, becomes unbearable if reason is made even for a moment the criterion of one's attitude to society, to one's wife, to one's health, or simply to oneself. Since the practice of reason is an impossible absurdity, it is better to participate in the comedy of social life. They perform this role either as professional *comédiens* such as Sganarelle (Dom Juan's valet) or Sosie, or as smiling reflective *comédiens*, such as Ariste, Chrysalde, Cléante, Philinte and Béralde.

It is from these principal vantage points that the plays mediate three views of reason to us. It is seen as being possessed *in toto* in the imagination of some, as a malleable object moulded by others for their own benefit, and as a potentially disruptive instrument to be kept under strict control in the affairs of life by others. A character becomes an *imaginaire* because he believes he possesses reason, and the more strongly he believes it the more comic does he become. The valet in *Dom Juan* provides a burlesque example of what Philinte refines to a philosophy in *Le Misanthrope*. The highest state of wisdom is the conscious or unconscious abandonment of reason, and the more naturally one can achieve this, the better *comédien* does one become, and consequently the wiser.

Although the comic vision of the Wise Fool is more complete than that of the *imaginaire* and the *fourbe*, he knows that he is merely a participant in the comedy and not the creator of it. If others present the spectacle of comedy to him, he is aware that the role which he plays may also appear comic in the eyes of others. Thus the greybeard Ariste is conscious that in the eyes of the reasoner Sganarelle he is deeply comic in his cultivation of youthful fashion. Chrysalde appears as immensely funny to Arnolphe in his refusal to countenance his scheme for educating his future wife. Cléante, with his plea for a religion that is less ostentatious and more humane, is the butt of Orgon's ponderous derision. Sganarelle is but a buffoon to Dom Juan, and to Alceste's sombre humour, Philinte is nothing more than an insipid actor in the social comedy which he intends to disrupt. To be aware of one's role within the comedy is the indispensable condition of the comic vision: one cannot understand the comedy of others if one is blind to the comedy of oneself.

But the comic vision has implications which go far beyond the bounds of individual and collective comedies. The purest example of the possibilities of the vision was seen in *Amphitryon*. There the Wise Fool, Sosie, becomes himself a Fool in the higher comedy which Jupiter offers at the expense of mortals, as his existence is made to evaporate before his eyes. Jupiter himself is placed in comic perspective by the debunking Mercure, and all their comedies are finally placed in higher comic perspective by Molière. The comic vision is a self-transcending phenomenon; one may after all be an *imaginaire* oneself when viewed in some superior perspective, just as one imagines that others are comic when seen in some lower perspective. Le Vayer, in a sentence in his *Petit*

Traité Sceptique lets us glimpse the possibility of a comic vision *ad infinitum:* '. . . je ne doute point que nous ne soyons bien plus ridicules aux Essences Divines dans la plupart de nos Actions, que les Singes ne le sont à notre égard en tout ce qu'ils font, lorsqu'ils tâchent de nous imiter.'[1] To keep faith with the comic vision, this possibility must always be kept open, otherwise one risks committing the original sin of Molière's comedy — that of *ultimately* taking oneself seriously. In a world of Fools and Wise Fools and *fourbes*, all of whom can be wise and foolish to varying degrees, the only element which cannot finally be superseded is the basis of comedy itself — comic irony.

The ascending comic strata in Molière's theatre must inevitably lead us back to their creator. His comic vision, however, remains true to itself and does not allow us to penetrate his thought on particular topics. For the thought and judgement, although unfailingly present in each character and situation, are compounded of an elusive irony. Whatever he envisages is seen in a double way: there may be two, three, four or more views presented on religion, marriage or social idealism. It is as though Molière were saying through each of these frequently contrasting views that 'man and life are too complex an interplay of unpredictable forces to be classified according to the language of reason: only the multifacetted language of paradox can encompass the contradictoriness of man.' Characters who categorize in his theatre occupy the lowest *échelon* in the hierarchy of the comic vision — it would be singularly clumsy to expect the master of comedy to do the same!

It is this 'conclusion' of the comic vision which gives to it the depth of a philosophic outlook, assuring the permanence of comedy even when it appears to be threatened most. In *Dom Juan* or *Le Misanthrope* we do not find the failure of comedy, as J. Guicharnaud has supposed, but the evolution of comedy to a way of seeing life steadily and seeing it whole.[2] Dogmatism about anything, whether it be about the necessity of practising truthfulness and integrity or about the non-existence of the supernatural, is irremediably comic because man presumes to dogmatize in areas where humility, hesitation and doubtfulness are seen to impose themselves. We cannot probe the motives of our fellows, still less can we claim knowledge of the supernatural. In its inconclusiveness, the comic vision is through and through a sceptical one, in the broadest sense of questioning and not restricting itself to a single view of the human condition. Another master of irony, André Gide, who is fully in line with the tradition of Rabelais, Montaigne, Le Vayer and Molière, came close to the essence of that sceptical vision when he wrote: 'Je ne prétends pas, certes, que la neutralité (j'allais dire: *l'indécision*) soit signe sûr d'un grand esprit; mais je crois que maints grands esprits ont beaucoup répugné à . . . conclure — et que bien poser un problème n'est pas le supposer d'avance résolu.'[3]

Notes

NOTES TO INTRODUCTION

1. *Molière*, (Paris, 1958) p. 6 (Reprint).
2. See G. Michaut, *La Jeunesse de Molière, Introduction*, (Paris, 1922), for a conspectus of views on Molière up to that date.
3. 'Maximes et Réflexions sur la Comédie', III, V, in *L'Eglise et le Théâtre* éd. Ch. Urbain et E. Levesque, (Paris, 1930) p. 172, pp. 184-5; 'Lettre d'un Théologien Illustre', ibid, pp. 67-119; Bourdaloue, *Chefs — D'Oeuvre Oratoires, Sermon sur l'Hypocrisie*, (Paris, 1910) pp. 273-96; *Lettre sur les Occupations de l'Académie française*, (Paris, 1883) p. 72; For a comprehensive view of clerical attitudes to Molière, see *L'Eglise et le Théâtre, Introduction*.
4. *Jugements des Savants sur les principaux ouvrages des auteurs*, (Paris, 1722) V, pp. 306 ff; *Lettre à M. D'Alembert Sur les Spectacles*, (Paris, 1907) pp. 54-70.
5. 'Dialogues des Morts' in *Oeuvres de Monsieur de Fontenelle*, (Paris, 1742) I, pp. 183-90; P. Bayle, *Dictionnaire Historique et Critique*, (Rotterdam, 1720) III, Art. Poquelin; *Encyclopédie, ou Dictionnaire Raisonné des Sciences, des Arts et des Métiers*, (Geneva, 1778) VIII, Art. Comédie; Voltaire, *Oeuvres Complètes*, (Paris, 1877-80) XIV, p. 105; XXXIII p. 354; III, p. 374; II, p. 458.
6. *Oeuvres de Marmontel*, (Paris, 1819) IV, p. 261; *Lycée, ou Cours de Littérature*, (Paris, 1799-1805) V, 3, pp. 429-50, where Rousseau's view of *Le Misanthrope* is systematically refuted.
7. Sainte-Beuve, *Portraits Littéraires*, (Paris, 1854) II, pp. 7 ff; G. Larroumet, 'La Comédie de Molière, l'auteur et le milieu', in *Revue des Deux Mondes*, (Oct, 1885) pp. 347-82; J. Lemaître, *Impressions de Théâtre*, I^e Série (Paris, 1886) pp. 35-74; L. Moland, *Vie de J-B. P. Molière*, (Paris, 1892); E. Faguet, *Dix-septième siècle : Etudes Littéraires*, (Paris, 1890); G. Lanson, *Histoire de la Littérature française*, (Paris, 1896) pp. 519 ff.
8. The first in *Molière et Bourdaloue*, (Paris, 1877); the second in *Etudes Critiques sur l'histoire de la littérature française*, (Paris, 1907) IVe Série pp. 179-242. His main ideas on Molière appeared originally in *Revue des Deux Mondes*, (1890). See also Perrens, *Les Libertins en France*, (Paris, 1899), p. 342.
9. A. Lefranc, 'La Vie et les ouvrages de Molière' in *Revue des Cours et Conférences*, 18 (1906) pp. 500-8. G. Lafenestre, *Molière* (Paris, 1909); E. Rigal, *Molière*, (Paris, 1908) I. pp. 181-3; the historian E. Lavisse aptly summed up current notions of the philosophy of Molière as follows: 'La morale de Molière est très modeste. On ne trouve point, dans tout son théâtre, un devoir qui commande un renoncement à soi, même un effort qui coûte, l'amour est une loi de la nature, la grande, l'essentielle loi, et Molière se soumet à la nature, la sachant plus forte que lui' *Histoire de France depuis les origines jusqu'à la révolution*, (Paris, 1900-11) VII, 2, p. 113.
10. Grimarest, *La Vie de M. de Molière* (édition critique par G. Mongrédien), (Paris, 1955) p. 39, n. 2.
11. *La Jeunesse de Molière*, (Paris, 1922), pp. 57-93. This reasoned conclusion is supported by R. Pintard, *Le Libertinage érudit dans la première moitié du 17e siècle*, (Paris, 1943), II, p. 624; G. Mongrédien, in *Pierre Gassendi, Sa Vie et son Oeuvre*, (Paris, 1955) pp. 128 ff; A. Adam, *Histoire de la Littérature française au 17e siècle*, (Paris, 1964) III, pp. 214-5, n. 4 (Reprint).
12. G. Michaut, *Les Luttes de Molière*, (Paris, 1925) pp. 108 ff; R. Fernandez, *La Vie de Molière*, (Paris, 1929) p. 164.

13. See C. S. Gutkind, *Molière und das komische Drama* (Halle, 1928); H. C. A. Lancaster, *A History of French Dramatic Literature in the 17th Century*, Part 3: *The Period of Molière*, 1652-1672 (Vols. I and II), (Baltimore, 1936).

14. W. G. Moore, *Molière A New Criticism*, (Oxford, 1949); R. Bray, *Molière Homme de Théâtre*, (Paris, 1954).

15. *Le Rire, Essai sur la signification du comique*, (Paris, 1900). For applications of this theory to Molière, see G. Brunet, 'Le Comique de Molière', *Mercure de France*, 153, (1922), pp. 289-320; C. D. Zdanowicz, 'Molière and Bergson's theory of laughter', *Wisconsin University Publications in Language and Literature*, (1924), 22, pp. 99-125; A. Thibaudet, 'Le Rire de Molière', *Revue de Paris*, (1922), pp. 312-33; Cf. also D. Romano, *Essai sur le comique de Molière*, (Berne, 1950), for a penetrating analysis of the comic structure in Molière in the light of more recent research into the phenomenon of the comic.

16. V. Vedel, *Deux Classiques français vus par un critique étranger*, (Paris, 1935); P. Bénichou, *Morales du Grand Siècle*, (Paris, 1948) pp. 156-218; D. Mornet, op cit; R. Jasinski, *Molière et Le Misanthrope*, (Paris, 1963) (Reprint); Adam, op. cit. III, Ch. 4.

17. J. D. Hubert, *Molière and The Comedy of Intellect* (Berkeley, 1962); J. Guicharnaud, *Molière une aventure théâtrale*, (Paris, 1963); L. Gossman, *Men and Masks, A Study of Molière*, (Baltimore, 1963).

18. See for example the group of articles dealing with questions of comic form in *Cahiers de l'Association Internationale des Etudes Françaises*, 16, (1964); also *Revue d'Histoire Littéraire de la France*, No. 5-6, (1972), *Molière*; '*Molière et le Théâtre Classique*', *Revue des Sciences Humaines*, (1973), 152; *Molière: Stage and Study*. Essays in Honour of W. G. Moore, ed. W. D. Howarth and M. Thomas, (Oxford, 1973); A. Eustis, *Molière as Ironic Contemplator*, (The Hague, 1973).

19. 'The Sceptical View of Marriage and the Comic Vision in Molière', *Forum for Modern Language Studies*, V, 1 (January, 1969) pp. 26-46; 'Un ami sceptique de Molière', *Studi Francesi*, No. 47-48 (1972) pp. 244-61.

NOTES TO CHAPTER I

1. *Molière A New Criticism*, ch. I; R. Bray, *Molière Homme de Théâtre*, Ch. II.

2. See the excellent *Introduction* of D. Mornet, op. cit.

3. This is one of the central points of Bray, op. cit. ch. VI.

4. See H. T. Barnwell, 'Some Reflections on Corneille's Theory of *Vraisemblance* as Formulated in the *Discours*', *Forum for Modern Language Studies*, I, 4, (Oct. 1965).

5. *Molière und das komische Drama*, pp. 90 ff; See the *Préface* to *Tartuffe* (1669) where Molière writes that '. . . l'emploi de la comédie est de corriger les vices des hommes . . .' in *Oeuvres de Molière*, *(Grands Ecrivains de la France)*, IV, p. 377. The abbreviation GE is used throughout to refer to this edition of the plays.

6. op. cit. p. 340, p. 370.

7. ibid. p. 355, pp. 360-2.

8. ibid. p. 349.

9. *The Life of the Drama*, (London, 1965), p. 104.

10. ibid. p. 115.

11. op. cit. pp. 21-2.

12. Many other critics have of course followed his approach, and I shall have occasion to refer to some of them in the chapters on individual plays (Part II).

13. *Les Débuts de Molière à Paris*, pp. 208-9; *Les Luttes de Molière*, pp. 108 ff, 227 ff.

14. *An Essay on Comedy and the Uses of the Comic Spirit*, (London, 1934), p. 34, (Reprint, first edition 1927).

15. This is the point of view of R. Fargher, who qualifies Philinte's attitude here as 'immoderate' and 'excessive' in 'Molière and His Reasoners', in *Studies in French Literature presented to H. W. Lawton*, (Manchester, 1968) p. 105.

16. 'Jamais Molière n'a dissimulé son opinion personnelle; toujours, au contraire, il a chargé un de ses personnages et quelquefois plusieurs, de la représenter, de l'exprimer très clairement. Dans les *Précieuses*, c'est La Grange . . . dans *L'Ecole des Maris*, Ariste; dans *L'Ecole des Femmes*, Chrysalde; dans *Le Tartuffe*, Cléante . . . dans *Les Femmes Savantes*, Henriette et Clitandre; dans *Le Malade Imaginaire*, Béralde'. *Les Luttes de Molière*, p. 227.
17. E. Bentley, op. cit. p. 4.
18. *Le Théâtre et l'Existence*, (Paris, 1952) p. 102; on identification, see E. Bentley, op. cit. Ch. 5; and the stimulating chapter on Illusion in *The Act of Creation*, by A. Koestler, (London, 1964) pp. 301-10.
19. *Le Rire, Essai sur la signification du comique*, (Paris, 1962) p. 4.
20. The text of the *Lettre* is to be found in GE IV, pp. 529-66; on the question of authorship, see C. S. Gutkind, op. cit., pp. 85ff, who believes that the author was a friend of Molière; R. Robert, in 'Des Commentaires de Première Main sur les Chefs-d'oeuvre les plus discutés de Molière', *Revue des Sciences Humaines*, 1956, pp. 27-32, argues in favour of Donneau de Visé as author; G. Poulet, who accepts that Molière is the author of the *Lettre*, centres his sensitive essay on the notion of the comic in Molière, see *Etudes sur le temps humain*, Edinburgh, 1949, pp. 116-24; for additional evidence in favour of Molière's authorship, see my article 'Un ami sceptique de Molière', *Studi Francesi*, 1972, p. 247.
21. ibid. pp. 560-1; p. 564; so quick is our imagination to seize upon the irrational, says the *Lettre* '. . . qu'en quelque autre lieu, quoique plus décent, que nous trouvions ces mêmes manières, nous sommes d'abord frappés d'un souvenir de cette première fois . . . lequel, se mêlant mal à propos avec l'occasion présente et partageant l'âme à force de plaisir qu'il lui donne, confond les deux occasions en une, et transporte dans la dernière tout ce qui nous a charmés et nous a donné de la joie dans la première; ce qui n'est autre que le ridicule de cette première.' ibid. p. 561.
22. *Essai sur le comique de Molière*, p. 57.
23. Quoted by W. G. Moore, op. cit. p. 23.
24. *The Act of Creation*, pp. 27-96.
25. *Le Rire*, p. 29; *Jokes and their Relation to the Unconscious*, translated by James Strachey, (London, 1966) p. 209 (Reprint). See D. Romano op. cit. for an interesting application of Freud's theory of the comic to Molière.
26. op. cit. pp. 38-44.
27. ibid. pp. 35-6, p. 45.
28. ibid. p. 35.
29. Cf. Freud's comment on this aspect of the verbal joke: 'Displacement habitually takes place between a remark and a reply which pursues the train of thought in a direction other than that in which it was started by the original remark.' op. cit. p. 54, n. 2.
30. op. cit. p. 56.
31. Cf. Bergson, op. cit. pp. 73-4: 'Une situation est toujours comique quand elle appartient en même temps à deux séries d'événements absolument indépendantes, et qu'elle peut s'interpréter à la fois dans deux sens différents.' See also Koestler, op. cit. p. 78.
32. ibid. pp. 61 ff.
33. Both Bergson and Freud underline the irrational origins of the comic. For Bergson, it is governed by 'une logique de l'imagination' which is related to the logic of dreams, ibid. pp. 32-3; and Freud writes that 'The comic arises from the uncovering of a mode of thought that is exclusively proper to the unconscious.' op. cit. p. 206.
34. op. cit. p. 15.

NOTES TO CHAPTER 2

1. *Vie de Monsieur de Molière*, (Paris, 1930) p. 16.
2. *La Littérature de l'Age baroque en France; Circé et Le Paon*, (Paris, 1954); see A. Adam, *Histoire* . . . III, p. 266-7 on the currency of these themes.

220   *Notes*

3. See GE II, pp. 147-54; G. Michaut, *Les Débuts de Molière à Paris*, pp. 80 ff.
4. *Les Nouvelles nouvelles*, (Paris, 1663) III, pp. 225-6.
5. It is true that several months later de Visé wrote *Zélinde ou La Véritable critique de l'Ecole des Femmes*, in which he says (Act I, Sc. 8) that some verses spoken by Sganarelle (Sc. 16, ll. 355-8) are taken from Ch. Sorel, *La Vraie Histoire Comique de Francion*, (1633) 8e livre. But the borrowing merely amounts to one isolated *boutade*, and it seems to have been in the nature of a proverbial remark made by husbands in danger of imminent cuckoldry, see also *Le Pédant Joué* (1654) by Cyrano de Bergerac, (Act II, Sc. 3). Grimarest does refer to 'Quelques personnes savantes' who said that Molière '. . . a pris toute cette Pièce chez les Etrangers', op. cit. p. 16. But G. Mongrédien, in his edition of Grimarest's biography affirms that no contemporary mentioned plagiarisms of any kind in connexion with this play. It seems that the first person to indicate a possible source was Riccoboni in 1736, who suggested that Molière knew *Arlequin cornu imaginaire*, an Italian play performed in 1716. There is some similarity in the 'plot' but it cannot be considered a source in any sense, since its date of composition is unknown.
6. *Essais*, (Paris, 1962) I, Livre II, Ch. 12, p. 603.
7. op. cit. p. 25.
8. See *Le Misanthrope*, Act IV, Sc. 3, ll. 1325-6, where Alceste tells Célimène

    Ce billet découvert suffit pour vous confondre,
    Et contre ce témoin on n'a rien à répondre.

    See also *Dom Garcie*, Act II, Sc. 5, which has a close similarity with the above episode.
9. Molière gives this attitude to his characters in different contexts; Tartuffe makes masterly use of it to produce a reversal of the situation where Damis accuses him of infamous conduct towards Elmire (Act III, Sc. 6, ll. 1074-86); Célimène, having dissolved Alceste's 'proof' of betrayal, hears him say 'C'est moi qui me viens plaindre, et c'est moi qu'on querelle!' (Act IV, Sc. 3, l. 1374).
10. The attempt of the comic hero to masquerade as a courageous warrior is of course a frequently exploited scene in farce, see Scarron's *Les Trois Dorothées ou Le Jodelet souffleté* (1647) where Jodelet engages in a lengthy dialogue between his cowardice and his valorous ambition (Act III, Sc. 1; Act IV, Sc. 7; Act V, Sc. 1). The most famous rationalization of honour is that made by Falstaff in Shakespeare's *Henry IV*, Part I, Act V, Sc. 1. The importance of Sganarelle's argument lies in its relation to the central theme of the play and not in the fact that it is simply a passage added for comic effect. On the comic aspect of Sganarelle, see the remarks of A. Adam. op. cit. pp. 268-9.
11. This view would seem to receive confirmation from Grimarest, op. cit. p. 65: '. . . Molière n'était bon que pour représenter le Comique; il ne pouvait entrer dans le Sérieux, et plusieurs personnes assurent qu'ayant voulu le tenter, il réussit si mal la première fois qu'il parut sur le théâtre, qu'on ne le laissa pas achever.' See also A. Adam, op. cit. III, p. 271; H. C. Lancaster, *A History of French Dramatic Literature* . . . Part III, The Period of Molière, (Baltimore, 1936) pp. 539-40.
12. W. D. Howarth, 'Dom Garcie de Navarre or Le Prince Jaloux', in *French Studies*, V (1951) pp. 140-8; cf. the reproduction of the title of the edition of 1682 in GE II, p. 234; F. R. Freudmann, in 'le comique dans *Dom Garcie de Navarre*', *Romanic Review*, LX (1969) pp. 251-64, sees the comedy in the hero's inability to perceive that Done Ignès is the sole object of Elvire's affection. I find this unconvincing, since it makes the hero a mere dupe rather than the self-duping *imaginaire*, whose temperament inclines him to a strictly subjective view of events; for an attempt to see the similarity between Dom Garcie and other characters, see M. Gutwirth, '*Dom Garcie de Navarre et Le Misanthrope*: de la comédie héroïque au comique du héros', *Publications of the Modern Language Association of America*, 83 (1968) pp. 118-29.
13. In the light of this *précieux* attitude, it seems difficult to accept Lancaster's statement that 'There is . . . nothing in the character of Elvire to justify his jealousy', op. cit.

p. 539; for a similarly favourable view of Elvire, see B. Rountree, '*Dom Garcie de Navarre*: Tentative de réconciliation avec les précieux', *Romanic Review*, LVI (1965) pp. 161-70.

14. In comparisons between the plays, I refer to the French translation of Cicognini's play, *Le Prince Jaloux*, published in Riccoboni's *Nouveau Théâtre Italien*, (Paris, 1733) III.

15. GE II, p. 232.

16. This view of temperament as the dominating factor in judgement is repeated by Elise in variant forms throughout the play, Act I, Sc. 1, ll. 89-99; Act II, Sc. 1, ll. 390-5; Act III, Sc. 1, ll. 770-81. It foreshadows the speech drawn from Lucretius which Eliante will make in *Le Misanthrope*, Act II, Sc. 4, ll. 711-30, just as the character of Dom Garcie foreshadows Alceste.

17. *Les Débuts . . .* p. 105; op. cit. p. 39. Michaut does admit, however, that in this scene 'sa jalousie pouvait avoir quelque raison d'être . . .' ibid. p. 105.

18. W. D. Howarth, art. cit. p. 144.

19. op. cit. pp. 104-5.

20. Cf. the verses spoken by Dom Garcie to Elvire prior to his first 'test', (Act I, Sc. 3, ll. 319-26).

NOTES TO CHAPTER 3

1. G. Michaut, *Les Luttes . . .* p. 98, stresses the different inspiration of the 1664 and 1669 plays.

2. GE IV, p. 392. For a detailed examination of the differences between the 1667 and 1669 versions see GE IV, pp. 325-31; G. Michaut, op. cit. pp. 82-5; H. d'Alméras, *Le Tartuffe de Molière*, (Paris, 1946) pp. 78-82.

3. *Molière, Oeuvres complètes*, (Paris, 1971) I, p. 838; see also the excellent article by the same person, 'L'Etat civil d'Armande Béjart, femme de Molière, ou historique d'une légende', *Revue des Sciences Humaines*, (1964) pp. 311-51.

4. On this aspect of the role see P. F. Butler, '*Tartuffe* et la direction spirituelle au XVIIe siècle', *Modern Miscellany* presented to E. Vinaver, (Manchester, 1969) pp. 48-63.

5. éd. cit. p. 847.

6. *Lettre . . .* in GE IV, p. 544, p. 550; see also Molière's description of him in the *Préface* of 1669, ibid. p. 375; Michaut, op. cit. p. 85, comes to the paradoxical conclusion that the satire of hypocrites was sharper in 1669 than in the second version.

7. *Le Registre de La Grange* 1659-1685, Ed. B. E. and G. P. Young, (Paris, 1947) I, p. 67.

8. Cf. the remark of G. Michaut, op. cit. p. 65 on this point: 'Le rideau peut tomber là-dessus.'

9. GE IV, p. 231.

10. *Molière*, (Paris, 1908) I, p. 261; See J. Lemaître, *Impressions de Théâtre*, (Paris, 1892) IV, pp. 38-44; G. Michaut, *Les Luttes . . .* pp. 128-31; R. Bray, Molière, *Homme de Théâtre*, pp. 352-3; A. Adam, *Histoire*, III, pp. 317-18. On the ambiguity of Tartuffe's role, and the ways in which it has been played, see M. Descotes, *Les Grands Rôles du Théâtre de Molière*, (Paris, 1960) pp. 151-202.

11. See *Lettre sur la Comédie de l'Imposteur*, GE IV, pp. 531-3.

12. Furetière, in his *Dictionnaire Universel*, gives the following definitions of these terms of abuse: '*Cagot*; faux dévot: hypocrite; qui affecte des apparences de dévotion: *Pied-plat*; On appelle pied plat, un rustre, un homme de rien qui a des souliers tout unis, et tout plats, comme en portent ordinairement les païsans. *Gueux*; On dit proverbialement, qu'un homme est gueux comme un rat d'Eglise, gueux comme un Peintre; pour dire qu'il est fort pauvre . . . On appelle aussi un gueux fieffé, un gueux qui s'attache à quelque endroit certain, à quelque coin d'Eglise pour y attendre l'aumône.'

13. GE IV, pp. 536-7.

14. ibid. p. 564.
15. *La Vie de Molière*, p. 76.
16. See H. Bergson, *Le Rire*, p. 32: 'Il y a donc une logique de l'imagination qui n'est pas la logique de la raison, qui s'y oppose même parfois, et avec laquelle il faudra pourtant que la philosophie compte, non seulement pour l'étude du comique, mais encore pour d'autres recherches du même ordre.'
17. *Les Luttes* . . . p. 129.
18. GE IV, p. 540.
19. See for example W. G. Moore, *Molière*, . . . p. 45: 'The mask falls at four points of the action, twice with Orgon, and twice with Elmire. Nowhere else in the play, as far as I can see, does Tartuffe pretend to be other than a holy man.' See also P. H. Nurse, 'Essai de définition du comique moliéresque', *Revue des Sciences Humaines*, (1964) pp. 21-24, who applies this principle to Dom Juan.
20. *Les Luttes* . . . p. 129.
21. op. cit. p. 45.
22. ibid. p. 46.
23. GE IV, p. 560; Cf. the article by Y. Delage on the comic in *Revue du Mois*, XX, (août 1919), pp. 337 ff: 'Pour qu'une chose soit comique, il faut qu'entre l'effet et la cause il y ait désharmonie.'
24. *Pensées*, éd. Lafuma, No. 131.
25. op. cit. p. 357.
26. See the commentary of the *Lettre sur la Comédie* on Tartuffe's ruse: '(Orgon) le trouve qui, bien loin d'entreprendre de se justifier, par un excellent artifice se condamne et s'accuse lui-même, en général et sans rien spécifier, de toutes sortes de crimes.' GE IV, p. 543.
27. op. cit. p. 46.
28. In his analysis of jokes, Freud gives an example which involves the hearer refusing to accept a perfectly truthful reply. His comments are illuminating in connexion with the development of Tartuffe's character at the end of Act III: '. . . the more serious substance of the joke is the problem of what determines the truth. The joke, once again, is pointing to a problem and is making use of the uncertainty of one of our commonest concepts. Is it the truth if we describe things as they are without troubling to consider how our hearer will understand what we say? Or is this only jesuitical truth, and does not genuine truth consist in taking the hearer into account and giving him a faithful picture of our own knowledge? I think that jokes of this kind are sufficiently different from the rest to be given a special position. What they are attacking is not a person or an institution, but the certainty of our knowledge itself, one of our speculative possessions. The appropriate name for them would therefore be 'sceptical' jokes.' *Jokes and their Relation to the Unconscious*, (London, 1960) p. 115.
29. GE IV, p. 545.
30. ibid. p. 547.
31. ibid. p. 548.
32. According to the *Lettre de la Comédie* the Panulphe of 1667 did attempt to reason with Orgon more fully than in 1669: 'Panulphe persiste donc dans sa manière accoutumée, et pour commencer à se justifier près de *son frère* (car il ose encore le nommer de la sorte) dit quelque chose du *dessein qu'il pouvoit avoir* dans ce qui vient d'arriver . . .' ibid. p. 549.
33. op. cit. p. 48.
34. GE IV, p. 549. (my italics).
35. op. cit. III, p. 320.
36. GE IV, pp. 551-2.
37. See the verses of Cléante, Act I, Sc. 5, l. 397, Act V, Sc. 3, ll. 1703-6, where he speaks of such *cabales*.
38. *Impressions de Théâtre*, IV, 4ᵉ partie, pp. 38-44. See also J. Rousset, 'A Propos de Tartuffe', in *La Littérature de l'Age baroque en France*, (Paris, 1954) pp. 248-50.

39. On the authorship of the *Lettre*, see Ch. 1, note 20.
40. The phrase is that of W. G. Moore, op. cit. p. 67.
41. *Essais*, (Paris, 1962) II, Ch. 15. Cf. the penetrating remarks of H. Friedrich in this connexion in his *Montaigne*, (Berne, 1949) pp. 195-204.
42. op. cit. II, Ch. 12, p. 587; this example is drawn from Cicero's *Academica*, II, Ch. XXIX. Cf. La Mothe Le Vayer: '. . . non seulement il arrive que nous disons quelquefois des choses fausses sans mentir, pour ce que nous croyons dire la vérité, mais il se peut faire aussi que nous mentirons en disant vrai . . ., d'autant que notre dessein sera d'imposer à nos auditeurs et de les repaître de bourdes.' In *Du Mensonge* in *Oeuvres de La Mothe Le Vayer*, (Dresden, 1756-9) III,(1re partie) 5e vol. pp. 157-8.
43. ibid. p. 634.
44. GE IV, p. 560, p. 564. (my italics).
45. See A. Levi, *French Moralists: The Theory of the Passions 1585-1649*, (Oxford, 1964) p. 28. Cf. also La Mothe Le Vayer: 'La Vertu morale est une habitude, ou une disposition constante, qui nous fait agir selon la raison. Cette définition nous donne à connaître celle du Vice, qui comme contraire à la Vertu, n'est rien qu'une habitude au mal, et à des actions déraisonnables.' op. cit. I, (2e partie), 2e vol. Ch. 12, p. 264.
46. GE IV, p. 553.
47. Cf. Julien-Eymard d'Anger's observation in his excellent article 'Stoïcisme et libertinage dans l'œuvre de François La Mothe Le Vayer', in *Revue des Sciences Humaines*, (1954) p. 266: 'Ce va-et-vient continuel d'une pensée qui se dérobe en s'affirmant sans cesse . . .' Cf. also R. Pintard, *Le Libertinage érudit dans la première moitié du 17e siècle*, (Paris, 1943) I, p. 505.
48. *Discours ou homilies académiques*, in ibid. III, (2e partie), 6e vol. p. 406.
49. ibid. VII, (2e partie), 14e vol. p. 28. Cf. Cléante's verses to Orgon on the difference between true and false religion:

> Estimer le fantôme autant que la personne,
> Et la fausse monnoie à l'égal de la bonne? (Act I, Sc. 5, ll. 337-8)

and Molière's reference to his enemies in the *Premier Placet* as 'ces faux-monnoyeurs', GE IV, p. 387.
50. *Opuscules ou petits traités*, (4e partie) in op. cit. III, (1re partie) 5e vol. p. 123.
51. *Discours ou homilies académiques* in ibid. III, (2e partie) 6e vol. pp. 297-9. For the same idea see also *Dialogue sur la Divinité* in *Deux Dialogues* (édition E. Tisserand), (Paris, 1922) p. 114; *Prose Chagrine* in ibid. III, (1re partie), 5e vol. p. 262.
52. ibid. V, (1re partie), 9e Vol. p. 103. Cf. Montaigne, op. cit. II, Ch. I, p. 370: '. . . l'estrangeté de nostre condition porte que nous soyons souvent par le vice mesmes poussez à bien faire, si le bien faire ne se jugeoit par la seule intention.'
53. *Préface*, 1669, in GE IV, p. 377.
54. *Du Mensonge*, in *Opuscules ou Petits Traités*, op. cit. III, (1re partie), 5e vol. pp. 125-6.
55. ibid. pp. 132 ff., p. 137.
56. G. Michaut uses the uncertain appearances of this episode to suggest that in the 1664 version Elmire was sympathetic to the hypocrite's declarations. But he bases his interpretation upon several remarks in the *Lettre sur la Comédie* which could also imply that she took *pity* on Panulphe, *Les Luttes . . .* pp. 77 ff. M. Descotes also stresses the equivocal nature of her behaviour, op. cit. p. 176, and a recent article even sees her as engaged in 'dalliance' with Tartuffe, see G. P. Orwen, 'Tartuffe Reconsidered', in *French Review*, 41 (1967-68) p. 613.
57. *Du Mensonge*, in op. cit. p. 132.
58. Sainte-Beuve, *Port-Royal*, (Paris, 1908) III, Ch. 15, p. 268. Cf. also R. Allier, *La cabale des dévots, 1627-66*, (Paris, 1902) and F. Baumal, *Molière et les dévots*, (Paris, 1919).
59. See 1669 *Préface*, GE IV, p. 378; also *Lettre sur la Comédie*, ibid. p. 548; Molière's remarks in the *Préface* make it very probable that he drew on the 7th letter of Pascal's *Provinciales* for Tartuffe's use of the direction of intention in Act IV, Sc. 5. Of this

method, Pascal's *bon père* says: 'Ce n'est pas qu'autant qu'il est en notre pouvoir, nous ne détournions les hommes des choses défendues; mais quand nous ne pouvons pas empêcher l'action, nous purifions au moins l'intention; et ainsi nous corrigeons le vice du moyen par la pureté de la fin.' *Oeuvres Complètes*, pp. 397-8.

60. *Prose Chagrin* in op. cit. III, (Ire partie), 5e vol. p. 252.

61. GE IV, p. 540.

62. *Du Mensonge*, op. cit. pp. 150-1: 'Je dirais volontiers à ceux qui inventent infinité d'autres circonstances requises pour être obligés à s'acquiter de ce qu'on a promis soumettant par ce moyen la Foi à leur raisonnement, que notre Foi n'a pas besoin d'être si mal gouvernée, ni assujettie à tant de règles, qui sont autant d'échapatoires pour ceux qui ne se soucient pas d'être infidèles pourvu qu'ils en évitent le nom.'

63. *Du Mensonge*, ibid. p. 160; Molière, *Préface*, 1669, GE IV, p. 381.

64. Cf. F. Brunetière, for whom *Tartuffe* was 'un acte d'hostilité déclarée,' *Etudes critiques* . . . pp. 205-22.

65. See GE IV, p. 375, p. 387, pp. 391-2; as J. Cairncross assumes in 'Tartuffe ou Molière hypocrite,' *Revue d'Histoire Littéraire de la France*, (1972) pp. 890-901.

66. Act IV, Sc. 5, intercalated between ll. 1487 and 1488. In spite of this, the view of Tartuffe as essentially sincere has received, and continues to receive, a measure of support; actors such as Coquelin *aîné* and Jouvet have emphasized his basic sincerity, see M. Descotes, op. cit. p. 167, pp. 170-2. Cf. also E. Rigal, op. cit. I. pp. 241-2. This view has come back into vogue, and is represented in the following articles: L. Jouvet, 'Pourquoi j'ai monté *Tartuffe*', *Témoignages sur le Théâtre*, (Paris, 1952) pp. 79 ff; P. Bourdieu, '*Tartuffe* ou le drame de la foi et de la mauvaise foi', *Revue de la Méditerranée*, 19 (1959) pp. 453-8; C. Roy, 'Sur Tartuffe', *Nouvelle Revue Française*, 137 (mai 1964) pp. 897-908; B. Dupriez, 'Tartuffe et la sincérité', *Etudes Françaises*, I (1965) pp. 452-67; I. Singer, 'The Shadow of Dom Juan in Molière', *Modern Language Notes*, 85 (1970), pp. 847 ff.

67. Cf. the *Lettre sur la Comédie* . . . GE IV, pp. 554-6, where approval of the play is taken as the pointer to a correct understanding and practice of religion.

68. ibid. p. 390, p. 387.

69. From Brossette's account of the encounter between Molière and M. de Lamoignon, as recounted to him by Boileau, who presented the playwright to the *Premier Président*. See ibid. pp. 318 ff.

70. ibid. p. 373, p. 375. Cf. also *Lettre sur la Comédie* . . . ibid. pp. 554-5.

71. ibid. p. 374.

72. *Lettre sur les Observations d'une comédie* . . . GE V, p. 243. On the authorship of this cogent defence of Molière, see R. Robert, art. cit. pp. 22-7.

73. GE V, p. 245.

74. ibid. pp. 252-5.

75. The paradoxical thesis that Orgon is meant by Molière to represent the true *dévot* is the basis for L. Veuillot's interpretation of the play, *Molière et Bourdaloue*, (Paris, 1877) p. 359.

76. op. cit. p. 158.

77. GE IV, p. 377; G. Michaut, *Les Luttes* . . . pp. 104-6.

78. op. cit. pp. 161-2.

79. op. cit. p. 318. In a stimulating article, '*Tartuffe* sans problèmes', H. Gouhier compares the radical conversion of a St. Cyran to that of Orgon: '. . . à travers la caricature qu'il (Orgon) en donne, il faut bien reconnaître qu'il s'agit de la même conversion.' *Table Ronde*, 197 (1964) p. 126. See also J. Calvet, *Molière est-il chrétien? Essai sur la séparation de la religion et de la vie*, (Paris, 1950) p. 64 ff.

80. 'Molière, Conférence faite aux Annales', in *Conferencia*, (juin, 1938), p. 662. Cf. also his *Molière et la comédie classique* (Paris, 1965) pp. 240-1.

81. op. cit. II, Ch. 12, p. 634. On Montaigne's attitude to reason, see A. Levi. op. cit. pp. 58-63.

82. *Dialogue Sur la Divinité*, p. 73.

83. ibid. p. 74. The words *folle sagesse* which seem to me to summarize Cléante's attitude are from the title of an article by H. Bremond: 'La folle sagesse de Pierre Charron' in *Le Correspondant*, CCLII (1913) pp. 357-64. On its origin, see Ch. 7, n. 43.
84. GE IV, p. 555.
85. *La Pensée religieuse française de Charron à Pascal*, (Paris, 1933) p. 3.
86. V, (1ʳᵉ partie), 9ᵉ vol. p. 61. On Le Vayer's opposition to Jansenism, see F. Wickelgren, *La Mothe Le Vayer, Sa vie et son Oeuvre*, (Paris, 1934) pp. 183 ff.
87. See J. Laporte, *La Doctrine de Port-Royal*, (Paris, 1923) II, p. 138; Pascal, *Pensées*, éd. Lafuma, No. 211.
88. See GE IV, p. 288; pp. 297-8.
89. See J. Laporte, op. cit. II, pp. 137-8.
90. V, (1ʳᵉ partie) 9ᵉ vol. p. 102.
91. For a detailed study of the Jansenist view of human actions, see Laporte, op. cit. II, pp. 132-53.
92. V, (1ʳᵉ partie), 9ᵉ vol. p. 106. For Montaigne's attitude to the moral absolutism of Stoicism, see op. cit. II, Ch. 11, p. 471; This is also Gassendi's position, see *Abrégé de la Philosophie de Gassendi*, (Lyon, 1678) VIII, Ch. 5; La Rochefoucauld, *Maximes*, No. 182; La Bruyère in *De l'Homme* dismisses the Stoic *sage* as 'ce fantôme de vertu', *Les Caractères*, (Paris, 1962) p. 297.
93. GE IV, p. 545.
94. See *Les Stoïciens, Textes choisis* par J. Brun, (Paris, 1957) pp. 98-101.
95. *Discours ou homilies académiques*, in *Oeuvres*, III, (2ᵉ partie) 6ᵉ vol. pp. 404-5. One of his most sustained attacks on the Stoic theory of the passions is to be found in *Prose Chagrine*, III (1ʳᵉ partie), 5ᵉ vol. pp. 352-4. See also *De l'Impassibilité*, in VII (2ᵉ partie), 14ᵉ vol. pp. 216-23; *La Connaissance de soi-même*, III, (2ᵉ partie), 6ᵉ vol. pp. 453-6. For a similar use of the *sage-fou* paradox in an anti-Stoic sense, see La Rochefoucauld, *Maximes*, Nos. 42, 207, 209, 231; Pascal, *Pensées*, éd. cit. No. 412, p. 549.
96. *Traité de la Comédie*, (Paris, 1961) ch. 3, p. 43. Cf. Bossuet, *Maximes sur la comédie* in *L'Eglise et le théâtre*, (Paris, 1930) pp. 175-89. The Prince de Conti, in his *Traité de la comédie et des spectacles*, (Paris, 1666) pp. 45-6, writes: 'le but de la Comédie est d'émouvoir les passions . . . et au contraire, tout le but de la Religion Chrétienne est de les calmer, de les abattre et de les détruire autant qu'on peut en cette vie.'
97. GE IV, pp. 382-3; Nicole, ibid. Ch. 3, p. 43. Cf. Le Vayer, *Promenades en neuf dialogues*, IV, (1ʳᵉ partie), 7ᵉ vol. pp. 177-8. In *Des Récréations Honnêtes*, Le Vayer justifies at length the moral worth of comedy, VI, (2ᵉ partie), 12ᵉ vol. On the similarity between this and Molière's *Préface*, see my article 'Un ami sceptique de Molière', *Studi Francesi*, (1972) p. 247.
98. ibid. ch. 9, pp. 69-73.
99. *Maximes sur la comédie*, . . . V, p. 183.
100. op. cit. Ch. 8, pp. 60-1.
101. GE IV, p. 383. Cf. Racine's *Lettre aux deux Apologistes de L'Auteur des Hérésies imaginaires*, (1666): '. . . car de me demander . . . si je crois la comédie une chose sainte, si je la crois propre à faire mourir le vieil homme, je dirai que non; mais je vous dirai en même temps qu'il y a des choses qui ne sont pas saintes, et qui sont pourtant innocentes. Je vous demanderai si la chasse, la musique . . . et quelques plaisirs . . . sont fort propres à faire mourir le vieil homme, s'il faut renoncer à tout ce qui divertit?' *Oeuvres de Racine*, GE (Paris, 1865) IV, p. 333.
102. *Essais*, III, Ch. 9, p. 432.
103. III, (2ᵉ partie), 6ᵉ vol. pp. 209-10. He paraphrases here *St Luke*, ch. XIV, v. 26, which reads: 'Si quelqu'un vient à moi, et s'il ne hait pas son père, sa mère, sa femme, ses enfants, ses frères et ses soeurs et même sa propre vie, il ne peut être mon disciple' (Version L. Segond). Cf. also *St Matthew*, Ch. X, v. 37, which shifts the emphasis from the hatred of one's kin for the sake of Christ to the danger of preferring them.
104. ibid. p. 210.

105. Although it should be noted that an equitable ecclesiastical writer, Mgr J. Calvet, has written of Orgon's words at this part of the play as follows: '. . . un chrétien fervent et éclairé ne peut pas entendre ces propos sans éprouver une gêne et un commencement de blessure.' op. cit. p. 78.
106. op. cit. p. 210.
107. *Oeuvres de Chapelle et de Bachaumont*, (Paris, 1854) p. 125. On Chapelle and Molière, see the well documented article by G. Mongrédien, 'Le meilleur ami de Molière: Chapelle', in *Mercure de France*, 329 (février, 1957) pp. 242-59; also *Les Libertins au XVIIe siècle. Textes choisis et présentés par A. Adam*, (Paris, 1964) pp. 245-51; Le Vayer is ironic also in his attitude to religious practices such as fasting, see *De l'Impiété*, VII, (2e partie), 14e vol. p. 98.
108. *Voyages de François Bernier*, (Amsterdam, 1699) II, p. 124. According to Grimarest, 'Ce fut au Collège qu'il (Molière) fit connaissance avec deux Hommes illustres de notre temps, Mr de Chapelle et Mr Bernier.' *Vie de M. de Molière*, p. 8.
109. This is the theme of Charpy's mystical treatise, *L'Eglise triomphante en Terre,*(Paris, 1657) p. 233.
110. *Morales du Grand Siècle*, pp. 203-4.
111. H. Bremond, *Histoire littéraire du sentiment religieux en France depuis la fin des guerres de religion jusqu'à nos jours*, (Paris, 1916-33) I, pp. 11-12.
112. H. Bremond, ibid. I, p. 72; *Traité de l'Amour*, I, 3.
113. *Introduction à la vie dévote*, (Paris, no date) p. 20. Many of his ideas on the Christian life may indeed be compared to Cléante's, see J. Plantié, 'Molière et François de Sales', *Revue d'Histoire Littéraire de la France*, (1972) pp. 902-27.
114. ibid. p. 192. One could compare this with Le Vayer's attitude, in *Des Jeux*, III (2e partie), 6e vol. pp. 37 ff.
115. Quoted in M. Magendie, *La Politesse Mondaine* . . . (Paris, 1925) I, p. 295; see *Introduction* . . ., pp. 196-7, 'Quand on peut jouer et danser.'
116. ibid. p. 192; 195-6. On the basic incompatibility of *honnêteté* and religion, see Julien-Eymard d'Angers, *Pascal et ses précurseurs*, (Paris, 1954) p. 25.
117. H. Bremond, op. cit. Ch. 1 and Ch. 8.
118. See H. Busson, op. cit. Ch. 1 , (3), pp. 45 ff.
119. Cf. *Pensée* no. 427, Lafuma.
120. *Deux Dialogues* . . . p. 92.
121. ibid. p. 86.
122. GE IV, p. 537.
123. op. cit. p. 160.
124. op. cit. p. 104.
125. GE IV, pp. 532-6. Cf. Act III, Sc. 7, l. 1141, where he says to Damis: 'Offenser de la sorte une sainte personne!'.
126. op. cit. II, Ch. 12, p. 571.
127. See *Dialogue sur la Divinité*, pp. 72 ff; *Apologie* . . . pp. 482 ff.
128. Quoted by H. Busson, *La Pensée* . . . p. 91. On his bizarre friendship with Molière, formed when the actor was touring the provinces, see GE X, pp. 126-8, pp. 164-9.
129. *Dialogue sur la Divinité* . . . p. 128.
130. On P. Charron see R. Popkin, *The History of Scepticism from Erasmus to Descartes*, (Assen, 1960) pp. 57-63.
131. *De La Sagesse*, (Paris, 1820-4) II, Ch. 5, pp. 134-5. Cf. Kant, *The Critique of Judgment*, Translated by J. Meredith, (Oxford, 1954) p. 114: '. . . religion is intrinsically distinguished from superstition, which latter rears in the mind, not reverance for the sublime, but dread and apprehension of the all powerful Being to whose will terror stricken man sees himself subjected, yet without according Him due honour. From this nothing can arise but grace begging and vain adulation, instead of a religion consisting in a good life.'
132. The text of *Les Quatrains* is to be found in *Les Libertins au XVIIe siècle* . . . pp. 88-109, see especially verses 60-1. See also H. Busson, op. cit. pp. 102-9.

133. Charron, op. cit. II, Ch. 5, p. 139.
134. op. cit. II, Ch. 12, p. 571; Cf. Le Vayer, *Dialogue sur la Divinité*, p. 73.
135. *Port-Royal*, III, Ch. 16, p. 289, n. 1.
136. Charron, op. cit. II, Ch. 5, p. 145.
137. op. cit. II, Ch. 12, p. 487.
138. op. cit. II, Ch. 3, p. 82.
139. GE V, pp. 244-5. The allusion to St Paul is from *Epistle to the Romans*, Ch. XIV, v. 10.
140. *De l'impiété*, in VII (2e partie), 14e vol. p. 93, pp. 99-100.
141. *Dialogue sur la Divinité* . . . p. 119.
142. *Le Libertinage érudit* . . . I, p. 539.
143. *De la Justice* in I,(1re partie), 1re vol. p. 31.
144. Cf. Charron, op. cit. II, Ch. 2, pp. 299-300: 'Le Prince doit soigner que la religion soit conservée en son entier selon les anciennes cérémonies et loix du pays, et empêcher toute innovation et brouille en elle . . . l'injure faite à elle, traîne avec soi un changement et empirement en la république.' Cf. also Gassendi, *Abrégé* . . . VIII, *Des principaux devoirs du souverain*, especially pp. 308-9.
145. *De la Religion*, I, (1re partie), 1er vol. p. 29.
146. ibid. pp. 27-31.

NOTES TO CHAPTER 4

1. I have observed the convention of referring to the general theme and the legendary hero as Don Juan, and to Molière's play and other seventeenth-century French works as *Dom Juan*.
2. *Impressions de Théâtre*, I, p. 57.
3. The first in *Observations sur une comédie de Molière intitulée le Festin de Pierre* par B.A. Sr de R(ochemont), avocat en Parlement, in GE V, pp. 217-32; the second in his *Traité de la comédie et des spectacles*, (Paris, 1666).
4. The first pamphlet is to be found in GE V, pp. 232-40, and the second in pp. 240-55. On the authorship of this letter, see R. Robert, art. cit. pp. 22-7.
5. The first opinion is represented by G. Michaut, *Les Luttes* . . . pp. 181 ff, and by R. Fernandez, op. cit. pp. 165 ff; the second by A. Adam, op. cit. III, pp. 333-4, and J. Cairncross, *Molière, Bourgeois et Libertin*, (Paris, 1963) Ch. 3.
6. See Despois and Mesnard, GE V, p. 6; J. Lemaître, op. cit. p. 59; W. G. Moore, op. cit. p. 93; A. Adam, op. cit. III, p. 322; J. Doolittle, 'The Humanity of Molière's *Dom Juan*,' *Publications of the Modern Language Association of America*, 68 (June 1953) p. 509; A. Simon, *Molière par lui-même*, (Paris, 1957) p. 106. The *marché de décors*, of 3 December 1664, is used by R. Pintard to show convincingly that Molière was already at that time in complete possession of his subject, 'Temps et Lieux dans le *Dom Juan* de Molière, *Studi in Onore di Italo Siciliano*, (Florence, 1966) Vol. II, pp. 997-1006; also H. G. Hall, 'Molière, *Dom Juan*: 'la scène du Pauvre", in *The Art of Criticism*, (Edinburgh, 1969) p. 84.
7. *Les Luttes* . . ., pp. 138-40.
8. See *Le Festin de Pierre avant Molière, Textes Publiés Avec Introduction, Lexique et Notes* par G. Gendarme de Bévotte, (Paris, 1907) pp. 148-9.
9. See E. Bentley, *The Life of the Drama*, p. 38, for the argument against this view.
10. GE V, p. 243.
11. For a complete history of the use of the legend in drama, see G. de Bévotte, *La Légende de Don Juan*, 2 Vols, (Paris, 1911); also J. Rousset, *L'Intérieur et l'Extérieur. Essais sur la poésie et sur le théâtre au XVIIe siècle*, (Paris, 1968) pp. 127-54.
12. See G. de Bévotte, op. cit. I, pp. 80-4; GE V, pp. 12 ff; G. Michaut, *Les Luttes* . . ., pp. 141-4.
13. See G. de Bévotte, ibid. I, p. 66.

14. For parallels between Molière's hero and seventeenth-century *libertins*, see F. Baumal, *Molière et les dévots*, (Paris, 1919), and A. Adam, op. cit. pp. 330 ff.
15. See E. Faguet, *En lisant Molière*, (Paris, 1914) pp. 39-42; G. de Bévotte, op. cit. I, p. 98; G. Michaut, *Les Luttes* . . . pp. 152-3.
16. ibid. pp. 186-7.
17. Among critics who have argued in favour of a comic Dom Juan are W. G. Moore, op. cit. pp. 93-7; H. G. Hall, 'A Comic Dom Juan', *Yale French Studies*, 23 (1959) pp. 77-84; H. Walker, 'The Self-Creating Hero in *Dom Juan*', *French Review*,(1962)pp. 167-74; L. Gossman, op. cit. pp. 37-65; R. Laufer, 'Le comique du personnage de Dom Juan de Molière', *The Modern Language Review*, LVIII (1953) pp. 15-20; P. H. Nurse, 'Essai de définition du comique moliéresque', *Revue des Sciences Humaines*, (1964) pp. 20-4; F. L. Lawrence, 'The Ironic Commentator in Molière's *Dom Juan*', *Studi Francesi*, 12 (1968) pp. 201-7; R. Fernandez, op. cit. pp. 165-7, and J. Doolittle, art cit. have represented the opposite viewpoint.
18. Rochemont notes in his pamphlet, *Observations sur une comédie*. . . 'Un Molière . . . habillé en Squanarelle (sic), qui se moque de Dieu et du Diable . . .', GE V, p. 226.
19. op. cit. p. 107.
20. Line references are to W. D. Howarth's edition of the play, (Oxford, 1958).
21. J. Arnavon, *Le Don Juan de Molière*, (Copenhagen, 1947). Tobacco, although in use from 1560 onwards, was still a subject of controversy with Church authorities and the Compagnie du Saint-Sacrement was at this time waging an energetic war against it.
22. This point is put well by A. Villiers in *Le Dom Juan de Molière*, (Paris, 1947) pp. 46 ff.
23. *Des Injures*, in *Oeuvres de François de La Mothe Le Vayer* (Dresden, 1756-59) III,(2ᵉ partie), 6ᵉ vol. pp. 96-7. Cf. Pascal's use of the paradox of the 'esprit fort' and the 'esprit faible': 'Rien n'accuse davantage une extrême faiblesse d'esprit que de ne pas connaître quel est le malheur d'un homme sans Dieu.' *Pensée* No. 427 in éd. Lafuma. In the same fragment, Pascal shows the same profound aversion for the pretensions of the *libertin* as Le Vayer: 'Il faut qu'il y ait un étrange renversement dans la nature de l'homme pour faire gloire d'être dans cet état, dans lequel il semble incroyable qu'une seule personne puisse être. Cependant l'expérience m'en fait voir un si grand nombre, que cela serait surprenant si nous ne savions que la plupart de ceux qui s'en mêlent se contrefont et ne sont pas tels en effet. Ce sont des gens qui ont ouï dire que les belles manières du monde consistent à faire ainsi l'emporté. C'est ce qu'ils appellent avoir secoué le joug, et qu'ils essayent d'imiter.' Cf. also La Bruyère, *Des Esprits forts*, in *Les Caractères*, (Paris, 1962), p. 458.
24. GE V, p. 228.
25. ibid. p. 247.
26. op. cit. pp. 331-4.
27. op. cit. p. 128.
28. A. Simon, op. cit. p. 107; cf. H. Walker, art. cit. pp. 168-9 for a similar view of Sganarelle's role.
29. Cf. Albert Camus' comment in *Le Mythe de Sisyphe* on donjuanism: 'Ce n'est point par manque d'amour que Don Juan va de femme en femme . . . Mais c'est bien parce qu'il les aime avec un égal emportement et chaque fois avec tout lui-même, qu'il lui faut répéter ce don et cet approfondissement.' In *Essais*, (Paris, 1965) p. 152. For a different view of Dom Juan see J. Rousset, *L'Intérieur et l'Extérieur*, pp. 136-7.
30. L. Gossman, op. cit. p. 37.
31. See J. D. Hubert's interesting analysis of the choice and function of words in *Dom Juan*, op. cit. pp. 118-22.
32. GE V, p. 226. See A. Adam, op. cit. pp. 332-3; L. Gossman, op. cit. p. 58.
33. Notably by Théodore de Banville, who saw Dom Juan as the author's *porte-parole*: 'au lieu d'être un impie sans croyance, Dom Juan devient un philosophe matérialiste, plein de foi au contraire, mais de foi dans les croyances qui seront la religion de l'avenir.' *Critiques*, pp, 185 ff, quoted in G. Michaut, *Les Luttes* . . . p. 180.

34. As for example Despois and Mesnard have supposed, see GE V, pp. 141-2, n. 8. Compare the following passage from Gassendi with Sganarelle's argument on the necessary and logical sequence of cause and effect in nature: 'Comment osera-t-on dire que le corps de l'homme soit l'ouvrage d'une cause aveugle, sans prudence, sans dessein, et sans intelligence? . . . le corps de l'homme, dis-je, dans lequel les pieds, les yeux, et les mains, dans lequel le coeur, le poumon, le cerveau et le foie, dans lequel les os, les muscles, et les veines . . . dans lequel toutes choses ne sauraient être plus artistement formées, plus convenablement mises et situées, ni plus utilement destinées? Si nous devons raisonner de l'effet à la cause ne devons-nous pas d'un sage et savant ouvrage inférer un sage et savant ouvrier, et de tous ces usages si propres et si commodes, inférer une Cause très intelligente qui se les soit proposés?' F. Bernier, *Abrégé de la Philosophie de Gassendi*, (Lyon, 1678) Vol. IV, Tome V, Livre V, pp. 428-9.

35. Cf. Boileau's condemnation of such *libertin* pretensions to *sagesse* in his IV.[e] *Satire*, dedicated to Le Vayer's son (it is interesting to note that his picture of the *libertin* follows his satire of the 'bigot orgueilleux'; both Molière and he would seem to have regarded *bigot* and *libertin* as contrary but equally blameworthy aberrations):

> Un libertin d'ailleurs, qui, sans âme et sans foi,
> Se fait de son plaisir une suprême loi,
> Tient que ces vieux propos de démons et de flammes,
> Sont bons pour étonner des enfans et des femmes. *Oeuvres* (Paris, 1961) p. 35.

36. op. cit. III, (1re partie) 5e vol., p. 462; On the *Petit Discours* see R. Pintard, op. cit. I, pp. 517-20. Cf. Pascal, *Pensées*, No. 83, éd. Lafuma: 'Les sciences ont deux extrémités qui se touchent, la première est la pure ignorance naturelle où se trouvent tous les hommes en naissant, l'autre extrémité est celle où arrivent les grandes âmes qui ayant parcouru tout ce que les hommes peuvent savoir trouvent qu'ils ne savent rien et se rencontrent en cette même ignorance d'où ils étaient partis, mais c'est une ignorance savante qui se connaît.'

37. See H. Busson, *La Pensée Religieuse* . . . Ch. III, (i), L'Immortalité de l'Ame, pp. 115 ff.

38. op. cit. p. 400.

39. Molière might well have been conscious of the parallel between this scene and the symbolic confrontation of good and evil in *Job* Ch. 2, and the temptation of Christ in *St Matthew* Ch. 4.

40. *Les Luttes* . . ., p. 186.

41. V, (2e partie) 10e vol. No. XXVI pp. 303-6.

42. III (1re partie) 5e vol., *Opuscules ou petits traités*, II, pp. 67-8. Molière may well have taken several details of his scene from this *opuscule*. When the *Pauvre* asks Dom Juan to succour him, as a recompense for his directions through the forest, the Dom says 'Ah! Ah! ton avis est intéressé, à ce que je vois' (l. 993). At the end of the scene he gives him a *louis d'or* saying 'je te le donne pour l'amour de l'humanité' (l. 1025). Le Vayer, discussing the opinion which decrees that all virtue must be disinterested, writes that 'C'est ce qui portait autrefois Aristote à soutenir qu'il fallait donner à l'humanité plutôt qu'à l'homme' (pp. 35-6). The Dom is saying that whereas the *Pauvre*'s actions have an ulterior motive, his are purely disinterested, and that is why he does not insist on making the *Pauvre* swear in order to gain the money.

43. J. Arnavon's comment on this aspect of Dom Juan's character is worth noting: 'Le méchant homme a disparu, on dirait que Molière l'a oublié', op. cit. p. 317.

44. III, (1re partie) 5e vol. *De l'Ingratitude*, p. 72.

45. ibid. p. 73.

46. ibid. p. 74.

47. ibid. p. 75.

48. VII, (2e partie) 14e vol. *Petits traités en forme de lettres écrites à diverses personnes studieuses*, p. 58.

49. ibid. p. 61.

50. Cf. Dom Louis' lines: 'Apprenez . . . que la vertu est le premier titre de noblesse; que je regarde bien moins au nom qu'on signe, qu'aux actions qu'on fait' (ll. 1468-71). In *Des Gentilshommes*, Le Vayer writes similarly: 'En effet, la noblesse d'une race est bien mieux fondée sur une suite d'actions vertueuses de ceux, qui en sont, que sur sa durée . . .' He expounds essentially the same ideas in his *De la Noblesse*, in *Opuscules ou petits traités*, in II, (2ᵉ partie), 4ᵉ vol. pp. 401-20.

51. ibid. p. 62.

52. art. cit. p. 522. Such an interpretation of this passage of Dom Louis would seem to be confirmed by reference to the French versions of Dorimond and Villiers. In both these plays, Dom Alvaros merely makes a passing reference to the fact that the virtue of a father is not always inherited by his son (ll. 118-22, and ll. 199-200 respectively). There is no question of interference on the part of a human in the affairs of heaven. See also G. de Bévotte, *Le Festin de Pierre avant Molière*, p. 170, n. 7.

53. G. Michaut, *Les Luttes* . . ., p. 186.

54. op. cit. pp. 55-6.

55. ibid. p. 62. For satire of those who ape the nobility see *Les Précieuses Ridicules, Le Bourgeois Gentilhomme*. Nobles who think themselves superior to others are ridiculed in *La Critique de l'Ecole des Femmes* and *L'Impromptu de Versailles, George Dandin, Monsieur de Pourceaugnac, La Comtesse d'Escarbagnas* etc; See R. McBride, 'Le Provincial dans la comédie de Molière', *Revue Marseille*, 101, 2 (1975) pp. 149-52.

56. *Maximes*, No. 256.

57. On the *dénouement* and its originality in Molière's play see A. Adam, op. cit. III, p. 327.

58. 'L'Inhumain Don Juan' in *La Table Ronde*, (novembre 1957) 119, p. 69.

59. art. cit. pp. 71-2. For J. Rousset '. . . l'intervention du Commandeur dans la pièce est insuffisamment motivée', op. cit. p. 141. But this is to overlook the final evolution of the character in Molière towards total dehumanization.

60. III, (1ʳᵉ partie), 5ᵉ vol., p. 49, pp. 51-2, pp. 58-60, p. 61.

61. op. cit. pp. 96-7. Jouvet has gone further, asserting that the hero is a man who sincerely seeks but cannot find God. *Molière et la Comédie Classique*, (Paris, 1965) p. 98.

62. Montaigne, op. cit. II, ch. 12, p. 545. On the way in which Pascal interprets this remark, see 'Pascal's use of *Abêtir*', by E. Moles, in *French Studies*, 1965, pp. 379-84.

NOTES TO CHAPTER 5

1. *Histoire de la littérature française* . . . III, p. 343.

2. G. Michaut, *Les Luttes de Molière*, pp. 225 ff.

3. R. Fernandez, *La Vie de Molière*, Ch. 6.

4. R. Jasinski, *Molière et Le Misanthrope*, p. 120.

5. R. Doumic, *Le Misanthrope de Molière*, (Paris, 1929) pp. 190-1.

6. A. Adam, op. cit., pp. 344 ff. Cf. the same thesis, although more nuanced, in D. Mornet, *Molière*, pp. 107-14.

7. Cf. P. Bénichou, *Morales du Grand Siècle*, pp. 214 ff; Cf. also the introduction to the edition of *Le Misanthrope* by E. Lop and A. Sauvage, Les Classiques du Peuple, (Paris, 1963).

8. See J. D. Hubert, *Molière and The Comedy of Intellect*, Ch. 13; L. Gossman, *Men and Masks*, Ch. 3; J. Guicharnaud, *Molière, une aventure théâtrale 3ᵉ partie*.

9. See P. J. Yarrow's article, 'A Reconsideration of Alceste', *French Studies*, (1959) pp. 314-31, for a comprehensive survey of critical opinion on the character of Alceste.

10. GE V, p. 440. This letter has been used by R. Robert, in his article 'Des Commentaires de première main . . .' to explain Molière's intentions in the play. But a **passage** from Grimarest's *Vie de M. de Molière* invalidates much of its authority:

'Mr. de . . . crut se faire un mérite auprès de Molière de défendre *Le Misanthrope*; il fit une longue lettre qu'il donna à Ribou pour mettre à la tête de cette pièce. Molière, qui en fut irrité, envoya chercher son libraire, le gronda de ce qu'il avait imprimé cette rhapsodie sans sa participation, et lui défedit de vendre aucun exemplaire de sa pièce où elle fût, et il brûla tout ce qui en restait; mais après sa mort on l'a réimprimée.' (Paris, 1930) p. 58.

11. J.-J. Rousseau, *Lettre à M. d'Alembert sur Les Spectacles*, (Paris, 1907) p. 57; A. de Musset, *Une soirée perdue*; A. Adam, op. cit. pp. 345-6; M. Descotes, *Les grands rôles* . . . p. 95; P. J. Yarrow, art. cit., R. Fernandez, op. cit.

12. See the somewhat similar views of P. Gaxotte, in 'Quand Alceste était jeune', *Le Figaro Littéraire*, (le 5 avril 1958). M. Magendie has expressed the modern attitude towards Alceste with clarity; 'On chercherait en vain, dans *Le Misanthrope*, un passage de quelque importance où nous aurions raison de rire d'Alceste', in 'Le véritable sens du *Misanthrope*', *Mélanges Hùguet*, (Paris, 1940) p. 285.

13. See Grimarest, op. cit. pp. 24-5, pp. 47-8; R. Jasinski, op. cit. pp. 61 ff.

14. Edition Ch.-L. Livet, (Paris, 1878) p. 4.

15. GE I, pp. XV-XVI.

16. op. cit. p. 59.

17. *Témoignages sur le Théâtre*, (Paris, 1952) p. 31.

18. *Elomire Hypocondre*, Act I, Sc. 3; Grimarest, op. cit. p. 46, pp. 47-8.

19. Cf. Grimarest, p. 47, who quotes remarks which he attributes to Molière in conversation with Rohaut and Mignard: 'J'aime la vie tranquille, et la mienne est agitée par une infinité de détails communs et turbulents . . .'

20. This passage forms part of his discussion of *L'Ecole des Maris*, op. cit. pp. 108-9. On the similarity between the *barbon* and Alceste, see P. Bénichou, op. cit. pp. 212-3.

21. R. Fernandez, ibid. pp. 188-9.

22. op. cit. pp. 259-75.

23. See III,(1re partie), 5e vol. of *Oeuvres* . . . pp. 254-5, pp. 268-78.

24. VII,(1re partie) 13e vol. pp.108-9. Solitude and misanthropy are recurrent themes throughout Le Vayer's works, see particularly *Neuf dialogues faits à l'imitation des anciens par Oratius Tubero* (1630-1), *De la Conversation et de la solitude*, in II, (2e partie) 4e vol., *Prose Chagrine* (1661), *Promenades en neuf dialogues* (1662-4), *Soliloques sceptiques* (1670).

25. GE V, pp. 430-1.

26. *Prose Chagrine*, p. 252.

27. Quoted by G. Michaut, *Les Luttes*, p. 208, n. 1.

28. C. Hoy, *The Hyacinth Room, An investigation into the Nature of Comedy, Tragedy and Tragicomedy*, (London, 1964) p. 6. See also the section on *Le Misanthrope*, pp. 156-61.

29. op. cit. p. 242; Cf. Saint-Evremond's observation of those who 'rencontrent une certaine volupté dans les plaintes', *Oeuvres Mêlées*, (Paris, 1865) I, p. 21.

30. One of the opening sentences in *Prose Chagrine* makes his detachment from what he is saying and is going to say explicit: 'En effet, le chagrin qui me possède présentement, m'envoie au cerveau des fumées si contraires à la conversation, que pour aucunement les dissiper, nonobstant leur agrément qui me flatte, ou pour en quelque façon les évaporer . . . il faut que je m'en décharge sur ce papier.' p. 241.

31. My italics: see Sextus Empiricus, *Outlines of Pyrrhonism*, Ch. XIV for the sceptical theory that all perception is conditioned by one's temperament. La Rochefoucauld expresses perfectly the sceptical view of the importance of humours in *Maxime* 297: 'Les humeurs du corps ont un cours ordinaire et réglé, qui meut et qui tourne imperceptiblement notre volonté; elles roulent ensemble et exercent successivement un empire secret en nous: de sorte qu'elles ont une part considérable à toutes nos actions, sans que nous le puissions connaître.'

32. My italics; such perverse delight in their *idée fixe* is characteristic of all the *imaginaires*; see Orgon in *Tartuffe*, Act II, Sc. 2, Argante in *Les Fourberies de Scapin*, Act I, Sc. 4, Argan in *Le Malade Imaginaire*, Act I, Sc. 5.

33. p. 338.

34. Furetière's *Dictionnaire Universel* gives the following definition of *atrabilaire*: 'Mélancolique; qui est d'un tempérament où la bile noire domine.' In *De l'Amour* (1648), Le Vayer foreshadows the situation of *Le Misanthrope* when he says that an atrabilious temperament is naturally inclined towards love.

35. op. cit. pp. 238-9.

36. *De l'amitié*, in III, (2e partie), 6e vol. p. 193. In another *opuscule* on friendship, he writes that '. . . la diversité de ce même tempérament . . . fait une différence . . . qui rend ce parfait consentement en toutes choses, . . . hors de toute apparence'; *De l'amitié*, in *Opuscules ou petits traités*, II, (2e partie) 4e vol. p. 144. Cf. J. Dubosc: '. . . comme des Arbres de différente espèce étant bien entés, ne laissent pas de porter du fruit: aussi l'Amitié qui se forme entre des personnes de diverses humeurs, ne laisse pas de réussir . . . l'affection s'engendre aussi bien dans l'inégalité des humeurs, comme l'harmonie se forme dans l'inégalité des voix.' *L'Honneste Femme*, (Rouen, 1643) I, pp. 226-7.

37. Alceste's recourse to what L. Gossman terms 'the myth of the irrationality of passion' (op. cit. p. 79) to defend his choice of Célimène, shows his partial awareness of this problem (Cf. ll. 247-8). But his subsequent attempts to reform her ways reveal clearly the limitations of his lucidity.

38. II, (2e partie), 4e vol. p. 138.

39. ibid. pp. 133-4.

40. Cf. Alceste's speech (ll. 277-84) with a paragraph in one of Le Vayer's *Petits traités* . . ., *De l'étude et du lien d'amitié* (1654): 'Je ne saurais m'empêcher d'abord de vous louer . . . pour ne vous pas engager mal à propos dans une affection, dont vous voulez observer les loix en homme d'honneur. L'on peut civilement ne s'y pas embarquer, mais depuis qu'on y est, le mauvais choix ne cause pas de petites amertumes; . . . Votre franchise d'ailleurs vous portant à imiter la Nature, qui commence son ouvrage du corps humain par le coeur, vous faites très prudemment de ne pas hasarder légèrement une partie, où l'on ne reçoit jamais de légères blessures.' VI, (2e partie) 12e vol. p. 180.

41. GE V, pp. 433-4.

42. op. cit. p. 344. Cf. D. Mornet op. cit. p. 112: '(Alceste) n'aime pas le sonnet d'Oronte et c'est assurément Molière qui parle par sa bouche'.

43. It seems to me dangerous to infer Molière's opinion of the sonnet on the basis of his probable opposition to the type of *précieux* affectation which characterizes Oronte's poem. D. Mornet has pointed out that Molière knew, as well as any *salon* poet, the art of writing such *précieux* poetry, op. cit. pp. 111-12.

44. Cf. H. Bergson, *Le Rire* . . . pp. 57-8.

45. Cf. R. Doumic, op. cit. p. 116; Cf. also F. W. Lindsay, 'Alceste and the sonnet', *French Review*, 28 (1954-5) pp. 395-402.

46. It is not difficult to imagine how ridiculous Alceste's hyperbolic and cumbersome language must have seemed to the *honnête homme* with his exact notion of *justesse*. In addition, Célimène draws attention to his outmoded aberration in dress, in Act V, Sc. 4. The costume worn by Alceste consisted of 'hault de chausse justeaucorps de brocart rayé or et soye gris, doublé de tabis, garny de ruban vert, la veste de brocart d'or, les bas de soye et jaretieres . . .' *Cent ans de Recherches sur Molière*, edited by M. Jurgens and E. Maxfield-Miller, (Paris, 1963) p. 568.

47. Shakespeare's Duke of Cornwall underlines finely the proximity of sincerity and insincerity in a tirade against the blunt-spoken Earl of Kent, in *King Lear*, (Act II, Sc, 2).

48. op. cit. p. 137.

49. Cf. the interesting article of M. Michel, 'Alceste ou Le Misanthrope', *La Nouvelle Revue Française*, (août, 1963) pp. 316-23, which sees as Alceste's characteristics 'une naïveté et une puérilité étonnantes', p. 323.

50. See L. Gossman on their relationship, op. cit. Ch. 3.

51. Saint-Evremond, *Oeuvres Mêlées*, II, 2, p. 532. Cf. the strictures on *coquettes* by J. Dubosc, op. cit. III, pp. 49 ff.

52. *Le Misanthrope de Molière*, (Paris, 1930) p. 111.

53. See Q. M. Hope, 'Society in *Le Misanthrope*', *French Review*, 32 (1959) p. 329.
54. *Prose Chagrine*, p. 263. *De l'Estime et Du Mépris* in II, (2ᵉ partie), 4ᵉ vol. p. 146. N. Faret, in *L'Honneste Homme ou L'Art de Plaire à la Cour*, (Paris, 1630) writes that such 'esprits opiniâtres', always full of 'contrariétés et de la mélancholie', will never please women, who are drawn towards 'humeurs gaies et divertissantes', p. 253.
55. Le Vayer makes frequent use of precisely this idea to undermine the view that there can be any objective norm of judgement, cf. *Petit Traité Sceptique sur cette commune Façon de parler N'Avoir Pas le Sens Commun* (1646) in V, (2ᵉ partie), 10ᵉ vol. pp. 150-2. Cf. also *Promenades en neuf dialogues* (1662-4), IV, (1ʳᵉ partie), 7ᵉ vol. p. 143. In *L'Honneste Homme*, Faret gives his pupil the same advice as Eliante. In the presence of a woman 'Elle n'aura point d'attrait de l'esprit qu'il ne loue . . . elle n'aura point de défaut qu'il ne déguise par quelque terme d'adoucissement. Si elle a le teint noir, il dira qu'elle est brune, . . . si elle est trop maigre et trop petite, elle en sera d'autant plus adroite et agile . . . il couvrira chaque imperfection du nom de la perfection la plus voisine.' pp. 171-3.
56. P. J. Yarrow, art. cit. p. 322.
57. Cf. the same maxim in metaphorical terms in *Prose Chagrine*, p. 341: 'Nous avons toujours la serpe en main pour couper la vigne des autres, qui jette toujours trop, ce nous semble; cependant que la nôtre demeure en friche faute d'être émondée.' Dubosc describes the *prude* in terms very applicable to Arsinoé. She is one of those people '. . . qui ne veulent blesser qu'avec des armes dorées; (elles) déguisent leur blâme sous quelque apparence de louange; s'(elles) disent du mal, (elles) veulent témoigner que c'est à regret; mais c'est pour imiter les Archers, qui tirent le trait à eux, afin de le mieux décocher au blanc.' op. cit. I, p. 160.
58. This is, in varying forms, the thesis of R. Jasinski, op. cit. p. 149; P. J. Yarrow, art. cit. p. 322; and J. Guicharnaud, op. cit. p. 436. Saint-Evremond describes Alceste at Court when he writes of '. . . des gens qui ne peuvent quitter la cour, et se chagrinent de tout ce qui s'y passe; qui s'intéressent dans la disgrâce des personnes les plus indifférentes, et qui trouvent à redire à l'élévation de leurs propres amis. Ils regardent comme une injustice tout le bien et le mal qu'on fait aux autres.' op. cit. I, p. 20.
59. P. J. Yarrow, art. cit. p. 322; G. Michaut, *Les Luttes . . .* p. 223. G. Rudler in his edition of *Le Misanthrope*, (Oxford, 1947) p. XVI.
60. GE V, p. 437.
61. R. Jasinski, op. cit. p. 153. This is also the view of P. J. Yarrow, art. cit. pp. 322-3, and of J. Guicharnaud, op. cit. p. 443.
62. op. cit. p. 39. Elsewhere, (*L'Ecole des Femmes*, Act V, Sc. 4) Molière uses the same device to keep Arnolphe farcical in a potentially serious situation. Cf. the remarks of Lysidas in *La Critique de L'Ecole des Femmes* (Sc. 6) where he speaks of Arnolphe's 'roulements d'yeux extravagants, . . . soupirs ridicules . . . larmes niaises qui font rire tout le monde.'
63. As set forth by G. Rudler, éd. cit. pp. 127-8; R. Jasinski, op. cit. pp. 166-87; P. J. Yarrow, art. cit. p. 323; Cf. also H. J. Hunt, 'Célimène: 'coquette' or 'coquine'?' *French Studies*, III (1949) pp. 324-34. For a presentation of the opposite point of view, see J. Guicharnaud, op. cit. pp. 442-53.
64. P. J. Yarrow, art. cit. p. 323.
65. Cf. the similar verses spoken by Arnolphe to Agnès in *L'Ecole des Femmes*, Act V, Sc. 4, ll. 1581-3, ll. 1596-7.
66. *De la curiosité*, in *Petits Traités en forme de lettres . . .* in VI, (1ʳᵉ partie), 11ᵉ vol. p. 152.
67. op. cit. p. 154; art. cit. p. 323.
68. p. 254.
69. éd. cit. p. 144.
70. For a very different view of Alceste's exit from the one proposed here, see J. Arnavon, *Le Misanthrope de Molière*, pp. 272-3; for M. Magendie 'C'est l'albatros qui échappe aux 'huées' des marins, et regagne les hauteurs solitaires, où il redevient un 'prince de nuées' art. cit. p. 286.
71. Indeed Philinte shares the same ideas as Alceste to such an extent that commentators

have spoken of him as being the true misanthrope, cf. E. Faguet, *En lisant Molière*, (Paris, 1914) pp. 192 ff. P. Gaxotte has made this view the basis of his interesting article, 'Quand Alceste était jeune', *Le Figaro Littéraire*, (5 avril, 1958).

72. I have studied this aspect of the play in 'Un ami sceptique de Molière', *Studi Francesi*, No. 47-48 (1972) pp. 249-54. The example of Clitandre and Chrysale in *Les Femmes Savantes* may also be quoted as proof that the difference between the *raisonneur* and the *ridicule* tends to be more nuanced than has sometimes been suspected (see Part II, Ch. 7 (3)).

73. Cf. G. Michaut, *Les Luttes* . . . pp. 228 ff; R. Jasinski, op. cit. p. 202; A. Adam, op. cit. 352; J. Guicharnaud, op. cit. p. 370. This interpretation of Philinte would appear to originate from D. de Visé's *Lettre Ecrite Sur la Comédie du Misanthrope*, where he writes: 'L'ami du Misanthrope est si raisonnable, que tout le monde devroit l'imiter'. GE. V, p. 441.

74. Cf. *Epistle to the Romans*, Ch. XII, v. 3; Montaigne, *Essais*, I, Ch. 30, p. 225: 'Ne soyez pas plus sages qu'il ne faut, mais soyez sobrement sages.'

75. References are to the Dresden edition, V, (2ᵉ partie), 10ᵉ vol.

76. On Erasmus see W. Kaiser, *Praisers of Folly*, (London, 1964) pp. 19-100; also P. H. Nurse, 'Essai de définition du comique moliéresque', *Revue des Sciences Humaines*, (1964) pp. 9-24.

77. op. cit. pp. 141-2. Le Vayer, in his characteristic style, is of course employing the same arguments as those used by Montaigne against man's presumption in his *Apologie de Raimond Sebond*.

78. ibid. pp. 143-50. The classical statement of this sceptical approach to knowledge is found in Sextus Empiricus, *Outlines of Pyrrhonism*, Ch. 14.

79. ibid. p. 181, p. 149.

80. ibid. pp. 165-6.

81. On the indivisibility of Stoic virtue, see *Les Stoïciens, Textes choisis* par J. Brun, p. 92. Alceste's attitude is similar to that of Orgon in this connexion, see Part II, Ch. 3 (4).

82. *Petit Traité* . . . pp. 168-71. Cf. Montaigne's remark: 'Je ne pense qu'il y ait tant de malheur en nous comme il y a de vanité, ny tant de malice comme de sotise;' op. cit. I, Ch. 50, p. 337.

83. ibid. p. 173.

84. A. Camus, *Le Mythe de Sisyphe*, in *Essais*, (Paris, 1965) p. 101.

85. op. cit. pp. 176-7. Cf. Boileau's Satire IV, 1664, dedicated to Le Vayer's son:

> En ce monde il n'est point de parfaite sagesse;
> Tous les hommes sont fous, et malgré tous leurs soins,
> Ne diffèrent entr'eux que du plus, ou du moins.

86. ibid. p. 177. Cf. Erasmus, who also sees the whole of life taking place under the beneficent aegis of *folie*: without it, life would be miserable for all 's'ils ne se maintenaient l'un l'autre dans l'illusion, s'il n'y avait entre eux tromperie réciproque, flatterie, prudente connivence, enfin le lénifiant échange du miel de la Folie'. in *Eloge de La Folie*, traduit par P. de Nolhac, (Paris, 1953) XXI, p. 41.

87. ibid. p. 178.

88. ibid. p. 179. Cf. Béralde in *Le Malade Imaginaire* who, having described medicine as 'une des plus grandes folies qui soit parmi les hommes', says 'je ne vois rien de plus ridicule qu'un homme qui se veut mêler d'en guérir un autre' (Act III, Sc. 3). Although his words carry a literal sense here, he would obviously share the same view of reformers as Le Vayer and Philinte. Cf. Boileau, *Satire* X: 'N'allons donc point ici réformer l'univers, Laissons là, croyez-moi, le monde tel qu'il est' and Saint-Evremond: 'Tant qu'on est engagé dans le monde, il faut s'assujettir à ses maximes, parce qu'il n'y a rien de plus inutile que la sagesse de ces gens qui s'érigent d'eux-mêmes en réformateurs. C'est un personnage qu'on ne peut soutenir longtemps, sans offenser ses amis et se rendre ridicule.' *Oeuvres Mêlées*, I, 3, p. 22.

89. ibid. pp. 192-3.

90. Cf. Boileau, Satire IV:

> Le plus sage est celui qui ne pense point l'être;
> Qui toujours pour un autre enclin vers la douceur,
> Se regarde soi-même en sévère censeur,
> Rend à tous ses défauts une exacte justice,
> Et fait sans se flatter le procès à son vice.

91. *Prose Chagrine*, pp. 340-1.

92. *Portraits de Femmes*, (Paris, 1854) p. 296.

93. Cf. J. Guicharnaud, op. cit. pp. 370-1; L. Gossman, op. cit. p. 99, n. 6.

94. Méré, *Oeuvres Complètes*, (Paris, 1930) III, p. 71; II, p. 13; Faret, op. cit. p. 166.

95. For an *honnête homme* such as Méré, religion and *honnêteté* interpenetrate. He writes that '. . . la dévotion et l'honnêteté vont presque les mêmes voies, et . . . elles s'aident l'une à l'autre.' op. cit. III, p. 101. Faret stresses that religion is an integral part of *honnêteté*, op. cit. pp. 66-7. On the fundamental incompatibility of the religious and *honnête* outlooks on life, see Part II, Ch. 3, (4).

96. op. cit. II, pp. 36-7; op. cit. p. 35. Y. Delègue makes the same observation with regard to Montaigne in his interesting article 'Du paradoxe chez Montaigne', *Cahiers de l'Association Internationale des Etudes Françaises*, (1963) p. 248: '. . . contre tous ceux qui 'artialisent la nature' il ne prétend pas renoncer à l'artifice; il ne veut que 'naturaliser l'art'.'

97. *Réflexions Diverses, De la Société*, in *Maximes*, (Paris, 1967) p. 185.

98. *Prose Chagrine*, p. 319. Cf. Méré, op. cit. II, *De l'Esprit*, p. 93. Faret criticizes the person who is rigidly attached to his opinions: 'Jamais il ne sait fléchir à propos, et s'est tellement assujetti à ses humeurs, et à ses opiniâtretés, qu'il s'imagine que tout ce qui les contrarie ne peut être conforme au bon sens.' op. cit. p. 167.

99. See La Rochefoucauld, op. cit. pp. 185-6: 'Il faudrait du moins savoir cacher ce désir de préférence, puisqu'il est trop naturel en nous pour nous en pouvoir défaire; il faudrait faire son plaisir et celui des autres, ménager leur amour-propre, et ne le blesser jamais.' Cf. Méré, op. cit. III, pp. 87-8.

100. *Les Luttes . . .* p. 229. Cf. R. Jasinski, op. cit. pp. 195-6, for the same view.

101. *En Lisant Molière*, p. 199.

102. Philinte is here once more the embodiment of Faret's *honnête homme*: '(il) n'a garde de se rendre si fort esclave de ses inclinations, qu'il ne puisse en tout temps les faire ployer sous celles de la personne à qui il aura envie de se rendre agréable'. It is the sign of consummate *honnêteté* on the part of a 'grande âme' 'd'être ainsi universelle, et susceptible de plusieurs formes'. op. cit. p. 168.

103. *Des bonnes et des mauvaises compagnies* in VI, (1re partie), 11e vol. p. 123.

104. *Des Louanges*, in III, (2e partie) 6e vol., pp. 72-3, p. 81. *Prose Chagrine*, p. 258. See also *De la Flatterie et de la Correction*, in VI (1re partie) 11e vol. pp. 350-2; Faret, op. cit. pp. 97-8; Dubosc, op. cit. II, pp. 13 ff.

105. *Des Nouvelles de la Cour*, in VI, (2e partie) 12e vol., p. 141. Cf. also La Rochefoucauld's remarks in favour of 'un silence éloquent' in *De la Conversation*, op. cit. p. 193, and Méré, op. cit. II, p. 77. Faret also gives similar advice. Only those 'qui savent se taire avec jugement, sachent parler de la même sorte.' op. cit. p. 181. Cf. Dubosc, op. cit. II, p. 34: 'Le Sage doit bien toujours penser à ce qu'il dit, mais il ne doit pas toujours dire ce qu'il pense.'

106. Jasinski, op. cit. p. 195; Cf. also Michaut, *Les Luttes . . .*, p. 229; For a completely different view of Philinte's motives here, see J. Guicharnaud, op. cit. p. 409.

107. *Du Temps et de l'Occasion* in VI, (1re partie), 11e vol. p. 264. Cf. La Rochefoucauld, *Des Goûts* in op. cit. p. 202: 'Il y en a qui, par une sorte d'instinct dont ils ignorent la cause, décident de ce qui se présente à eux, et prennent toujours le bon parti.'

108. J. Guicharnaud describes his attitude at this point as constituting 'une nouvelle trahison' of Alceste, op. cit. p. 412.

109. *De la Flatterie et de la Correction,* in VI, (1^{re}partie), 11e vol. pp. 354-5. Cf. Méré, op. cit. III, pp. 91-2: 'Je remarque . . . que les gens si concertés, qui jamais ne relâchent de leurs maximes, quoiqu'elles soient pleines d'honneur, sont souvent tournés en ridicules comme l'était Caton d'Utique, le plus grave et le plus vertueux de son temps.' On the importance of observing what is proper to a particular occasion and company, see La Rochefoucauld, *De la Conversation,* in op. cit. p. 194, n. 4. Cf. Dubosc, op. cit. II, pp. 31-2: '(Ceux) qui ont de l'inclination à contredire, en ont aussi à corriger et à réformer toutes choses; mais ils sont inutiles aussi bien qu'importuns.' Faret makes the same point, when he writes that the most sensible things in the world can be ridiculous if proffered 'à contre-temps', op. cit. p. 194.
110. VI, (1re partie), 11e vol. p. 267.
111. op. cit. p. 198; *Les Luttes* . . . p. 229.
112. *Dialogue sur le mariage* is found in the second volume of *Neuf Dialogues faits à l'imitation des anciens,* entitled *Quatre Autres Dialogues du mesme Auteur,* (Francfort, 1716). The passage quoted is on p. 361. On this dialogue and its analogies with Molière's plays, see 'The Sceptical View of Marriage and the Comic Vision in Molière, *Forum for Modern Language Studies,*V, 1 (January, 1969) pp. 26-46.
113. op. cit. I, p. 42.
114. *Greek Tragedy,* (London, 1928) p. 240.
115. Thomas Mann, *Doctor Faustus,* quoted by C. Hoy, op. cit. p. 22.
116. III (1re partie), 5e vol. p. 385, p. 367.

NOTES TO CHAPTER 6

1. op.cit. p. 60; see also A. Adam, op.cit. III, pp. 367-8.
2. This has been done, notably by J. Jarry, *Essai sur les oeuvres dramatiques de Jean Rotrou,* (Lille and Paris, 1868); 'GE VI, pp. 311-45;
3. References are to *Amphitryo* by Plautus in *The Rope and òther Plays,* Translated by E. F. Watling, (London, 1964) and *Les Sosies* by Rotrou in *Théâtre Choisi* edited by F. Hémon, (Paris, no date).
4. On this point, see J. Rousset, *L'Intérieur et l'Extérieur, Essais sur la poésie et sur le théâtre au XVIIe siècle,* (Paris, 1968) p. 144. It is interesting to remember what these characters are brought to say of love, in the light of what Mercure says about Jupiter. Tartuffe confesses to Elmire that '. . . pour être dévot, je n'en suis pas moins homme' (Act III, Sc. 3, l. 966). Alceste analyses his *foiblesse* and admits that he is human after all, (*Le Misanthrope,* Act V, Scène dernière, ll. 1754-6). Armande the *précieuse* couches her admission of her humanity in subtle terminology which is designed to absolve her of human weakness (*Les Femmes Savantes,* Act IV, Sc. 2, ll. 1237-40).
5. *De la Prudence,* in *Discours ou homilies académiques,* in III (2e partie) 6e vol. p. 405.
6. Quoted by J. Rousset in *La Littérature de l'Age baroque en France: Circé et le Paon,* (Paris, 1954) p. 69.
7. R. Fernandez writes of the play as follows: 'La vision comique, dans *Amphitryon,* apparaît à l'état de représentation pure. Je veux dire qu'elle ne sert point à démontrer ni à corriger, qu'elle se joue purement d'elle-même. La vision double, essence du comique, est le thème essentiel d'*Amphitryon.*' op. cit. p. 199.
8. See *Les Sosies,* Act II, Sc. 1; *Amphitryo,* pp. 250-3.
9. op. cit. p. 163.
10. Cf. the remarks by Hubert on this episode, in op. cit. pp. 187-8. Also P. L. Cornett 'Doubling in "Amphitryon"', *Essays in French Literature,* 7, (1970) pp. 16-29.
11. *L'Avare,* Act IV, Sc. 7.
12. Sosie's reply to Mercure, to the effect that the gods have given him his name and that it is not in his power to change it, is original to Molière's play. Plautus and Rotrou both treat the encounter of Sosie and Mercure as nothing more than a highly amusing duplication of identity, leading to Sosie's confusion and flight. The effect of Molière's

introduction is obviously to make more explicit the imminent reversal of established truth by Mercure.

13. In Shakespeare's *The Comedy of Errors* there are also two identical masters and valets who are twins. Like Sosie, one of the servants, Dromio, is brought to the stage where he doubts his identity, asking himself: 'Am I Dromio? Am I myself?' (Act III, Sc. 2).

14. Descartes, *Oeuvres et Lettres,* (Paris, 1953) p. 272. See the article by R.-L. Hébert, 'An Episode in Molière's *Amphitryon* and Cartesian Epistemology', *Modern Language Notes,* 70 (1955) pp. 416-22, and L. Gossman, op. cit. pp. 1-34, who make interesting analogies between Descartes and Molière, considering them primarily from a philosophic standpoint as opposed to the dramatic point of view adopted here.

15. *La Littérature de l'Age baroque,* pp. 61 ff.

16. ibid. p. 66.

17. ibid. p. 62.

18. in III, (1re partie), 5e vol. p. 253.

19. Discussing the philosophy of Montaigne, he says that the Sceptics, although believing that God has made us capable of attaining truth, only believe this fideistically; they still open the possibility in their arguments that we were created by 'un être faux et méchant', bent on deceiving our reason and senses. *Oeuvres Complètes*, p. 294.

20. op. cit. pp. 147-8. One Sceptic whom Descartes probably had in mind was Le Vayer. In a letter dated 6 May 1630 and written to Mersenne, Descartes speaks of a 'méchant livre' which contains extremely dangerous implications for religion. He himself thought of writing a reply to it, defending Christianity. The book to which he refers is without doubt *Cinq dialogues faits à l'imitation des Anciens* par Oratius Tubero, published in 1630, which contained his dialogue *De la divinité:* in it Le Vayer adduces all the reasons he can think of for not believing in the existence of God, before protesting that such belief must be accepted fideistically. See R. Popkin, *The History of Scepticism from Erasmus to Descartes,* (Assen, 1960) pp. 176-7; Descartes, op. cit. p. 933, pp. 935 ff.

21. Cf. R. Lefèvre: 'Ce qui importe à Descartes, c'est de sortir du Cogito plus encore que d'y entrer,' *La Métaphysique de Descartes,* (Paris, 1959) p.20.

22. *Petit Traité Sceptique sur cette Commune Façon de parler . . .* in V, (2e partie), 10e vol., p. 168.

23. The traditional *bastonnade* of farce is a certain means of conquering the comic character's doubts about reality. In Sc. 5 of *Le Mariage Forcé* (1664), Sganarelle asks the Sceptic Marphurius whether or not he will be cuckolded by his future wife. He is so exasperated by the philosopher's cryptic replies that he applies a cudgel to him, which has the effect of restoring fully the philosopher's perception of reality.

24. op. cit. p. 147.

25. ibid. pp. 274-5.

26. *Méditation Seconde* in ibid. p. 275.

27. R.-L. Hébert, on the contrary, sees this scene as ending in the defeat of Sosie, who 'seeks in vain a "clarté fidèle"', art. cit. p. 422.

28. The full title of Gassendi's treatise is *Disquisitio Metaphysica Seu Dubitationes et Instantiae Adversus Renati Cartesii Metaphysicam et Responsa.* I refer in the text to the French translation of the *Disquisitio* of B. Rochot, (Paris, 1962). On the quarrel between the philosophers see in particular Pintard, *Le Libertinage érudit . . .* I, pp. 482-6; Popkin, op. cit. pp. 204 ff; H. Berr, *Du Scepticisme de Gassendi*, (Paris, 1960) pp. 87-93.

29. The scepticism of Gassendi is different from the scepticism of the *libertin érudit* such as Le Vayer, whose doubt seeks to undermine religious truth. As Rochot has shown, there is nothing in Gassendi's *Syntagma philosophicum* in any way incompatible with his religious vocation. See his 'Le Cas Gassendi' in *Revue d'Histoire Littéraire de la France,* 47 (1947) pp. 289-313. For the opposite view of Gassendi as *libertin érudit* see Pintard, 'Modernisme, Humanisme, Libertinage, petite suite sur le 'cas

Gassendi', in the same review, 48 (1948) pp. 1-52, and his *Le Libertinage érudit* . . . I, pp. 476-504.

30. *Disquisitio*, p. 10: 'Je les propose donc, [ces raisons] mais sans autre intention que précisément de les proposer . . . en les faisant porter non pas contre les choses mêmes que vous avez entrepris de démontrer, mais contre la méthode et le genre de preuve [dont vous usez] pour [les] démontrer.'

31. ibid. p. 56; p. 28; p. 30; further in the *Disquisitio* Gassendi writes that '. . . l'esprit humain répugne, quand il cherche à excuser son ignorance, à s'imaginer un Dieu trompeur . . . parce qu'en l'absence d'une telle fiction, il est possible de chercher et de trouver les causes naturelles et véritables des erreurs qui se produisent dans nos sensations.' p. 50.

32. ibid. p. 70.

33. 'Le Banquet Sceptique', in *Cinq Dialogues faits à l'imitation des anciens*, (Francfort, 1716) pp. 163-4.

34. Cf. Gossman, op. cit. pp. 20 ff. on this point.

35. in V, (2ᵉ partie), 10ᵉ vol. p. 136; cf. Montaigne, op. cit. I, ch. 27: 'C'est Folie de Rapporter Le Vray et Le Faux A Nostre Suffisance'; in the *Apologie* he writes that 'Tout ce qui nous semble estrange, nous le condamnons, et ce que nous n'entendons pas', I, Ch. 12, p. 515; Charron in *De la Sagesse*, I, Ch. 41, p. 289, takes over Montaigne's view literally; Cf. also La Rochefoucauld, *Maxime* 347.

36. ibid. pp. 143-50; he takes these tropes from his acknowledged master, Sextus Empiricus, *Outlines of Pyrrhonism*, Ch. XIV.

37. *Contre la Cinquième Méditation*, in op. cit. p. 502; cf. also Popkin, op. cit. pp. 204 ff.

38. The argument of Jupiter (ll. 1669 ff) to the effect that appearances do not favour Amphitryon is to be found neither in the corresponding scene of Plautus nor in that of Rotrou, Act IV, Sc. 4.

39. op. cit. p. 283; Act V, Sc. 5.

40. Molière selects the following two lines spoken by Rotrou's Sosie and gives them ironic amplification:

Cet honneur, ce me semble, est un triste avantage:
On appelle cela lui sucrer le breuvage (Act V, Sc. 6)

Cf. his Sosie, ll. 1928-43.

41. In *De la Curiosité*, Le Vayer writes that we should content ourselves with the opinion that we have, and thus avoid perverse self-affliction brought on by curiosity: 'sans vouloir pénétrer jusques dans l'intérieur des autres par une curiosité d'autant plus ridicule, qu'elle nous serait tout à fait désavantageuse si nous la pouvions satisfaire.' In VI, (1ʳᵉ partie) 11ᵉ vol. p. 152.

NOTES TO CHAPTER 7

1. E. Faguet, *Propos de Théâtre*, quoted by G. Lafenestre, *Molière*, (Paris, 1909) p. 157; P. Brisson, *Molière, Sa Vie dans ses Oeuvres*, (Paris, 1942) p. 257; A. Adam, *Histoire* . . . III, p. 392.

2. D. Mornet, *Molière*, pp. 121-2; G. Reynier, *Les Femmes Savantes*, (Paris, 1962) p. 91, p. 227; P. Brisson, op. cit. p. 276; A. Adam, op. cit. III p. 392.

3. *L'Ecole des Femmes*, Act III, Sc. 2; *Les Femmes Savantes*, Act III, Sc. 2.

4. See 'The Sceptical View of Marriage and the Comic Vision in Molière', art. cit.

5. Cf. her role in Act III, Sc. 2.

6. *De la différence des esprits* in *Oeuvres*, VII, (1ʳᵉ partie) 13ᵉ vol. p. 405. In *Dom Garcie* Élise says to Dom Garcie

. . . nous avons du Ciel ou du tempérament,
Que nous jugeons de tout chacun diversement. (Act IV, Sc. 6, ll. 1182-3)

Notes

239

Diversity of temperament and individuality are two major themes in Montaigne, op. cit. I, ch. 42; II, ch. 12.

7. *Oeuvres Complètes, II, Des Agrémens*, pp. 18-19.
8. *Réflexions Diverses, Du Faux*, in *Maximes*, p. 208. Earlier theoreticians of *honnêteté* had already given great prominence to this principle, cf. N. Faret, *L'Honneste Homme*, p. 35; J. Dubosc, *L'Honneste Femme*, I, pp. 215-16. In *La Prétieuse ou Le Mystère des Ruelles* (1656-8) by the Abbé de Pure, the *précieuse* Eulalie admonishes her friends thus: 'que chacune de nous tâche à faire valoir ses talents, sans vouloir les forcer par des principes estrangers ny les confondre avec les talents d'autrui, . . .' éd. E. Magne, (Paris, 1938) I, p. 47.
9. ibid. p. 209.
10. op. cit. II, *Des Agrémens*.
11. *Les Promenades en Neuf Dialogues*, in *Oeuvres*, IV, (1ʳᵉ partie), 7ᵉ vol. pp. 118-19.
12. ibid. p. 121. The analogy between the *Promenades* and Molière's plays forms a part of 'Un ami sceptique de Molière', art. cit. pp. 254-7.
13. Cf. Lanson's memorable definition of a comic character in Molière's world: '. . . une nature puissamment unifiée par la domination d'une passion ou d'un vice qui détruit ou opprime toutes les autres affections et puissances de l'âme, et devient le principe de toutes les pensées et de tous les actes du personnage.' 'Molière et la Farce', *Revue de Paris*, (mai 1901) p. 145.
14. Saint-Evremond, *Le Cercle*, in *Oeuvres Mêlées*, (Paris, 1865) II, 2, p. 534. The expression was also used by Scarron in 1659, see R. Lathuillère, *La Préciosité, Étude Historique et Linguistique*, (Paris, 1966) I, pp. 52-3, p. 122.
15. op. cit. III, p. 395.
16. III, (2ᵉ partie) 6ᵉ vol. p. 231. Le Vayer quotes the fable of the Ox and Camel 'qui cheminaient de compagnie' to illustrate the reciprocal function of mind and body (Cf. Clitandre, l. 1218).
17. IV, (1ʳᵉ partie) 7ᵉ vol. p. 121.
18. ibid. p. 123.
19. ibid. pp. 118-20.
20. *Epître aux Colossiens*, ch. III, v. 2 (L. Segond translation).
21. See V. Cousin, *La Société Française au 17ᵉ siècle*, (Paris, 1858) II pp. 289-90; F. Baumal, *Le Féminisme au temps de Molière*, (Paris, 1923) pp. 84 ff; H. Cottez, 'Molière et Mlle de Scudéry', *Revue d'Histoire de la Philosophie et d'Histoire Générale de la Civilisation*, (1943) pp. 340-64; R. Lathuillère, op. cit. I, pp. 119 ff.
22. *Histoire de la Littérature Française Classique*, (Paris, 1947) pp. 25-39.
23. ibid. p. 37.
24. F. Baumal, op. cit. p. 77; *La Prétieuse*, I, 2ᵉ partie, p. 276.
25. F. Baumal, ibid. pp. 70-1.
26. op. cit. II, *Le Cercle*, p. 535.
27. See G. Reynier, op. cit. pp. 190-1; see also GE IX, p. 34.
28. Furetière defines 'clartés' as 'connaissance', 'instruction'.
29. Cf. Arnolphe's description of an ideal wife, *L'Ecole des Femmes*, Act I, Sc. 1, ll. 124 ff.
30. IVᵉ *Promenade*, p. 136. Molière and Le Vayer doubtless found this *boutade* in Montaigne, who ascribes it to François Duc de Bretagne: 'comme on luy parla de son mariage avec Isabeau, fille d'Escosse, et qu'on luy adjousta qu'elle avoit esté nourrie simplement et sans aucune instruction de lettres, respondit, qu'il l'en aymoit mieux, et qu'une fame estoit assez sçavante quand elle sçavoit mettre difference entre la chemise et le pourpoint de son mary.' *Essais*, I, ch. 25, p. 150. J. Dubosc makes contemptuous reference to this anecdote, op. cit. I. p. 140.
31. In *Des Femmes* (1659) Le Vayer had already written that in many families intelligence was on the side of women, VII, (1ʳᵉ partie) 13ᵉ vol. pp. 394-5.
32. IVᵉ *Promenade*, pp. 135-6; In Le Vayer's *Dialogue sur le mariage*, Philocles is made to aver that *femmes savantes* are to be avoided '. . . soit qu'elles veuillent faire les savantes, elles qui ignorent tout ce qu'elles pensent savoir, et ne savent que ce qu'elles feignent ignorer.' *Neuf dialogues faits à l'imitation des anciens*, (Francfort, 1716) II, p. 455.

33. V. Cousin, op. cit. II, p. 179; cf. J. Dubosc; '. . . comme les Dames qui n'ont point d'étude ou de lecture sont véritablement stériles; aussi celles qui en ont sont quelquefois un peu confuses et importunes.' For a similar view to that of Cousin, see H. Cottez, art. cit. pp. 349-50.

34. V. Cousin, ibid. p. 180; the dreaded reputation attaching to the *femme savante* was very real in the seventeenth century, see Méré, op. cit. I, p. 9, and *La Prétieuse*, I, p. 13, p. 8, pp. 126 ff, where it is constantly stressed that women must at all costs conceal learning.

35. This dialogue forms part of the second volume of *Neuf Dialogues faits à l'imitation des anciens* par Oratius Tubero, (Francfort, 1506) (sic).

36. ibid. p. 11, p. 17.

37. ibid. p. 19.

38. ibid. p. 20. Cf. J. Brun, *Les Stoïciens*, II, pp. 90 ff: 'La Vertu repose sur la Raison'.

39. ibid. pp. 23-4.

40. ibid. p. 27.

41. ibid. p. 29, pp. 29-32. Cf. also *De l'Ignorance* in *Homilies Académiques*, III, (2ᵉ partie) 6ᵉ vol. pp. 170-1. Montaigne makes the same point in his lengthy criticism of contemporary education: '. . . le soing et la despence de nos peres ne vise qu'à nous meubler la teste de science; du jugement et de la vertu, peu de nouvelles'. I, Ch. 25, p. 144. Charron repeats this in *De la Sagesse*, III, Ch. 14, pp. 87 ff. See also N. Faret, op., cit. p. 59.

42. III, (2ᵉ partie) 6ᵉ vol. p. 173. For the same argument, see *De la lecture des livres et de leur composition*, II, (2ᵉ partie) 4ᵉ vol. pp. 488 ff; *Prose Chagrine*, III, (1ʳᵉ partie) 5ᵉ vol. pp. 294-5; on the ambivalent nature of knowledge, see Montaigne, op. cit. I, Ch. 25, p. 150.

43. op. cit. I, Ch. 25, p. 145. The theory of learned ignorance (*la docte ignorance*) has of course a very long and varied history. Socrates made it the basis of his teaching method (*c.* 400 B C) and St Paul christianizes it in many of his letters (notably in *1st Epistle to Corinthians*, Ch. I-III). Sextus Empiricus (*c.* A D 200) grafts it on to his scepticism, and directs it specifically against the Stoic *sage*. Nicolas of Cusa (*De docte ignorantia*, 1440) and Thomas à Kempis (*Imitatio Christi*, 1441) use it as justification for the Christian fool opposed to scholasticism. Erasmus also uses it satirically against scholasticism in *Encomium Moriae* (1511) as does Martin Luther. See E. Rice, *The Renaissance Idea of Wisdom*, (Oxford, 1958) pp. 134-43. Agrippa von Nettesheim puts it to similar use in *De Incertitude et vanitate scientiarum* . . . (1526). Montaigne in his *Apologie de Raimond Sebond* and in the *Essais* makes great play with *l'ignorance doctorale*, and Charron follows him in *De la Sagesse*, 1601. For an outline of the idea of the wise fool in the Mediaeval and Renaissance periods, see W. Kaiser, *Praisers of Folly*, (London 1964) pp. 1-16.

44. Cf. the first of his *maximes supprimées*, éd. J. Truchet, (Paris, 1967) pp. 133-6.

45. II, (2ᵉ partie) 4ᵉ vol. p. 69. Cf. *Les Précieuses Ridicules*, Sc. 9.

46. ibid. pp. 71-3.

47. ibid. p. 78.

48. Faret, in his advice to the *honnête homme*, counsels him to avoid following the example of importunate poets, op. cit. p. 64. Boileau, in *Satire* X, describes the *salon* as the last repair of all 'les fades auteurs': 'Là, tous les vers sont bons, pourvu qu'ils soient nouveaux.'

49. *Le Misanthrope*, ll. 285-97. In *Clélie*, Mlle de Scudéry writes: 'Je vous assure qu'il n'y a rien de plus incommode que ces gens qui font de mauvais vers sans le savoir et qui, croyant qu'ils donnent autant de plaisir aux autres qu'ils s'en donnent à eux-mêmes en récitant ce qu'ils ont fait . . .' Quoted by H. Cottez, art. cit. p. 358.

50. III, (2ᵉ partie) 6ᵉ vol. p. 169.

51. VII, (1ʳᵉ partie) 13ᵉ vol. p. 225, p. 135.

52. *De quelques Compositions* in ibid. pp. 129-30.

53. ibid. p. 231.

54. *D'un mauvais Déclamateur,* in VI, (2ᵉ partie) 12ᵉ vol. p. 290.
55. See P. Brisson, op. cit. pp. 281-2; A. Adam, op. cit. III, p. 394.
56. *D'un mauvais Déclamateur,* VI, (2ᵉ partie) 12ᵉ vol. p. 287; *De quelques Compositions,* pp. 131-2.
57. *De la lecture des livres et de leur composition,* II, (2ᵉ partie) 4ᵉ vol. p. 517. La Bruyère, *Des Ouvrages de l'Esprit,* in *Les Caractères,* (Paris, 1962) p. 67.
58. *De quelques Compositions . . .* p. 132.
59. *Vie de Monsieur de Molière,* (Paris, 1930) p. 9.
60. For a comprehensive list of 'sources' and Molière's treatment of them see GE IX, pp. 35-47; G. Reynier, op. cit. pp. 57-74; R. Bray, *Oeuvres Complètes de Molière,* VIII, pp. 275 ff.
61. *D'un mauvais Déclamateur . . .* p. 284; *Du Récit d'un Ouvrage,* VII, (1ʳᵉ partie), 13ᵉ vol. pp. 274-5; In *Les Précieuses Ridicules,* Sc. 9 and *L'Impromptu de Versailles,* Sc. 1, the bombastic diction of 'les grands comédiens' of the Hôtel de Bourgogne is ridiculed.
62. *D'un mauvais Déclamateur . . .* p. 293. Mlle de Scudéry likewise finds such affectations blameworthy on account of their obscurity, see H. Cottez, art. cit. p. 358.
63. F. Baumal, *Molière auteur précieux,* (Paris, 1924); D. Mornet, *Molière,* pp. 111-2.
64. *D'un mauvais Déclamateur . . .* pp. 293-4; *D'une dispute,* VII, (1ʳᵉ partie) 13ᵉ vol. p. 258.
65. On the development of the *Académie littéraire* and the *salon,* see A. Adam, op. cit. I, pp. 213-84.
66. VI, (2ᵉ partie) 12ᵉ vol. pp. 19-21, p. 56, p. 62.
67. ibid. pp. 64-5.
68. On the importance of words and images in the play, see J. D. Hubert, *Molière and The Comedy of Intellect,* Ch. 20.

NOTES TO CONCLUSION

1. *Petit Traité Sceptique sur cette commune Façon de parler, N'Avoir pas le Sens Commun,* in *Oeuvres . . .* V (2ᵉ partie) 10ᵉ vol. pp. 167-8.
2. *Molière une aventure théâtrale,* pp. 524-6.
3. *L'Immoraliste, Préface,* in *Romans, Récits et Soties.* (Paris, 1958) p. 367.

Bibliography

The number of critical works on Molière and of editions of the plays is immense, and I have therefore listed only those bibliographical items which have been of greatest use in the course of the preparation of this study.

Editions of Molière's plays

Oeuvres complètes Edition Despois et Mesnard, Grands Ecrivains de la France, 13 Vols., (Paris, 1873-1893). All quotations are from this edition except where otherwise stated.
Oeuvres complètes Edition R. Bray, 8 Vols., (Paris, 1935-52).
Théâtre complet Edition R. Jouanny, 2 Vols., (Paris, 1962).
Oeuvres complètes Edition G. Couton, 2 Vols., (Paris, 1971).

General Bibliography

Adam, A. *Histoire de la littérature française au XVIIe siècle*, 5 Vols., (Paris, 1964). (Reprint) Vol. III, *L'Apogée du siècle, Boileau-Molière*.
Les libertins au XVIIe siècle: Collection Le Vrai Savoir, (Paris, 1964).
Allier, R. *La cabale des dévots*, 1627-1666, (Paris, 1902).
Alméras, H. d'. *Le Tartuffe de Molière*, (Paris, 1946).
Angers, Julien-Eymard d' . 'Stoïcisme et libertinage dans l'oeuvre de François La Mothe Le Vayer', *Revue des Sciences Humaines*, 75 (1954) pp. 259-84.
Pascal et ses précurseurs, (Paris, 1954).
Attinger, G. *L'Esprit de la commedia dell'arte dans le théâtre français*, (Neuchâtel, 1950).
Auerbach, E. *Mimesis, Dargestellte Wirklichkeit in der abendländischen Literatur*, (Berne, 1946), tr. W. Trask, (Princeton, 1953).
Baumal, F. *Molière et les dévots: la genèse du Tartuffe*, (Paris, 1919).
Bénichou, P. *Morales du Grand Siècle*, (Paris, 1948).
Bentley, E. *The Life of the Drama*, (London, 1965).
Bergson, H. *Le rire, essai sur la signification du comique*, (Paris, 1962). (Reprint).
Bernier, F. *Abrégé de la philosophie de Gassendi*, 8 Vols. (Lyon, chez Anisson et Posuel, 1678).
Berr, H. *Du scepticisme de Gassendi.* Traduction de Bernard Rochot, (Paris, 1960).
Bevan, E. *Stoics and Sceptics*, (Oxford, 1913).
Bévotte, G. de. *Le Festin de Pierre avant Molière, textes publiés avec introduction, lexique et notes par G. de Bévotte*, (Paris, 1907).
La légende de Don Juan, 2 Vols., (Paris, 1911).
Boileau-Despréaux, N. *Oeuvres*, Edition de G. Mongrédien, (Paris, 1961).
Bossuet, J. B. *Maximes et réflexions sur la Comédie, précédées d'une introduction historique et accompagnées de documents contemporains et de notes critiques par Ch. Urbain et E. Levesque*, in *L'Eglise et le théâtre*, (Paris, 1930).
Bourdieu, P. 'Tartuffe ou le drame de la foi et de la mauvaise foi', *Revue de la Méditerranée*, 19 (1959) pp. 453-58.
Bray, R. *Molière homme de théâtre*, (Paris, 1954).
Bremond, H. *Histoire littéraire du sentiment religieux en France depuis la fin des guerres de religion jusqu'à nos jours*, 12 Vols., (Paris, 1916-36).

Brisson, P. *Molière, sa vie dans ses oeuvres*, (Paris, 1942).

Brody, J. '*Don Juan* and *Le Misanthrope*, or The Esthetics of Individualism', *Publications of the Modern Language Association of America*, 84 (1969) pp. 558-76.

Brun, J. *Les Stoïciens*, Textes choisis, (Paris, 1957).
Le Stoïcisme, (Paris, 1963).

Brunetière, F. 'La philosophie de Molière', *Revue des Deux Mondes*, C. (1890) pp. 649-84.
Etudes critiques sur l'histoire de la littérature française, (Paris, 1907) Vol. 5.

Burgess, G. S. 'Molière and the Pursuit of Criteria', *Symposium*, XXIII 1 (1969) pp. 5-15.

Busson, H. *La Pensée religieuse française de Charron à Pascal*, (Paris, 1933).

Butler, P. 'Orgon le dirigé', *Gallica*, (Cardiff, 1969) pp. 103-19.
'*Tartuffe* et la direction spirituelle au XVIIe siècle', *Modern Miscellany*, presented to E. Vinaver (Manchester, 1969) pp. 48-63.

Cairncross, J. *Molière bourgeois et libertin*, (Paris, 1963).

Centre International de Synthèse, Pierre Gassendi, sa vie et son oeuvre, 1592-1655, (Paris, 1955).

Chapelle, C.-E. *Oeuvres de Chapelle et de¹ Bachaumont*, (Paris, 1854).

Charpy de Sainte-Croix, N. *L'ancienne nouveauté de l'Ecriture sainte ou l'Eglise triomphante en terre*, (Paris, 1657).

Charron, P. *De la Sagesse*, 3 Vols., (Paris, 1820-24).

Cicognini, A. G. *Il Principe Geloso (Le Prince jaloux)*, in *Nouveau Théâtre Italien*, (Paris, 1733) Vol. IV.

Conti, Prince de. *Traité de la comédie et des spectacles, selon la tradition de l'Eglise tirée des Conciles et des Saints Pères*, (Paris, 1666).

Cornett, P. L. 'Doubling in 'Amphitryon", *Essays in French Literature*, 7 (1970) pp. 16-29.

Cottez, H. 'Molière et Mlle de Scudéry', *Revue d'Histoire de la Philosophie et d'Histoire générale de la Civilisation*, (1943) pp. 340-64.

Cousin, V. *La Société française au XVIIe siècle d'après Le Grand Cyrus de Mlle de Scudéry*, 2 Vols., (Paris, 1858).

Couton, G. 'L'Etat civil d'Armande Béjart, femme de Molière, ou historique d'une légende', *Revue des Sciences Humaines*, (1964) pp. 311-51.
'Réflexions sur 'Tartuffe' et le péché d'hypocrisie 'cas réservé", *Revue d'Histoire littéraire de la France*, (1969) pp. 404-13.

Delègue, Y. 'Du paradoxe chez Montaigne', *Cahiers de l'Association Internationale des Etudes françaises*, 14 (1963) pp. 241-53.

Descartes, R. *Oeuvres et Lettres*, (Paris, 1953).

Descotes, M. *Les grands rôles du théâtre de Molière*, (Paris, 1960).

Doolittle, J. 'The humanity of Molière's Dom Juan', *Publications of The Modern Language Association of America*, 68 (1953) pp. 509-34.

Doumic, R. *Le Misanthrope de Molière, étude et analyse*, (Paris, 1929).

Dubosc, J. *L'Honneste Femme*, 3 vols., (Rouen, 1643).

Dupriez, B. 'Tartuffe et la sincérité', *Etudes Françaises*, 1 (1965) pp. 452-67.

Erasmus, D. *Eloge de la Folie*, traduit par Pierre de Nolhac, (Paris, 1953).

Eustis, A. *Molière as Ironic Contemplator*, (The Hague, 1973).

Faguet, E. *En lisant Molière: l'homme et son temps, l'écrivain et son oeuvre*, (Paris, 1914).

Faret, N. *L'Honneste Homme ou l'art de plaire à la Cour*, (Paris, 1630).

Fargher, R. 'Molière and his Reasoners', in *Studies in French Literature presented to H. W. Lawton*, (Manchester, 1968) pp. 105-19.

Fernandez, R. *La Vie de Molière*, (Paris, 1929).

Freud, S. *Jokes and their Relation to the Unconscious*, tr. J. Strachey, (London, 1960).

Freudmann, F. R. 'Le comique dans *Dom Garcie de Navarre*', *Romanic Review*, LX (1969) pp. 251-64.

Friedrich, H. 'Pascals Paradox, das Sprachbild einer Denkform', *Zeitschrift für Romanische Philologie*, LVI (1936) pp. 322-70.

Montaigne, (Berne, 1949).

Furetière, A. *Dictionnaire Universel, contenant généralement tous les mots françois tant vieux que modernes, et les termes de toutes les sciences et des arts.* 4 Vols., (La Haye, 1727).

Gassendi, Pierre. *Dissertations en Forme de Paradoxes contre les Aristotéliciens. (Exercitationes Paradoxicae adversus Aristoteleos).* Texte établi, traduit et annoté par Bernard Rochot, (Paris, 1959).

Disquisitio Metaphysica, seu Dubitationes et Instantiae adversus Renati Cartesii Metaphysicam et Responsa, Texte établi, traduit et annoté par Bernard Rochot, (Paris, 1959).

Gill, A. '"The Doctor in the Farce" and Molière' *French Studies,* II (1948) pp. 101-28.

Goldmann, L. *Le dieu caché. Etude sur la vision tragique dans les Pensées de Pascal et dans le théâtre de Racine,* (Paris, 1955).

Gossman, L. *Men and Masks, A Study of Molière,* (Baltimore, 1963).

Gossen, E. J. "Les Femmes savantes': Métaphore et mouvement dramatique', *French Review,* XLV (1971) pp. 37-45.

Gouhier, H. *Le théâtre et l'existence,* (Paris, 1952).

'L'inhumain Don Juan', *Table Ronde,* 197 (1964) pp. 122-29.

Grimarest, Jean Léonor Gallois Sieur de. *Vie de Monsieur de Molière,* (Paris, 1930).

La Vie de M. de Molière, édition critique par Georges Mongrédien, (Paris, 1955).

Guicharnaud, J. *Molière, une aventure théâtrale,* (Paris, 1963).

Gutkind, C. S. *Molière und das komische Drama,* (Halle, 1928).

Gutwirth, M. *Molière ou l'invention comique: la métamorphose des thèmes, la création des types,* (Paris, 1966).

'*Dom Garcie de Navarre et Le Misanthrope:* de la comédie héroïque au comique du héros', *Publications of The Modern Language Association of America,* 83 (1968) pp. 118-29.

Hall, H. G. 'A Comic Dom Juan', *Yale French Studies,* 23 (1959) pp. 77-84.

Molière: Tartuffe, (London, 1960).

'*Molière: Dom Juan*: La scène du pauvre', in *The Art of Criticism: Essays in French Literary Analysis,* (Edinburgh, 1969) pp. 70-87.

'The Literary Context of Molière's *Le Misanthrope*', *Studi Francesi,* No. 40 (1970) pp. 20-38.

'Molière's *Le Misanthrope* in The Light of D'Aubignac's 'Conseils d'Ariste à Célimène' and Other Contemporary Texts', *Kentucky Romance Quarterly,* 19 (1972) pp. 347-63.

Hébert, R.-L. 'An Episode in Molière's *Amphitryon* and Cartesian Epistemology', *Modern Language Notes,* 70 (1955) pp. 416-22.

Hope, Q. M. 'Society in *Le Misanthrope*', *French Review,* (1959) pp. 329-36.

'The Scene of Greeting in Molière', *Romanic Review,* (1959) pp. 241-54.

Howarth, W. D. 'Dom Garcie de Navarre ou le Prince jaloux?' *French Studies,* V (1951) pp. 140-48.

Howarth, W. D. and Thomas, M. (Editors) *Molière: Stage and Study.* Essays in Honour of W. G. Moore, (Oxford, 1973).

Hunt, H. J. 'Célimène, coquette or coquine?' *French Studies,* III (1949) pp. 324-34.

Janet, P. 'La philosophie de Molière', *Revue des Deux Mondes,* XLIV (1881) pp. 323-62.

Jasinski, R. *Molière et Le Misanthrope,* (Paris, 1963).

Molière, (Paris, 1971).

Jouvet, L. 'Molière, conférence faite aux Annales', *Conferencia,* 31 (septembre 1937) pp. 281-99; 32 (juin 1938) pp. 655-75.

Témoignage sur le théâtre, (Paris, 1950).

Jurgens, M. and Maxfield-Miller, E. *Cent ans de recherches sur Molière, sur sa famille et sur les comédiens de sa troupe,* (Paris, 1963).

Kaiser, W. *Praisers of Folly: Erasmus, Rabelais, Shakespeare,* (London, 1964).

Koestler, A. *The Act of Creation,* (London, 1964).

Krailsheimer, A. J. *Studies in Self-Interest from Descartes to La Bruyère,* (Oxford, 1962).

Lafenestre, G. *Molière*, (Paris, 1909).

La Grange, Charles Varlet Sieur de. *Le Registre de La Grange, 1659-1685*, reproduit en fac-similé avec un index et une notice sur La Grange et sa part dans le théâtre de Molière, Edition de B. E. et G. P. Young, 2 Vols., (Paris, 1947).

La Mothe Le Vayer, François de. *Cinq dialogues faits à l'imitation des anciens, par Oratius Tubero*, (Francfort, 1716).

Quatre autres dialogues du mesme auteur, faits comme les précédens à l'imitation des anciens par Oratius Tubero, (Francfort, 1716).

Oeuvres de François de La Mothe Le Vayer, conseiller d'Etat ordinaire, 14 Vols., (Dresden, 1756-59).

Deux Dialogues sur la divinité et l'opiniâtreté, Introduction et notes par Ernest Tisserand, (Paris, 1922).

Lancaster, H. C. A. *A History of French Dramatic Literature in the XVIIth Century*, (Baltimore, 1929-42). Part 3, Vols. 1 and 2, *The Period of Molière*, 1642-72.

Lanson, G. 'Molière et la farce', *Revue de Paris*, (mai 1901) pp. 130-53.

Laporte, J. *La doctrine de Port-Royal*, 2 Vols., (Paris, 1923).

La Rochefoucauld, F. de. *Maximes*, Edition de J. Truchet, (Paris, 1967).

Lathuillère, R. *La Préciosité, Etude Historique et Linguistique*, (Paris, 1966) Vol. 1.

Laufer, R. 'Le comique du personnage de Dom Juan de Molière', *The Modern Language Review*, LVIII (1963) pp. 15-20.

Lawrence, F. L. *Molière: The Comedy of Unreason*, Tulane Studies in Romance Languages and Literature, 2 (1968).

'The Ironic Commentator in Molière's *Dom Juan*', *Studi Francesi*, 12 (1968), pp. 201-7.

Lea, K. M. *Italian Popular Comedy, a Study in the commedia dell'arte, (1560-1620)*, 2 Vols., (Oxford, 1934).

Lemaître, J. *Impressions de théâtre*, première série, (Paris, 1892), Vol. 1, quatrième série, Vol. 4.

Levi, A. *French Moralists, the Theory of the Passions, 1585-1649*, (Oxford, 1964).

Lindsay, F. W. 'Alceste and the sonnet', *French Review*, 28 (1954-55) pp. 395-402.

McBride, R. 'The Sceptical View of Marriage and the Comic Vision in Molière', *Forum for Modern Language Studies*, V 1 (January, 1969) pp. 26-46.

'Un Ami sceptique de Molière', *Studi Francesi*, No. 47-48 (1972) pp. 244-61.

'Le Provincial dans la comédie de Molière', *Revue Marseille*, 101, 2 (1975) pp. 149-52.

Magendie, M. *La politesse mondaine et les théories de l'honnêteté en France au XVIIᵉ siècle, de 1600-1660*, 2 Vols., (Paris, 1925).

'Le véritable sens du *Misanthrope*', *Mélanges Huguet*, (Paris, 1940) pp. 281-6.

Magne, E. *Une amie inconnue de Molière, suivi de Molière et l'université: documents inédits*, (Paris, 1922).

Méré, Chevalier de. *Oeuvres Complètes*, texte établi et présenté par Charles H. Boudhors, 3 Vols., (Paris, 1930).

Meredith, G. *An Essay on Comedy and the Uses of the Comic Spirit*, (London, 1927).

Michaut, G. *La Jeunesse de Molière*, (Paris, 1922).

Les Débuts de Molière à Paris, (Paris, 1923).

Les Luttes de Molière, (Paris, 1925).

Michel, M. 'Alceste ou Le Misanthrope', *Nouvelle Revue Française*, (août, 1963) pp. 316-23.

Moles, E. 'Pascal's Use of *abêtir*', *French Studies*, XIX (1965), pp. 379-84.

Mongrédien, G. 'Le meilleur ami de Molière: Chapelle', *Mercure de France*, 329 (février, 1957) pp. 242-59.

Montaigne, Michel de. *Essais*, Edition de M. Rat, 2 Vols., (Paris, 1962).

Moore, W. G. ''Tartuffe' and The Comic Principle in Molière', *The Modern Language Review*, XLIII, (1948) pp. 47-53.

Molière, A New Criticism, (Oxford, 1949).

'*Dom Juan* reconsidered', *Modern Language Review*, LII (1957) pp. 510-17.

'Reflections on *Le Misanthrope*', *Australian Journal of French Studies*, IV 2 (1967) pp. 198-203.

'The Comic Paradox', *Modern Language Review*, 68 (1973) pp. 771-75.

Morel, J. 'Molière ou la dramaturgie de l'honnêteté', *L'Information Littéraire*, 15 (novembre-décembre 1963) pp. 185-91.

Mornet, D. 'La Signification et l'évolution de l'idée de préciosité en France au XVIIe siècle', *Journal of the History of Ideas*, I (1940) pp. 225-31.

Histoire de la littérature française classique 1660-1700, (Paris, 1947).

Molière, (Paris, 1958). (Reprint).

Nicole, P. *Traité de la Comédie*, présenté par G. Couton, (Paris, 1961).

Nurse, P. H. 'Le rire et la morale dans l'oeuvre de Molière', *Bulletin de la Société d'Etude du XVIIe siècle*, 52 (1961) pp. 20-35.

'The Role of Chrysalde in *L'Ecole des Femmes*', *Modern Language Review*, LI (1961) pp. 167-71.

'Essai de définition du comique moliéresque', *Revue des Sciences Humaines*, (janvier-mars, 1964) pp. 9-24.

Orwen, G. P. 'Tartuffe Reconsidered', *French Review*, 41, (1967-68) pp. 611-17.

Pascal, B. *Oeuvres Complètes*, présentation et notes de Louis Lafuma, (Paris, 1963).

Picard, R. '*Tartuffe*, production impie', in *Mélanges Lebègue*, (Paris, 1969), pp. 227-40.

Pintard, R. *Le libertinage érudit dans la première moitié du XVIIe siècle*, 2 Vols., (Paris, 1943).

'Temps et Lieux dans le *Dom Juan* de Molière', *Studi in Onore di Italo Siciliano*, (Florence, 1966) Vol. II, pp. 997-1006.

Plautus. *The Rope and other plays*, translated by E. F. Watling, (London, 1964).

Popkin, R. H. *The History of Scepticism from Erasmus to Descartes*, (Assen, 1960).

Poulet, G. *Etudes sur le temps humain*, (Edinburgh, 1949).

Pure, l'abbé Michel de. *La Prétieuse, ou le Mystère des Ruelles*, éditée par E. Magne, 2 Vols., (Paris, 1938).

Revue d'Histoire Littéraire de la France, No. 5-6, (septembre-décembre, 1972), Molière.

Revue d'histoire du théâtre, No. 1-3, (janvier-septembre, 1974), Molière.

Revue des Sciences Humaines, Molière et le Théâtre Classique, 152, (octobre-décembre, 1973).

Reynier, G. *La Femme au XVIIe siècle, ses ennemis et ses défenseurs*, (Paris, 1929).

Les Femmes Savantes de Molière, étude et analyse, (Paris, 1936).

Rice, E. F. *The Renaissance Idea of Wisdom*, (Harvard, 1958).

Rigal, E. *Molière*, 2 Vols., (Paris, 1908).

Robert, R. 'Des commentaires de première main sur les chefs-d'oeuvre les plus discutés de Molière', *Revue des Sciences Humaines*, (1956) pp. 19-49.

Romano, D. *Essai sur le comique de Molière, Studiorum Romanicorum Collectio Turicensis*, IV (Berne, 1950).

Rountree, B. '*Dom Garcie de Navarre*: Tentative de réconciliation avec les précieux', *Romanic Review*, LVI (1965) pp. 161-70.

Rousset, J. *La Littérature de l'Age baroque en France, Circé et le Paon*, (Paris, 1954).

L'Intérieur et l'Extérieur, essais sur la poésie et sur le théâtre au XVIIe siècle, (Paris, 1968).

Roy, C. 'Sur Tartuffe', *Nouvelle Revue Française*, 137, (mai, 1964) pp. 897-908.

Saint-Evremond, C. de. *Oeuvres mêlées, Edition de Ch. Giraud*, 3 Vols., (Paris, 1865).

La Comédie des Académistes, Edited by G. L. van Roosbroeck, (New York, 1931).

Sales, F. de. *Introduction à la vie dévote*, (Paris; Flammarion, no date).

Salomon, H. P. *Tartuffe devant l'opinion française*, (Paris, 1962).

Scherer, J. *Structures de Tartuffe*, (Paris, 1966).

Sur le Dom Juan de Molière, (Paris, 1967).

Sells, A. L. 'Molière and La Mothe Le Vayer', *Modern Language Review*, XXVIII (1933) pp. 352-67, pp. 444-55.

Sextus Empiricus. *Works,* with an English translation by Rev. R. G. Bury, 4 Vols., (Cambridge, Mass., 1935-53).

Simon, A. *Molière par lui-même*, (Paris, 1957).

Spink, J. S. *French Free-Thought from Gassendi to Voltaire*, (London, 1966).

Stern, A. *Philosophie du Rire et des Pleurs*, (Paris, 1949).

Tallemant des Réaux. *Les Historiettes*, Edition de Monmerqué et Paulin, 6 Vols., (Paris, 1862).

Thibaudet, A. 'Le rire de Molière', *Revue de Paris*, (1922) pp. 99-125.

Vedel, V. *Deux classiques français vus par un critique étranger; Corneille et son temps. Molière*, (Paris, 1935).

Villiers, A. *Le Dom Juan de Molière, un problème de mise au point*, (Paris, 1947).

Walker, H. 'The Self-creating Hero in *Dom Juan*', *French Review*, 36 (December, 1962) pp. 167-74.

Wickelgren, F. *La Mothe Le Vayer, sa vie et son oeuvre*, (Paris, 1934).

Yarrow, P. J. 'A Reconsideration of Alceste', *French Studies*, XIII (1959) pp. 314-31.

Zdanowicz, C. D. 'Molière and Bergson's theory of laughter', *Wisconsin University Publications in Language and Literature*, 20 (1924) pp. 99-125.

Index